The Idea and Practice

of

General Education

The Idea and Practice

of

General Education

An Account of the
College of The University of Chicago

By

PRESENT AND FORMER MEMBERS
OF THE FACULTY

THE UNIVERSITY OF CHICAGO PRESS

THE UNIVERSITY OF CHICAGO PRESS, CHICAGO 37
Cambridge University Press, London, N.W. 1, England
W. J. Gage & Co., Limited, Toronto 2B, Canada

Foreword

As this book is published, the College of the University of Chicago finds itself in a position to which it has not long been accustomed. In the nation, "general education" is at last in vogue. Its principles bid fair to become the operative educational theory of the remainder of this century. At the University of Chicago the long struggle* of the College to control, define, and construct an intelligible and effective curriculum in general education has passed through its uphill stage. A period of fruition has been entered upon, and a national concern has been added to the local preoccupations of the recent past.

What is needed now is communication among those who are engaged in general education in the nation, to the end that the sins which were committed in the name of the elective system may not be matched by different, but no less shoddy, deeds done in the name of general education. The major purpose of this book is to contribute to this communication, by placing before those who are concerned about the new form of undergraduate education in America an account of the academic program of the College as it is today, after nearly two decades of debate and development.

Of course, as several of the authors make clear, both debate and development continue vigorously in the College. Indeed, it cannot even be assumed that all the details of this account will have survived its publication. Yet experience would be quite pointless if nothing were learned from it, and the College faculty has learned enough in twenty years to be fairly sure at present of the lines along which its next experiments and advances will be directed. What may be done in the more remote future, in the

---

* Described in its many aspects by Messrs. Faust and Frodin in this book and by former Deans Boucher and Brumbaugh in an earlier volume, *The Chicago College Plan*, by C. S. Boucher and A. J. Brumbaugh (rev. ed.; Chicago: University of Chicago Press, 1940).

v

College at Chicago and in other colleges now planning and testing new curriculums, may well depend upon the degree of rigor
and energy with which discussion and appraisal of the possible
forms of general education are carried on during the next few
years.

The College has another, parochial reason for publishing this
book. The pioneer is always isolated and usually misunderstood.
In its isolation, the College has been widely misunderstood, and
it should be an effect of the publication of this book to remove or
lessen certain misconceptions about what the College is and what
it is trying to do. At present, these misconceptions appear to rest
upon a number of confusions: confusions between the College of
the University of Chicago and St. John's College in Annapolis,
Maryland; between the College of the University of Chicago and
the University of Chicago's "Great Books" program for adults;
between what Chancellor Hutchins has said about Bachelors of
Arts and what he has said about Doctors of Philosophy; between
liberal and aristocratic education; between informed and whimsi-
cal academic and vocational choices; between requiring studies
and imposing doctrines; between acquiring arts and memorizing
answers; between the interdisciplinary courses which are now
given in the College and "survey" courses; between students who
are interested in their studies and students who work too hard;
confusion, even, between not playing intercollegiate football and
not playing football at all. The reader of this book may weigh
for himself the distortions of the College which have resulted from
these confusions. Perhaps, when he has finished reading, he may
be led to echo the words of a recent British visitor, who, in reporting to his fellow-scientists in England upon his study of higher education in America, told them that he ". . . found many of the
statements made by outside Americans concerning the College
course of the very volcanic University of Chicago bore little or no
relation to the facts observable within the College."

The period of fruition referred to above has been marked by
the publication of a number of articles written by members of the
faculty of the College about "the facts observable within the College." Suitably revised, these articles constitute a part of this vol-

ume.* Other portions have been written especially for the present occasion. Thanks are due to all these authors and colleagues for their willing collaboration in contributing to this book. I am particularly grateful to Mr. Clarence Faust and Mr. Reuben Frodin for the first two chapters, prepared during a time when both were busy with heavy tasks assumed following their administration of the College. I can only hope that their authorship of these chapters has not tended to conceal the real extent to which the quiet, insistent excellence of Mr. Faust's leadership was responsible for the major accomplishments of the College during the years 1941–47.

Special thanks should also go to my associates in the College Dean's Office, Mr. Hugh Davidson, Miss Margaret Perry, and Mr. Eugene Northrop, without whose editorial assistance this book would never have reached the printer.

F. CHAMPION WARD

February 1, 1950

* Portions of the following chapters have been adapted from published articles: chap. 3: *Journal of General Education*, II (1948), 121–28; chap. 4: *ibid.*, II (1948), 251–58; chap. 5: *Science in General Education*, ed. Earl J. McGrath (Dubuque: Wm. C. Brown Co., 1948), pp. 60–64; chap. 6: *American Mathematical Monthly*, XLII (1945), 132–37, and LV (1948), 1–7; chap. 11: *Journal of General Education*, III (1949), 210–15, and IV (1950), 221–33; *School Review*, LV (1947), 526–33.

Contributors

F. CHAMPION WARD: Dean of the College and Professor of Philosophy in the College

CLARENCE H. FAUST: Dean of the College, 1941–47, now Dean of Humanities and Sciences, Stanford University

REUBEN FRODIN: Assistant Dean of the College, 1943–46, now Editor of *The Journal of General Education*, Adviser on Special Projects in the Central Administration and Lecturer in the Department of Political Science

RUSSELL THOMAS: Associate Professor of the Humanities in the College and Chairman of the College Humanities Staff

MILTON B. SINGER: Professor of the Social Sciences in the College and Chairman of the College Social Sciences Staff

JOSEPH J. SCHWAB: Professor of the Natural Sciences in the College and Chairman of the College Natural Sciences Staff

MERLE C. COULTER: Professor of Botany and Associate Dean of the Division of Biological Sciences

EUGENE P. NORTHROP: Associate Dean of the College, Professor of Mathematics in the College, and Chairman of the College Mathematics Staff

HENRY W. SAMS: Associate Professor of English in the College and Chairman of the College English Staff

JAMES C. BABCOCK: Associate Professor of Spanish in the College and Chairman of the College Spanish Staff and of the Staff of Language 1

WILLIAM H. MCNEILL: Assistant Professor of History in the College and Chairman of the College History Staff

WILLIAM O'MEARA: Professor of Philosophy in the College and Chairman of the College Observation, Interpretation, and Integration Staff

ALBERT M. HAYES: Associate Professor of English in the College

BENJAMIN BLOOM: Associate Professor of Education and College Examiner

JANE ALLISON: Assistant to the University Examiner

PAUL B. DIEDERICH: Associate Professor and Examiner

JOHN R. DAVEY: Dean of Students in the College and Associate Professor of the Humanities in the College

Table of Contents

xi

PART I

On Theory and History

1

The Problem of General Education

CLARENCE H. FAUST

THE history of American education illustrates, among many other things, that preoccupation with the practical may, in the long run, be dangerously impractical. One of our basic needs as a nation is a generally educated citizenry, for the success of our democracy depends ultimately upon the wisdom of our people. Yet this crucial need for general education, that is, for the kind of education that will prepare men to deal with the problems which confront all members of a democratic society, has been largely overlooked at the higher levels of education in this country because of our concern with more restricted needs, especially our interest in developing competence for occupations and professions. Many of our earliest colleges were designed to prepare men for the ministry. Some later institutions, such as the academy set up in Philadelphia at the suggestion of Benjamin Franklin, were established with an eye to the preparation of youth for various other vocations. Specialized training has been wonderfully successful in this country. Our law schools, medical schools, and engineering schools have developed efficient programs of preparation for professional practice, and the academic departments of our universities have become expert in producing specialists. But between these and the elementary schools, which provide education in the basic skills of reading, writing, and arithmetic, there is a gap which it has not seemed practically important to fill. It has

3

been found possible to advance students from elementary training directly into specialization, without providing for the development of the wisdom concerning the common problems of mankind which the members of a democratic society need to acquire. Having failed to develop this wisdom, we complain about the indifference or lack of intelligence of American voters and are discouraged by the blind and unreasoning ways in which elections are managed and national policies formulated. We bemoan the low state of our national culture as revealed in the movies, the radio, and the comic book. And we are alarmed by the evidence of our scientific illiteracy as exposed in the success of various pseudo-scientific quackeries.

One of the great needs of the country, therefore, is the development of effective programs of higher general education, and it is the attempt of the College at the University of Chicago to meet this need that makes its philosophy and plan of operation interesting; for the College at Chicago has been formally charged by the University with the responsibility for doing "the work of the University in general higher education." It has performed this function in the University for almost two decades. The program of general education which it offers did not spring fully fledged into being when the College was established in 1931, nor did it emerge in anything like final form from the deliberations of its first curriculum committee. It has been developed over the years as the result of the thought, discussion, and experimentation concerning general education which have flourished in the College since its beginning; and the degree of clarity and coherence achieved in its program of general education has been the result of increasing insights into the nature, the ends, and the means of general education.

The College has not had to prove to itself, or to the University, or to the educational world at large that general education is a good thing. Almost no one denies its value. Everyone seems to grant that all our citizens need it and that those who, as specialists, will occupy particularly influential places in our society need it perhaps most of all. But the term "general education," like the terms "liberty" and "equality," has acquired a wide range of meanings, including some irreconcilable ones. It cannot be defined by the simple device of pointing to examples of it. Almost every college in the country, if presidents, deans, and catalogues are to be believed, provides a general or liberal education for its undergraduates; but it is impossible to discover any substantial, common element in the educational programs of our colleges. The requirement of a course in English composition, one in history, and one in the natural sciences would come closest, perhaps, to meeting this test; but even this agreement proves, upon examination, to be apparent rather than real, for the courses labeled "English," "History," and "Science" in various colleges exhibit such differences of content, method, and purpose—and, indeed, such contradictory differences—as to leave little hope of defining general education by references to what is being done about it.

The faculty of the College at Chicago has been driven, therefore, to consider all aspects of the question afresh. It has been obliged to consider the relation of the College to other parts of the educational system, to formulate its purposes precisely, to determine in the light of them the proper contents of its curriculum, and to devise effective methods of instruction. Inevitably, it has sometimes hesitated between two or even more opinions, has sometimes fumbled, and sometimes been mistaken; but, over the twenty years of its operation, many hesitations have been resolved, and many false starts corrected.

The role of the College in the educational system as a whole has become increasingly clear. The College stands between two other parts of that system. Its work lies between the elementary training provided by the schools from which its students come and the specialized training furnished by the graduate schools and the professional schools into which many of its students go. It is the chief function of elementary and secondary schools to lay the general foundations of education, that is, to teach reading, writing, and arithmetic and to provide basic information in geography, history, and the political institutions of our country. The task of professional and graduate schools is to train specialists, that is, to prepare able students to perform special kinds of work in our society—to construct roads, bridges, and homes; to cope with cancer, tuberculosis, and heart disease; to resolve difficult questions of law; to handle various parts of our complex economy; to extend the frontiers of knowledge through research in the natural and social sciences and in the humanities; and, in short, to meet the various special demands of our increasingly complex and specialized society.

Between these two parts of the American educational system lies an important area of responsibility for the liberal arts college. Its function is to prepare young people, in whom the foundations of education have been laid by grade schools and high schools, to deal not with the special problems parceled out in our society to the members of various occupations and professions— to the chemist and the carpenter, the architect and the accountant, the doctor, the merchant, and the housewife—but with the problems which confront all members of our society alike, such problems as our domestic and foreign policies, our political leadership, our individual relations with the physical universe, our personal philosophies. General education appears from this point of view to be the preparation of youth to deal with the personal and social problems with which all men in a democratic society are confronted.

This is in many respects a task of great importance and of extraordinary difficulty. It is important because the course that this nation takes in both domestic and international affairs is determined by the judgments of its citizens, however far it may seem at moments to slip from their control; and whether the course it takes is wise and good or foolish and evil will be determined ultimately by the quality of judgment that our citizens exercise. It is therefore one of the important functions of general education to prepare people to exercise wisely the power which will be thrust upon them as citizens of a democracy. General education cannot provide young people with ready answers for all political and social problems. For one thing, we do not possess satisfactory answers for some of the most important of them. Nor, if we did possess them, should they be simply imposed upon each new generation. General education must undertake, therefore, to prepare people to think profitably for themselves.

The need of such education was never greater. The problems of democracy have become increasingly complex, and so has the machinery of politics and of government. There is an increasing tendency to suppose that many of these problems can be solved only by specialists and that, as things stand, they are now viciously resolved by the manipulations of politicians. If democracy collapses in this country, it is most likely to do so under the pressure of these opinions. From trusting the specialist, whose judgment is supposed to be superior to that of the mass of the people and whose decisions seem to deserve precedence over the manipulations of politicians, to belief in the dictator, whose decisions all must blindly approve, is a short and easy road, and one which America is much more likely to follow than that of simple demagoguery if it turns its face against democracy.

The importance of general education is not limited, however, to the need for wise citizens. The urgency of the social and political problems with which we are at present confronted permits us easily to forget that society is not an end in itself. We desire a strong, well-organized, smoothly functioning society, not in and for itself, but as a means to the realization of men's potentialities as individuals. We judge the goodness of a society, indeed, by determining whether it provides the conditions for the pursuit of truth, for freedom of speech and action, and for the flowering of men's creative powers in literature and the arts. Something must be wrong with a society, no matter how powerful, which can maintain its power only by denying these goods to some of its members or by denying them to other nations. Something would be wrong, moreover, with a society in which a lawyer could be a successful lawyer or a merchant could be a successful businessman only by ceasing to be a successful human being. The development of men and women in whom the best possibilities of human nature are realized to the limit of each individual's capacity is a primary concern of general education. These possibilities include the development of social and political wisdom; the capacity to appreciate and enjoy the products of man's creative activity in literature, music, and art; and man's capacity for reflective thought concerning the nature of the universe and of man's place and role in it. The development of these possibilities is not and cannot be the chief concern of professional schools, whose task is to train competent specialists, men in whom the power to do something extraordinarily well is realized. It is, however, the chief concern of the liberal arts college.

Great as is the importance of this task, its difficulties are even greater. Many of the major developments of American education over the last three or four generations have been inimical to it, often unconsciously so, and have introduced purposes, produced methods, and established kinds of academic organization which make general education difficult. One of the most important of these is the departmental structure of colleges and universities. As subject matters have been developed for the pursuit of research and the training of specialists, universities have been progressively compartmentalized. Departmentalization has great virtues: it has encouraged and aided the development of rigorous and precise disciplines, and it has provided conditions for the training of extremely competent specialists for the purposes of research and graduate instruction. But these achievements have been accompanied by a tendency in both teaching and research to mistake the lines which have come to circumscribe the activities of academic departments for divisions in the nature of reality. This is a mistake which the most energetic and imaginative research specialists have been least likely to make. In the great research centers of the country, the transgression of departmental lines illustrated in the rise of new departments, such as biochemistry, biophysics, and radiobiology, is evidence of the discovery on the part of research scientists that the boundaries of academic departments do not mark off basic differences in the nature of the things to be known. Yet departmentalization along the lines fixed in the development of various academic disciplines tends to maintain itself belatedly in secondary schools and in liberal arts colleges. As the demand for more highly trained teachers has quite properly increased, teachers have been more and more trained to handle departmental specialties, and, as the number of these teachers has increased in colleges and even in secondary schools, curriculums have been splintered along departmental lines and have become more elaborate and unrealistic and less effective for the purposes of general education.

The problem thus presented to colleges concerned about general education is anything but simple. A solution by means of a curriculum consisting of vaguely generalized courses, handled by vaguely educated teachers, will not do. What is needed, however difficult it may be to secure, is general courses which deal rigorously with basic principles under the direction of teachers who have been educated not merely in departmental specialties but in the fundamental disciplines common to the field of the social sciences or the humanities or the natural sciences. Any serious attempt to meet this need must ultimately produce a radical reformation of our system of training teachers. Meanwhile, the College at Chicago has met the problem as best it could, and with surprising success, by enlisting in its faculty men rigorously trained in the present system and yet possessed by an interest in adapting their special knowledge and competence to the purposes of general education and by a willingness to work hard at this task. Men trained in zoölogy, for example, have undertaken to examine, for the purposes of general education, the foundations of the natural sciences; men trained in classical philology, to study the basic disciplines of the humanities; and men trained in economics, to explore the basic disciplines of the social sciences. The work they have done in devising and making effective a more general and liberal curriculum has been as difficult and demanding as traditional research and graduate training.

The departmentalization of graduate study, which has reflected itself in the training of teachers and ultimately in the fragmentation of the curriculums of general education in both the high school and the college, has led to an extremely serious difficulty for high-school and college students. As departmental courses have been multiplied under the influence of the departmentalization of graduate schools and of programs for training teachers, the number of courses in high schools and colleges has constantly increased. The courses in natural philosophy, common some generations ago, have been replaced by courses in physics, chemistry, geology, botany, zoölogy, physiology, etc. The course in political philosophy has been replaced by courses in economics, sociology, public administration, anthropology; and the course in rhetoric and belles-lettres has been replaced by courses in Chaucer, Shakespeare, the Romantic poets, Colonial American literature, the short story, etc. Obviously, no student can take all these courses. Yet faculties have been unwilling or unable to designate some of them as essential. The answer everywhere seized upon was the elective system. Schools became educational cafeterias, providing a bewildering variety and number of dishes from which a student was permitted or forced to select as best he could. He could hardly be blamed for selecting unwisely, experiencing intellectual indigestion, and failing to obtain healthy intellectual maturity. If his teachers were unable to determine what is essential to his education, it was unreasonable to expect that he would be able to do so. He would, indeed, have needed the wisdom that a liberal education is designed to give him in order to discover for himself what is essential for his education.

Too often the student makes his choices for trivial reasons, such as the convenience of the class hour or the reputation of the instructor as an amusing or generous fellow. It is true that many colleges, recognizing the dangers of such haphazard selection as the student is driven to and dissatisfied with the ill-balanced patchwork of courses which often results from it, have limited the range of choice somewhat, requiring that one or more courses be taken in each of the several larger groups into which the curriculum is divided. Each student may be required to take one course in the physical sciences, for instance, one in the social sciences, and one in literature. But this device is frustrated by another difficulty of departmentalization. Since each of the courses in the physical sciences is, in large part, planned as the first step toward specialization in a departmental field, it can only incidentally and accidentally serve as an introduction to the physical sciences as a whole, though such an introduction is precisely what is needed for the purposes of general education. It is, in fact, not uncommonly the chief pride of good teachers in such courses that their students have achieved remarkable success in graduate school. The professor of chemistry teaching a hundred students each year may cite the successful graduate careers of a half-dozen of them over a period of several years as evidence of the excellence of his course, without apparently asking himself about its effects upon the great majority of his students who have no intention of becoming professional chemists and whose only profit from the course must be their understanding of the problems of knowledge concerning the natural world, the methods for achieving it, its proper fruits, and its limitations.

Faced with the difficult cluster of questions which the departmentalization of education raises, the faculty of the College at Chicago has undertaken to determine the essentials of a liberal education and to devise an integrated system of courses to provide them. The program of the College is consequently not elective. To become eligible for the degree of Bachelor of Arts, the student must pass examinations which test his competence in the basic principles, the major concepts and methods, and the salient facts in the natural sciences, the social sciences, the humanities, and mathematics, and his ability to express himself clearly.

This is not to say that the College has relieved students of responsibility or denied them opportunities for choice. Class attendance and the performance of class assignments are voluntary. Although a student may not be able to foresee the consequences of choosing to take Chaucer rather than labor problems, or chemistry rather than abnormal psychology, and consequently cannot profit from being given freedom to do so, he is able to make a reasonable estimation of the consequences of attending class or not and of carrying out class assignments. Responsibility for such decisions is therefore a useful freedom. But responsibility for determining the ingredients of general education is assumed by the faculty.

Although it would probably have been impossible at any time in the history of the College to secure unanimous and detailed agreement concerning what it is essential for every student to acquire in college, there has been general agreement that the College ought to provide all students with the means for acquiring, and demand of all students evidence of having acquired, the understanding of society and social institutions, the knowledge of the physical world in which they live and the grasp of the methods employed in the natural sciences, the competence to understand and appreciate literature and the arts, and the ability to express themselves clearly and effectively which all members of our democratic society, regardless of occupation or profession, ought to acquire. These have seemed to the faculty of the College the components of general education, the kind of education men need as men and human beings rather than as specialists.

In entertaining these general purposes, the College has, of course, not been unique. Its uniqueness has emerged in its attempt to define them precisely, to discover what they involve, and to formulate in the particular circumstances of the University a plan to achieve them. The program of general education which it has worked out over almost twenty years differs in several important ways from the undergraduate programs traditional in American colleges. It begins two years earlier than that of other colleges, admitting students who have finished two years of high school rather than four. The curriculum consists of an integrated system of courses covering the major areas of knowledge rather than a collection of departmental elective courses. It admits students and places them in its program on the basis of examination rather than on the basis of units of entrance credit and grades; and it measures the achievements of students and determines their eligibility for the degree of Bachelor of Arts by means of college-wide, comprehensive examinations rather than by adding up credits earned in separate college courses.

A college curriculum which is not simply the product of historical accidents must be based upon an educational philosophy. What is taught and how it is taught, the inclusion of this subject (or one of its aspects) rather than that in the curriculum, and the choice of this rather than that method of instruction, unless these are explicable simply as the persistence of tradition or as unthinking imitation, will reveal by implication the philosophy of education which a faculty more or less consciously holds. It may be a very simple philosophy, such as that no valid ground can be found for regarding any subject as more valuable than any other or any method as better than any other, which in its simplest form results in permitting students to take what they please, so long as they accumulate 120 semester-hours of credit. Or the educational philosophy reflected in a curriculum may embrace contradictions, such as those exhibited in a program consisting of departmental courses, each of which has been designed as the first step toward a departmental specialization but among which the student is forced to choose at least one in each of several groups as a device to insure a general education.

What too often happens is that preoccupation with one aspect of college education leads to neglect of other important aspects of it, and thus to oversimplification of the problems of general education. A well-considered college program must take into account the nature and needs of students as human beings, the extent and character of the wisdom which has been accumulated in Western culture, the role of the college in the social order, and the circumstances of the interests and training of the available faculty. Fixation upon one of these as the guiding principle of college education may lead, as in the case of Sarah Lawrence, which centers upon the individual differences of students, or Antioch, which centers upon the college's service to society, or St. John's, which centers upon the heritage of wisdom in the great books, to an unfortunately amputated curriculum. At the other extreme in educational theory lie those programs, such as that indicated in the Harvard report, *General Education in a Free Society*, in which, by a sweeping eclecticism, almost all current ideas, proposals, and projects are favorably regarded, with the consequence that no basis is provided for the elimination of the false and unnecessary or even for the determination of the relative importance of various educational proposals.

The curriculum of the College at Chicago is neither traditional nor imitative. Nor is it eclectic. There are some unresolved contradictions in it despite the faculty's constant re-examination of it, but the chief elements of a reasonably full and coherent educational philosophy may be quite clearly made out in it. Of the major considerations which should enter into the formation of a college plan, it has placed heaviest emphasis upon the demands of subject matters and upon its particular historical circumstances as an institution rather than upon the individual traits of students or upon the particular demands of society.

The curriculum of the College reflects the belief, for one thing, that the kind of wisdom which general education aims at cannot be produced by developing in students even a high degree of competence in a narrow field—that a knowledge of sociology or economics, for example, is an inadequate general education with

respect to social institutions, activities, and behavior. The economist and the sociologist, like the chemist and the mathematician,
have limited their problems to bring them within the grasp of the
kind of detailed and precise examination which will make possible new excursions into limited areas of the unknown. The specialist in these fields, commanding the techniques of research,
may throw light into the hitherto dark aspects of the subject or
may manage to order more fully, more systematically, and more
intelligibly a collection of hitherto chaotic facts. General education attempts, however, to develop the capacity for wise decisions
in those matters with which everyone must be concerned: the
broad area of human relationships and human institutions, for
example, or the broad area of literature and the arts. It is impossible to give every undergraduate all the knowledge that specialists have developed. To give him a part of the specialized knowledge that has been accumulated in one section of the social sciences, of the humanities, or of the physical sciences (the device of
the elective system) is not likely to give him the well-balanced
understanding of social problems or the ability to appreciate literature and the arts or the understanding of natural phenomena
which every educated man should possess. Nor, on the other
hand, will a piece of economics, a piece of sociology, a piece of
political science, and a piece of anthropology, brought together
in a single survey course on the social sciences, serve the purpose.
Great as the value of these departmental disciplines for research
and the training of specialists may be, no one of them and no
mere piecing-together of a number of them can constitute a general education.

This is not to say that the difference between specialized and
general education is a matter of precision and rigor in the one and
vague generality in the second. The curriculum of the College at
Chicago is based upon the principle that certain major divisions
of knowledge may be distinguished and defined on the basis of
traits common to the various separate departmental disciplines
into which universities and colleges have split them. It recognizes, on the one hand, that the process of thought for reaching
truth about one subject matter differs from the processes of
thought required to reach truth in another; that the methods of

reasoning appropriate and fruitful in one field may be inappropriate and unproductive in another; and that we may easily run up blind alleys in the pursuit of knowledge if we fail to recognize this fact—if, for instance, we apply statistical methods where such methods cannot provide the truth we seek, supposing that, if data concerning a social or political problem could be collected and reduced to tables and charts, the problem would be solved; or if we transpose a social or aesthetic question into biological or physical terms, in the mistaken opinion that the clarity of the statements thus achieved is a guaranty of their truth and usefulness. It recognizes, on the other hand, that the subject matter, the methods, and the aims of disciplines which have come historically to be dealt with in separate academic departments fall into certain groups having fundamental and essential traits in common and that these common traits make possible a treatment broader than that of individual, academic departments. Physics and chemistry from this point of view fall together; so do anatomy, physiology, botany, and zoölogy; so, too, do political science, sociology, economics, and anthropology; so, likewise, do literature, art, and music. The members of these groups fall together by reason of certain basic likenesses, while the groups themselves are separated by basic differences. The area of knowledge commonly assigned the social sciences is related to a subject matter different from that of the natural sciences, in that what is examined in the social sciences is the product of man's desires, intentions, thoughts, and activities rather than the product of forces outside man. Moreover, a common purpose animates the work of the social sciences—that of determining what is best, or at least better, in human activities and in the institutions which men devise. The methods of the social sciences for acquiring knowledge of this subject for this purpose have, therefore, certain basic likenesses by contrast with those of the natural sciences. Indeed, the terms "social sciences," "natural sciences," and "humanities" reflect our awareness of the common elements of the subject matter, ends, and methods of the various departmental disciplines of which each one is composed. This awareness is further reflected in the administrative organization in many universities, in the development of "area" studies, in the formation of learned societies which the professors of various related disciplines have organized for the purpose of exchanging ideas, and in the publications of learned journals dealing with several related fields. The recognition of traits common to the departmentalized disciplines which are brought together in schools of the social sciences in American universities or related in the establishment of the Social Sciences Research Council and the similar recognition of common traits in the departmentalized disciplines which are brought together in schools of the humanities or related in the establishment of the Modern Language Association and its publications point to the solution of one of the major problems of general education.

On the principle which these phenomena reflect, it is possible to construct general courses which are not accumulations of selected conclusions from various departmental fields or vaguely general formulations of widely general problems but are exact, penetrating treatments of the basic principles of such an area as the social sciences or the humanities. Thus the development in the area of the humanities of the kind of understanding and appreciation of literature and the arts which the doctor, the engineer, the lawyer, the chemist, and the businessman should have, may be undertaken not by a "survey" of world literature into which the conclusions of dozens of research workers are packed or by a course in eighteenth-century English literature reporting the discoveries of research workers in this field but by a course in which students are led to consider the fundamental problems in interpreting literature and are given practice in the understanding and appreciation of literature through the reading and discussion of an appropriate variety of literary works. A like approach to the problems and methods of the social sciences and of the natural sciences might be expected to produce general courses which, while providing a wider training than introductory departmental courses can reasonably be expected to furnish, would deal precisely and rigorously with the basic principles and methods of each of these areas.

The construction of such courses is far from simple or easy. It requires the co-operation of specialists who have undertaken to determine what is basic in a group of related subjects and to work out and to correct, in the light of experience, the materials and methods by which students may be led to acquire a grasp of the fundamental principles and methods of thinking needed to form sound judgments in the social sciences, the natural sciences, and the humanities. The attempt to develop courses of this sort has been the major concern of the College of the University of Chicago for the last two decades, and the descriptions of the general courses which this volume contains reveal the progress which the faculty has made in this direction.

The general courses of the College reflect, furthermore, the College's concern with teaching students to think for themselves rather than with providing a mass of information on a host of subjects concerning which it might be pleasant to have students informed, or even with a set of general truths. It is not the purpose of the College to instruct members of the rising generation what to think but, rather, to teach them how to think. Its purpose is not indoctrination but the development of power to form sound judgments with respect to those questions which are the concern of everyone. This principle has, over the years, assumed increasing importance in the College's continuous re-evaluation of the curriculum. It has not been thought sufficient in the application of this principle to develop the student's powers of logic in the sense of teaching him either to avoid common logical fallacies or to analyze in terms of formal logic his own or other people's arguments. It is not a matter, so to speak, of developing a smartly functioning logical machine. What is required in general education can best be described by the term "wisdom" rather than by the popular term "straight thinking"; for what students need is not merely guidance in avoiding error, or even smoothness in mental operations, but the competence to establish an adequate relation of the mind to the things which it undertakes to grasp. This kind of competence, like skill in swimming, cannot be developed by learning rules but only by exercise; and, since the methods by which problems regarding the natural world are formulated and resolved differ from the formulation and resolution of problems in the interpretation of lyric poetry—and both of these differ from the methods of formulating ethical standards—education in the formation of sound judgments in these various areas requires practice in thinking about different subject matters.

The chief means of education which the College has, over the years, evolved for this purpose is the careful reading and discussion of well-argued approaches to basic problems in the social sciences and the natural sciences and the study of master-works in the humanities. What is aimed at is the capacity to formulate clearly the differences between the conflicting lines of argument and to locate the critical point at which determination of the relative merit and soundness of different approaches may be profitably undertaken. The best materials for the purpose are the outstanding writings of natural and social scientists and the great works of literature and art. The study of these—the careful and close examination of them, the analysis of them by reference to appropriate principles and criteria—is the best method that the College has discovered for developing the student's competence to think profitably for himself.

Such study cannot be induced by the lecture system. It can be managed only by the method of discussion. One of the most disillusioning experiences of the teacher is that of discovering from examination papers what has happened to the ideas that he has presented in lectures, no matter how skilfully and even brilliantly his lectures have been worked out. The distortions which inevitably occur as the student sets down in his notebook what he supposes the lecturer has said, and then records on his examination what he supposes, from a review of them, his lecture notes mean, are likely soon to destroy the instructor's confidence in the lecture method of education for undergraduates. There is another and more serious objection to the lecture system. Except under the best circumstances, that is, with the most stimulating teacher and the most eager students, the lecture method places the learner in a passive role, where it is least likely that he will exercise his powers of thought and expression or learn to discipline his judgment. The lecture may be useful in conveying information not to be found in print and in providing excitement and stimulus for the study of a subject, but in the education of the judgment it must yield to the method of class discussion, where the student is obliged to engage actively in formulating a position, giving cogent reasons for it, and defending it against objection.

This method is sometimes attacked on the superficially convincing ground that it makes education merely verbal, whereas education must proceed by experience. The truth is that experience by itself is far from being the best teacher or, perhaps, even a good teacher. A student exposed for eight hours a day to the playing of a phonograph could quite conceivably learn little or nothing about the nature of music. A student placed for eight hours a day in a well-equipped chemistry laboratory might, if he were active, have exciting experiences without learning anything about chemistry. Experience is more likely to be a buzzing, unintelligible confusion than an educational process unless one comes to it equipped with ideas in the light of which it may be grasped, ordered, and understood. Thus the student who is taken to the local police court or is induced to witness the activities of a local election is not educated by the process unless he has been led to think about these things sufficiently to analyze his experience. In large part, college education must function to prepare students for experience—to provide them with concepts, ideas, and principles by which experience, as it comes to them, may be rendered intelligible and by means of which they may, within the limits of human power, master and control it. Premature or artificially induced experience may hinder, rather than aid, this process. For one thing, education involves the acquisition of general principles for illumination and guidance in particular cases. These are not obvious in the mass of particulars which constitute an individual experience, and preoccupation with these particulars may, in practice, block the discovery of basic principles. The best way to prepare a student to profit from experience—to discover guiding principles in it—is to prepare him for it by inducing him to read thoughtfully what the best thinkers about the problems of man and society have to say.

There are other decisive reasons for insisting upon the basic position of careful reading and discussion in education. The fact is that many of the most important decisions which men have to make must be made not on the basis of direct experience but on the basis of verbal and written reports and arguments. When the people of this country select every four years a chief administrative officer for our government, they cannot do so from direct experience of the men who offer themselves for this position or of the range of problems on which they have announced their programs. Determining for whom to vote in a presidential campaign is not like deciding on the basis of a taste-test that one prefers Chesterfields to Camels or chocolate to vanilla ice cream. What happens to us in a presidential campaign is that we are bombarded by sounds and symbols as the radio, newspapers, and magazines, and even our acquaintances, present claims and counterclaims for the candidate and urge us one way or another. Judgments in these cases, as indeed in most social problems, must be made very largely through analysis of the written or spoken word. To be realistic in education, therefore, we must undertake to prepare students to cope with this situation. Men cannot be intelligible among themselves or reach agreement on what is true or right, except by the use of language, and consequently what is sometimes dismissed as verbalism is, in truth, essential to education. There is, of course, always the danger that men will mistake neat verbal formulations for wisdom; but this error is to be avoided not by a futile attempt to forego verbal expression but by disciplining the mind to such analysis of words and discourse as will bring out clearly the relation of language to ideas and to things.

The objection to verbalism is sometimes combined with another objection to the kind of education which the College has developed, namely, that men make most of their decisions not on the basis of reason but on the basis of feeling or emotion and that it is consequently the chief task of education to inculcate right attitudes in students rather than to teach them to reason. It is undoubtedly true that men's emotions and prejudices often distort their judgment and that men's decisions often rest upon feeling rather than upon logic, but this is not a reason for dismissing the attempt to teach people wisdom, unless we are prepared to take the view that reason plays no role at all with respect to attitude and emotion. It is true that men act only when their feelings are to some extent committed, but it is the part of reason to provide criticism of attitudes, prejudices, and feelings and, consequently, guidance and correctives for attitudes and emotions; and, however narrow may be the scope of reason's operation, it is within the sphere of these operations that mankind's only hope lies. To reject this hope is to leave to education only the task of imposing attitudes and feelings, arbitrarily selected as desirable, upon the rising generation. Unless, moreover, we are to assume that educators are in some strange way exempt from the general slavery to emotion or, in some way not open to other men, capable of discriminating reasonably between desirable and undesirable emotional states, the attitudes that they will select to inculcate will themselves have emotional determinants; and it is difficult to see how, in this view of the matter, we should escape the philosophy of education which prevailed in Nazi Germany in the thirties. As the College views the question, then, its primary task is the education of judgment.

These major aspects of the educational philosophy of the College at Chicago reveal themselves in the system of general courses developed by the college faculty. Recognizing that students do not have time to take introductory courses in all the departmental disciplines as a way of securing a general education and convinced, in any case, that introductory courses designed as the first step toward specialization in a departmental area are not the most effective means of general education, the College has set up an integrated sequence of general courses dealing with the basic problems and methods of major areas of human knowledge. Three such fields are distinguished in the College curriculum—the humanities, the social sciences, and the natural sciences. The general courses provided in these areas have placed increasing dependence upon the reading and discussion of original writings of scientists and of masterpieces of literature rather than upon textbook summaries and lectures.

Much thought has been given, for example, to the problem of developing in students the insight into the methods and results of science, which, in an age dominated by science, they need as part of general education. It has seemed clear that a mere array of facts, however impressive, would not serve the purpose. For one thing, the sheer mass of knowledge accumulated by science is too great; but, even if this were not the case and even if a wise selection from the vast accumulation of facts could be made, science refuses to stay fixed, and much of the science of today will be obsolete tomorrow. Even those facts, moreover, which maintain their scientific status cannot be truly grasped and really understood as mere items of information retained in memory. They come to be intelligible, come to be truly known and significant, only through understanding the methods by which they have been established. For all these reasons, but perhaps especially for the last, the College curriculum in the natural sciences has increasingly provided for the study of the nature, methods, and role of science rather than for the presentation of the present state of knowledge in such subjects as physics, chemistry, geology, zoology, botany, etc. For this purpose it has increasingly turned from the textbooks on science to the writings in which scientists themselves report their discoveries and announce and defend their theories, and it has turned from the memorization of textbook facts to the analysis in class discussion of the ways in which scientists have formulated their problems, the nature of the principles they have used, the methods of argument and proof they have employed. It is not expected that such study will produce original scientists but, rather, that it will bring students to an understanding of the nature, processes, possibilities, and limitations of science and will prepare them to distinguish between scientific sense and mere quackery. Experience has meanwhile shown that students retain a larger number of facts from courses pursuing this method than from the traditional textbook and lecture courses.

The College courses in the humanities have likewise been evolved through wrestling with the problem of general education in literature and the arts. What has been aimed at with increasing clarity is the development of the student's competence to understand, appreciate, and enjoy the achievements of man's powers of reflective thought, imagination, and artistic creation. The history of human culture, that is, the organization in an intelligible, chronological sequence of man's achievements in philosophy and the arts, has come to seem much less useful for general education than the careful study and discussion of excellent

examples of these achievements. Without a broad base of analyzed experience with particular works of literature, music, and
art, historical information which may be conveyed to students
about these matters is hardly intelligible—certainly is not real
knowledge—and, above all, provides students with little preparation for that proper understanding, intelligent criticism, and
appropriate enjoyment of man's arts for which general education
should prepare them. The humanities courses of the College have
therefore depended less and less upon lectures and histories of
various arts and cultures and have tended more and more toward
the active analysis and discussion of great works of art.

In the social sciences, too, the curriculum of the College has
come to depend increasingly upon the discussion of important
writings on political, economic, and social problems rather than
upon lectures and textbooks. It is one of the functions of general
education to prepare young people to exercise wisely the freedom
and power with which they will be intrusted as members of a
democratic society. For this purpose they need to develop competence to make sound judgments concerning society and the programs of action proposed to it. A knowledge of the history of human institutions does not, of itself, accomplish this purpose. Information, however detailed, precise, and even statistical, concerning the existing state and operations of society is not sufficient.
The rigorous analysis of writings which are rich in ideas and
exemplary in method has been found the most rewarding way of
attempting to attain the ends of general education in the field of
human relations and social institutions.

Finally, the College recognizes its obligation to equip the student with the knowledge and intellectual disciplines necessary
for the integration of the different fields of knowledge. To this
end he is called upon to practice integration in two modes,
one analytical and the other historical. The course in the interrelationships of the fields of knowledge seeks to increase the
student's ability to raise and answer questions about the constitution, methods, and principles of the various arts and sciences,
and to do so consistently and with awareness of the advantages
and disadvantages of alternative approaches. Like the other general courses, it abstains from simple indoctrination, preferring, in-

stead, the analysis, comparison, and application to one another of original papers which deal with identical or similar problems in different ways. Another species of integration is undertaken in the course treating the history of Western civilization. In addition to providing a knowledge of the major events, institutions, and personalities, it places historically ideas and materials used elsewhere in the College and constantly invites the student's critical judgment of particular formulations of history.

What has made the work of the College exciting to those who have taken part in the planning and development of its program has been the sense of participation in a task of great importance. The most enthusiastic would not assert that the plan has attained perfection or that it has reached its final form. The program is constantly being re-examined as the theory of general education comes to be more precisely articulated, and it is almost constantly revised as experience, reviewed in the light of more fully developed educational philosophy, dictates. It is one important principle of that philosophy that education is a practical science in which insight into particular circumstances must be combined with general principles. In this sense, the educational philosophy of the College is not frozen; and the energy, intelligence, and venturesomeness of its faculty can be counted upon to make the next decades of its existence as importantly useful to a general education as its operations over the last twenty years have been.

2

"Very Simple, but Thoroughgoing"

REUBEN FRODIN

THE lawyer, Henry Adams once said, "is required to give facts the mould of a theory; the historian need only state facts in their sequence." Years later, grown cynical of his calling, he wrote: "Historians undertake to arrange sequences—called stories, or histories—assuming in silence a relation of cause and effect."[1] This chapter is the story of the development of an institution within an institution—the College of the University of Chicago. It might be called a lawyer's history of general education, because there is a "mould of theory" in which sequences of facts have been arranged. The theories, or assumptions, are mainly three. Given certain conditions which we already have—or can have—in a democracy, every young man and woman should have a fair chance to get a general, or liberal, education. Certain educational institutions with the means to do so, like the University of Chicago, have a special mission to seek out the ends of collegiate education, and to practice achieving them—as well as to advance knowledge by research. Finally, it is assumed that the administrator in an educational institution has a responsibility to take an active role in these processes.

The simplest, and by far the most interesting, way to tell any story of education is to tell of the men who have made the colleges and universities. At Chicago the story must start with William Rainey Harper, who built the mould of the University of

Chicago. Examination of the first president's letter files and of the University's printed bulletins and records reveals how many decisions he actually made regarding the detailed operation of the institution. This is understandable, for probably no one except the energetic little scholar and teacher himself knew all that he was trying to do. In a note he would propose a scholarly journal to a professor. He would review the "thought" of an educational scheme in a quarterly convocation statement. He would make a trip East to secure new members for the faculty. He alone was sure that the year-end deficit would somehow be taken care of.

President Harper came to Chicago as a young man with ideas, and he was in a hurry. He once said about his efforts at Chicago, "There isn't much time." He was thinking about his poor health and all the educational plans he was trying to effect. Harper's achievement of successfully presenting his ideas to John D. Rockefeller and of keeping Rockefeller with him on a difficult road is one of the great stories of American education. In large part the achievement was the result of Harper's enormous energy and his ability to put together scores of extant educational notions into one comprehensive program.[2] There was the idea of the quarter system, which would keep the institution running throughout the year; a press with its own printing plant to publish scholarly work; an elementary school, an academy, and a college or two as laboratories of the university; coeducation at the university level; extension work (away from the campus and by mail); and, most important, graduate and professional work in a great many fields.

In the 1880's leading Baptists all over the country were pressing Rockefeller to found a sectarian institution. Rockefeller probably wanted to settle for a college; in fact, correspondence of the organizing group shows that "a college to begin with" was the scheme for the new university in Chicago. But Harper, with plaint and purpose, told the "oil king" on the eve of being offered the presidency of the institution in September, 1890, that "it seems a great pity to wait for growth when we might be born full-fledged." Rockefeller accepted Harper's assurance that his plan for a university in the Middle West was "very simple, but thoroughgoing."[3] Harper also told the founder of the University that the plan and its execution would "revolutionize university study in this country." The revolutionary aspects did not concern Rockefeller—those were for the educators; what appealed to him were the freedom of inquiry which Harper promised, the efficiency of a plant that would run the year around, the provision for giving a student the kind of work he wanted, and Harper's infectious salesmanship. Harper won out over Augustus H. Strong, president of the Rochester (N.Y.) Theological Seminary and a lifelong friend of Rockefeller's, who wanted to build a $20,000,000 sectarian school in New York City. Strong was initially disdainful of Harper's plan. "The mongrel institution in Chicago—neither fish, flesh, nor fowl, neither University, College, nor Academy," he said, "would not create even a ripple in the educational sea." But Strong was a man of vision, and he soon conceded that the plan was an imposing one, writing President Harper: "I doubt whether anyone but yourself could carry it out. . . . If it succeeds, it will unquestionably attract the widest attention both at home and abroad."

One of Strong's objections to the Chicago plan was the proposal to carry on both graduate and undergraduate training in the same institution. He wrote to Harper: "You . . . ignore the lessons of the past by attempting to combine in one institution both postgraduate and academical work. . . . The best work cannot be done by teachers who teach both [under]graduates and postgraduates together—nor is the effect upon students good. . . ."[4] Harper had plans to meet these difficulties. He proposed at the outset "to make the work of investigation primary, the work of giving instruction secondary." "Promotion of younger men in the department will depend more largely upon the results of their work as investigators than upon the efficiency of their teaching, although the latter will by no means be overlooked."[5] His placing of research first, in the fashion of the German university—as Daniel Coit Gilman had done at Johns Hopkins, and G. Stanley Hall at Clark—was the key to Harper's plan. Harper himself was a researcher with an insatiable curiosity and a contagious interest which inspired others. He was also a great teacher, who had an intense desire to disseminate knowledge. At Yale the authorities had to assign to his Hebrew class the largest lecture-rooms available; his long-continuing participation in Chatauqua summer sessions demonstrated his concern with adult education.[6] So the statement that teaching "will by no means be overlooked" in considering promotions was an important addendum to the rules of practice of a research institution. The ground that Harper laid for a good teaching tradition at Chicago, while it has had its fallow seasons, was well laid. But it is clear from the early annual reports that there was never enough money to employ both a great research faculty and a great teaching faculty and that, when both qualities were found in the same individual, teaching tended to yield under the pressure for research.

That the problem of instruction troubled Harper, although he never stated it so explicitly as others did, is obvious from the amount of attention he gave to it in writing about the organization of the undergraduate years at Chicago. In one of his original "bulletins" written before the new institution opened, he divided the work of the four undergraduate years into two units: the freshman and sophomore years, called the Academic Colleges and subsequently designated the Junior Colleges, and the junior and senior years, called the University Colleges, subsequently designated the Senior Colleges. The work of the last two years was to "be done in connection with the various Graduate Schools."[7] In his *President's Report* for 1898–99 Harper reviewed the reasons for this division between the Junior and Senior Colleges and for the award of the title or degree of Associate in Arts to mark the completion of the work of the Junior College. This title had been approved by the faculty and the Board of Trustees in 1898. Harper stated that it was "very generally recognized that no important step" was taken at the end of the high-school course and that the work of the freshman and sophomore years differed little in content and method from that of the secondary school, except that it was somewhat more advanced. At the beginning of the junior year, on the other hand, students received greater liberty in the choice of subjects, "higher methods of instruction" were employed, and, in short, specialization began. Harper argued, moreover, that the end of the sophomore year was a convenient terminal point of formal education for those students who were either unable to profit further by university work or were without financial means to do so. Others, of marked ability but small means, might be encouraged to complete the two remaining years.

From the point of view of the University—Harper continued, in this remarkably farsighted document of fifty years ago—several points had been considered before decisions had been reached: (1) many secondary schools are able to do, at least in part, the work of the freshman and sophomore years; (2) if high schools and academies "could so perfect their work that freshman and sophomore courses might be offered, many people would be enabled to pursue their education to at least this higher point" locally; (3) "a large number of so-called colleges, which have not sufficient endowment to enable them properly to do the work of the junior and senior years, should limit their work to that of the freshman and sophomore years. . . . These institutions in many cases would be disposed to limit their work to the lower field, if it were made possible for them to do so. They find it necessary, however, to give a degree." If they could give appropriate recognition of the work of the lower years, Harper concluded, they would be ready to adopt the arrangement of work which he suggested.[8]

To carry out his general plan of organization, which he had conceived before the first classes met at the University of Chicago in October, 1892, President Harper arranged to have the Junior Colleges administered by a board under the general faculty. After the first year, however, a separate faculty was set up, composed of all instructors offering courses intended primarily for Junior College students. Thus it is clear that Harper perceived the importance of an independent faculty to guide the curriculum and programs of the freshman and sophomore years, although it is not clear whether he expected the Junior College faculty ever to contain persons who were not, at the same time, members of the departments devoted to advanced and graduate work. The faculty of the Junior College was made up of members of departments in which "the work of giving instruction [was] secondary"—senior men who had an interest in teaching and younger men whose promotion was to "depend more largely upon the results of their work as investigators than upon the efficiency of their teaching." The basic problem of the makeup of an independent faculty for general education was not to be solved until nearly fifty years had elapsed.

While the general shape of the curriculum could be legislated by the faculty, control of the Junior College courses was in the hands of the departments which offered work in the freshman and sophomore years. Debates concerning the curriculum developed when these departments sought to get more of the student's time through increased requirements in a given department. Thus, in 1898–99 there was a conflict of views between the arts and the science faculties over the requirement of Latin. The science faculties wanted to increase the amount of time which a student could spend in science courses in the early undergraduate years. President Harper attempted mediation by enlarging the issue. He proposed that the faculty accept "as its fundamental principle . . . that an essential element in the education of every man, and especially in that of the scientist, is a study of the great heritage we have received from the past." A curriculum reform embodying this policy, Harper contended, would mean that students be required to take "a specified number of courses in the study of the history, the institutions, and perhaps the literature of the past." Some of the faculty will object, he said, "(1) that after all, the student is not allowed to study the subject which he prefers, namely, science; (2) that at the most important age for the cultivation of observation and for the training which science furnishes, he is deprived of the privilege of such training; (3) that the connection is broken between the work in science which may have been done, and . . . later work. . . . A careful study of these objections shows that they affect the case slightly, if at all. . . . It is not proposed that at any stage in the career of the student he should be deprived of the possibility of doing work in science. . . . If the scientist demands all of the time of a student from an early age, he is demanding what will in the end prove injurious to the student and injurious to the cause of science; and with such demands there can be no sympathy on the part of one who is interested in the development of other departments of human knowledge."[9]

The location of responsibility for the curriculum and the nature of its content were two important aspects of collegiate education which presented problems over the years. Another was the standards of admission to collegiate work. In 1892 the University announced that all students who sought admission must pass entrance examinations in English, foreign languages, history, and mathematics. Admission to college, it was believed, should be based on the student's ability to do college work, and examinations should measure his preparation for such work. But, as George E. Vincent, Dean of the Junior Colleges (later President of the University of Minnesota and of the Rockefeller Foundation), reported in 1902: "Soon after the opening in 1892 it became evident that a strict examination policy in a region where . . . [certification to college from high school without examination] had been universally adopted would for a long time at least isolate the University and seriously retard its growth in numbers and influence." The University, therefore, "conformed to the system." "An examination of the high school system," he added, "soon made it plain that a large number of subjects were being taught which were not recognized by the University. The institution therefore enlarged the list of [acceptable] entrance subjects." Dean Vincent also reported the modification of the Junior College curriculum to meet the requirements of the programs of the departments of the Senior College and the professional schools: "While almost all discussions of the curriculum [of the Junior College] bring forth sporadic proposals for a practically free elective system, there has been no serious movement in that direction. The changes . . . have rather taken the form of gradual adaptation to situations as these have arisen."[10]

This gradual adaptation to situations as they arose soon carried the University from its original plans. In his report of 1904–5 Dean Vincent stated that the Junior College had adopted a revised curriculum. The Junior College was to be continued as a "clearing house" between the high school and the Senior College, but the core curriculum—that is, a certain number of specific requirements—would give way to "requirements in larger groups thus permitting a greater degree of flexibility"; and, to offset the increase in amount of elective work, "continuity and thorough-

ness in some one Department or group of Departments" would
be secured by prerequisites for advanced work "which will make
a mere scattered choice of introductory courses impossible."[11]

Thus, by the time of William Rainey Harper's death in 1906,
it was possible for a student to enter the University of Chicago
without examination on the basis of a high-school record containing a wide variety of courses; elect one of numerous programs,
which were restricted only in having to satisfy "group requirements" (one science course, for example, from a variety of introductory science courses); work off prerequisites for advanced
work in a departmental field; and receive the title of Associate in
Arts after two years of work. Harper's plan to relate the work of
the Junior College years to basic subjects in the last two years of
high school and to unify the first two college years had been aban-
doned. Harry Pratt Judson, who succeeded Harper as President,
expressed his view of the matter in his first report: "It is the duty
of college officers to see to it that the college curriculum . . . in-
terposes no inflexible bar against . . . advancement. . . . It is
quite possible to attain general culture in a college course and yet
so to plan a good part of the work that it will lead directly toward
a profession already chosen." Judson seems to have assumed (1)
a unity of the curriculum through the four college years (freshman through senior); (2) that there was nothing to be gained by
the development of a program through the late high-school years
and the Junior College, although he repeated Harper's view that
"it would seem that a boy ought to be ready to enter college by
the time he is sixteen"; (3) that a student definitely knows what
profession he will enter when he comes to college; and (4) that
most early college courses should lead directly to specialized
work.[12] The seventeen years of Judson's administration were to
see the almost complete submersion of the college or undergraduate program under the dictates of the graduate schools.

Bulletin Number Thirty of the Carnegie Foundation for the
Advancement of Teaching, *Studies in Early Graduate Education*
(1939), makes the following statement in summarizing the development of the University under the administration of Harper:
"One problem that was not solved in Harper's day and has not
been solved since is that of the relationship between less advanced

and more advanced students. . . . The problem . . . has proved to be much more complicated than it appeared to be to President Harper and others at Chicago. For one thing, it has had to be recognized as much more than an organizational matter. In nearly all the discussions of the time a quantitative concept of education was tacitly accepted, with a gradation based on number of years of subject matter covered. Such a concept would be more and more questioned today. . . . The experience . . . [at Chicago and elsewhere] would be cited as evidence of the ability of 'undergraduates' under certain conditions to meet the most exacting intellectual standards and achieve the independence assumed to be characteristic of graduate work."[13] Almost a decade before this statement was made, and four decades after Harper had announced his plans for the University, the College of the University of Chicago had begun to build a curriculum and a faculty to make that curriculum effective which offer a solution to the problem of the relationship between general or liberal education and specialized or professional education.

A recital of a partial roster of departmental heads at the time of President Harper's death provides the background for understanding the course of education at Chicago until the late 1920's. There was James R. Angell in psychology; James H. Breasted in Egyptology; Carl D. Buck in philology; Ernest DeWitt Burton in New Testament; Thomas C. Chamberlin in geology; John M. Coulter in botany; Edwin B. Frost in astrophysics; William G. Hale in Latin; James Parker Hall in law; Ludvig Hektoen in pathology; Harry Pratt Judson in political science; J. Laurence Laughlin in political economy; Andrew C. McLaughlin in history; John M. Manly in English; A. A. Michelson in physics; Eliakim H. Moore in mathematics; John U. Nef in chemistry; Paul Shorey in Greek; Albion W. Small in sociology; James H. Tufts in philosophy; and Charles O. Whitman in zoölogy. That funds available to Harper had been used to build up a strong research faculty is obvious. These heads of departments were a group of exceptionally able men. Both by virtue of their headships and through the machinery of the University Senate—composed of the professors of full rank—they wielded great power. Harper was, however, the guiding force in the University during his presidency. After his death, presidential leadership was lacking for a long period, and departmental power and authority determined both the strength and the weaknesses of the educational and research programs of the University.[14]

When Albion Small retired as Dean of the Graduate School in 1923 after twenty years in the office, he wrote: "The 'autonomy of departments' has been not only our theory but our practice. . . . It would be a calamity . . . if the essentials of that theory and practice ever fell into disregard. Like our fundamental democratic idea 'liberty,' however, the academic concept 'departmental autonomy' cannot be absolute. We all understand that it has more than one dimension. . . . At present, if one of the . . . Deans were to inquire of the officer representing a given department as to the wisdom of a certain schedule of courses, as to the most effective distribution of duties within the staff, as to the quality of work performed by certain members of the staff, and similar subjects, that department would be within its constitutional rights if it regarded the Dean as an intruder and an interloper." Small's recommendation was that the "entire economy" of the institution might be benefited if the Deans were given more duties and rights.[15]

The "autonomy of departments," the emphasis on research, and the freedom of the professor to investigate what he wished were among the American expressions of the model of the German university, which contributed to the fruitful development of specialized education and, at the same time, hampered the development of liberal education. In a convocation address upon the occasion of the granting of honorary degrees to a number of eminent German scientists, scholars, and statesmen in March, 1904, John M. Coulter, head of the Department of Botany and one of the leading American botanists, discussed the contribution of Germany to higher education in the United States.[16] Among other things, he spoke of the idea that the professor must be both investigator and teacher, which, he said, "has met with such wide acceptance in American universities that it is the general custom to select at least the leading instructors from those who are known as investigators, without any serious question as to their ability to teach. In fact, the doctrine has stimulated the

effort to investigate where both the training and the ability are
lacking; and has been applied to colleges where the chief function of the teacher is to teach. The atmosphere of the university,
however, is investigation, and the method of instruction is
through companionship in investigation. The appropriation of
previous knowledge is no longer the chief purpose, but is entirely
subsidiary to the discovery of additions to knowledge; and the
ability to stimulate students to investigate becomes the only problem of teaching." But, the scientist continued, such a view of the
university "involves certain dangers that must be faced. One is
that an exaggerated devotion to research may blind the instructor to the need of good teaching. . . . Another . . . arises from the
fact that most of our students expect to become teachers, and experience has proved that to make an investigator is not the only
thing necessary in making a teacher. . . . A third thing we are in
danger of losing sight of in our eagerness to make universities the
centers of investigation . . . [is the achievement of] 'general scientific and moral culture, together with mastery of one special
department of study.' "

That the University of Chicago—like most of its sister-institu-
tions of the first rank—paid inadequate attention to the curriculum which might have helped the undergraduate student achieve
a greater degree of "general scientific and moral culture" during
most of its history cannot be denied. Whitman in zoölogy, for
example, let new members of his staff know that undergraduate
teaching was to encroach as little as possible on research.[17] The
undergraduate curriculum lacked unity, and, despite the fact
that there were many good teachers—Coulter was one—there
were never enough to provide adequately for the needs of three
thousand, and later forty-five hundred, undergraduate students.
The emphasis of President Judson's administration is to be judged
from his statement in 1920 that "one of the difficulties of university administration is to effect a proper distribution of funds as
pertaining to graduate work . . . and undergraduate instruction.
. . . The number of undergraduates tends to increase to a very
large extent and of course undergraduate instruction must be
provided. The inevitable tendency is to siphon off funds from
more advanced work to the great embarrassment of this essential

part of university activities."[18] As early as 1907 Robert Morss Lovett, for a number of years Dean of the Junior Colleges, complained in his annual report about the large size of the undergraduate classes, contrary to Harper's original plan for small classes.[19] He also pleaded for year-long courses for the Junior College rather than quarter courses, so that the curriculum might have greater continuity for the college students.

President Judson felt that there was "considerable waste" of time in the elementary and high school and that the student ought to be able to begin college work at the age of sixteen. Because of the duplication of some high-school and college work, he suggested that "the best thing to do with the freshman year is to abolish it."[20] This was not done, but in 1912, at the suggestion of Charles Hubbard Judd, head of the Department of Education, the University Elementary School eliminated Grade VIII.[21] Thus, while the University had difficulty escaping the "8-4-4 pattern" (eight years of elementary education, four years of secondary education, and four years of college work) which largely prevailed throughout the United States, it was able, in its own schools, to make the first step toward shortening the time-span of preliminary schooling. This was directly in line with William Rainey Harper's original plan that the University's Elementary School, High School, and Colleges should be "laboratories for the University." The "6-4-4 pattern" of organization, although not realized at Chicago until 1937, was the logical outcome of President Harper's desire to push back the point in school life at which the student would begin college-level work.[22]

The position of Dean of the Faculty of Arts, Literature, and Science had been created in 1894, a move which resulted in the gradual alteration of jurisdiction for the Deans of the Junior and Senior Colleges, leaving them little more than officers in charge of advisory systems which registered students and verified the satisfaction of requirements for the "major" and "minor." An informal advisory system had been adopted in the autumn of 1901, but, being voluntary, it did not work out as had been hoped, and gradually a more formal system was adopted. In 1913 James R. Angell, the Dean of the Faculty of Arts, Literature, and Science, who later became President of Yale University, reported that the student would thereafter be under the jurisdiction of the same adviser from the beginning to the end of his course. "The curricula at present in force," Dean Angell stated, "throw upon the student [early in the second year of residence] the obligation to choose a principal [i.e., major] and secondary [i.e., minor] sequence of courses to be pursued throughout the last three years of the college course."[23] In his report for 1917–18 Dean Angell recommended that the jurisdiction of the Junior Colleges be reduced to the freshman year and that the final three years of college be organized as the Senior Colleges of Arts, Literature, and Science. He also suggested the elimination of the Associate's title—the recognition for the completion of the required work of the Junior Colleges, which President Harper had introduced. Faculty action to these ends was adopted, and President Judson recommended changes in the statutes to the Board of Trustees. The enlargement of the jurisdiction of the Senior Colleges was approved but was never put into effect.[24] The "paper" separation of Junior and Senior Colleges—each encompassing two years of work—remained until 1931. The meaninglessness of this organizational structure in practice was underlined in Dean Lovett's one-paragraph report for 1919: "I beg to recommend that in the future the reports of the registration by departments in the Senior and Junior Colleges be combined. The distinction between Junior College and Senior College courses is no longer a vital one."[25]

The large influx of students to the University of Chicago after the first World War—there were 11,385 different students registered during 1920–21, 3,659 of them classified as graduate—intensified the long-standing debate over the maintenance of a college by the University. President Judson pointed out in his report of 1919–20 that the "tendency [was] to siphon off funds from more advanced work" when undergraduate enrolment increased,[26] without mentioning that large tuition revenue came from these students. A year later he again discussed the relationship between the colleges and graduate departments: "Some ardent advocates of the Graduate Schools are inclined to lament that the University has also a large College. On the other hand, influential college alumni often complain that the College [is] submerged. . . . The College and the Graduate School began simultaneously. It has been our experience on the whole that the presence of the Graduate School has had a reflex influence on the College which is decidedly beneficial. The larger ideas which characterize the Graduate School cannot fail, to some extent at least, to affect the College students."[27] On the other hand, there were heard expressions of a more mundane defense of the collegiate function. The new Dean of the Colleges of Arts, Literature, and Science, David Allan Robertson, who later became President of Goucher College, expressed a utilitarian view of undergraduate education in his first report to the President. "The general function of the Colleges," he said, "is to provide training for efficiency in labor for one's self and for society and for the enjoyment of leisure by one's self and in society. Efficiency in labor . . . is ordinarily developed for the purpose of securing the largest and easiest pecuniary reward for efforts. . . . Even courses which are not contributions to a technical skill in making a living may appeal to selfish interest in success."[28]

It is difficult to see how such a view of the college program could foster the development of a truly liberal curriculum, one which would develop the student's ability to think for himself and which might be expected to produce good men and good citizens. A program which indicated the way to the "largest and easiest pecuniary reward" seems, in retrospect, characteristic of the 1920's, yet grossly inadequate as an educational goal. For, as William Rainey Harper said in 1905, "the purpose of the college . . . is . . . to develop in the man systematic habits; to give him control of his intellectual powers. . . . Special training looking toward a particular profession or line of work is not the province of the college."[29] A college program in which the first year or two were largely spent in making up for the deficiencies of preliminary education and the last two or three were devoted to professional work could scarcely achieve the objective set up by the first President. Yet Dean Robertson declared in his 1920–21 report that "each college student must have an individual curriculum such as will prepare him for his peculiar labor and leisure. . . . A study of student records shows, however, that too many, although they have satisfied . . . requirements for the baccalaureate degrees, have pursued badly balanced curricula."[30]

Twenty years later, in 1942, Robert M. Hutchins reasserted the original idea of the college before the American Council on Education. The college, he said, "must resolutely face the question of what is important and what not. It cannot teach everything that any student thinks he would like to hear about or that any teacher thinks he would like to talk about. It cannot pile course on course. . . . It must set up clear and comprehensible goals for its students to reach. It must articulate its courses, squeezing out waste, water, and duplication. It cannot tolerate education by the adding machine, that system by which we mark the intellectual progress of the young by the arithmetical averages they have achieved on a medley of miscellaneous courses. . . . More than all, [the college] that wishes to solve the problem how to develop and administer a liberal education must have a faculty devoted to this task."[31] The lack of group concern for the improvement of the curriculum in the years immediately following the first World War can be illustrated by the fact that in a dozen faculty meetings during a two-year period the average attendance was 9.7 and the agenda contained only one matter of curricular significance. In this instance, with twenty-two members of the faculty present, the recommendations were approved on the ground that they were "primarily departmental questions."[32]

In *The Chicago College Plan*, Chauncey Samuel Boucher described the situation which existed after the first World War as follows: "Undergraduate work was grossly neglected; even worse, the College came to be regarded by some members of the family as an unwanted, ill-begotten brat that should be disinherited. Nearly all finally agreed that we had reached a situation that necessitated a decision either to abandon the College or to develop it. . . ."[33] One group defended the College because (1) it provided the departments with an opportunity to select promising research students; (2) it brought revenue which helped pay for research and graduate instruction; and (3) it attracted contributions from college alumni—since it was this group, rather than graduate-school alumni, which had greater wealth.[34] The formally adopted view of the University Senate at the end of 1922 was: "The time has come to base our policy more definitely upon the obvious truth that this University can perform its most distinctive service to education through its graduate and professional schools. The limitation of undergraduate instruction appears to be complementary to this. . . ."[35]

President Judson retired in February, 1923, and was succeeded by Ernest DeWitt Burton, a New Testament scholar, a member of the faculty since 1892, and Director of the Libraries from 1910 to 1924. President Burton had large views of what the University should be and do, and, as his biographer says, "initiative and wisdom to devise great measures . . . energy to push these measures to accomplishment . . . and administrative ability of the first order."[36] During the two years of his presidency a major development campaign was inaugurated, and some $10,000,000 were secured to carry through various building and other programs. Unlike the great majority of his professorial colleagues, he felt that the University had "an unusual opportunity to develop a type of undergraduate life not yet presented in any modern university," and, as President, he told the Senate (of which he had been a member since 1892) that "the development of . . . [the undergraduate] division of the University is no less obligatory than the development of the work of the Graduate and Professional schools."[37] In his first annual report he said: "The University of Chicago was thought of by its founders as a College. Before it opened its doors, however, their ideal had, under the influence of President Harper's dominant personality, been displaced by that of a University in which graduate work should hold the place of eminence, but in which undergraduates should also have place and consideration. . . . That there are advantages in this plan need not be denied. But that it has serious disadvantages is beyond dispute. The ideals and purposes of a graduate school are in important respects different from those which properly characterize college work. . . . I wish to emphasize . . . that we have reached a stage in our development when of the two great fields of the University's work . . . each must stand on its own merits, each must receive that discriminating attention which its own character demands, neither must be hindered by the other." The decisive factor in this decision, President Burton stated, was the fact that "the University is dominated by the idea of research, and that such research must be carried on in all the social sciences, and surely not least in education."[38]

Burton's position on undergraduate work at that period in the University's history and the support of it by the Board of Trustees were important. Enrolments were large; teaching of freshmen and sophomores was at its lowest ebb. The departments had turned the Junior College into a training ground for their graduate students; at the time that Burton took office, approximately a hundred graduate students were teaching elementary courses, and the annual turnover in the staff of these courses was 40 per cent. A faculty report in 1924 said: "Our elementary teaching, while it is probably as good as that prevailing in any other similar institution . . . is on the whole far from satisfactory."[39] One remedy adopted by a single department, but not copied, was to discontinue its elementary courses. Romance languages had dropped beginning courses in 1920, and instruction in them was assumed by a "junior college division" of the Laboratory Schools of the School of Education. A staff specifically interested in teaching and in the development of teaching methods was assembled; it initiated and perfected the "reading method" of instruction in foreign language, a development having wide effect throughout the country. The organizational device was clumsy, however, and no similar transfers of jurisdiction were made.[40]

In the autumn of 1923 President Burton appointed Ernest Hatch Wilkins, a scholar in Romance languages, Dean of the Colleges of Arts, Literature, and Science, and, as President Burton's biographer remarks, "the morale of the Colleges soon showed a marked improvement."[41] During his first year in office Dean Wilkins carried through several reforms in the handling of college students and set in motion some thinking about the curriculum. The growth of the student body after the first World War provided an opportunity for a more selective admission system and led to an enlarged advisory staff to deal with the educational guidance of large numbers of students with varying backgrounds and interests. More individual attention was given to superior students. An "orientation week" for freshmen was instituted, preceding the opening of the autumn quarter, in which new students were introduced to the educational community and made to feel a part of it. This commonplace feature of every American college today was an innovation widely commented upon in 1924—an indication of how peripheral was the concern of large universities of that time for their undergraduate students.

On the larger problems of curriculum, organization, and facilities, there was much talk and no action. For one part of his overall planning program President Burton went to the Board of Trustees in September, 1923, and asked for the formation of a commission on the future development of the Colleges, to consist of seven members of the faculties appointed by him and three members of the Board. Burton told the commission that he was preparing the development program in terms of needed buildings and endowments; the commission decided that it could not plan physical requirements for undergraduates until it did "considerable investigation of educational policies." The moving figures in this inquiry were Dean Wilkins and Henry C. Morrison, Professor of Education and a specialist in the curriculums of secondary schools. By April, 1924, a report had been prepared which recommended a plan of undergraduate development which was radical for the 'twenties but not unlike William Rainey Harper's unrealized "blueprints." The organization of eight years of general education at the University of Chicago beyond six years of elementary schooling was to be divided between an enlarged University High School and a (junior) College separated from the senior college, in which specialization began. A student was to proceed into the College when he had demonstrated his ability in the high school, but it was expected that the completion of half the total program would usually signify such readiness.[42] The commission said that it favored a certificate to mark the completion of the College program, although "if any existing degrees must be awarded to graduates of the College, we submit that the attainment of intellectual, cultural, and volitional independence is worthily marked by the award of the bachelor's degree." The College was to be physically separated from the existing quadrangles, with sixteen large residential units for men and women to house twelve hundred, and an instructional quadrangle of buildings to accommodate a total of fifteen hundred, students. The report aroused opposition in the faculty because it "created an impression that the paramount interest of the University was in the colleges," because the basic educational theory behind the report—the division between general and specialized training—had not been formally accepted within the various faculties, and because the physical plan was "grandiose as compared with existing plans for graduate work."[43] The Board of Trustees received the report but took no action on it.[44]

Although prospects for a thoroughgoing revision of the curriculum grew dimmer during 1924, Dean Wilkins proposed to introduce a series of "survey" courses for freshmen, designed to orient the student in fields of knowledge which crossed artificial boundary lines created by the departmental structure. He quoted President Burton as saying that one of the purposes of the college was "to help each student to acquire such a knowledge of the physical universe, of the history of the race, of the structure of society, and of the nature of the individual, that . . . he may have a sense of where he is."[45] The desire of Dean Wilkins to enlist the aid of the best men on the faculty for teaching freshmen and sophomores, coupled with the knowledge that the "Contemporary Civilization" course at Columbia and the "Evolution" course at Dartmouth were succeeding, helped the survey proposal along. Whatever the faults of the survey course, it was an improvement over the typical departmental introductory course for the needs of most students and a necessary development in general education at the junior college level. The junior college line of "cleavage" from the senior college, advocated so strongly by Harper, had, during the 'twenties, become a fact in 55 per cent of the independent colleges, 80 per cent of the endowed universities, and 90 per cent of the state universities.[46] As Boucher described the situation which brought forth the survey course: "It seemed that nearly every department framed its curriculum as though the intellectual sun rose and set within its boundaries, as though every worthy student must desire to specialize in that department, and as though that department had a life-long vested interest in every student who elected its introductory course."[47]

The first survey course at Chicago was "The Nature of the

World and of Man," under the direction of Horatio Hackett Newman, Professor of Zoölogy. This course, extending over two quarters, was offered for the first time in the autumn of 1924. It was primarily a lecture course, in which the University's leading scientists lectured on the nature and properties of matter, the character of chemical properties, the origin of the earth, the evolution of the plant and animal kingdoms, and the evolution of man. The course was successful: enrolment (of selected applicants among freshmen and, later, sophomores) increased so rapidly that there was some embarrassment to the staff and the Dean's office; and the lectures were published in a book, which the American Library Association selected as one of forty notable books of 1926.[48] Dean Wilkins' plans for other survey courses, including one in the humanities entitled "The Meaning and Value of the Arts" and one in the social sciences entitled "Man and Society," were offered but did not meet with enough faculty support to become established in the curriculum. But the impetus generated by his proposals and, in particular, by the success of "The Nature of the World and of Man" greatly assisted curriculum reform in the following years.

Max Mason, a distinguished mathematical physicist from the University of Wisconsin, succeeded Burton as President on October 1, 1925, after the latter's death. Mason's great interest in research was revealed in his expressions about the development of the University of Chicago. "One of the greatest duties that we have to perform," he said, "is to create . . . a university in which participation in scholarship is pleasant, looked for, and appreciated by the undergraduate body. . . . With the research background of this institution there seems to be clearly indicated a type of performance in education which it is our specific duty to try—education by participation in research. We cannot drive that to the limit. There must be . . . a training in the technique for that participation, and . . . means for obtaining general information. It seems clear that the last two can be left to the individual students without nearly so much detailed supervision as in the past, if they are stimulated to real interest by contact with our creative scholars."[49] And on college education: "We are in a period of wholesome self-examination and experimentation for

means of vitalizing the intellectual life of the undergraduate. . . .
Our goal will be reached when . . . the intellectual work of the
College becomes a 'student activity.' Under such conditions the
. . . College will stimulate, as it is stimulated by, the work in
graduate teaching and research. The interest and appreciation
of students in the Junior College has been increased by the orientation courses. . . . Such courses may well prove of the greatest
value in fixing the temper of the work of general education in the
Junior College, when supplemented by courses of specific training." [50]

Contemporary expressions of faculty opinion and committee
activity revealed divergent interpretations of Mason's position
on undergraduate education—reflecting, of course, existing divisions of faculty sentiment. Dean Wilkins revived consideration of
a document entitled "A Theory of Education" which had been
prepared as a detailed argument to establish the desirability of
a new administrative unit for general education within the University.[51] This unit would have a dean with power over appointments and a faculty possessing, "as an indispensable qualification," interest in teaching. Julius Stieglitz, Chairman of the Department of Chemistry, spoke for the scientists when he proposed
that the existing junior college be improved "with decidedly
enlarged opportunities for underclassmen to receive inspiration
by work under, and contact with, men who, by their research
work, are contributing to the boundaries of human knowledge."[52]
At the same time, however, the Dean of the Graduate School,
Gordon J. Laing, was saying: "Not even in the best [university]
is the graduate work on the scale or the quality that would be
possible if the institution were entirely free from undergraduate
entanglements."[53] The conflicting philosophies with regard to the
place of general education in a university were not to be easily
settled. Wilkins tried vigorously to get the faculty of the Colleges
to adopt a position which would clarify administrative, faculty,
and curriculum matters in this regard, but the resulting document—adopted in January, 1927—was a compromise report
which left the existing situation largely unchanged.[54]

Boucher followed Wilkins as Dean of the Colleges in 1926[55] and
continued the kind of "self-examination and experimentation"

which his predecessor had started. His immediate approach to the problem was to hammer away at the quality of teaching, telling the President that instruction was being given "slight attention and no real supervision" by many departments. Teaching done by graduate students, Boucher stated, was "simply a means of keeping the pot boiling while they give their best efforts . . . on graduate courses and a doctoral dissertation," and young instructors with the Ph.D. believed quite accurately "that their advancement in rank and salary will depend . . . upon their research productivity."[56] Dean Laing held the position that the teaching burden caused by the relatively large undergraduate enrolment—there were forty-one hundred undergraduates in arts and sciences in 1926–27—cut research productivity in two.[57] Nevertheless, as a result of Dean Boucher's argument, departmental and administrative officers making appointments were charged "to bear in mind both the possession of creative power in a particular field and the ability to teach."[58] Some departmental faculties showed an increased interest in survey courses and, at the request of the College, undertook revision of introductory courses to meet the needs of students not specializing in their departments. Also during 1926–27 the University took the important step of requiring all freshmen to enter the Junior College of Arts, Literature, and Science; none could immediately enrol in a professional school, such as business administration or education.

President Mason, in 1927, publicly questioned the desirability of continuing the slavish adherence to course units and course credits as the basis of awarding degrees—the now widely condemned "academic bookkeeping" by which intelligence and progress are bought and sold across the American collegiate counter. Dean Boucher told the President that he was convinced that the faculty would welcome an opportunity for a fundamental revision of the course-unit and course-credit system—the system which meant, as he put it, that when a student was half the way to his Bachelor's degree he was registered on a white instead of a yellow card.[59] To consider these problems and related curriculum matters, President Mason, in March, 1928, appointed a strong Senate committee on the undergraduate colleges, consisting of nine members, with Boucher as chairman.[60] The committee went to work promptly; its report was ready on May 1, 1928, and was mailed to the faculty. The report was a step toward the goal of resolving the character of collegiate education: it proposed the abolition of the existing system of counting credits both for admission to the Senior College and for the award of the Bachelor's degree and the substitution therefor of comprehensive examinations. The requirements for the Bachelor's degree were to be stated in terms of three comprehensive examinations, one covering the major field and two for minor fields, all of which might be taken whenever the student felt he was ready. The Junior College requirements were stated in terms of five comprehensive examinations: (1) English composition and literature; (2) foreign language; (3) natural science and mathematics; (4) social science; and (5) an elective that might represent the early stages of specialization in some field of particular interest to the student.[61] The exact character and length of the courses to prepare for these examinations were not specified but were to be determined by the Junior College faculty. Establishment of a board of examiners was also recommended.

This report was not acted upon because of the announcement of President Mason's resignation on May 7, 1928. Instead, it was referred for further study by the faculty to two boards, one for the Junior College and one for the Senior College. The boards were asked "to have in mind, as ends to be attained": the substitution of fields of study for course units, the employment of comprehensive examinations as tests of accomplishment, and provision for exceptional students to make more rapid progress.[62] Mason referred to the situation on the occasion of his farewell address to the faculty on June 1, saying: "I have spoken much before Faculty dinners of the undergraduate problem. Most of the *support* has gone to the graduate work; a good many of the *words* have gone to the undergraduate department. I hope it will be treated with the seriousness it deserves."[63]

The academic year 1928–29 was a difficult one for those interested in undergraduate education at the University. At the end of the year Boucher felt that the faculty was no nearer a solution of basic questions than it had been six years before. While the

Senior College board considering the May 1 report was "fairly in agreement" on the notion of Bachelor's comprehensive examinations, the Junior College group was "shot through with disagreement."[64] The major points of attack on the proposals were three, none of them new: survey courses were attacked as less desirable than departmental introductory courses; limitation on early specialization was bemoaned; and there was vigorous disagreement over the question of what faculty group was to control the Junior College. The uncertainty was heightened by the fact that the University was without a president. This difficulty was removed soon after April 17, 1929, when Robert Maynard Hutchins, Dean of the Yale School of Law, was named by the Board of Trustees to be the fifth President of the University of Chicago. Thus began twenty years of significant development for undergraduate education, as well as distinguished progress in graduate education and research.

Boucher early presented the Senate Committee report to the new President and found that he was in sympathy with its objectives.[65] President Hutchins addressed himself to the public on the subject of undergraduate education at Chicago for the first time in his inaugural address, November 19, 1929: "The emphasis on productive scholarship that has characterized the University from the beginning and must characterize it to the end has naturally led to repeated question as to the place and future of our colleges. They could not be regarded as training grounds for the graduate schools, for less than 20 per cent of their graduates went on. . . . Nor did the argument that we should contribute good citizens . . . make much impression on distinguished scholars anxious to get ahead with their own researches. They were glad to have somebody make this contribution, but saw little reason why they should be elected for the task. At times, therefore, members of the Faculty have urged that we withdraw from undergraduate work, or at least from the first two years of it. But we do not propose to abandon or dismember the colleges. . . . If the University's function is to attempt solutions of difficult educational problems . . . it cannot retreat from the field of undergraduate work. . . . The whole question of the relation of the first two years of college to the high school on the one hand and the Senior College on the other is one of the most baffling that is before us."[66] The President also made suggestions for broadening the program of early collegiate education and proposed definite steps for improving the preparation of college teachers. The faculty knew from this inaugural address and from the series of actions and speeches which followed in the next few years that the President was, as the statutes of the University say, "the executive head of the University in all its departments, exercising such supervision and direction as will promote the efficiency of every department." Furthermore, he had ideas.

It is not easy to characterize all that happened at the University of Chicago in the first two years of Hutchins' presidency. In respect to the Senate committee report on the College, he urged the two boards to assemble for study and discussion sample sets of comprehensive examinations for administration to students completing the Junior College. There was considerable talk about the kinds of courses that would be suitable to prepare students for these examinations; and it became clearer that a wholesale and wholesome attack on academic bookkeeping was under way. Budgetary support to the Junior College was provided, to substitute regular instructors for "the Coxey's army of graduate student assistants."[67] But more important than that, however, was the decision of the President that improvement in the work of the University could be accomplished only after a radical reorganization of its structure and administration. A number of factors led to the shaping of the reorganization plan. An outside committee, financed by the General Education Board, was at work on a large-scale survey of the University.[68] The report of the Senate Committee on Undergraduate Colleges itself suggested the seemingly irreconcilable attitudes of the generalists and the specialists, referred to in the President's inaugural address.

It was decided that the major educational objective of the Junior College (the freshman and sophomore years) should be general education, with, as Dean Boucher put it, "reasonable provision for the pursuit of special interests."[69] With the support of Deans Boucher, Laing, and Henry Gordon Gale, the latter the Dean of the Graduate School of Science, President Hutchins proposed to the University Senate on October 22, 1930, a divisional organization of the work in arts, literature, and science, which was designed to improve administration by reducing the number of officers reporting to the President and increase the responsibility of deans, promote research, co-ordinate teaching, and open the way to experiments in general education.[70] There was to be the College division to "do the work of the University in general higher education"; and, upon completion of the College, the student could enter one of four divisions for specialized study in arts, literature, and science. These were to be the Division of the Biological Sciences, the Division of the Humanities, the Division of the Physical Sciences, and the Division of the Social Sciences, each administered by a dean. Existing departments were to be assigned by the President to one of the four divisions, and the divisions were to assume the responsibility of recommending candidates for the Bachelor's, Master's, and Doctor of Philosophy degrees. Students from the College were also to be admitted to the professional schools, Business, Divinity, Law, Library, Medicine, and Social Service.[71] The College was to award a certificate (subsequently, the restored Associate of Arts title) to mark the completion of its program. The desirability of awarding the Bachelor's degree was advanced by the President, but no proposal was put to vote in a legislative body.

President Hutchins' proposal for reorganization, which was only one typewritten page in length, was immediately adopted by the Senate and approved by the Board of Trustees.[72] The task of remaking curriculums—or of leaving them alone—in each division fell to the divisional faculties. Provision was made for a College faculty and a College budget. "The budget of the College would consist of that portion of the salaries of the members of the faculty that represented the share of their time and attention that was devoted to College work. Each member of the College would be a member of some other division."[73] The faculty of the College was not yet independent of departmental control, but it had more chance of guiding its own destiny than ever before. Boucher was named Dean of the College. He immediately appointed a curriculum committee, which reported to the faculty of the College a completely new program, which the faculty adopted on March 5, 1931.[74] Completion of the College requirements was stated solely in terms of educational attainment as measured by comprehensive examinations, and not in terms of course credits. To receive the College certificate, the student was to pass seven examinations, five of them specified. A student could take these examinations whenever he felt that he was prepared; class attendance was to be optional. The task of advising students —along with all nonacademic activities devoted to the welfare of students—was transferred to a newly established University officer, the Dean of Students.[75]

In order that completion of the College requirements should signify "a wholesome balance between breadth and depth of educational experience," the College faculty stated that the examinations were to demand "the attainment of the minimum essentials of factual information and an introduction to the methods of thought and work in each of the four divisional fields—the humanities, the social sciences, the physical sciences, and the biological sciences—such as may be expected of a student who has pursued a general course through an academic year" in each field (requirements *one*, *two*, *three*, and *four*). The new "introductory general courses" were to be a further development of the "survey course" but were to be broader in scope and deeper in penetration. In addition to these four examinations, a student was to pass examinations in two of the four divisional fields "as may be expected of" a student who has taken two year-long divisional or subject sequences of courses[76] recommended by the faculty of one of the four upper divisions and approved by the College faculty. This meant that a student would take examinations (requirements *five* and *six*) over two one-year courses—or prepare independently for them—offered in art, literature, music, philosophy, or a foreign language; social sciences (political science, economics, and sociology); chemistry, geography, geology, mathematics, or physics; biological sciences (botany, zoölogy, and physiology).[77] The *seventh* requirement was an examination to measure "the student's ability to express himself with clarity and accuracy in written English"; and a year course, replacing a one-quarter course, was set up to prepare for this examination. There were also separate foreign language and mathematics requirements, measured by two high-school units each, which nearly all entering students at Chicago offered for admission.[78]

The College faculty adopted its new program (widely referred to as the New Plan) in March, 1931. The plan called for a system of comprehensive examinations to be constructed by independent examiners. In the same month the University Senate approved the establishment of an all-University Board of Examinations which was to be responsible for "determination of policies to be used in the formulation and administration of comprehensive examinations" in the College, the Divisions, and, on request of the faculty involved, the professional schools.[79] A University Examiner and a Chief Examiner were to be in charge of the preparation of examinations, with the assistance of (a) a technical staff and office force and (b) members of the instructional staff who had shown interest and competence in the problems involved. The examination program has been fully effective in the College since 1931.[80]

At least three other features of the new College program, the first courses of which were offered in the Autumn Quarter of 1931, should be mentioned. The College curriculum committee report stated: (1) "Experimentation with methods of instruction shall be encouraged"; (2) "placement tests . . . to determine a student's competence for enrolment in a course . . . shall be encouraged"; and (3) "for each of the courses . . . a syllabus with appropriate bibliographical material, and sample examinations, shall be published."[81] The idea of experimentation, so significant to the growth of the University as a whole throughout its history, was to be a basic principle of the new College. The idea of placement tests for incoming students, which President Harper had advanced as the correct way to place students properly in a scheme of collegiate education—instead of high-school credits— was again recognized. However, with the exception of placement in English composition, the device was not immediately used. The idea of a syllabus for every course, to encourage independent work by the student, resulted in the publication of a score of useful detailed outlines (many with selected readings) of courses which have attracted the attention of hundreds of institutions to the kind of integrated general courses constructed at Chicago.

Similarly, the publication of examinations has shown students the kinds of questions and the scope of the materials on which they would be examined and has demonstrated to educators the possibilities of comprehensive examinations.

To get the introductory general courses into operation in the autumn of 1931, the College faculty devoted, as Dean Boucher reported,[82] "immense amounts of time, careful study, pointed discussion, and downright hard work" to the weighing of objectives, the choice and organization of appropriate subject matter, and the selection of instructional materials. A new organizational device, the staff, came into being for each of the general courses; there were to be no departments. Under course directors appointed by the Dean, the staffs shaped the general courses. Members of the faculties trained in the various disciplines met to agree on what a course should contain, worked together on the syllabi and other instructional materials,[83] and reached agreement (together with the examiners) on what the examination should expect of the student. As individual instructors they then went into the classrooms to conduct their courses with a great degree of freedom as to techniques and approaches.

It was thus that the New Plan got under way. The fact that students did not have to attend classes did not cut down attendance. The fact that they could proceed as rapidly as they wanted did not materially change the pace; in the first three years of the program thirty-four students completed their work for the College certificate in less than the usual time, but one hundred and eighteen took longer than the usual two-year period. The curriculum, President Hutchins said in 1935, "succeeded in keeping the individual up against work that is stimulating and challenging to him."[84]

By the end of the first year in which the New Plan had been in operation, the President was determined to take some steps to resolve the question of the relationship between the first two years of college and the last two years of high school, a problem which he had said in his inaugural address needed a solution. Support for the proposal that he had made to incorporate the last two years of the University High School into the College by removing them from the jurisdiction of the Department of Education and the Division of the Social Sciences came largely from the educators and the social scientists, with some approval in the humanities and the professional schools, and very little from the natural scientists.[85] On November 19, 1932, after favorable consideration by the deans and by its policy committee, the University Senate approved by a very substantial majority the President's proposal to extend the work of the College in general education into the last two years of the University High School, under the jurisdiction of the College faculty. The Senate also abrogated the requirement that all members of the College faculty be members of departmental faculties in the four upper divisions of the University. The Dean of the College was empowered to recommend to the President appointments to the College faculty without departmental status.[86]

Hutchins then carried the proposal to the Board of Trustees. He pointed out to them that the organization of education in America on the plan of eight years of elementary school, four years of high school, and four years of college was the result of a series of historical accidents and was coming apart at the joints. The elementary school was becoming a six-year unit; the junior high school had been developed and was taking over Grades VII and VIII from the elementary school and sometimes Grade IX from the high school. Superior students in numerous areas were being admitted to college without having been graduated from high school. Two-year junior colleges, most of them publicly supported, numbered four hundred and fifty in 1932. The two-year unit was unsatisfactory, the President argued, because it was difficult to frame a unified curriculum in an institution which must lose 50 per cent of its student body by graduation every year.[87] In January, 1933, the Board of Trustees approved the transfer of jurisdiction over the last two years of the University High School from the Department of Education to the College but was unwilling to call the four-year unit the College and did not want extensive publicity given to the move because the University had so recently embarked on its reorganization program.[88]

Opposition in the College faculty to the proposed four-year arrangement began to develop immediately. The College curriculum committee took the position that the faculty had, within the preceding two years, worked out an entirely new curriculum, which had just been put into operation. A number of the faculty felt that the College staff would be made into high-school teachers. One senior member of the faculty, while approving of the change in jurisdiction over the last two years of high school, said that he did not favor any attempt to "push much of our college work down to the level of high school students in their third and fourth years," but added, "of course, that could be done with a degree of success." Other faculty members took the view expressed by one of them as follows: "I am interested in the College only as an integral part of the University which aims to provide the individual student with the best possible preparation for the successful prosecution of his subsequent [specialized] work." From the High School came a report that its faculty was already at work on curriculum revision; the implication was that the teachers in the last two years did not want to be swallowed up by the College faculty. As a result, in March, 1933, the College faculty and the University Senate approved the recommendation of the College curriculum committee that "pending further development of our program, the designation of the last two years of the University High School . . . continue." A slightly modified curriculum was approved which was "designed to serve the needs of those [high-school students] who enter other institutions as well as those who enter the University of Chicago." "Though at some indefinite time in the future," the curriculum committee's report stated, "it may be advisable to frame a continuous and completely integrated program for a consolidated four-year unit, it would seem inadvisable to attempt to do so at the present time."[89] While members of the upper high-school teaching staff became members of the College faculty and qualified high-school students were permitted to take work in the College when they were prepared to do so, President Hutchins and the substantial group which supported the change were, in 1933, unable to offer the country the example of a four-year college curriculum beginning after the end of the sophomore year in high school. Progress would have to await the gradual building-up of a faculty interested in perfecting such a program of general education.[90]

By 1934 the work of the freshman and sophomore years had at

long last become respectable; although the result had not been sought or expected, the introductory survey courses had come to be regarded as "harder" than their predecessors. The quality of teaching had improved markedly; three $1,000 awards were made annually for the most effective college teaching. The administration encouraged the annual revision of the published syllabi for the various courses and, for the first time, made provision for a separate College library—which circulated approximately 125,000 books each academic year. An elaborate questionnaire to one thousand students verified general observations that students were enthusiastic about the new courses and about what they got from them. In general, they rated the biological science and humanities courses above the physical science and social science courses.[91]

The general courses and the use of comprehensive examinations in place of course credits to measure academic achievement had great influence upon other colleges and universities. Nevertheless, it was apparent by 1935 that the President expected more progress to be made in developing the curriculum. He has said that he thought of having an outside agency make a survey to spur further experiment but rejected the idea because he doubted that such an inquiry would have much effect on the faculty. Early in 1936 he wrote the lectures on higher education delivered at Yale University in April, which, when published as *The Higher Learning in America*,[92] had an impressive influence upon educational thinking throughout the United States. Termed "militant, rebellious, positive, and important" by one reviewer after another, the book naturally had impact and reaction on the quadrangles of the University of Chicago. Hutchins' prescription in the *Higher Learning* for administering general education in time became a reality, as this narrative tells in detail. "Let us assume," the President said in 1936, "that we have an intelligible organization of education under which there is a four-year unit, beginning at about the beginning of the junior year in high school and ending at about the end of the sophomore year in college. Let us assume that we are going to try to teach in that unit everybody who can learn from books. Let us assume further that the conclusion of their work in this unit will mark the end of formal instruction for most students. They will not go on to the university. Nevertheless we must have a curriculum which will, in the main, do as well for those who are going on as those who are not."[93] He then asked: "What shall the curriculum be?" and gave his answer: "A course of study consisting of the greatest books of the Western world and the arts of reading, writing, thinking, and speaking, together with mathematics, the best exemplar of the processes of human reason. If our hope has been to frame a curriculum which educes the elements of our common human nature, this program should realize our hope. If we wish to prepare the young for intelligent action, this course of study should assist us; for they will have learned what has been done in the past, and what the greatest men have thought. They will have learned how to think themselves. If we wish to lay a basis for advanced study, that basis is provided. If we wish to secure true universities, we may look forward to them, because students and professors may acquire through this course of study a common stock of ideas and common methods of dealing with them. All the needs of general education in America seem to be satisfied by this curriculum."[94]

Publication of *The Higher Learning in America*—as with many of Hutchins' five hundred different statements during twenty years of educational leadership—brought forth at least three generalized reactions to his theories among the faculty. One group has felt that Hutchins' criticisms of higher education were correct but that his positive proposals were wrong or, at best, untimely. A second group has taken Hutchins' proposals as immediate goals to be effected at the first opportunity, with little attempt to relate them to existing situations. A third group has been keenly aware that Hutchins' leadership and ideas have made possible a College within, and of, the University of Chicago in which a program of general education could be developed; it is this group which, stimulated by him to work out a meaningful program, has built the College.

The diverse roles of these groups were very apparent in the years 1936–37. With a view to stimulating the study of the curriculum in the College and in the Division of the Humanities, there was established in the latter a committee to consider the place of the "seven liberal arts"—grammar, rhetoric, logic, arithmetic, geometry, music, and astronomy—in modern education. Stringfellow Barr, a historian, and Scott Buchanan, a philosopher, both at that time of the University of Virginia, were made visiting professors, and a committee of their choosing set to work to frame a curriculum based on a study of the great books of Western civilization. President Hutchins said at the time: "In view of the state into which . . . [some] disciplines have fallen, the vocational attitudes of most students, and the . . . hostility of many professors, it is doubtful whether . . . [the seven liberal arts] can be adapted to contemporary conditions. The difficulties of framing a program of general education without some resort to them, however, justify the attempt."[95] The presence of this committee on the liberal arts on the Chicago quadrangles caused a furor far out of proportion to the usual campus reaction when a committee tries to wrestle with an intellectual problem. Those faculty members who objected to Hutchins' educational views were joined in objection to the committee's activities by those who felt that one major revision of a curriculum (i.e., the College's) in a short span of years was enough. The group interested in continuous study and revision of the liberal arts program was, as is usual in "crisis" situations, inarticulate by comparison with the objectors. What happened is told somewhat bitterly by Scott Buchanan: "The University of Chicago saw red, and they almost burned our books so that we couldn't read. Our presence made . . . [the] Dean of the Humanities a great deal of trouble. It was a great relief for everybody but the donors of the money for this project when St. John's [College in Annapolis, Maryland] called the members of the Liberal Arts Committee to put its program into operation."[96] Actually, the place of great books in the College curriculum at Chicago had, previous to the existence of the Barr-Buchanan committee, and has since, received study and attention; the results may be judged by program descriptions in later chapters of this book.[97]

During the period from 1934 to early 1937 the curriculum committee of the College had intermittently devoted time and energy to the construction of an "ideal" program for the four-year College which began after two years of the traditional high school. This was an attempt to achieve concretely the objectives of the paper reorganization which had been approved by the Trustees in January, 1933, but not effected by the faculty. The work of the curriculum committee was accelerated after October 1, 1935, when Aaron J. Brumbaugh, Professor of Education and Dean of Students in the College, was appointed Dean of the College, to succeed Chauncey Boucher, who resigned to become President of West Virginia University. Since 1933 more and more members of the College faculty had come to believe that the work of the College could be carried back into the last two years of high school; more understood that youths sixteen years of age who had finished ten years of adequate schooling were physiologically and psychologically ready for college work. The curriculum committee, headed by Brumbaugh and consisting of twenty-seven members of the faculty, brought in a report during the winter of 1937 setting forth a new four-year program;[98] a separate smaller committee, at the same time, made a detailed study of factors involved in granting the Bachelor's degree at the end of the College course but made no recommendations to the College faculty.[99]

The curriculum recommended by the curriculum committee and adopted by the College faculty on March 9, 1937, was based on the principle that "the end of general education can be achieved best by helping students to master the leading ideas and significant facts in the principal fields of knowledge, with a view to the development of intelligent action." All students in the four-year College were to follow the same basic program, with time "available . . . in which to follow special interests or to acquire a greater mastery of the subjects and techniques needed for advanced work."[100] The following courses were to be provided to prepare students for the comprehensive examinations, fifteen in number: A three-year course in the humanities (requirements *one*, *two*, and *three*), including material from history (ancient, medieval, modern European, and American), the fine arts, and literature; a three-year course in the natural sciences (requirements *four*, *five*, and *six*), which would be offered in two variations: two years of biology and the existing Introductory General Course in the Physical Sciences, or two years of physical science and the existing Introductory General Course in the Biological Sciences; a three-year course in the social sciences (requirements *seven, eight,* and *nine*), a study of society in its political, economic, and social aspects; a three-year course in reading, writing, and criticism (requirements *ten, eleven,* and *twelve*), in which there would be intensive reading of selected texts in the subject-matter areas of the curriculum, coupled with extensive exercises in oral and written expression; a one-year course in philosophy (requirement *thirteen*) designed to encourage active critical reflection and interrelations of subject matters previously considered; two departmental elective courses (requirements *fourteen* and *fifteen*), as in the existing two-year College curriculum; and, finally, mastery of mathematics and a foreign language equivalent to two high-school entrance units each. Physical education requirements were set for students in the first two years of the program.

The curriculum committee and the College faculty, which adopted the committee's report, did not expect in 1937 that the four-year program would have immediate effects on the two-year program. There were common elements in the two curriculums, but most members of the College faculty believed that the task of the "Four-Year College" was one of building a program for the one hundred students annually finishing Grade X of the University High School[101] and for a few students from the immediate environs of the University. Nevertheless, attention could be called to several important features in the program: the establishment of three-year units of study; the development of the courses in reading, writing, and criticism; and the provision for an integration course. The inadequacy of the provision for mathematics and foreign language instruction found in the two-year program was not corrected.

Classes in the "Four-Year College" began in the autumn of 1937.[102] The small size of sections made it possible to use a wide variety of instructional methods; laboratory work was called for in the science courses—something which had not been considered feasible in the large introductory general courses in the biological and physical sciences for freshmen and sophomores. Increased emphasis was placed on the advisory services, including individual diagnosis of reading difficulties and study habits, and remedial work where necessary. The instructional staff for the first two years of the four-year unit consisted of teachers who had been working with Grades XI and XII, supplemented in the succeeding years with several new appointments. Rarely, during the years between 1937 and 1941, did the faculty of the traditional freshman and sophomore years participate in actual course construction and teaching, although a member of the Department of Philosophy was called upon to organize and teach the fourth-year course in philosophy (requirement *thirteen*), which was called "Methods, Values, and Concepts." One member of the faculty teaching in Grades XI and XII was elected to the newly created College Committee on Policy and Personnel.[103] During the succeeding ten years this committee became the only standing committee of the College faculty, one in which all important matters pertaining to the development of programs and the organization of courses and staffs were discussed prior to faculty action.

Two matters which were to have continuing importance in the development of the College came before the Policy Committee and the faculty during 1939 and 1940. One dealt with the functions of the faculty members who were directors of general courses. A minority of the committee maintained that the director was merely a presiding officer, who carried out the "will of the staff"; but, after considerable discussion, the Policy Committee adopted a statement of agreement which provided that, thereafter, directors were to be called "chairmen," were to engage in democratic consultation with the staff, and were responsible for carrying on negotiations with the Dean of the College—including recommendations about the course under their charge, appointments, and promotions. Members of the staff were at liberty to consult the dean with regard to individual views.[104] The other issue of importance was a proposal brought forward at a faculty meeting by members who represented divisional interests, that quarterly course grades could be allowed as substitutes for the grade received on the comprehensive examination covering a full year's work in the specialized sequence courses.[105] The reasons advanced were that the comprehensive examinations shortened the Spring Quarter instructional time, that the examination system produced "loafing" in class, that there were some subjects which did not lend themselves to comprehensive examinations, and that the testing and rating of students were not a primary function of the university.

The issue thus raised with some force after nearly ten years of the New Plan divided the faculty, and for six months there were meetings of the Policy Committee, exchanges of letters, and the preparation of reports pro and con on the comprehensive examination system. The majority of the Policy Committee—and subsequently of the faculty—took the view that any relaxation of the comprehensive examination requirements was an undesirable return to less objective testing and a lowering of standards. A report adopted by the faculty approved existing legislation on examinations and called for greater effort on the part of the faculty in the preparation of better and different types of examinations; it also reaffirmed the faculty's view that the examinations were an integrating factor in larger units of subject matter and that they created a better relationship between student and teacher (who did not grade them).[106]

In the early part of the autumn of 1941, Brumbaugh, who had served six years as Dean, was appointed Dean of Students in the University, and President Hutchins selected Clarence Henry Faust to succeed him. Faust had taught courses in composition, linguistics, and American literature in the College and the Department of English for eleven years, and at the time of his appointment as Dean he was made Professor of English. At his first meeting with the Policy Committee, in answer to a question about his views of the duties of a dean, Dean Faust stated that he believed that a dean should (1) perform routine duties of administration; (2) act as a clearing-house for faculty proposals, directing them to appropriate faculty channels—already provided—for action; and (3) initiate new ideas on College policy and advance them through regular procedures. He further suggested a complete reconsideration of the objectives of the College, beginning with a review of statements of policies and aims prepared by staff chairmen. He stated that he believed that general education, usually defined negatively as "nonvocational" or "nonspecialized," should receive more positive definition in terms of ends to be served and functions to be performed.[107] During the five years that he was Dean, Faust worked toward this goal, eventually demonstrating that a truly integrated curriculum could be constructed and that a first-rate faculty could be devoted to the tasks of general education.[108]

During the eighteen months prior to the attack on Pearl Harbor, the University had co-operated with agencies of the federal government in conducting projects—mostly research—in connection with the program of national defense. Late in the summer of 1941 several training programs were begun, and after December 7, 1941, every effort was made to provide the maximum use of the University's resources and the maximum opportunity for students to get an education before entering military service or to get training for special warwork in the shortest possible time. President Hutchins, in a speech to the faculty on January 7, 1942, stated that he believed the time to be propitious to award the Bachelor's degree to mark the completion of the program of general education offered by the College.[109] This would enable the student to reach a definite educational goal before entering military service. He reminded the faculty that the proposal was neither novel nor drastic for the University of Chicago, that the matter had been discussed in 1930, in 1932, and again in 1937, when the four-year program of the College had finally been adopted. He stated that it was his belief that the development of the four-year college program for the Bachelor's degree would remove the last obstacle to the clarification of the University's educational program, thus completing a process begun fifty years before under William Rainey Harper.[110] In discussing the matter with the deans and with the elected Senate Committee on University Policy later in January, the President elaborated his view that the building of significant programs to the Master's degree in the three-year period of study in the divisions would materially improve the quality of specialized training. After hearing argument that the proposal be postponed until after the war, the Senate Committee voted eight to five to recommend to the full Senate that the College be empowered to award the Bachelor's degree for "completion of general education as redefined by the College Faculty."[111]

In the Senate—constituted of professors of full rank—the battle over the President's proposal was intense. Sentiment in the humanities and social sciences tended to favor the change; in the natural sciences, particularly the physical sciences, to oppose it; and in the professional schools, to be rather evenly divided. The argument against the relocation of the degree rested primarily on three grounds. The first was tradition. It was held that the Bachelor's degree had a commonly accepted significance in American colleges and universities—a four-year program, including specialization in a major field of study, based upon a four-year course of study in secondary school. It was further argued that students would have difficulty in transferring to other institutions from the College at Chicago. The second principal line of argument, advanced by the physical scientists, was that there was a recognized content in the program of studies leading to the Bachelor of Science degree in such subjects as chemistry and mathematics. The third line of argument was that the process of general education was not limited to the span of work in the College—that it extended through the period of specialized divisional or graduate work.[112]

Proponents of the change traced the evolution of the educational program of the University of Chicago from 1890 to 1930 and from 1930 to 1942, emphasizing the nation-wide acceptance of the junior college idea pioneered by Chicago and the more recent development of the four-year period of college work following the completion of ten years of primary and secondary schooling. This group also pointed out, supporting their view with a historical summary of the development of liberal education to the Bachelor's degree in the United States and Europe, that tradition likewise called for the award of a degree for the completion of general studies. To the arguments of the scientists, the social science group replied that the Bachelor of Science degree programs were not in line with the principal objectives of the divisions—advanced training and research—and, further, that the development of the three-year programs of specialization for the Master's degree was a desirable and necessary goal.

With regard to the idea that general education was a continuing process, two points were made. It was recalled that by its action in the reorganization of 1930–31 the Senate charged the College to "do the work of the University in general higher education." It was admitted that the process of general education did not stop with the College. As President Hutchins was later to phrase the position: "No program of liberal education, whether it ends at eighteen or twenty-two, can produce a man who will never have to learn anything more. A liberal education should communicate the leading facts, principles, and ideas which an educated man should possess, together with the intellectual techniques needed to acquire, understand, and apply more facts, principles, and ideas. This, and only this, the College pretends to do. Education is a lifelong process. We are not so deluded as to suppose that educational institutions, by any age, can do what only a full life of study, reflection, and experience can accomplish."[113]

After discussion and debate at two extended meetings, the Senate voted on January 22, 1942, by a vote of 63 to 48, "that the Bachelor's degree be awarded in recognition of the completion of general education, as redefined by the College faculty." At the same time, the power to award the degrees of Bachelor of Arts and Bachelor of Philosophy was taken away from the Divisions of the Humanities and Social Sciences and from the professional schools, while for the "continuation of the national emergency" the Divisions of the Biological Sciences and the Physical Sciences could award the degree of Bachelor of Science.[114]

The task of redefining general education and revising the course of study was thus given to the College faculty. Dean Faust reported the action of the Senate to the College Policy Committee on January 26, and on March 10—preceding a full meeting of the faculty called for March 19—the recommendations of the majority and minority of the committee concerning the program for the Bachelor's degree were transmitted to the faculty. During the six weeks devoted to the preparation of the report, fourteen lengthy meetings of the committee were held, a preliminary report was circulated among the faculty, and written communications were solicited and received from those members of the faculty wishing to communicate their views to the Policy Committee. The discussions revealed the continuing differences of opinion with regard to the amount of required work and the amount of free election for the student, the distribution of time between science and nonscience courses, the role of sequence courses taught by the divisional departments, the provision for mathematics and foreign languages, and the desirability of an integrating course of a philosophical character. Whether comprehensive examinations should be retained as a key feature of the College plan, whether there should be a different course of study for those students for whom the program would be terminal and for those who expected to pursue advanced work, whether there should be more than one Bachelor's degree (and what the degree should be)—these were among the other important issues which were discussed and debated in the Policy Committee.

The report of the Policy Committee set up a single four-year college program to which students who had completed two or more years of secondary-school work would be admitted. The majority recommended that high-school graduates entering the final two years of the College would meet the same examination requirements as the four-year students in these years; the minority report provided for general courses which might differ from those taken by four-year students. The majority recommended doubling the requirement in the last two years in the humanities and the social sciences. The majority—a different one in composition—recommended that "for special needs of some pre-divisional students an examination covering a year's work in a special field may be substituted for that covering a year's work in the general course in that field," while the minority recommended that all general course examinations be required of all students.[115] It was on this last issue—the early preparation for specialization by the substitution of elective courses for general courses—that the ultimate compromise in the faculty was reached at the meetings of March 19 and 20, 1942.

Dean Faust's position throughout the Policy Committee's discussions had been for a prescribed curriculum of general courses in a "merged" four-year program. With the Dean not voting, the committee had voted six to five that only one degree should be awarded, and also for three electives.[116] After the committee's reports were circulated and before the faculty meeting, the Dean accepted the fact that, to achieve the combination of the Four-

Year College and the Two-Year College, the possibility of some electives would need to be provided, and it was agreed to set up two degree programs—one without electives leading to the Bachelor of Arts degree and the other including two electives leading to the degree of Bachelor of Philosophy. The faculty voted[117] that the completion of the requirements for the Bachelor's degree would be measured by comprehensive examinations upon which the student's average grade must be nearer C than D; that entering students, whether they had completed two, three, or four years of high school, should be expected to present evidence of completion of two years of work in mathematics and two years of a foreign language;[118] and that the comprehensive examinations call for the knowledge and competence which would be expected of students who had taken the following courses. For students who enter the College after two years of high school:

a) *Biological Sciences.*—A two-year course of four hours a week or, for students who take the examination over the two-year course in the Physical Sciences listed below, a one-year course of four hours a week.

b) *Physical Sciences.*—A two-year course of four hours a week or, for students who take the examination over the two-year course in the Biological Sciences listed above, a one-year course of four hours a week.

c) *Social Sciences.*—A three-year course of four hours a week.

d) *Humanities.*—A three-year course of five hours a week in the first year and of four hours a week in the second and third years.

e) *English.*—A three-year course, meeting three hours a week, in reading, writing, and criticism, and the last year more largely to English composition.

f) *Observation, Interpretation, and Integration.*—A one-year course in the methods and relationships of the fields of knowledge, meeting three or four hours a week.[119]

For students who enter after graduation from high school:

a) *Biological Sciences.*—A one-year course, meeting four hours a week.

b) *Physical Sciences.*—A one-year course, meeting four hours a week.

c) *Social Sciences*—A two-year course, meeting four hours a week.

d) *Humanities.*—A two-year course, meeting four hours a week.

e) *English Composition.*—A one-year course, meeting three hours a week.

f) *Observation, Interpretation, and Integration.*—A one-year course, meeting three or four hours a week.

Students completing these examinations—either eight or fourteen in number, depending upon whether a student had finished two or four years of high school—were to be awarded the Bachelor of Arts degree, having followed a program in which there was no election. At the same time, and as part of the same motion, the faculty voted to award the degree of Bachelor of Philosophy to students who were to be allowed to substitute for two examinations covering general course areas (humanities, social sciences, or integration) two examinations over one-year elective sequences.[120]

In accordance with University statutory procedure, the College actions were reported to the Senate, which, by taking no action, permitted the curriculum changes to become legislation. By a vote of 48 to 32, however, the Senate referred back to the College faculty for consideration the award of two Bachelor's degrees, expressing once again the split in the Senate over the use of the traditional degree names.[121] The College faculty met again and reaffirmed its action on the programs leading to two degrees.[122] An attempt was again made in the Senate to overturn this faculty action, but a motion to rescind the approval of January 22 failed by the narrowest margin,[123] and the programs outlined were ready for execution.

On the surface—at least to the nonparticipant observer of this College-wide and University-wide conflict in the committee and legislative sessions—the 1937 and 1942 curriculum specifications were not dissimilar. In fact, it may fairly be said that the 1942 action was merely a rationalization of the previous reforms. The new elements, however, were significant. First, the Bachelor's degree was awarded. Second, the two programs were merged: there were to be one faculty and one set of courses, apart from the electives. Third, there was to be additional work in the humanities, in the social sciences, and in the integration of the fields of knowledge in the Bachelor of Arts program. The majority of the faculty, however, was not prepared to eliminate some elective, specialized work. Still unresolved by the faculty was the question of the place and the amount of mathematics and foreign languages in the program: admittedly, the eight-examination prescription for the high-school graduate prevented requirements in these areas. Some members of the faculty, including the Dean, staff members who had participated in the four-year program, and the University Examiner, realized at the time that only a reconsideration of the entrance requirements and placement of students in the College according to their competence would permit further development of the curriculum in mathematics and language.

Following the adoption of the new curriculum requirements, the College faculty's immediate tasks were the revision of the humanities and social science programs and the development of the course called Observation, Interpretation, and Integration. The science courses and the course in English composition were not immediately altered. Dean Faust became acting chairman of the humanities in the College and proposed three new courses. The first, called Humanities 1, a course designed primarily for students who entered the College after two years of high school, introduced them to various kinds of literature, art, and music, covering a fairly large number of less difficult examples of each. By means of discussion meetings, the course sought to train students in the art of reading and in the elements of art and music, in order to lay the foundations for sensitive and intelligent understanding and enjoyment. The second, called Humanities 2 and first offered in the autumn of 1942, replaced the Introductory General Course in the humanities which had been given since 1931—a course which used the materials of history as a foundation and framework for the presentation of the literature, philosophy, religion, and art of civilizations which have contributed conspicuously to the contemporary outlook on life. The new course centered attention on the arts of interpretation needed for the full understanding of historical, rhetorical, philosophical, dramatic, and fictional works rather than on historical information; and it undertook to lay the foundations for critical and appreciative reading. To this end, discussion meetings were devoted to training in careful analysis and proper appreciation of the histories, dramatic literature, and works of fiction which were read. A subordinate role was assigned to the historical approach and to history itself; the Policy Committee took the view that instruction in history was a joint responsibility of the social scientists and the humanists. The new third-year course in humanities, Humanities 3, offered for the first time in the autumn of 1943, was to be devoted to lyric poetry, philosophy, art, and music, with emphasis on the theoretic side of humanistic study. Besides practical training in the arts required for understanding and appreciating poetry, philosophy, art, and music, the course work was to turn to the study of the theories which have been used to explain the origin, nature, and effect of humanistic works.[124]

The course in Observation, Interpretation, and Integration, planned by a committee, of which Richard P. McKeon, Professor of Philosophy and Greek and Dean of the Division of the Humanities, was chairman, was offered for the first time in the autumn of 1943. This course was designed to clarify for students the relationships of the subject matters of the general courses in which they had been working. It led students to analyze and compare the methods of acquiring and testing knowledge in the natural sciences, the social sciences, and the humanities, and it dealt with the history of the relations between the various fields of human knowledge, tracing the ways in which one field or another has achieved independence or dominance or has been subordinated or even absorbed by another. It was the final aim of the course to prepare students to distinguish clearly the essential and characteristic differences in the manifold problems which they would encounter as individuals and citizens and to prepare them to determine the kinds of information and approach needed for the solution of each.[125]

In the area of the social sciences Dean Faust proposed to the staff that the existing first-year course in the four-year curriculum be revised drastically and that the two courses in the two-year curriculum—Introductory General Course in the Study of Contemporary Society and the elective second-year course—become the second and third-year courses in the new three-year program in the area. Beginning in the autumn of 1944, Social Sciences 1 shifted from a more or less conventional course in government to one devoted to the study of some of the leading ideas which have expressed and influenced the historical development of the United States. The materials used for this course, subsequently published in book form after five years of experimentation,[126] are taken from primary sources which present a series of major problems faced by the American people in the development of their political and economic institutions. A textbook in American history became supplementary reading (for chronology and continuity) to the study and discussion of some seventeen hundred pages of the writings of such men as John Locke, Thomas Paine, Abraham Lincoln, Alfred Thayer Mahan, Woodrow Wilson, and Herbert Hoover; and such documents as the Declaration of Independence, *Marbury* v. *Madison*, and the United Nations Charter. The second- and third-year courses were subsequently revised by the staffs to improve the sequential character of the social science program; Social Sciences 2 became concerned with a study of the relations of human nature and society, and Social Sciences 3 with problems of the choice of ends and means in matters of public policy.[127]

The academic year 1943–44, in which the first phase of the reorganization of the College curriculum was completed, coincided with the period during World War II when the University of Chicago offered instruction to a peak enrolment of military, naval, and air-force personnel. In January, 1944, there were 4,839 men and women in uniform receiving instruction on the campus; and during the entire academic year 1943–44, 25,583 different students—civilian and military—attended the University of Chicago. The College had been assigned the responsibility for two service programs, the so-called "pre-meteorology" course of the Army Air Forces and the basic course of the Army Specialized Training Program (ASTP). Dean Faust served in an advisory capacity at the national level in the formulation of both programs, and the regular College faculty, with some supplementation, taught the courses at Chicago.

The experience of a substantial number of the College faculty with the war programs, when coupled with knowledge of the way achievement examinations had worked in the regular curriculum, speeded the consideration of entrance requirements and placement tests for regular students in the College. The desire on the part of the faculty to get the men in uniform adjusted to academic work, regardless of details of their background, and the satisfactory results obtained with various groups demonstrated better than hours of faculty discussion could have done what was needed in placing students in any collegiate curriculum. The fact that the Office of the University Examiner was constructing tests for all branches of the armed services, as well as for the Armed Forces Institute, likewise tended to make the entire faculty examination-conscious. The development of the placement-test program in the College grew out of a restatement of the requirements for admission to the College which the faculty had adopted in the spring of 1943.[128] In what is perhaps the shortest statement of admission standards of any American college, these key sentences were chosen by the faculty to express its educational position on one phase of academic bookkeeping: "Admission to the College is based upon evidence that the student is intellectually and socially prepared to benefit from the work of the College. Such evidence may be found in the quality of his academic achievement as reported by his high school, the judgments concerning the student to be found in recommendations of his high school principal, teachers, or other persons who know him, and scores made on standard scholastic aptitude tests. . . . Each student will be given placement tests to help fit him into the College courses, whatever the amount or kind of high school work he has had."

The primary considerations underlying the policy of requiring no specified subjects for admission were (1) that the secondary school should control its own curriculum and (2) that research had repeatedly shown no correspondence between completion of courses usually required for college admission and success in college.[129] While it is doubtful whether many members of the faculty were familiar with William Rainey Harper's proposals in the 1890's that admission to the Junior Colleges be based on entrance examinations demonstrating the students' ability to do college work, it might truly be said that the passage of fifty years was required for the abandonment of counting units of high-school work as the primary device for admitting students to college and permitting them to undertake a program of college work.[130]

It took several years for the faculty and the Office of the University Examiner to put into operation the courses and examinations which were designed to realize the faculty's objective in merging the two-year and four-year programs. By the end of the academic year 1945–46 the College had, in reality, become a four-year program in which students were placed on the basis of their performance on examinations, irrespective of whether they had spent two, three, four, or five years in high school or even a year or two in another college or in an army training course. For example, high-school graduates were no longer given credit for the first year's work in the social sciences on the basis of a year's course in American history. On the other hand, students who, as a result of independent work, had mastered a portion of a given area of subject matter deemed a part of general education by the faculty were not held for College comprehensive examinations merely because they lacked "paper credits." Such a procedure, of course, was complementary to an existing practice—adopted in 1931—of permitting students to take comprehensive examinations whenever they felt ready for them. One of the several noteworthy results which the scheme of placement brought forth was the means to handle the veterans who came to the University in great numbers in 1946 and 1947. A twenty-two-year-old veteran could be placed in the same class with a sixteen-year-old student just finished with his sophomore year of high school—both knowing that they had been judged by the same standards as needing a certain program of studies. Further, if the veteran, as a result of his maturity, was able to prepare himself for a comprehensive examination—say, in the physical sciences—after three months of residence, he could take the examination and, if successful, satisfy the requirement, while the youngster plugged away in classes acquiring knowledge of science and the ability to deal with scientific problems.

The adoption of the principle of placement examinations to

determine what a student's College program should be paved the way for undertaking the second phase of the redefinition of the curriculum which followed the relocation of the Bachelor's degree. The areas in which Dean Faust proposed changes to the Policy Committee were, successively, mathematics, foreign languages, and natural sciences. For a dozen years there had been numerous discussions in committee and faculty meetings on mathematics and foreign languages in a program of general education. The proposals that were made never received enough support to insure legislative action. In the curriculum proposals made by the Policy Committee in 1942 there had been provision for examination requirements in both mathematics and a foreign language, but these had not been adopted because (1) it was felt that there was not enough "room" in the program of the high-school graduate and (2) there was continued feeling on the part of a majority of the faculty that the existing courses were merely "manipulation-skill" or "tool" courses. During the year 1943–44 a new course in mathematics was devised and taught, on an experimental basis, by Eugene P. Northrop, Assistant Professor of Mathematics in the College, to a group of first-year college students who had had two years of high-school mathematics—the amount of preparatory work, in fact, which most high-school graduates presented when admitted to the College. With the success of this course, designed to fill the needs of students who intended to proceed further in mathematics as well as those for whom the year's work was terminal in the subject, Dean Faust and the Policy Committee recommended to the faculty in the spring of 1944 that an examination requirement in mathematics be added to the program for the Bachelor's degree. The faculty voted unanimously to accept the recommendation,[131] and the number of comprehensive examinations required for graduation from the College was increased from thirteen to fourteen. The objectives of the course to prepare students for the examination, Mathematics 1, were (1) thorough understanding of the nature of the problems and the structure of a variety of theories in mathematics and (2) mastery of certain fundamental methods. Since the autumn of 1945 a second general course in mathematics has been offered by the College for students who intend to do further work in calculus and post-calculus subjects in the Department of Mathematics.[132] The examination for this course, Mathematics 2, was not made a requirement for the Bachelor's degree.

The place of foreign languages in the American collegiate curriculum has been the subject of debate and discussion, not to mention invective and tears, for more than a generation. The requirement in language for graduation disappeared from Chicago, as from many other institutions, before 1930, the result of pressures from the natural and social sciences. Many language scholars would have agreed with one member of the Chicago faculty that requirements of curriculums no longer allowed "the kind of academic training which a generation ago produced Greek, Latin, Romance and German scholars who contributed to the greatness of our universities." But the attitude of the majority of the University faculty, divisional as well as College, was that foreign languages had, partially as a result of poor teaching at the secondary and collegiate level throughout the United States, come to be taught as an end in themselves or, in the case of some modern languages, as instruments of South American trade or conveniences for European travel. Dean Faust took this view of the situation generally, but he also believed that, rightly taught, foreign languages provide an opportunity for insight into the nature of language (including English), for increase in a student's capacity for expression (oral and written), and for providing direct contact with the literature and culture of other nations and peoples. In 1944 and 1945 a small committee of the College faculty reviewed the problem and considered a proposal for an integrating unit to be taught simultaneously with each foreign language and to consist of lectures, readings, and discussions on the following topics: language as a system of vocal sounds; history and relationships of languages; grammar; and problems of meaning and translation. While it was recognized that only a limited achievement could be expected in the one academic quarter proposed as the course length, the committee foresaw additional benefit in the particularization of these topics in each different language course.

The fact that there had long been a tradition of competent language teaching in the College created a favorable context for discussion when the proposal for a foreign language requirement went to the faculty in the spring of 1945. The modern language staffs, independent of the graduate departments since 1920, had perfected the "reading method" of instruction and had published an extensive and widely adopted series of French, German, and Spanish texts and readers.[133] Experimental teaching of the work in general problems of language during 1944–45 demonstrated what more could be done within the time which might be made available in the curriculum for all students. It was not surprising, then, that the College faculty, when the proposal was put to a vote in the spring of 1945, approved a one-year foreign language requirement, including the examination in the general problems of language.[134] Whereas formerly the somewhat pious require- ment of two units of high-school language work represented the level of achievement of all College students not continuing their language work by election, beginning in 1946 all students were placed in a foreign language of their choice on the basis of exami- nation. As in the case of mathematics, the existence of the place- ment-examination machinery assisted in carrying out the kind of language program proposed. Time in the curriculum was pro- vided by a reduction by one-third of the requirement in English composition, so that the maximum number of comprehensive examinations for which a student could be held remained con- stant at fourteen. Foreign language instruction in the College has been offered in French, German, Greek, Italian, Latin, Russian, and Spanish.

At the same meeting of the faculty (June, 1945) at which the language requirement was adopted, the science requirement for students who entered the first year of the College was restated. Since 1937, students who entered the College after two years of high school had to pass comprehensive examinations covering two years of the biological sciences and one year of the physical sciences *or* two years of the physical sciences and one year of the biological sciences. The course preparation for these examina- tions, as indicated earlier in this narrative,[135] employed the one- year survey courses as the third year of work for students who entered the first year of the College. Substantially unchanged since their introduction into the curriculum in 1931, these two courses had been very successful survey courses; the course in the biological sciences had been widely imitated across the country, and the textbooks which had been written for both courses had been hailed as "wonders of the textbook world." The desire of some members of the faculty to explore more searchingly the nature of scientific knowledge at the expense of some "coverage" of the fields, and the desire to experiment with additional types of science courses—a feature of thinking about the curriculum since 1931—led to a reconsideration of the science program. The policy committee accepted the view, following committee investigation and some course experimentation during 1944–45, that a single, three-year, integrated natural science course to follow the year of mathematics was a desirable program for students entering the first year of the College.

The proponents of the new course maintained that some of the artificial separations of physical and biological problems could be removed; that the students would, as in the existing courses, acquire a knowledge of major current conceptions of the organic and inorganic worlds; and that they would acquire an understanding of the methods by which such knowledge comes to be. The question "What should be the content, teaching materials, and methods of courses for undergraduates that attempt to reveal scientific questions and methods as they really are?" was squarely faced by the committee proposing the new course, the chairman of which was Joseph J. Schwab, Associate Professor of the Biological Sciences in the College and a member of the biology general-course staff since 1935.[136] Such general subjects—and scientific problems—as the forms of energy and the laws governing their operation or the structure and function of the living organism would be the scientific problems of the student. The primary textual materials for the course would be original writings of the great scientific thinkers and investigators who had asked and answered such questions. Laboratory work would provide techniques of firsthand observation, designed to help the student understand the papers read and to pose for him the problems of science in such a way that he would recognize them as problems. The conventional textbook, the "cookbook" laboratory exercise, and the magic-like demonstration of a scientific experiment were to be put aside. As one member of the College faculty put it: "The demonstration experiment which generally works, the laboratory experiment of two hours duration which validates the theory, the problem which neglects friction, are well-tested teaching devices that exhibit the skill of the magician without revealing his secrets."[137]

The proposals to the faculty which embodied the new three-year course met with opposition. It was said that the new course was antiquarian, in that it dealt with certain scientific discoveries and experiments which had been superseded by later work and, further, that it did not present "a unified picture of the world." The majority of the College faculty, however, was willing to approve the experiment and voted for a science comprehensive-examination requirement covering three years' work in the natural sciences. For the high-school graduate, the existing two-year program was retained.[138]

The adoption of the alternative natural sciences requirement in 1945 brought to completion the second phase of the curriculum reform in the post-1942 College. During the academic year which ended with this faculty action, the Dean, the College Policy Committee, and the course chairmen (seventeen members of the faculty in all) met with President Hutchins and the Dean of Faculties for a review of College problems.[139] The discussion indicated that a desirable size for the College was between two thousand and three thousand students, the optimum being at perhaps twenty-seven hundred;[140] that a continuing demonstration of the significance of the College's program of general education could best be accomplished with a group which was not highly selected or composed only of the intellectually gifted; and that additional facilities were needed for students and for faculty. The Dean reported on the development of the faculty, noting that in a faculty of approximately one hundred and twenty-five the number devoting full time to College work had more than doubled in five years and that the educational background of the faculty—both in training and in experience—for work in general higher education was the "best" in the history of the College.

In the autumn of 1945 Faust proposed to the Policy Committee that it recommend to the faculty the abolition of the Bachelor of

Philosophy degree—the compromise method adopted in 1942 by which the College requirements could be satisfied by the substitution of two departmental sequence courses for two College general courses. The recommendation that there be only one degree—the Bachelor of Arts—awarded by the College was presented as a "natural, next step in the development of the College." The Dean stated that it was his conviction, and that of the majority of the College faculty as well, that the system of general courses as devised in the College provided the best means for achieving an effective program of general education. It was undesirable, Faust argued, for the College to perfect placement examinations which placed a student in the three-year humanities program, for example, and then permitted him to substitute a course in chemistry for the third year's work in the humanities. Under this arrangement it was impossible to build effective three-year sequences in the humanities and in the social sciences, since the second year's work must be terminal for some students. The abolition of the two-elective choice would remove these difficulties.[141]

The objections to the proposal, which were presented on various occasions during the six months that the matter was before the University academic bodies, were (1) that the nonelective curriculum deprived the student of freedom; (2) that the Bachelor of Arts program left insufficient time for the student to satisfy prerequisites for further specialized study, as in medicine; (3) that some specialized study was desirable; and (4) that the elimination of departmental electives would tend to make a "gap" between the College and departmental faculties.[142]

After four lengthy meetings, the College faculty voted, on February 6, 1946, by a vote of 65 to 43, that "the College award only the degree of Bachelor of Arts as at present defined to students entering after the Summer Quarter 1946."[143] The action, since it was interpreted as "affecting other ruling bodies [i.e., divisional faculties] and the general interest of the University," went to the Council of the University Senate—the newly organized elective body of the entire faculty which had replaced the old Senate as the supreme academic body. At its meeting of March 5 the Council voted, 30 to 10, to "request the College to reconsider its action of February 6, 1946, by designating a committee to confer with a committee of the Council concerning the possibility of resolving the issues between the College and other parts of the University in such a way as to conserve, through greater flexibility in the requirements for the Bachelor of Arts degree, both the objectives of general education and the interests of students intending to enter the Divisions or Schools."[144] Hutchins, who had assumed the office of Chancellor of the University on July 1, 1945, had the power to veto an action of the Council; in such a case, under the University statutes, the matter, if the action were reaffirmed by the Council, went to the Board of Trustees for decision. On March 7 Hutchins vetoed the action of the Council,[145] the first—and only—veto since the establishment of the veto machinery. He called the suggested consultative committee "instructed" to bring in a different program, and this, he said, was an attack on the autonomy of the College. "The policy of the University is," the Chancellor stated in his veto, "to place great responsibilities on the several faculties and to expect them to take the initiative in developing the educational program in the area committed to their care. The actions of a faculty in its area are not to be rejected or seriously delayed unless they are in conflict with established policy or are clearly unsound. To hold otherwise is to dampen the ardor of the groups on which the University must rely for its educational vitality."

The veto went to the Council, where the original action was reaffirmed by a vote of 33 to 12 on March 19.[146] This action was an expected one because the Chancellor had called in question the power and authority of the Council; but it was clear at the meeting that the matter of autonomy of a faculty affected more bodies than the College and that some way should be found to keep a strictly educational question from going to the Board of Trustees for decision. The suggestion was made in the Council that the veto be recalled by Chancellor Hutchins. What then happened was that the Council joined with the Chancellor in withdrawing from the trustees the actions of the Council of March 5 and 19 and the Chancellor's veto of March 7, thus bringing to the Council *de novo* the College's action with regard to the abolition of the Ph.B. degree. A week later the Council accepted a suggestion contained in the Chancellor's veto message by voting for a joint Council-College discussion on the relation of the College one-degree action "to Divisional programs of study," meanwhile staying the College action of February 6.[147] The College faculty agreed to such discussions.[148]

Five meetings were held during the month of May, and these led to the formulation by the College Policy Committee of five amendments to the one-degree action of February 6. They were: (1) the postponement for one year of the effective date of the abolition of the Ph.B.—until 1947; (2) the addition of a one-year course entitled "General Physics" as an alternative mode of preparation for the examination in the physical sciences—a "plus" course for students going on in the Division of the Biological Sciences (including the School of Medicine); (3) plans for offering the third year of the humanities program in certain foreign languages—a means of accelerating preparation in language while satisfying the humanities requirements; (4) agreement to study the problem of including general history in the requirement of fourteen comprehensive examinations for the Bachelor of Arts degree; and (5) provision for joint residency in the College and an upper Division while fulfilling College requirements.[149] These amendments were accepted by the Committee of the Council, by the College faculty with only one dissent, and by the Council unanimously, thus bringing to a close a controversy which had strained College-Divisional relationships and had threatened to bring an educational issue to the Board of Trustees for settlement.[150]

The controversy over the elimination of the last two electives in the work for the Bachelor's degree and the jousting for "time" in the resulting curriculum were caused by natural, conflicting pressures within the University. In an interesting way the conflict mirrored the curriculum fight which President Harper had mediated in 1898–99, previously recounted in this narrative.[151] At that time the defenders of classical education were arguing for Latin; the scientific departments were advocating the beginning of specialized training in science at the earliest possible time. Harper proposed a middle ground—a series of required courses "to gain a certain familiarity with the life and thought of the various nations which have contributed most to our modern civilization." If, Harper had said, the scientist demands all the student's time from an early age, this will in the end prove injurious both to the student and to science. He added: "The student will never know what subject or subjects may be in accordance with his natural taste and ability and what may be distasteful to him, unless he shall have made an earnest effort in subjects which represent the various groups of the curriculum."[152]

In the 1945–46 controversy the graduate foreign language faculty joined the scientists in trying to preserve electives, so that the student who wanted to take extended work in language or devote himself to a scientific education could do so at the earliest possible time—with the partial exclusion of work in certain other areas of knowledge. On the ground that it knew better than the student what was the best curriculum in general education the College faculty decided upon a required program. Elective courses could be taken in any field, along with the required general courses but not as substitutes for them.

The work in history which was added to the curriculum was, like that proposed by President Harper in 1899, "a study of the great heritage we have received from the past." The reintroduction of a course with a primary historical emphasis was, however, in no way a radical innovation. The older, historically oriented humanities course was dropped in 1942 in response to the need for a course with greater emphasis on modes of analysis of the various arts, including history.[153] The introduction of the course in American institutions (Social Sciences 1) illustrated another method of dealing with the historical development of political, economic, and social thinking, as well as with events. The work in the history of Western civilization which a committee of the College faculty devised in the period after 1946 was a one-year course to provide the student with historical knowledge of the occurrence and the cultural context of problems and changes in the sciences, arts, literatures, and philosophies. Parts of the course were devoted to tracing the history of a group of ideas and problems drawn from the fields covered by other College courses; an effort was made to select problems in which a maximum amount of material familiar to the student might be used. Other parts contemplated an emphasis on historical facts and a knowledge of historical connections among facts, problems, and persons consonant with the primary objectives of instilling "a sense of the continuity of Western civilization" and achieving a historical integration.[154]

Provision for history in the list of fourteen comprehensive examinations for the Bachelor's degree necessitated a reduction somewhere else in the list of examinations. This was done by (1) reducing the requirement in writing from two examinations to one, (2) a reorganization of the third year's work in the humanities to provide for more writing, and (3) an organized effort through a committee to increase the amount of writing by College students in courses other than English and the humanities.[155] Students in the last year of the College were encouraged to write and submit to the faculty a "Bachelor's Essay," which, if of superior quality, led to the award of the Bachelor of Arts degree with honors upon the completion of the examination requirements with high standing. The third-year course in the humanities, while retaining a literary approach and an emphasis on criticism and critical theories, became, in fact, an intelligently planned terminal year for the work both in the humanities and in English. The alternative presentations of the third year's work in the humanities in four foreign languages—French, German, Greek, and Spanish—seemed not to be at odds with the increase in writing in Humanities 3 because students who were linguistically inclined—so that they wanted to work in a foreign language —were usually more advanced in their ability to write. In June, 1950, the humanities-in-a-foreign-language courses were still regarded as experimental, but they had demonstrated another aspect of the flexibility of the College program and inventive pedagogy on the part of the faculty.

Immediately after the Council of the University Senate had approved the revised statement of requirements for the degree of Bachelor of Arts in the College, Faust informed Chancellor Hutchins of his desire to resign as Dean of the College. He told the Chancellor that he felt that the task he had undertaken five years before—reorganization of the curriculum and rebuilding of the faculty—was done. Faust's resignation was accepted, as of October 1, 1946, when he was appointed Dean of the Graduate

Library School, although he remained as acting dean of the College until his successor was selected.[156] Frederick Champion Ward, a graduate of Oberlin and Yale who had joined the College faculty in 1945 as an assistant professor of philosophy, was appointed Dean of the College on February 1, 1947. To him fell the task of carrying out the modifications in the curriculum approved the preceding June. In his first two and one-half years as Dean he steered to completion the planning of the new history, physics, and humanities-writing courses. He continued personnel practices initiated by Faust to insure the quality of the faculty.[157] Most important for the future of the College program, Ward encouraged the various staffs in the College to raise fundamental questions about the nature of those disciplines which supply the materials, problems, and methods in the existing curriculum.

The names of the courses which make up the curriculum are meaningful only in the context of their history. In schematic summary, the course of study is simple:

First Year	*Second Year*
Social Sciences 1	Social Sciences 2
Humanities 1	Humanities 2
Natural Sciences 1	Natural Sciences 2
English	Mathematics

Third Year	*Fourth Year*
Social Sciences 3	History
Humanities 3	Observation, Interpretation,
Natural Sciences 3	and Integration
Foreign Language	

The achievement of this curriculum and the other aspects of the plan of the College at the University of Chicago has required a thoroughgoing reform in ways of meeting many of the problems of higher education. The issues dealt with are always old, and always new. Required courses and free electives. Distribution of work among fields of knowledge and concentration in a major field. Textbooks and original source materials. Lectures and discussions. Admission requirements and placement examinations. Course credits and comprehensive examinations. Faculties for research and faculties for teaching, faculties for teaching and research. Liberal education and specialized education. General education and professional training. The university superimposed on the college, and the college a burden to the university.

The process of transforming the American college of the nineteenth century into the university of the twentieth was a complex one. The place where the minister and the gentleman had been educated became the center for scholarship, scientific investigation, and professional training. Emulation of the German conception of the university at a time when the inadequacies of the American college had been recognized and the impact of natural —and subsequently social—sciences upon classical and theological learning produced the elective system. Historically, the elective system was a necessary tool for the broadening of an educational system which had been narrow; and it was the tool which paved the way for the inevitable professionalization of training for the specialties of modern industrial society. In the process of university-building, the collegiate function—the education of the man and the citizen—was neglected, although not lost sight of.[158]

William Rainey Harper wanted the University of Chicago to be a university *and* a college; he wanted the college to be part of the university. This chapter has been the story of the development of the collegiate function at Chicago—a history of what faculties and administrators have done to develop the idea and practice of general, liberal education in one university. It has been an account of how a faculty of teachers has been given the responsibility for the collegiate function; how that faculty has defined the objectives of liberal education; and how the relocation of the Bachelor's degree has permitted a reorganization of the course of collegiate study so that students who have completed ten years of preliminary schooling may profitably engage in such study. In a discussion with Harper and Nicholas Murray Butler, of Columbia, nearly fifty years ago, Charles W. Eliot, the great president of Harvard, defended the Harvard faculty's reduction to three years of the time required to secure a Bachelor of Arts degree with these words: "We must get forward in education as in politics by a perpetual contest and a series of compromises. . . . Let us have the conflict of . . . experiments, and the result will be the working out of a solution by compromises from year to year, or from decade to decade."[159]

Notes

1. Henry Adams, *History of the United States of America*, III (New York: Charles Scribner's Sons, 1890), 45; *The Education of Henry Adams* (Boston: Houghton Mifflin Co., 1918), p. 382.

2. For a summary of Harper's program see W. Carson Ryan, *Studies in Early Graduate Education* (Carnegie Foundation for the Advancement of Teaching, Bull. No. 30 [New York, 1939]), pp. 91–138. Of the main features of the Chicago plan, Ryan reminds us that "comparatively few even of the main features strike us as novel or original today, partly, no doubt, because the Chicago experience has accustomed us to take for granted much that seemed new at the time" (p. 114). See also Thomas W. Goodspeed, *A History of the University of Chicago, 1891–1916* (Chicago: University of Chicago Press, 1916), pp. 130–57.

3. Quoted in Goodspeed, *op. cit.*, pp. 121 and 168.

4. A. H. Strong, *The Church and the University* (Rochester: E. R. Andrews, 1889), p. 81; Letter, A. H. Strong to W. R. Harper, December 23, 1890, Harper Letter File, Archives, University of Chicago.

5. Unfinished MS of Harper's projected "First Annual Report," Archives, University of Chicago, p. 149.

6. Cf. George E. Vincent, "William Rainey Harper," in *The William Rainey Harper Memorial Conference*, ed. Robert N. Montgomery (Chicago: University of Chicago Press, 1938), pp. 6–7.

7. *Official Bulletin*, No. 2, April, 1891, pp. 2 and 13.

8. *The President's Report, 1898–99* (Chicago: University of Chicago Press, 1900), pp. xx–xxi. In this report there is the genesis of the philosophy of the junior college and of the more recently advocated "community college."

Until 1930 the annual reports of the President and other officers of the University were published by the University of Chicago Press in the following year.

9. *Ibid.*, pp. xxiv–xxvi.

10. *The President's Report, 1892–1902*, pp. 108–13.

11. *The President's Report, 1904–5*, p. 34; see also *Report, 1897–98*, p. 85, and *Report, 1892–1902*, p. 109.

12. *The President's Report, 1905–6*, p. 6; see also Harper in *Report, 1898–99*, p. xxii.

13. Ryan, *op. cit.*, pp. 132–33.

14. In 1909–10 a standing faculty committee was asked to make a survey of faculty, student, and alumni opinion on "actual conditions and methods employed in college work." The report found that "the great proportion of instruction is regarded as excellent." Of interest was the finding that 71 per cent of the alumni queried preferred the discussion class to the formal lecture as a method of instruction.

The report asked the question, "What is the best agency for discovering and remedying defective instruction?" and gave its answer: "It may easily be the case that in some departments our past method of administration, in which the head has usually been selected for his eminence in research, has not been favorable for securing due attention to the needs of undergraduate instruction. In fact it has been no one's business. . . . The Deans of the colleges are necessarily confronted with evidences of unfortunate instruction, but . . . [they] have understood their duties to be the administration of Faculty regulations respecting students, and the incidental character of the office . . . does not encourage or permit the assumption of additional responsibility. The President . . . is necessarily dependent largely upon the recommendations of Heads of Departments. . . . There is no official, in these modern colleges which are parts of great universities, who has specific responsibility in respect to the particular problem of college instruction" ("Present Problems of Instruction in the University of Chicago: Report of the Committee on Instruction," *University of Chicago Magazine*, III [December, 1910], 58–86, esp. 81–83).

15. *The President's Report, 1922–23*, pp. 4–5. Deans were given additional duties and powers in the reorganization of 1930–31 (see text, p. 50). In 1940, on the occasion of a general revision of the statutes, the following enactment was voted: "Each Dean supervises in general the administration in his School, Division, or College, under the direction of the President, and is empowered to act as the executive officer and representative of his Faculty, and, with regard to educational policy, to take the initiative in proposing plans to the Faculty, and to carry into effect plans adopted by the Faculty" (Minutes of the University Senate, June 7, 1940; Minutes of the Board of Trustees, June 13, 1940).

16. "The Contribution of Germany to Higher Education," *University Record*, VIII (March, 1904), 348–53. Professor Coulter lists as contributions of the German universities: (1) the concept of the modern university; (2) freedom for the professor; (3) freedom for the student to study what he chooses; (4) the pursuit of knowledge, particularly scientific inquiry, for its own sake; and (5) the idea that the professor must be both an investigator and a teacher.

17. H. H. Newman, "History of the Department of Zoology in the University of Chicago," *Bios*, XIX (December, 1948), 220–21.

18. *The President's Report, 1919–20*, p. 6.

19. *The President's Report, 1907–8*, p. 96.

20. E.g., *The President's Report, 1905–6*, p. 6; *Report, 1911–12*, p. 10. Two less extreme alternatives were considered by James R. Angell, Dean of the Faculty of Arts, Literature, and Science, in an extensive report on the curriculum to the President in December, 1912 (*University Record*, I [n.s., January, 1915], 26–43). One was the removal from the undergraduate program of that work which was decidedly elementary (beginning modern languages, algebra, history, and others), without doing away with the freshman year as such. This was put into operation on a limited scale in 1919 (see text, p. 41). The second and more feasible alternative, according to Angell, was a reduction of credit obtained for elementary courses taken beyond the junior college level. Following Angell's lead, the faculty of the Colleges of Arts, Literature, and Science voted on June 3, 1914, to apply this principle to a number of elementary courses in political science, history, foreign languages, English, mathematics, physics, chemistry,

and geology (Minutes of the Faculty of the Colleges of Arts, Literature, and Science, June 3, 1914; Minutes of the University Senate, June 8, 1914).

21. *The President's Report, 1911–12*, p. 7; *Report, 1912–13*, p. 56.

22. John A. Sexson and John W. Harbeson, in their book *The New American College* (New York: Harper & Bros., 1946), pp. 27–28, state that George A. Merrill, the principal of the Wilmerding School of Industrial Arts of the University of California, "might well be called the father of the 6-4-4 plan of . . . school organization." Mr. Merrill reformulated the curriculum of three technical schools, starting in 1894, and his report to the president of the University of California in 1908 presents an excellent analysis of the need for regrouping the school years in a 6-4-4 plan. See also Leonard V. Koos, *Integrating High School and College: The Six-Four-Four Plan at Work* (New York: Harper & Bros., 1946). As this narrative has indicated, all President Harper's early writings on organization, including his *President's Report* of 1898–99, pointed toward the initiation of collegiate work after ten years of school.

23. *The President's Report, 1912–13*, p. 44.

24. *The President's Report, 1917–19*, p. 96; Minutes of the Board of Trustees, July 5, 1918.

25. *The President's Report, 1917–19*, p. 121.

26. *The President's Report, 1919–20*, p. 6.

27. *The President's Report, 1920–21*, pp. 3–4.

28. *Ibid.*, p. 23.

29. William Rainey Harper, *The Trend in Higher Education* (Chicago: University of Chicago Press, 1905), pp. 272–73.

30. *The President's Report, 1920–21*, p. 26.

31. "The University of Chicago and the Bachelor's Degree," *Educational Record*, XXIII (July, 1942), 569.

32. Minutes of the Faculty of the Colleges of Arts, Literature, and Science, April 10, 1920.

33. Chauncey S. Boucher, *The Chicago College Plan* (Chicago: University of Chicago Press, 1935), p. 1. Boucher was Dean of the Colleges of Arts, Literature, and Science from 1926 to 1932, Dean of the College from 1932 to 1935, and subsequently President of West Virginia University and Chancellor of the University of Nebraska.

34. Cf. *The President's Report, 1920–21*, pp. 3–4 (President Judson), and p. 26 (Dean Robertson).

35. Minutes of the University Senate, December 18, 1922. The Senate outlined desirable goals in research and recommended the establishment of more institutes like the Oriental Institute, in which teaching obligations were minimal (cf. Robert M. Hutchins, *No Friendly Voice* [Chicago: University of Chicago Press, 1936], pp. 179–80). Such institutes in areas of science which received great impetus from the controlled release of atomic energy at Chicago were established in 1945.

36. Thomas W. Goodspeed, *Ernest DeWitt Burton* (Chicago: University of Chicago Press, 1926), p. 81.

37. Minutes of the University Senate, February 24, 1923.

38. *The President's Report, 1922–23*, pp. xv–xvi. On another occasion Burton said: "The central business of a college is, I believe, to develop, not ideas in the abstract, nor the human tools of the trades, but personalities capable of a large participation in life and of a large contribution to life. One argument only I advance for this opinion, viz., that personalities of this type are the world's greatest need, and that the college rightly administered is capable of producing them—not, indeed, of finishing their training, but of starting them in the right direction. The process of education will necessarily be lifelong" ("The Business of a College," *University Record*, X [n.s., January, 1924], 59).

39. Minutes of the Faculty of the Colleges of Arts, Literature, and Science, January 31, 1925.

40. *Ibid.*, April 10, 1920. This separate "faculty" was reincorporated into the Colleges in 1927 but was not put under departmental auspices.

41. Goodspeed, *Ernest DeWitt Burton*, p. 82.

42. The commission distinguished three stages of education: the primary stage (the first six years of elementary school); the secondary stage ("not at present represented in any single institution" but covering two years in elementary school, four years of high school and the junior college), "a period of general education which insures the proper adjustment of the individual to the environment in which he is to live"; and the tertiary stage (part of the senior college, and the graduate and professional school), a period of specific training. Being concerned with the secondary stage of approximately eight years, the commission distinguished "three types of powers" necessary to adjust the student to his environment: (1) independence in thinking in the major fields of knowledge; (2) appreciation of the fine arts; and (3) attainment of independence in moral living. The commission then attempted to specify the abilities which each of these powers should command and the general subject matters which should occupy the courses of study for the eight-year period. An appendix to the report contained a list of twenty-nine units of study, calculated on four units yearly for eight years, in eighteen subject matters of the broad fields of knowledge ("The Report of the Commission on the Future of the Colleges," 1924, Archives, University of Chicago).

43. Minutes of the University Senate, June 11, 1924; also letter, Albion W. Small to Henry W. Prescott, May 15, 1924, Archives, University of Chicago.

44. Minutes of the Board of Trustees, October 16, 1924.

45. *The President's Report, 1924–25*, pp. 21–22.

46. Floyd W. Reeves, "The Junior College Curriculum in Colleges and Universities," in William S. Gray (ed.), *The Junior College Curriculum: Proceedings of the Institute for Administrative Officers of Higher Institutions*, I (Chicago: University of Chicago Press, 1929), 81.

47. *The President's Report, 1928–29*, p. 33. Robert M. Hutchins later commented on academic departmentalization in the 1920's as follows: "The Junior Colleges also aroused a conflict over whether they were to prepare students for advanced work or to give them a general education. The attitude varied

from department to department. In general, however, it is accurate to say that the departments taught all their courses from the first year on as though every student in them were planning to devote his life to the subject. Yet the median number of courses taken by a student in a single department was one" ("Report of the President, 1930–34" [unpublished, University of Chicago, 1935], p. 19).

48. H. H. Newman (ed.), *The Nature of the World and of Man* (Chicago: University of Chicago Press, 1926).

49. *The President's Report, 1925–26*, p. xiv.

50. "The President's Convocation Statement, June 15, 1926," *University Record*, XII (n.s.) (July, 1926), 181.

51. "A Theory of Education" was prepared by Dean Wilkins and some of his associates in the autumn of 1924 and presented to the faculty for discussion in January, 1925. Developing the theory of "three stages" of education accepted as the basis of the 1924 commission report (n. 42 *supra*), the document met with extensive opposition, counterproposals, and moves to table it. In March, 1925, it was referred to committee for study, but this committee, with Wilkins as chairman, was not appointed until November, 1926—the death of President Burton, the appointment of Mason, and the illness of Wilkins intervening.

See also Wilkins' excellent paper on the relationships of the senior college to the junior college and to the graduate school, "The Relation of the Senior College to the Graduate School," *Journal of the Proceedings of the Association of American Universities*, XXVIII (1926), 59–70. In it he argued effectively for the removal "of any line of demarcation between the Senior College and the Graduate School." "Deletion of the line," he said, "would presumably mean either the abandonment of the B.A. degree, or its award at the end of the Junior College. . . . The B.A. has signified historically the completion of a general education; it would therefore seem appropriate that the B.A. should be given at the end of the Junior College."

52. Letter, Julius Stieglitz to E. H. Wilkins, November 26, 1926, Archives, University of Chicago.

53. "The Standards of Graduate Work," in *Problems in Education: Western Reserve University Centennial Conference* (Cleveland: Western Reserve University Press, 1927), p. 201.

54. Minutes of the Faculty of the Colleges of Arts, Literature, and Science, January 19, 1927.

55. Wilkins resigned from the University on June 30, 1927, to become President of Oberlin College.

56. *The President's Report, 1925–26*, pp. 24–25.

57. *The President's Report, 1926–27*, p. 7.

58. *Ibid.*, p. 28.

59. *The President's Report, 1927–28*, p. 29; Boucher, *op. cit.*, p. 4.

60. The other members were Edson S. Bastin, Anton J. Carlson, and Julius Stieglitz (scientists); Charles H. Judd and Leon Carroll Marshall (social scien-

tists); and T. V. Smith, David H. Stevens, and Archer Taylor (humanists). Boucher's field was American history.

61. Boucher, *op. cit.*, pp. 4–5.

62. Minutes of the Faculty of the Colleges of Arts, Literature, and Science, May 15, 1928; see also the statement of Acting President Frederic C. Woodward, *The President's Report, 1927–28*, p. xx.

63. "President Mason—Hail and Farewell," *University Record*, XIV (n.s.) (July, 1928), 152.

64. *The President's Report, 1928–29*, p. 38.

65. Boucher, *op. cit.*, p. 7.

66. "The Inauguration of President Hutchins," *University Record*, XVI (n.s.) (January, 1930), 12–13.

67. *The President's Report, 1929–30*, pp. 44–47.

68. The survey, under the directorship of Floyd W. Reeves, of the University of Kentucky, was begun in October, 1929, and completed in April, 1933. The results were published in twelve volumes under the general title *The University of Chicago Survey* (Chicago: University of Chicago Press, 1931–33).

69. Boucher, *op. cit.*, p. 8.

70. Minutes of the University Senate, October 22, 1930.

71. The School of Medicine was made an integral part of the Division of the Biological Sciences, which the College student could enter for the completion of his premedical work. The College of Education (for the preparation of teachers) was abolished in 1930. In 1933 an all-University committee was appointed for the administration of that program. At the same time the School of Education was combined with the Department of Education in the Division of the Social Sciences. The name of the School of Business was changed from Commerce and Administration in 1932.

72. Minutes of the Board of Trustees, November 13, 1930.

73. Minutes of the University Senate, October 22, 1930.

74. Minutes of the College Faculty, March 5, 1931. The College Curriculum Committee's report, in many ways a document of historical importance in American collegiate education, is set forth in Boucher, *op. cit.*, Appendix A, pp. 259–67.

75. A full description of the functions of this office, the creation of which Hutchins recommended to the University Senate in December, 1930, falls outside the scope of this chapter (see Robert M. Strozier, "The Office of the Dean of Students," in Norman Burns [ed.], *The Administration of Higher Institutions under Changing Conditions: Proceedings of the Institute for Administrative Officers of Higher Institutions*, XIX [Chicago: University of Chicago Press, 1947], 50–59). The proper operation of activities under the Dean of Students has been of highest importance in the success of the College program (see *infra*, chap. 12).

76. The terminology here needs to be clarified. "Divisional sequence" was defined as "three one-quarter courses in two or three departmental or subject fields." "Subject sequence" was defined as "three one-quarter courses in a subject," which, in fact, meant three departmental courses in one department.

77. These departmental courses provided what Dean Boucher called "reasonable provision for the pursuit of special interests" (*supra*, p. 49). Most, if not all, members of the faculty regarded these courses as the necessary first steps in specialization, and inclusion of them in the 1931 curriculum was a political necessity. The debate over these courses for the last twenty years, while not always sharply pointed up, has been whether such courses should be "counted" to satisfy general education requirements. Hutchins' position has been: "I believe that departmental courses of all kinds should be excluded from a general education" ("Report of the President, 1930–34" [unpublished, University of Chicago, 1935], p. 22). He has never said that introductory courses in a specific discipline should not be offered to students who wanted or needed them; his view has been that such courses are not a substitute for general education.

78. The full import of the Chicago requirements of an examination in English composition and four examinations in the three broad fields of knowledge (the humanities, the social sciences, and the natural sciences) may perhaps be made clearer by a reference to the chaotic state of requirements in 100 colleges and universities, as evidenced by a study made in 1929. The number of colleges (out of 80 independent colleges, 10 colleges in endowed universities, and 10 colleges in state universities) requiring the following subjects of all students was:

English	78	History	20
Science	58	Mathematics	20
Foreign language	57	Speech	11
Physical education	47	Psychology	3
Social science	42	Fine arts	2
Religion	31	Philosophy	2
Hygiene	23		

(Adapted from Reeves, in Gray, *op. cit.*, p. 83.)

79. Minutes of the University Senate, March 9, 1931.

80. The program is described in detail in chap. 11. From 1931 to 1941 the Dean of Students was also University Examiner. In the latter year the offices were separated, and the position of Chief Examiner was combined with that of University Examiner. Ralph W. Tyler, who had been Chief Examiner, became University Examiner.

81. Boucher, *op. cit.*, Appendix A, p. 262.

82. *Ibid.*, p. 38.

83. Among the instructional materials developed to meet the needs of the survey courses in the biological and physical sciences was a series of textbooks published by the University of Chicago Press. Ralph Buchsbaum, *Animals without Backbones* (rev. ed., 1948); Anton J. Carlson and Victor Johnson, *The Machinery of the Body* (rev. ed., 1948); Merle C. Coulter, *The Story of the Plant Kingdom* (1935); Alfred S. Romer, *Man and the Vertebrates* (3d rev. ed., 1941); Walter Bartky, *Highlights in Astronomy* (1935); Carey G. Croneis and William C. Krumbein, *Down to Earth* (1936); Harvey B. Lemon, *From Galileo to the Nuclear Age* (rev. ed., 1946); Mayme I. Logsdon, *A Mathematician Explains* (2d ed., 1936); Reginald J. Stephenson, *Exploring in Physics* (1935).

84. "Report of the President, 1930–34" (unpublished, University of Chicago, 1935), p. 17.

85. Charles H. Judd, Henry C. Morrison, Frank N. Freeman, Leonard V. Koos, George A. Works, and Floyd W. Reeves, of the Department of Education, provided the President with a wealth of historical and analytical material on the development of the American educational system supporting the 6-4-4 reorganization. William E. Dodd, Charles E. Merriam, and Beardsley Ruml were among the social scientists who favored the move.

86. Minutes of the University Senate, November 19, 1932. The Senate added the following to its resolution about the power of the Dean of the College to appoint faculty members without departmental status: "It is understood that members of the faculties of the other divisions will continue to teach in the College. . . . For the guidance of the Dean it is considered desirable that a large proportion of the College faculty be members of departmental and divisional faculties." See also Minutes of the University Senate, June 7, 1940.

87. Minutes of the Board of Trustees, December 8, 1932.

88. *Ibid.*, January 12, 1933.

89. Minutes of the College Faculty, March 16, 1933; Minutes of the University Senate, March 22, 1933.

90. See Robert M. Hutchins, *No Friendly Voice*, pp. 188–97, for his summary account of the developments between 1931 and 1934.

91. Chauncey S. Boucher and A. J. Brumbaugh, *The Chicago College Plan* (Chicago: University of Chicago Press, 1940), pp. 397–406. This is a revision and enlargement of Boucher's book published in 1935.

92. New Haven: Yale University Press, 1936.

93. *Ibid.*, p. 77.

94. *Ibid.*, p. 85.

95. "Report of the President, 1935–36" (unpublished, University of Chicago, 1937), pp. 21–22.

96. Scott Buchanan, "The Crisis in Liberal Education," *Amherst Graduate's Quarterly*, XXVII (February, 1938), 117.

97. Cf. the statement of Alexander Meiklejohn: "When the dominating idea and purpose of a course of study have once been accepted, the problem becomes largely that of finding books which will express the idea and serve the purpose. And from the very beginning [of the Experimental College at the University of Wisconsin] it has been taken for granted by the [faculty] that, just so far as possible, the books selected should be 'great,' should represent the work of the human mind in its highest quality as well as in relation to its most significant themes. We are certain that one of the greatest educational influences is found in this closeness of contact with the leaders in human intelligence. Teaching rests largely in the hope that greatness of mind may be contagious" (*The Experimental College* [New York: Harper & Bros., 1932], p. 107).

98. The curriculum committee was appointed January 16, 1933, and operated through subcommittees in the various subject-matter areas. In response to a request from a subcommittee concerned with the synthesis of suggested courses

into an "ideal" four-year program, Hutchins set forth his views as follows: "The object of general education is to train the mind for intelligent action. The question is how this can best be done. My own view is that the best method of achieving this aim is to help the student to master the leading ideas in the principal fields of knowledge, to see to it that he reads and understands the greatest books, and to help him to learn to read, to write, and to think. (. . . these are not three different methods, but merely three ways of saying the same thing.) . . . I should say that an 'ideal' program . . . might be more or less as follows:

1. The History and Science of Society—four years
2. Natural Science—four years (not taught historically)
3. The Fine Arts and Literature—four years (not taught historically)
4. Philosophy—four years (not taught historically)
5. Mathematics—first two years
6. Reading, writing, thinking—last two years."

(Memorandum, Robert M. Hutchins to A. J. Brumbaugh, February 7, 1936, files of the College, University of Chicago).

The final report was adopted by the curriculum committee on January 30, 1937, and was prepared for presentation to the College faculty.

99. Minutes of the College Committee on Policy and Personnel, January 22, 1937. Statement of the Joint Committee on the Granting of the Bachelor's Degree by the College, October 18, 1937, files of the College, University of Chicago. George A. Works, Dean of Students, was chairman. For a summary of some of the committee materials see George A. Works, "Arguments in Favor of Granting a Bachelor's Degree at the End of the Junior College Period," in William S. Gray (ed.), *Six Current Issues in Higher Education: Proceedings of the Institute for Administrative Officers of Higher Institutions*, IX (Chicago: University of Chicago Press, 1937), 3–13.

100. Minutes of the College Faculty, March 9, 1937. The action was approved by the Senate (Minutes of the University Senate, April 7, 1937).

101. Grade VIII had been abolished in the University Elementary School in 1913, as was previously noted. From 1913 until 1919 there was a seven-year Elementary School and a four-year High School. From 1919 until 1937 the University maintained a six-year elementary unit and a five-year secondary unit. In 1937, when the last two years were actually transferred to the College, one grade was restored; since 1945 the ten years above kindergarten have been operated as a single unit, the Laboratory School.

102. The average size of the class entering the first year of the College for the years 1937–38 through 1942–43 was 108. For enrolment in the College since 1942–43 see *infra*, n. 140.

103. Minutes of the College Faculty, June 11, 1936.

104. Minutes of the College Committee on Policy and Personnel, May 18, 1939.

105. Minutes of the College Faculty, May 2 and December 4, 1940.

106. Minutes of the College Faculty, January 14, 1941. At another meeting of the College Faculty a report on progress toward revising examination methods and schedules was asked for. This was prepared by the various instructional staffs and the Policy Committee but was never submitted to the faculty. (Minutes of the College Committee on Policy and Personnel, December 16, 1941).

107. Minutes of the College Committee on Policy and Personnel, October 16 and November 4, 1941.

108. For Faust's philosophy of general education see *supra*, chap. 1.

109. "The University at War," *University of Chicago Magazine*, XXXIV (January, 1942), 3 ff.

110. Robert M. Hutchins, Memorandum to the Faculty, January 19, 1942; see also "The University of Chicago and the Bachelor's Degree," *Educational Record*, XXIII (July, 1942), 567–73, and "Education at War," *North Central Association Quarterly*, XVII (October, 1942), 173–79.

111. Minutes of the Senate Committee on University Policy, January 16, 1942.

112. Minutes of the University Senate, January 21 and 22, 1942.

113. Robert M. Hutchins, "The University in War and Peace," *American Association of University Professors Bulletin*, XXIX (February, 1943), 24.

114. Minutes of the University Senate, January 22, 1942. For interpretative rulings see Minutes of the Senate Committee on University Policy, April 16 and May 22, 1942, and January 5, 1943.

115. Agenda of the College Faculty, March 19, 1942.

116. Minutes of the College Committee on Policy and Personnel, February 25 and March 6, 1942.

117. Minutes of the College Faculty, March 19–20, 1942. An amendment was carried to the effect that the question of comprehensive examination in elective courses would be left open.

118. The Policy Committee recommendation of examinations covering a year's work in both mathematics and a foreign language was rejected (see text, p. 74).

119. This course, which had been rejected by one vote in the Policy Committee, was added on motion made from the floor at the faculty meeting of March 19, 1942.

120. In the biological sciences there was a one-year course combining botany, zoölogy, and physiology. In the humanities the following one-year courses were available: art, English, French, German, Greek, history, Italian, Latin, music, philosophy, and Spanish. In the physical sciences one-year courses were offered in chemistry, geography, geology, mathematics, and physics. In the social sciences the one-year courses were geography and history.

121. Minutes of the University Senate, March 30, 1942.

122. Minutes of the College Faculty, April 6, 1942.

123. Minutes of the University Senate, April 9, 1942. The vote on the motion was 58 to 58.

124. For a description of the humanities courses see *infra*, chap. 3. The

description of the humanities survey given between 1931 and 1942 will be found in Boucher and Brumbaugh, *op. cit.*, pp. 44–45. Arthur P. Scott (historian) was the chairman of this course from 1931 to 1942.

125. For a description of the course in Observation, Interpretation, and Integration see *infra*, chap. 9.

126. *The People Shall Judge*, ed. Staff of Social Science 1, College of the University of Chicago (2 vols.; Chicago: University of Chicago Press, 1949).

127. For a description of the social science courses see *infra*, chap. 4. Harry D. Gideonse (economist), subsequently President of Brooklyn College, was chairman of the courses from 1931 to 1938, and Walter H. C. Laves (political scientist), subsequently Deputy Director-General of the United Nations Educational, Scientific, and Cultural Organization, was chairman from 1938 to 1942.

128. Minutes of the College Faculty, June 9, 1943. For a description of the placement-examination program see *infra*, chap. 11.

129. This does not mean that the College faculty believed that it made no difference what course of studies a student pursued in high school. If a student had given his time to trivial activities, placement tests might cause him to spend perhaps as much as two additional years in the College. If a student had a good mind, he could learn what the College taught; but if his previous training had been inadequate, it might take him longer to do so.

130. A study made in 1949 of the placement of 750 students entering the College with ten, eleven, and twelve years of previous schooling showed that 45 per cent of them were placed at a level which might have been expected from an analysis of transcripts of previous work, 25 per cent were excused from examinations for which they would have been held on the basis of customary evaluation of records, and 30 per cent were required to do more work.

Assuming that students proceed with their work in the College at a normal pace—taking four courses and four comprehensives each year—analysis of their programs prescribed by the placement tests has shown the following: Of students who enter the College after two years in high school, 54 per cent will spend three and one-half years in the College, 42 per cent will spend three years, and 4 per cent will spend two years or less; and, of students who have been graduated from high school, 60 per cent will spend three years, 36 per cent will spend two years, and 4 per cent will spend one and one-third years or less (see *infra*, chap. 11).

131. Minutes of the College Committee on Policy and Personnel, May 3, 1944; Minutes of the College Faculty, June 2, 1944.

132. See *infra*, chap. 6, for a discussion of the mathematics courses. A text prepared by the College Mathematics Staff, *Fundamental Mathematics*, appeared in 1945 and was in a third edition by 1949 (3d ed.; 3 vols.; Chicago: University of Chicago Press, 1948).

133. The work of Otto F. Bond and Peter Hagboldt was especially significant in the area; see, e.g., Otto F. Bond's forthcoming book, "The Reading Method: An Experiment in College French," describing thirty years' experience; and Peter Hagboldt, *Language Learning* (Chicago: University of Chicago Press, 1935):

134. Minutes of the College Faculty, June 8, 1945. For a description of the foreign language program see *infra*, chap. 8.

135. See *supra*, pp. 59–60, 67. Merle C. Coulter (botanist) was chairman of the general course in the biological sciences from 1931 to 1948. Hermann I. Schlesinger (chemist), Harvey B. Lemon (physicist), and Reginald J. Stephenson (physicist) were chairmen in the physical sciences from 1931 to 1945.

136. For a significant discussion of science in general education see Joseph J. Schwab, "The Nature of Scientific Knowledge as Related to Liberal Education," *Journal of General Education*, III (July, 1949), 245–66.

137. Aaron Sayvetz, "The Physical Sciences in General Education," *American Journal of Physics*, XIII (October, 1945), 303.

138. Minutes of the College Faculty, June 8, 1945. For a description of the College science program see *infra*, chap. 5. Between 1945 and 1950 both sequences of science courses were taught. During this period there was an increased understanding among the faculty as to what could be accomplished in a unified science program in which the original records of scientific research were used as the basis for study and discussion. There was an exchange of personnel in the different courses, giving various members of the staff an opportunity to teach in both programs. In the winter of 1950 the College faculty approved a union, proposed by the physical sciences staff and the natural sciences staff, of the physical sciences component of the two programs (Minutes of the College Faculty, February 22, 1950).

139. Minutes of the College Committee on Policy and Personnel, November 7, 1944.

140. The average annual enrolment of different students in the College for the years 1930–31 through 1941–42 was 1,830. For the years since 1942–43 enrolment has been as follows:

1942–43	1943–44	1944–45	1945–46	1946–47	1947–48	1948–49	1949–50
2,193	1,834	2,402	3,011	3,421	3,204	2,837	2,650

The number of Bachelor's degrees awarded by the College has been as follows:

1942–43	1943–44	1944–45	1945–46	1946–47	1947–48	1948–49	1949–50	Total
42	134	232	442	783	840	664	626	3,763

141. Minutes of the College Committee on Policy and Personnel, October 22 and November 30, 1945; January 4, 1946; Minutes of the College Faculty, December 17, 1945, and February 6, 1946; Memoranda, C. H. Faust to the Committee of the Council, February 12 and 21, 1946, appended to the minutes of the Committee of the Council of the University Senate for February 12 and 21, 1946.

142. Cf. "Documents Pertaining to the College Proposal of February 6, 1946" (unpublished, University of Chicago, April 1, 1946).

143. Minutes of the College Faculty, February 6, 1946.

144. Minutes of the Council of the University Senate, March 5, 1946.

145. Memorandum, Robert M. Hutchins to the members of the Council,

March 7, 1946, in Agenda of the Council of the University Senate, March 19, 1946.

146. Minutes of the Council of the University Senate, March 19, 1946.

147. *Ibid.*, April 9 and 16, 1946.

148. Minutes of the College Faculty, May 3, 1946.

149. Minutes of the College Committee on Policy and Personnel, May 15, 1946. As it affected the College, the provision for joint residency was a formalization of existing procedures. "While students in the College may, with the approval of their advisers, take courses in the Divisions, they may not take examinations for advanced degrees until they have fulfilled the College requirements" (University of Chicago, *Announcements of the College and the Divisions* [1944–45], p. 45).

150. Minutes of the Committee of the Council of the University Senate, May 29 and June 5, 1946; Minutes of the College Faculty, June 4, 1946; Minutes of the Council of the University Senate, June 11, 1946.

151. *Supra*, p. 30.

152. *The President's Report, 1898–99*, pp. xxv–xxvi.

153. See, e.g., the report of the College Committee on Policy and Personnel, March 10, 1942, and the discussion noted in the minutes of the Policy Committee, June 14, 1945.

154. For a description of the College history course see *infra*, chap. 9.

155. Minutes of the College Faculty, December 16, 1946, and March 16, 1948.

156. On September 1, 1947, Faust became Director of the Libraries and Professor of English at Stanford University, and a year later he became Dean of Humanities and Sciences. During part of 1949 he was acting president of Stanford.

157. In the autumn of 1949 there were 162 persons on the staff of the College. Of these, 122 were on a full-time basis (and 28 of the 40 on part-time were giving service in other parts of the University). The full-time equivalent was 129 persons, made up as follows: professors, 3; associate professors, 22; assistant professors, 55; instructors, 40; lecturers and visitors, 4; and teaching assistants, 5. The average age of the College faculty was thirty-seven (professors, fifty years of age; associate professors, forty-four; assistant professors, thirty-seven; instructors, thirty-two).

It is the expectation of the administration that the faculty of the College will include: (1) members appointed solely on the recommendation of the College faculty; (2) members jointly of departments, upper divisions, or schools, and the College; and (3) members of departments, upper divisions, or schools who will devote part time or full time to the work of the College.

158. The challenge to those who have responsibility for the execution of the collegiate function has been stated in various ways but seldom, perhaps, more aptly than by Henry Smith Pritchett, astronomer, sometime president of Massachusetts Institute of Technology (1900–1906) and first president of the Carnegie Foundation for the Advancement of Teaching (1906–30). In 1908 he said:

"The pressure of economic, no less than educational, influences will demand a solution of American educational organization more efficient, better proportioned, and less wasteful of time. . . . In the reorganization which will sooner or later come . . . the college will take account of both freedom and discipline. Its professors will be, first of all, teachers, and its function will be to lead boys out of the rule of the school into the freedom of the university; out of the tutelage of boyhood into the liberty of men. If the college does not fill this function, it will in the end be squeezed out between the reorganized secondary school and the fully developed university" ("The College of Discipline and the College of Freedom," *Atlantic Monthly*, CII [November, 1908], 603).

159. National Educational Association, *Journal of Proceedings and Addresses, Boston, Massachusetts, 1903* (Winona, Minn.: Published by the Association, 1903), p. 516.

74/54

PART II

On Curriculum

3

The Humanities

RUSSELL THOMAS

THE curriculum of the College of the University of Chicago recognizes three basic sets of disciplines which are addressed to the solution of three distinct kinds of problems. These problems define the subject matter of the natural sciences, the social sciences, and the humanities. The problems which define the humanities are those which arise in the formulation of judgments which are concerned with the appreciation of the arts of mankind. The humanities sequence in the College has, therefore, been organized with a view to training students in the exercise of the disciplines which contribute to an intelligent appreciation of the arts.

This definition of the subject matter and the instructional ends of the humanities in general education can be distinguished from other definitions which have determined the organization of many humanities courses. Some courses appear to define the humanities in terms of a specific and restricted body of works, usually imaginative literature, music, and the visual arts. In such courses, *Hamlet* and the poems of Wordsworth are allocated to the humanities, while Mill's essay *On Liberty* and Galileo's *Two New Sciences* are excluded, as falling wholly within the scope of the social sciences and the natural sciences, respectively. But the poetic achievements of mankind are not exclusively the province of the humanities, and, on the other hand, all the great products of intellectual inquiry yield to humanistic treatment. A work such as Lucretius' poem, *De rerum natura*, raises problems examinable

103

by the methods of the natural sciences when concern is with the adequacy of its proofs of the physical structure of the universe. It raises problems examinable by the methods of the social sciences when concern is with the effects of the poet's ethics upon the social institutions and behavior of his times. It raises problems examinable by the methods of the humanities when concern is with the effectiveness of the poem's use of the arts of communication. Elaborate studies of the great tragic heroes of drama and fiction have been made in recent years by various kinds of psychologists; but, while these have sometimes been useful in explaining motives of human behavior, they have seldom contributed to the appreciation of the works as great tragic poems.

The practice of defining the humanities in terms of kinds of artistic products has contributed to some confusion in determining the relations of the humanities courses to other parts of a program of general education. On the assumption that the study of imaginative works of literature is the province of the humanities, some schools have sought to integrate the humanities and the social sciences by joining the study of selected novels and poems with the study of problems in social and political organization. In such a scheme an examination of the problems of a regimented society might be enlivened by the introduction of such works as *Brave New World* and *Nineteen Eighty-four*. It seems probable, however, that a discussion of these works in the given context would lead only to the application of disciplines suitable to the social sciences and that no real integration would be achieved. Integration of knowledge is a desirable end of general education, but integration is best achieved when students recognize and relate to one another the several ends which the great achievements of mankind serve.

Among other organizing schemes represented in college humanities courses, there are two which are widely used, each of which has many variants. One of these is the "history-of-culture" course; the other is found in courses which are organized about ideas and concepts. It is no disparagement of the values which such courses may achieve to point out that they impose limited methods of interpretation. To examine a work solely as a cause or consequence of a cultural pattern is to restrict the study of the humanities to historical methods. Without an understanding of other humanistic disciplines, students are unable to grasp much more than the events which surround the production of a work. What is culturally significant about the poetry or painting of a period can be only partially grasped when a student has no understanding of either the ends or the media of these forms. This state is conspicuously evident in the visual arts and music. When a student is unable to understand musically the structure of a sonata or a symphony, the content of Mozart and Brahms is meaningless; he therefore has no basis for examining distinctions about their significance in the culture of the eighteenth and nineteenth centuries. This fact perhaps explains why music has been commonly neglected in many history-of-culture courses.

Where the humanities have been treated in terms of an examination of ideas and courses have been organized about such themes as "The Conflict of Freedom and Authority" or "Concepts of Justice," another limitation of method occurs. All expression tends to become one in kind, measured in terms of its adequacy as statement of external truths. Significant distinctions between various forms of expression seldom emerge; and the values peculiar to poetic achievement as distinct from historical and philosophical achievement are undiscovered.

In organizing the sequence of humanities courses in the College, we have sought principles which, on the one hand, would permit distinctions between the proper role of the humanities and those of the other areas of knowledge and, on the other, would avoid a too narrow conception of humanistic subject matter and method.

The humanities sequence consists of three courses, each extending through one academic year. The courses contribute progressively to the following objectives: (1) increasing the experience of students with the great products of the arts by the examination of a considerable body of the best works in the fields of literature, the visual arts, and music; (2) training students in the exercise of analytical methods appropriate to humanistic ends; and (3) training students in the use of the arts of criticism which will enable them to recognize some of the differences in values ascribed to works and the kinds of interpretations of the arts which lead to the assertion of these values and, in the light of this recognition, to make responsible and sensitive criticisms.

The foundation of appreciation is extensive familiarity with and interest in a great variety of works of art. Each of the courses contributes to the enlarging of the experience with great literary works, and each contributes, though in different ways, to the development of analytical skills. The enlarging of experience with music and the visual arts, as well as the development of the simplest analytical skills, is reserved primarily for Humanities 1, and the literary experience of the students in that course is relatively more extensive than in the others. The development of systematic methods of analysis of different literary forms is the principal task of Humanities 2, while the study of the arts of criticism is undertaken in Humanities 3.

Humanities 1 meets five hours each week, one hour of which is devoted to a general lecture which provides an outline or demonstration of the nature of the week's discussion problem. The remaining four hours are devoted to discussion in class groups of about twenty students each. Since the course is an introduction, extensive in the scope of its materials, to poetic literature, the visual arts, and music, the classrooms have been equipped to meet the needs of its varied subject matter. Each classroom is provided with a piano, a record-player, projectors, and screen.

The method of instruction is to present a sequence of general topics in terms of which each of the arts is subject to analysis. This course is the first experience which many students have had with an analytical approach to the arts; hence the instruction, particularly in the visual arts and music, must begin at an elementary level. The following topics form the sequence which is studied during the year:

1. Some relations between nature and art
2. Elements and form in the arts
3. Application of the principles studied (in Topic 2) to one complex work in each of the arts
4. Principles of differentiation within the arts
5. Tradition in the arts; its growth, elaboration, and change
6. Contemporary trends in the arts

In the study of each of these topics the classes devote approximately equal periods of time to each of the three fields of art. A single instructor guides each class through the discussions of all three media.

The first of these topics, which is examined very briefly, is intended primarily to permit students, who have long been accustomed to regard works of art as very literal representations of the natural world, to explore questions about the limitations of this point of view, about some of the functions which are unique to each art, and about intentions which lead to abstraction and symbolism in each of the arts.

The second of the topics directs attention, first, to the basic elements of the visual arts: color, line, volume, mass, texture; their uses in different media; and their interrelation in examples of painting, sculpture, and architecture. Afterward the study turns to the properties and uses of tone, intrinsically and in combinations, so that students may begin to hear distinctions in pitch, volume, and timbre and to recognize various harmonic, melodic, and rhythmic organizations. The materials for study are, at first, very simple folk songs, which are followed by slightly longer and more complex compositions. In the last division of the topic the study turns to literature. Here work begins with a study of the significative and nonsignificative functions of language. The functions of the sound-values of language (rhythm, rhyme, assonance, etc.) are studied, and particular uses of them are related to the significative content of several narrative poems. These poems also provide the means of introducing the elements of plot and character in narrative constructions.

The third topic is at once a review of the subject matter considered in the second topic and an application of the analytical procedures to a single complex work chosen from each field. For example, the classes may spend two weeks in the study of the uses of visual elements in a painting such as Seurat's "La Grande Jatte." Since the original is available in the Art Institute of Chicago, the work of the classroom is aided by the opportunity of direct examination. Brahms's *Variation on a Theme by Handel* has sometimes been studied as a complex organization and treatment of melody, harmony, and rhythm. *Richard II* might be chosen for the first study of a complex literary work in terms of its uses of the formal elements of dramatic narrative.

The fourth topic makes no attempt to exhaust the principles of differentiation which are employed in defining various types and functions of the arts. Each field of the arts provides materials for illustrating certain principles. Thus the visual arts have been used to illustrate differentiations in terms of materials and techniques, while music has provided materials for distinctions in terms of function and forms and literature has given material for distinctions in terms of types of expression.

The fifth topic should in no sense be construed as constituting a history of the arts. The purpose of the topic is to develop an understanding of how forms, styles, and techniques develop, expand, and are modified and of some of the factors which modify established traditions and lead to the invention of new patterns.

The final topic, which is closely related to the fifth, is, as the title suggests, an introduction to some of the developments in function and forms which have characterized the products of the present century.

The work of the classroom is aided in numerous ways by extra-class activities. A studio workshop, under the direction of a member of the staff, is open to all students. There they may learn, through actual use of the artist's materials, the importance of visual elements in relation to the problems of organization. Occasional assignments require the student to employ some medium of his choice in the preparation of a work. An essay which explains his use of visual elements or the relation of his chosen technique to his purpose completes the assignment. The director of the workshop is available for suggestion and criticism while the student prepares his assignment. Students are required to study special exhibitions at the Art Institute and other local galleries, as well as works in their permanent collections. Examinations include questions on original works which students see for the first time during the examination.

The classroom work in music is supplemented by the use of extra-class hours set aside for free listening periods. A staff member is available to aid the students in clarifying problems of musical structure. Attendance at concerts given under the direction of the University's Department of Music is also required. For those students who enter the course totally uninformed about music, a few hours are set aside at the beginning of the year, where they may learn something about the rudiments of music, a provision which is necessary because of the immense disparity between the best-informed and the poorest in every class.

In Humanities 2, the second course in the sequence, the subject matter is the arts of interpretation useful in the understanding and appreciation of a selection of modes of literary expression: history, rhetoric, drama and fiction, and philosophy. While the area of study is thus narrowed to literature, it introduces forms not studied in Humanities 1, and the study is much more intensive.

The course meets four days each week. One hour is given to a general lecture and the remaining three to discussions, which are based upon the student's reading of particular assigned works. The lectures are planned to aid the students by giving them essential data about the historical background of the works read and demonstrations of methods of analyzing passages. For example, a series of three lectures on rhetorical writing might deal with (1) a historical account of theories about the art of rhetoric, (2) a demonstration of a method of analyzing a rhetorical text, (3) an argument for the utility of the study of rhetoric for the modern student. Approximately eight weeks are given to the study of historical writings, three to works of rhetoric, eleven to drama and fiction, and nine to philosophy.

Instruction in the course aims at developing a recognition of distinctions with respect to the primary ends of works which determine their formal organization and permit the application of definitive terms such as "history," "tragedy," and "comedy." At the same time, instruction seeks to make clear that great works yield to more than one mode of analysis and may be examined variously in terms of historical, poetic, or philosophical ends. For practical purposes, however, it seems better to use historical works for the study of the disciplines of historical interpretation, to use poetic works for the study of the disciplines of poetic analysis, and so on.

In the study of historical writings we seek to develop an understanding of the nature of a historical construction and the elements which are the essence of all historical literature. Since all histories are accounts of the past and since the measure of the values of a history is the adequacy of its account of the past, students must know how to examine the elements which are the key to its values. Study, therefore, is directed to discovering the historian's aims; the kinds of data which he regards as relevant to his aims; the kinds of causes by means of which he explains the relationship of events; the sources of his evidence; and the philosophical assumptions, if any, which have determined his view of the nature of historical action. A knowledge of the past is indispensable to the citizens of a free society and is an important part of a general education; but the utility of history is largely determined by the capacity of the reader to assess the values of the accounts of the past upon which most of our knowledge depends. The ability to analyze such accounts would therefore seem to be a prerequisite to general courses in cultural and political history.

The study of rhetoric is perhaps even more unfamiliar to most students than the study of historical writing. Given a piece of persuasive literature, the student will tend to look for the conclusions of the author and argue for or against them as his own opinions may direct. Our effort is to direct his attention to the *arts* of persuasion. Through such models of deliberative rhetoric as Milton's *Areopagitica* and selections from *The Federalist* we raise questions about the manner in which the author adapts his arguments to the character of his audience, the character which he gives both to himself and to his audience, the relationship of diction or "style" to the effectiveness of the argument, and the logical structure and the rhetorical ordering of arguments. In a democratic society, where the deliberations of free citizens are assumed to play an important role in determining the courses of political action, the study of the arts of persuasion would scarcely seem to need justification as part of a liberal education. The prevalence of bad and dishonest practitioners of the art is merely an additional argument for its study and proper use by honest men.

The study of the disciplines of aesthetic appreciation, which was begun in Humanities 1, is limited in Humanities 2 to drama and fiction. Young and inexperienced readers often find it difficult to make judgments about these works without reference to the truths of the external world which they may be thought to express. Humanities 2, however, seeks to bring about an understanding and appreciation of dramas and novels as self-contained works. Study is directed to the particular pleasures which are the ends of each species of poetic works and to the kinds of subject matter, the means, and the manner which are appropriate to the achievement of each kind of pleasure. A quotation from the syllabus of the course may help to clarify the approach:

"Fiction and drama differ from historical and philosophical writing in that they do not purport to be accounts of anything existing outside of themselves. Many individual works, certainly most of those generally considered to be great, do convey what seem to be true insights into human life and character, combining (as some critics would have it) the particular truths of history and the universal truths of philosophy. Indeed the greatness of these works depends in no small degree on their embodiment of these kinds of truths. Yet Shakespeare's Hamlet is not a historical character as he is presented in the play, and his philosophical remarks possess their maximum truth or force only in the fictitious situation imagined by the dramatist. . . .

"Accordingly, the primary analysis of an imaginative or poetic work does not treat it as a historical, philosophical, or rhetorical statement of its author; but assuming it to be a self-sufficient work of art, seeks to investigate its nature as a created thing. We might begin, therefore, by observing that works of drama and fiction can best attain their proper self-sufficiency only if they are so unified that nothing can be taken from them without setting up a feeling of incompleteness, nor can anything be added to make them more complete. In other words there must be in an imaginative work some unifying or organizing principle which determines what must be included or excluded, some essential principle which makes the work a self-sufficient whole. In one sense the whole task of analysis of drama and fiction consists in discovering this organizing principle and in understanding how everything in the work is related to it and accounted for by it."

The inquiry concerning the unity of works of drama and fiction leads to questions about the kinds of action which works represent. This involves the making of distinctions between tragedies, comedies, and other species of action in terms of the particular ends of each. It will also involve considerations of the interrelations of plot, character, thought, and diction and of the adaptation of these elements to the particular aesthetic pleasure which is the end of any chosen work. In this way the significance of incident and statement in terms of the whole or unified action of a work becomes a matter of primary interest.

The study of philosophical texts leads to the development of the disciplines by means of which students are able to examine the adequacy and cogency of proofs which authors submit in the demonstration of universal propositions about the nature of things. The first task is to direct attention to the ends or truths which the philosopher seeks to demonstrate. But students must also be taught to seek the assumptions underlying arguments, the modes of developing arguments, and the relationships between the ends which texts seek to demonstrate and the kinds of proofs offered. The texts studied are chosen, in part, for their usefulness in illustrating different dialectical methods. No attempt is made to survey the field of philosophical inquiry or to examine any single problem in the fields of metaphysics, ethics, or logic. Students should know some of the great concepts about the nature of knowledge, virtue, justice, etc.; but true knowledge of the concepts follows only from the capacity to trace the course of the intricate reasoning which leads to their formulation. The arts of reading which develop this capacity have a claim on students' time which is prior to the comparison of systems of ethics and epistemology or to the study of the history of philosophy.

The disciplines of rhetorical, historical, aesthetic, and philosophical interpretation are complementary, and a part of our task is to enable students to grasp the ways in which each discipline may support the uses of another. An understanding of the poetic devices which Herodotus employs in his *History* and Plato uses in his dialogues will aid in understanding the historical and philosophic intentions of these authors. Proper use of the arts of rhetorical analysis can aid in understanding the function of the speeches upon which Thucydides depends in his historical accounts. The dramatic function of the episode of the Grand Inquisitor in *The Brothers Karamazov* will be clarified by a careful analysis of the philosophic position assumed in the episode.

We cannot, of course, expect that, in a single year, our students will have achieved perfection in the exercise of the analytical skills which are the subject matter of the course. We hope, however, to have developed some methods and habits of inquiry which will improve with continued application.

Humanities 1 and 2 have established certain methods of analysis of the poetic arts, the visual arts, and music; within the framework of these methods the students have discussed the excellences and the limitations of the works which they have studied. Humanities 3, the final course in the sequence, takes cognizance of the fact that there are different conceptions of the functions of the arts and that the various, and often conflicting, judgments which we make of works derive from different methods of interpretation. One task of the course, therefore, is to train the student to recognize the character of his own critical judgments and the principles from which they stem. A second task is to train the student in the arts of expressing his own criticisms. This involves training in the arts of writing at a more advanced level than that which is undertaken in the course in English composition. The course is therefore a joint enterprise of the staffs of Humanities and of English.

Since the primary concern is with the arts of criticism, both its theory and its practice, supplemented with the arts of writing, the choice of the particular objects of art upon which the students may apply their efforts in practical criticism can be very wide. We have, therefore, undertaken to meet a considerable variety of interests by developing several versions of the course. In the original or parent version of the course, the first quarter is devoted to a study of a few texts which develop different critical theories or aspects of problems of criticism which influence judgments about works. This quarter is followed by two quarters in which the students read and make their own critical evaluations of a selection of lyric poems, novels, and dramas. Attention is directed to the analysis of the critical principles explicitly developed or implied in these exercises. The works studied in all three quarters are read in the English language. In addition to this version, we have developed the following variant forms: Humanities 3 (French), Humanities 3 (German), Humanities 3 (Greek), Humanities 3 (Latin), Humanities 3 Spanish), Humanities 3 (Art), and Humanities 3 (Music). In the foreign language versions of the course, some of the theoretical texts and all the works used for purposes of practical criticism are read in the foreign language. A nucleus of texts, common to all versions, is read in English. Students are admitted to any of the foreign language versions who have had at least the equivalent of one year of the language in the College and can demonstrate ability to read at the advanced level. Admission to the art and music versions of the course presupposes a knowledge of these arts equivalent to that achieved by students who have completed the requirements of Humanities 1. The work for students in the art and music versions does not differ in the first quarter from that of the parent course. In actual practice, only students of more than average competence in a language, in art, or in music have elected to prepare for the examinations in these versions. A large majority of the students choose to take the parent version of the course.

The critical texts selected for reading include some which treat of the philosophic bases of the arts, others which treat of a critical method, and some which apply principles of criticism to particular works. For example, the reading of all the students may include selections from Croce's *Aesthetic*, Aristotle's *Poetics*, and Plato's *Phaedrus*. Students in the parent version may read, in connection with their study of novels, Elizabeth Bowen's essay, "Notes on Writing a Novel," and, in connection with their study of a lyric poem, e.g., Keats's "Ode on a Grecian Urn," two or three critical analyses of the poem which present quite different critical approaches. Students in the several variants will read other critical texts, some in English and some in the particular language of their choice, which will parallel in kind the ones read in the parent course.

The study of the critical texts leads to the raising of questions such as the following:

1. Is a work of art known and judged in terms of its reference to something external to itself? If so, what is that external thing, and by what argument does the critic demonstrate the relationship?

2. To what extent is a knowledge of the artist essential in judging a work of art? Is the author treated as an intuitive genius or as the product of social forces which he consciously or unconsciously represents, or is he treated in any other discoverable terms?

3. Is a work of art treated as representative of a species of created thing, whole and complete in itself, producing effects appropriate to its species? How is its wholeness or unity known, and how are its proper effects known?

4. Is a work of art known and judged in terms of its effect on its audience? Are any criteria imposed upon audiences which qualify them to judge? Are any absolute criteria imposed upon the works of art, or do the values of works vary with the audiences?

The answers to these and related questions ought to clarify the grounds upon which different evaluations of works of art rest and should aid the students in making explicit the bases of evaluation in the critical essays which they write after the study of different poems, novels, paintings, or musical compositions. The whole course will assist, we hope, in leading students away from an easy dogmatism rooted in a limited perspective of the basis of appreciation of the arts and away from a relativism which regards the taste of each individual as neither better nor worse than another. It can do this if the students are able to see how different methods of inquiry lead to different standards of values and if they discover the limitations of each and the ways in which they complement one another.

Humanities 3 meets three days each week; there are no general lectures. A reasonable proportion of the poetry, drama, fiction, art, and music is chosen from contemporary work, in part, because the earlier courses have given more attention to classical works and in part because the critical problems presented by contemporary works have an immediate appeal.

The objectives of Humanities 3 impose a need for more writing by the students and for more careful attention to the problems of effective writing than do the other courses. Writing assignments are made in each of the courses, however; and some of these are completed under supervision, others independently. In each course a considerable portion of readings (or works of music and visual art) is assigned for independent study, upon which about half of all comprehensive examinations is based. Since our subject matter is the disciplines of analysis and criticism which lead to appreciation, we can best find proofs of the power to exercise the disciplines in the students' independent application of them.

Reading Lists

HUMANITIES 1

In addition to the *Humanities 1 Handbook* (4th ed.; Chicago: University of Chicago Press, 1950), which is used throughout the year, the following list is representative of the materials studied:

LITERATURE

Selections of folk ballads; poems by SPENSER, SHAKESPEARE, MILTON, WORDSWORTH, COLERIDGE, SHELLEY, KEATS, TENNYSON, BROWNING, DICKINSON, ROBINSON, FROST, YEATS, SANDBURG, JEFFERS, ELIOT, AUDEN, SPENDER, and others, in LOUIS UNTERMEYER, *The Book of Living Verse* (New York: Harcourt, Brace & Co., 1945).

SHAKESPEARE, WILLIAM, *Romeo and Juliet, Macbeth, The Tempest,* and *Henry IV (Part 1),* in *Shakespeare: Major Plays and the Sonnets,* ed. G. B. Harrison (New York: Harcourt, Brace & Co., 1948).

SYNGE, J. M., *The Playboy of the Western World* and *Riders to the Sea;* SEAN O'CASEY, *Juno and the Paycock,* in *Five Great Modern Irish Plays* ("Modern Library" [New York: Random House, 1941]).

WILDER, THORNTON, *The Skin of Our Teeth* (New York: Samuel French, 1944).

The Bible: selections from Ecclesiastes, Ruth, Psalms, Genesis, the Gospel according to St. Luke.

HOMER *The Odyssey,* trans. T. E. Shaw (New York: Oxford University Press, 1932).

TURGENEV, IVAN, *Fathers and Children,* trans. R. Hare (New York: Rinehart & Co., 1948).

HAWTHORNE, NATHANIEL, *The Scarlet Letter;* MELVILLE, HERMAN, *Billy Budd;* TWAIN, MARK, *Huckleberry Finn;* JAMES, HENRY, *Daisy Miller,* in *Four Great American Novels,* ed. R. W. Short (New York: Henry Holt & Co., 1946).

JOYCE, JAMES, *The Dubliners* ("Modern Library" [New York: Random House, 1926]).

ART

[Space does not permit a complete listing of all the artistic works which are studied in Humanities 1. Original works and reproductions of works from various periods in the history of painting, drawing, print-making, sculpture, and architecture are put before the students during the year. The following list of works of art are those which have received particular attention.]

Paintings, drawings, and prints: Originals in the Art Institute of Chicago: El Greco, "Assumption of the Virgin"; Sebastian Schel (School of Innsbruch), "Madonna and Child with Saints"; Rembrandt, "Young Girl at an Open Half-door"; Poussin, "St. John on Patmos"; Delacroix, "Lion Hunt"; Turner, "Val d'Aosta"; Courbet, "Mère Grégoire"; Corot, "Interrupted Reading"; Manet, "Le Journal"; Monet, "Still Life with Apples"; Renoir,

"Rowers' Lunch"; Van Gogh, "Montmartre," "Sunny Midi," "La Ber-
ceuse"; Gauguin, "Mahana no Atua"; Cézanne, "Madame Cézanne,"
"Auvers," "Still Life with Fruit"; Seurat, "Sunday Afternoon on the Island
of the Grande Jatte"; Toulouse-Lautrec, "Au Moulin Rouge"; Picasso,
"Family of Saltimbanques," "Still Life"; Matisse, "The Plumed Hat";
Modigliani, "Gypsy Woman"; De Chirico, "Conversation among Ruins";
Braques, "Le Jour." *Reproductions:* Giotto, Arena Chapel frescoes; Michelan-
gelo, Sistine Chapel frescoes; Orozco, Baker Library frescoes (at Dartmouth
College); Dürer, woodcuts and engravings; Rembrandt, etchings; Hogarth,
engravings; Goya, etchings; Daumier, lithographs.

Sculpture: "Assyrian Winged Human-headed Bull" (Oriental Institute, Chicago); Parthenon frieze; Chartres Cathedral, west portal; thirteenth-century
"Italian Virgin and Child" (Art Institute of Chicago); Ghiberti, Baptistry
doors, Florence; Donatello, selected sculpture; Alsatian "St. Margaret of
Alexandria" (Art Institute of Chicago); Michelangelo, Medici tombs, Florence; Roccatagliata, "St. Francis" (Art Institute of Chicago); Lachaise,
"Standing Women" (Art Institute of Chicago); Pattison, "Kneeling Wom-
en" (Art Institute of Chicago); Faggi, "Stations of the Cross" (Church of St.
Thomas the Apostle, Chicago); Bernini, selected sculpture; Lipchitz, selected sculpture; Calder, selected sculpture; Henry Moore, selected sculpture.

Architecture: Parthenon; Santa Sophia; Chartres; Sullivan, Carson, Pirie, Scott
department store (Chicago), Auditorium Building (Chicago); Wright, Robie
house (Chicago); Goodhue, Rockefeller Memorial Chapel (University of
Chicago); Mies van der Rohe, Illinois Institute of Technology buildings
(Chicago), Promontory apartment building (Chicago).

MUSIC

Palestrina, selection of *Motets;* Bach, *Inventions*, Fugues from the *Well-tempered
Clavier, Chorales, Magnificat;* Handel, *Concerto Grosso in G Major*, No. 1;
Haydn, *Quartet in G Minor*, Op. 74, No. 3; Mozart, *Symphony in E Flat Major*,
No. 39, *Piano Concerto in C Minor*, No. 24, *Don Giovanni;* Beethoven, *Piano
Sonata in E Minor*, Op. 90, *Quartet in B Flat Major*, Op. 130; Schubert, *Die
Winterreise;* Chopin, *Préludes;* Brahms, *Variations on a Theme by Handel;* Wag-
ner, "Prelude" and "Love-Death" from *Tristan und Isolde;* Moussorgsky-
Ravel, *Pictures at an Exhibition;* Debussy, *Afternoon of a Faun, Clouds, Fêtes,
Chansons de Bilitis;* Ravel, *Mother Goose Suite, Daphnis and Chloe*, Suite No. 2;
Prokofieff, *Classical Symphony;* Hindemith, *Kleine Kammermusik*, Op. 24, No. 2;
Sibelius, *Tapiola;* Berg, *Lyric Suite;* Copland, *El Salón México;* Milhaud,
Suite Provençal; Stravinsky, *Dumbarton Oaks Concerto;* Harris, *Symphony No. 3;*
Britten, *Variations on a Theme by Purcell;* Bartók, *Piano Concerto No. 3; Hun-
garian Folk Tunes.*

HUMANITIES 2

HISTORY

HERODOTUS *The Persian Wars*, trans. George Rawlinson ("Modern Library"
[New York: Random House, 1947]), Book i.

GIBBON, EDWARD, *The History of the Decline and Fall of the Roman Empire* (New York: Harper & Bros., 1880), chaps. i, ii, iii, iv, v, xv, and "General Observations on the Fall of the Roman Empire in the West."

TAWNEY, R. H., *Religion and the Rise of Capitalism* (New York: New American Library of World Literature, 1947).

TROTSKY, LEON, *The History of the Russian Revolution*, trans. Max Eastman (New York: Simon & Schuster, Inc., 1932), I, Preface and 3–15, 33–51, 101–35, 458–61; III, 276–301.

THUCYDIDES *The Peloponnesian War*, trans. Richard Crawley ("Modern Library" [New York: Random House, 1934]), Books i, ii, v (chap. 17).

RHETORIC

FRANKLIN, BENJAMIN, "On the Slave-Trade," in *Benjamin Franklin: Representative Selections*, ed. F. L. Mott and C. E. Jorgenson (New York: American Book Co., 1936), pp. 510–13.

MILTON, JOHN, *Areopagitica*, in *Areopagitica and Other Prose Writings*, ed. William Haller (New York: Macmillan Co., 1927).

NEWMAN, JOHN HENRY, "Knowledge Its Own End," in *The Idea of a University*, ed. Charles Frederick Harrold (New York: Longmans, Green & Co., Inc., 1947), pp. 88–109.

DRAMA

SOPHOCLES *Oedipus the King*, trans. David Grene, in *Three Greek Tragedies in Translation* (Chicago: University of Chicago Press, 1942).

SHAKESPEARE, WILLIAM, *King Lear* and *Othello*, in *Shakespeare: Major Plays and the Sonnets*, ed. G. B. Harrison (New York: Harcourt, Brace & Co., 1948).

JONSON, BEN, *The Alchemist*, ed. G. E. Bentley (New York: F. S. Crofts & Co., 1947).

IBSEN, HENRIK, *An Enemy of the People*, in *Ghosts, An Enemy of the People, The Wild Duck* (New York: Rinehart & Co., 1948).

FICTION

AUSTEN, JANE, *Emma* ("Everyman's Library" [New York: E. P. Dutton & Co., Inc., 1906]).

DOSTOEVSKI, FEODOR, *Crime and Punishment*, trans. Constance Garnett ("Modern Library" [New York: Random House, n.d.]).

FORSTER, E. M., *A Passage to India* (New York: Harcourt, Brace & Co., 1924).

CONRAD, JOSEPH, *Victory* ("Modern Library" [New York: Random House, n.d.]).

PHILOSOPHY

DEWEY, JOHN, *Essays in Experimental Logic* (Chicago: University of Chicago Press, 1916), pp. 75–102, 220–29, 230–49.

PLATO *Phaedo* and *Protagoras*, trans. B. Jowett, in *The Works of Plato*, ed. Irwin Edman ("Modern Library" [New York: Random House, n.d.]).

ARISTOTLE *Metaphysics*, trans. W. D. Ross, in *Introduction to Aristotle*, ed. Richard McKeon ("Modern Library" [New York: Random House, 1947]), i. 1–7.

——— *Posterior Analytics*, trans. G. R. G. Mure, *ibid.*, i. 1–3.

——— *On the Soul*, trans. J. A. Smith, *ibid.*, i. 1; ii. 1 and 2.

―――― *Nichomachean Ethics*, trans. W. D. Ross, *ibid.*, i. 13; ii (entire).

Some of these readings are reprinted in the volume *Humanities 2: Selected Readings* (5th ed.; Chicago: University of Chicago Press, 1949).

HUMANITIES 3

CRITICISM

ARISTOTLE *Physics*, trans. R. P. Hardie and R. K. Gaye, in *The Basic Works of Aristotle*, ed. Richard McKeon (New York: Random House, 1941), ii. 1.

―――― *Metaphysics*, trans. W. D. Ross, *ibid.*, vii. 7–9.

―――― *Poetics*, trans. I. Bywater, in *Introduction to Aristotle*, ed. Richard McKeon ("Modern Library" [New York: Random House, 1947]).

PLATO *Phaedrus*, trans. B. Jowett, in *The Works of Plato*, ed. Irwin Edman ("Modern Library" [New York: Random House, n.d.]).

HUME, DAVID, "Of the Standard of Taste," in *Essays and Treatises on Several Subjects* (London, 1760), I, 363–95.

CROCE, BENEDETTO, *Aesthetic as Science of Expression and General Linguistic*, trans. Douglas Ainslie (2d ed.; London: Macmillan & Co., Ltd., 1922), pp. 1–38, 67–73, 78–81, 87–103, 111–39.

ARNOLD, MATTHEW, "The Study of Poetry," in *Representative Essays of Matthew Arnold*, ed. E. K. Brown (New York: Macmillan Co., 1936), pp. 156–68.

TAINE, HIPPOLYTE, Introduction, in *History of English Literature*, trans. H. Van Laun (Edinburgh: Edmonston & Douglas, 1871), pp. 1–21.

PATER, WALTER, "The School of Giorgione," in *The Renaissance: Studies in Art and Poetry* (London: Macmillan & Co., Ltd., 1910), pp. 130–54.

BOWEN, ELIZABETH, "Notes on Writing a Novel," *Orion*, II (1945), 18–29.

LITERARY WORKS

Short Stories for Study, ed. R. W. Short and R. B. Sewell (New York: Henry Holt & Co., 1941).

MARK TWAIN, *Huckleberry Finn* (New York: Rinehart & Co., 1948).

FITZGERALD, F. SCOTT, *The Great Gatsby* (New York: Bantam Books, Inc., 1945).

PROUST, MARCEL, *Swann's Way* ("Modern Library" [New York: Random House, 1928]).

HUXLEY, ALDOUS, *Point Counter Point* ("Modern Library" [New York: Random House, n.d.]).

BUTLER, SAMUEL, *The Way of All Flesh* (New York: Rinehart & Co., 1948).

EURIPIDES *Hippolytus*, trans. David Grene, in *Three Greek Tragedies in Translation* (Chicago: University of Chicago Press, 1942).

SHAKESPEARE, WILLIAM, *Measure for Measure*, in *Shakespeare: Major Plays and the Sonnets*, ed. G. B. Harrison (New York: Harcourt, Brace & Co., 1948).

IBSEN, HENRIK, *The Wild Duck*, in *Ghosts, An Enemy of the People, The Wild Duck* (New York: Rinehart & Co., 1948).

GOLDSMITH, OLIVER, *She Stoops To Conquer*, ed. T. H. Dickinson (Boston: Houghton, Mifflin Co., 1936).

THOMAS, WRIGHT, and BROWN, STUART G. (eds.), *Reading Poems* (New York: Oxford University Press, 1941), selections.

Most of the critical texts have been reprinted in the volume *Humanities 3: Selected Readings* (4th ed.; Chicago: University of Chicago Press, 1948).

HUMANITIES 3 (ART; MUSIC)

During the fall quarter students in these variants read the works of criticism listed above under the parent course. The sections diverge in the winter and spring quarters.

Art.—Additional readings in criticism include selections from Ruskin, Veron, Tolstoy, Bosanquet, Freud, Spengler, Bell, Santayana, Dewey, Parker, and Ortega y Gasset. The list of original works of art, which is designed to take advantage of the resources of the city of Chicago, includes paintings by Claesz, Chardin, Manet, VanGogh, Cézanne, Monet, Picasso, and Braque; drawings by Rembrandt, Ingres, VanGogh, Cézanne, and Seurat; sculpture by Mestrovic, Faggi, and Moore; and architectural works by Wright and Mies van der Rohe.

Music.—Additional readings in criticism include selections from Plato, Aristotle, Boethius, Beattie, Mozart, Wagner, and Tovey. The musical works studied are the following: Bach, *Brandenburg Concerto No. 6* and *Passacaglia and Fugue in C Minor;* Haydn, *Symphony in G*, No. 88; Mozart, *Don Giovanni* (final scenes); Beethoven, *Quartet in F Minor*, Op. 95; Schumann, *Dichterliebe;* Wagner, *Die Meistersinger* (Act III); Brahms, *Piano Concerto in B Flat;* Tchaikovsky, *Romeo and Juliet;* Debussy, *Chansons de Bilitis;* Williams, *Serenade to Music;* Berg, *Wozzeck* (excerpts); Bartók, *Quartet in A Minor*, No. 2; and Britten, *Serenade* for Tenor, Horn, and Strings.

HUMANITIES 3 (FOREIGN LANGUAGES)

All the foreign language variants read the selections from Aristotle, Plato, and Hume listed above. Aristotle and Plato are read in the original by Humanities 3: Greek; in English by the other variants.

French.—Additional critical texts are by BOILEAU and HUGO. Imaginative works include: MOLIÈRE, *Le Misanthrope;* RACINE, *Phèdre;* BEAUMARCHAIS, *Le Barbier de Séville;* HERVIEU, *La Course du Flambeau;* MIRBEAU, *Les Affaires sont les affaires;* STENDHAL, *Le Rouge et le noir;* BALZAC, *Le Père Goriot;* Rolland, *Jean-Christophe: L'Aube;* and MAUROIS, *Climats.* The students also read a few short stories and an extensive list of lyric poems.

German.—Additional critical texts are by GOETHE, SCHILLER, JEAN PAUL, and KLEIST. Imaginative works include: GOETHE, *Egmont* and *Hermann und Dorothea;* KLEIST, *Prinz Friedrich von Homburg;* KELLER, *Romeo und Julia auf dem Dorfe;* and MANN, *Tonio Kröger.* The students also read a collection of short stories and an extensive list of lyric poems.

Greek.—Additional critical texts are by LONGINUS and DIONYSIUS OF HALI-CARNASSUS. Imaginative works include HOMER *The Odyssey* (Books vi, ix, and xi in Greek, the remainder in translation); AESCHYLUS *Prometheus Bound* (in translation); ARISTOPHANES *The Frogs* (in translation); and EURIPIDES *Hippolytus* (in Greek). A number of lyric poems complete the reading list.

Latin.—An additional critical text is by HORACE. Imaginative works include PLAUTUS *Menaechmi*, and JUVENAL *Satires*. A number of lyric poems complete the reading list.

Spanish.—Additional critical texts are by AZORÍN and UNAMUNO. Imaginative works include BENAVENTE, *Los Malhechores del Bien;* GARCIA LORCA, *Bodas de Sangre;* PÉREZ DE AYALA, *Tigre Juan;* and PÉREZ GALDÓS, *Misericordia.* The students also read an extensive list of lyric poems.

4

The Social Sciences

MILTON B. SINGER

IN THE social sciences there is a three-year sequence which parallels the three-year sequences in the humanities and in the natural sciences. Since the present sequence is the product of almost twenty years' practice and discussion in the College, a brief historical comment may help the reader see it in perspective; after all, none of us can quite escape from our histories, much as we may later rationalize them.

In its earliest form the social sciences program consisted of a two-year sequence, the first year of which was required and the second year elective. Both these courses attempted introductory "surveys" of certain social sciences, particularly economics, sociology, and political science. Within each course senior lecturers from the departments concerned took major responsibility for their respective fields, while junior staff members handled the smaller discussion sections.

After fewer than five years' experience with these "surveys," both senior and junior staff members became dissatisfied with them on the grounds that they were too "thin," that they slighted several social sciences areas, that they lacked integration and significant focus. As a consequence, both courses were reorganized around "themes" or "problems." The first-year course came to deal with the industrial revolution and its social effects; the second-year, with the problem of "freedom and order."

An immediate result of this reorganization was a shift in staff orientation away from departmental curriculums. As these new

123

"themes" and "problems" led the staff and students across conventional departmental lines, it became evident that units of instruction were emerging which did not always mirror the organization of topics in departmental introductory courses. This reorientation was critical for the further development of the general social sciences courses, for it showed the staff that their task went beyond mere simplification and popularization of departmental fields and included the far more creative and challenging task of constructing an interdisciplinary program within a framework of liberal education.

In 1942, when the College became a four-year College awarding the B.A. degree, another year was added to the existing social sciences sequence, and the staff was now given the assignment of developing an integrated three-year program. For the first year in the sequence it revised an older College course on American political institutions, for the second year a new course on personality and culture was developed, and the "freedom-and-order" course was revised for the third year. Opportunity for individual and independent work in the social sciences has also been provided with the introduction of an honors program and special "preceptorial" versions of the Social Sciences 3 course. The honors work may be undertaken in addition to the regular course work, while the preceptorial is in part a substitute for the regular course.

These changes, which are still continuing, do not in one sense introduce any new principle beyond the conviction that the program must be interdisciplinary and must be adapted to the needs of liberal education. But in the detailed application of this principle the staff has made many advances beyond its earlier departures from the general survey courses. The most notable of these advances has been in the conception and organization of the program's objectives.

Although suspicious of general formulations of objectives separated from specifications of means, the staff nevertheless feels that its experience warrants several negative and several positive judgments concerning the nature of a social sciences program in general education. Negatively, it would reject the introductory survey of departmental fields as ineffective in its

own terms and inappropriate for the purposes of general education. It would also be quite reluctant to teach an over-all theoretical or conceptual "synthesis" of the social sciences, since it
does not believe that the social sciences are yet ready for such a
synthesis, nor does it believe that such a synthesis, if it did exist,
would necessarily be the most appropriate subject matter for
general courses. Short of such a synthesis, there exist, it believes,
many interdisciplinary "problems" and "themes" which are
appropriate for a general education.

Since there is a current tendency to consider any interdisciplinary project intrinsically valuable, it is important to insist on this
requirement of appropriateness. But what is the criterion of appropriateness for general education? It is education in those
things which are of general significance for the student, that is,
not merely of significance to him as doctor, lawyer, businessman,
engineer, economist, or labor leader, but of significance to him as
a citizen and as a human being. In this sense general education
is not superficial education about "things in general" but is
thorough education about those things that matter most to the
individual. The staff is, of course, aware that general education
in this sense is shared with the family, the lower schools, the
church, and other social agencies. It is also aware that educators
differ in their judgments of what every citizen and every person
should know. Nevertheless, it does not regard these circumstances as sufficient to exempt it from the responsibility of discriminating between the significant and the insignificant or from
the effort of constructing a curriculum of the widest possible
significance. While it does not claim infallible judgment in such
matters, it believes that an understanding of the democratic
tradition as a method of resolving political conflicts, of the expression of human personality under varying social and cultural
milieus, and of the conditions necesssary for a free world—the
subject matter of the present three-year sequence—will rank
high on any scale of general significance.

The organization of this material into instructional units will
be further clarified if we describe briefly each course in the sequence. A complete reading list for each course will be found at
the end of this chapter.

The development of American democracy is a story which cannot be told completely in a single college course. Fortunately, by the time that students get to the College, they have already heard a good part of this story. It is therefore possible in Social Sciences 1 to be selective and to avoid repeating the work of earlier years. We have selected for special study a number of situations in which the American people have had to face critical problems of government: e.g., declaring independence from Britain, organizing a Federal Constitution, fighting one civil and two world wars, regulating an industrial economy. These situations are viewed as large-scale instances of deliberation, decision, and action analogous to the deliberations that Americans engage in today. Through a wide use of original documents, the student is encouraged to study these events as they appeared to the participants in them. The documents are chosen to bring out how these participants interpreted the events in question; what issues of principle were raised and debated; what problems were raised by attempts to apply general principles to particular cases; how major groups of the population reacted; which groups and individuals initiated new lines of policy; and what the outcome was in the form of new political, social, and economic arrangements. Viewing historical events in this way, the student not only comes to understand how the democratic tradition has been built and renewed through physical and intellectual struggle but also learns to be on the lookout for the "lessons" of the past that apply to the present.

The special habits which the student is expected to develop in Social Sciences 1 are connected with the reading and interpretation of these texts and documents. We do not, however, intend to make the student an antiquarian or a historical specialist. The skills he learns here are of general significance and will be required not only in later college and university work but throughout his life. They are the same skills that are required for intelligent reading of the daily newspaper, a best-seller on public affairs, or a political speech. They are the skills involved in identifying an author's argument, analyzing it into its elements and seeing their interrelations, probing hidden assumptions, evaluating the inner consistency of the argument, testing it by the conflicting views of other authors, isolating basic issues of disagreement, and appreciating the kinds of evidence required to resolve such conflicts.

There are, unfortunately, no simple rules for learning such skills. The student is asked to prepare himself for classroom discussion by careful reading and critical analysis of the documents. It is hoped that, in doing this, he will exercise historical imagination, clear thinking, and judicious evaluation. But the ultimate reliance for the development of these skills must remain the persistent practice of the art of discussion in the classroom and out of it.

When he has completed the first course in the social sciences sequence, the student should have begun to develop a historical sense of the democratic tradition in the United States. That is, he should have become acquainted with the basic constellation of ideas in the tradition—"freedom," "equality," "natural rights," "property," "representative government," "minority rights," "general welfare"—and with the wide range of interpretation and reinterpretation to which these ideas have been subjected by different individuals and groups and in different historical contexts. He should also understand how these ideas helped to create new political, economic, and social institutions. The student emerges wiser not only about the "facts" in his country's evolution but about the deliberative processes of human beings "making history," the beliefs and values involved in their reasoning as they do so, and with a beginning sense of some of the uniformities in human behavior which he will soon explore systematically.

In the division of labor among the three courses, the task of examining the possibilities and limitations of studying human nature and society in a scientific spirit falls largely to Social Sciences 2. This task is focused on the relation of an individual's personality to his culture, a problem which naturally interests the student at this stage of his life. And it so happens that this is one of the liveliest fields in the social sciences, with many established classics available on our own and other cultures and many relevant works appearing in cultural anthropology, psychology, and sociology. Moreover, it is a field in which scientific analysis can and does lead to better human understanding of interpersonal and intergroup relations.

Some of the questions raised by the readings in this field are: What is "human nature"? To what extent is it inborn and to what extent acquired? How does a child learn the acquired part? What is the nature of the personality differences—if any— among individuals, among social classes, among racial and national groups? Is there such a thing as a "national character"? Has industrial civilization produced any distinctive personality types whose traits find expression in specific economic, religious, and political institutions? What is the relation of social and cultural change to changes in personality? How far can and should one go in eliminating "undesirable" and creating "desirable" personality traits? What are the sources of standards of "normal" and "abnormal" personality?

Unlike the first course, Social Sciences 2 is concerned not exclusively with the student's own society and culture but with societies in general and with widely contrasting types of culture. The student is thus led to view his own society as but one member of the species "society" and to look for the common characteristics of all societies, as well as for those characteristics which differentiate one society and culture from another. He is further led to investigate the question of whether these fundamental similarities and differences of different societies and cultures are reflections of a universal human nature or whether there are as many "human natures" as there are different cultures. The culture of Western industrial society is intensively examined from this point of view and compared with pre-industrial cultures. Its family organization, class and caste structures, economic division of labor, centers of political power, and religious systems are analyzed, and the consequences for individual development and social cohesion are traced.

Finally, the question of deliberate social change and maintenance is raised. Although this is, strictly speaking, no longer a theoretical but a practical question, its major elements are identified and related to the preceding theoretical analysis. All proposals for deliberate change of course presuppose some system of values on the basis of which an existing situation is judged undesirable and the proposed change desirable. In analyzing such proposals, it thus becomes necessary to inquire into such presuppositions and to compare them with alternative systems of value. In this analysis the question naturally arises as to whether there is a system of values that is valid for all men and for all cultures and why, even within a single culture, there are widely differing estimates of the desirability and possibility of changing human nature and culture. The consideration of such questions invites the student to look at his society's development in broad perspective and to start thinking about the problems of policy which he will encounter in Social Sciences 3.

As in the case of the other two courses, the staff has avoided major reliance on textbooks in Social Sciences 2. Most textbooks deprive the student of the opportunity to exercise just those habits of thought which it is the end of a general education to develop. They present him with highly simplified summaries of results and practically no insight into the methods and processes by which these results were achieved. They seldom communicate to the student any of that passionate sincerity or integrity to be found in the original works. They do not really contain knowledge but are a kind of conventionalized gossip about knowledge which is thought to be sufficient for beginners. There are, of course, exceptions, but most textbooks conform to this pattern.

In reading originals, on the other hand, the student has an opportunity to watch first-rate minds at work and to retrace the development of a significant idea or theory. The objection that this may lead to a neglect of later revisions and corrections of the original statement is easily met by adding some of these revisions and corrections to the readings. The student is thus given the added opportunity to follow the living growth of scientific thought. He can then see where an original formulation was obscure or overgeneralized or in need of greater precision and qualification. And he can also see how, despite defects of this character, original formulations usually possess a fruitfulness and a suggestive power that are far superior to the later refinements. Selections from the works of Durkheim, Freud, Malthus, Marx, Owen, Sumner, Veblen, and Weber are read in this spirit and are supplemented by writings of Benedict, Knight, Myrdal, Notestein, Warner, and other significant contemporary writers.

The attitudes and skills contributed to the student's development by Social Sciences 2 are implicit in the foregoing. In the first place, the student should have become convinced of the value of disinterested inquiry into the nature of man and society and should have developed some desire and ability to cultivate such a study for himself. Foremost in this ability is the discrimination between the scientific mode of thought and such nonscientific modes as folklore, superstition, and special pleading. The student should be aware of the actual difficulties involved in making this discrimination and the moral courage required to practice the scientific mode. Further, he should be familiar with the elementary operations of scientific reasoning not merely in the abstract or in terms of artificial classroom examples but as actually applied in the scientific study of society. That is, he should be acquainted with alternative attempts to define precisely such basic concepts as "society," "culture," "human nature," "personality," "class"; and he should be able to use these concepts in particular cases. He should also be familiar with some of the outstanding theories and hypotheses relating these concepts into explanatory systems and be able to appraise these theories with respect to such requirements of scientific method as clarity, consistency, adequacy in explaining facts, and fruitfulness. Finally, he should know something about the major sources and kinds of evidential data relevant for testing these theories, how they are gathered, and how accuracy and representativeness of the data can be assured.

The application of theoretical social science to practical issues of social policy is not the primary concern of Social Sciences 2. But in this course the student is made aware of the practical conditions and consequences of scientific inquiry and of the ethical presuppositions involved in any attempt to apply theoretical knowledge to practice.

The student who has acquired the foregoing attitudes and skills not only will have realized his instructor's fondest hopes but will also have acquired some theoretical understanding about his own and other cultures, about how the individual—and he himself, as a case in point—comes personally to learn and embody the pattern and ideals of a given culture, and about the possibilities or impossibilities of changing a given pattern of personality and culture by deliberate individual or collective effort.

In the first two years of the social sciences sequence the student has learned something of the history of his country and of what science can contribute to an understanding of man and society. In the terminal course of the sequence, Social Sciences 3, he is introduced—with the help of those analytical disciplines that deal with problems in the choice of means and ends (political science, political economy, political sociology, ethics, and social philosophy)—to the habit of deliberating rationally on problems of public policy.

We do not share the assumption underlying most "current-events" and "problems" courses in the social sciences: that it is feasible to appraise in the classroom the desirability and practicability of day-to-day political decisions. The students—and the instructor—do not have the necessary detail of experience or the responsibility for action to decide in the classroom which candidate should be elected in a forthcoming election or whether an impending strike is justified. What can be done in the classroom is to provide a background of relevant historical and scientific knowledge, an analysis of general principles, and some concrete exercises in deliberative thinking about well-prepared specimen cases on which history has already passed some judgment. Such exercises must, of course, remain vicarious, but they can help to develop practical judgment about public policy and to clarify general criteria for policy formation.

The conditions of freedom in the contemporary world define the particular set of issues studied in Social Sciences 3. The student is introduced to these issues through a dialectical comparison of the philosophies of freedom in J. S. Mill's essay *On Liberty* and in Plato's *Republic*. A special study of freedom as a social ideal in England in the nineteenth century fills in recent historical background. This case study amplifies what the student has already learned about the development of freedom in the United States. The conditions for the preservation of freedom in the contemporary world are studied with the help of political, economic, and sociological analysis. Alternative policies for attaining freedom are examined, and the price of these policies in terms of other values is appraised. Systems of social organization and social philosophies which sacrifice freedom to security and to other social values are also studied. What the student has already learned in Social Sciences 2 about human nature and culture is, in Social Sciences 3, specialized and elaborated with reference to particular nations and to international organization. A more concrete idea of the approach used in the third course may be given by considering a typical problem of policy which is treated in the course, namely, freedom of the press.

If we are to deliberate intelligently and responsibly about this problem, we must first know the meaning and grounds of the doctrine of a free press. This we can get from a study of the historic struggle for a free press and from a reading of the classical attempts to interpret the doctrine both in theory and in practice (for example, Milton's *Areopagitica*, J. S. Mill's *On Liberty*, U.S. Supreme Court cases). Next, we should have to know whether the existing state of affairs in the United States and in other countries is in general accord with that doctrine or not. This leads us into a factual analysis of newspapers, radio, motion pictures, and mass communication in general.

Further, if we accept for the sake of the argument a diagnosis like that contained in the report of the Commission on Freedom of the Press—that the existing state of affairs is not entirely in accord with the traditional principles of a free press—it becomes necessary to consider how this discrepancy is to be resolved—whether by government regulation, government operation, a laissez faire policy, or by some other means. And, in respect to each of the proposed measures, we should have to appraise its most probable consequences, both in the light of the desired objective of a free press and in terms of the general system of values of a free society.

The commission's report, incidentally, is in many ways an excellent example of the process of deliberation which we are describing. It cannot, however, be used by the student as a substitute for that process. For if he himself is to develop habits of deliberation and practical understanding, he must study the history of the doctrine of a free press, its principles, its application to the present scene—in short, go through the same process which the members of the commission went through.

Other major policy problems of modern society are treated in the same spirit: bureaucracy, full employment, the compatibility of socialism with democracy, international organization, etc. Readings are always selected to include three types of material: (1) classic philosophic formulations of doctrine—for example, Plato's *Republic*, Hobbes's *Leviathan*, Kant's *Perpetual Peace;* (2) analyses by contemporary social scientists—e.g., Frank H. Knight, *Economic Organization and the Price System*, Robert Redfield, *The Folk Society*, Henry Simons, *A Positive Program for Laissez Faire* and *Reflections on Syndicalism*, Max Weber, *Bureaucracy;* and (3) case materials drawn from Supreme Court opinions, congressional hearings, labor-management negotiations, and so forth.

These materials are so organized that in the case of each major problem the student is encouraged—almost compelled—by the materials themselves to put together what he knows of the historical background, the philosophic arguments concerning the ultimate values, and the scientific theory and facts, for the purpose of drawing or appraising conclusions on practical policy, in the concrete case before him. We hope in this way to train the student to integrate philosophic, scientific, and case methods of analysis.

With this emphasis upon the habit of rational and informed deliberation, the three-year sequence in the social sciences achieves its culmination. There is also, as in Plato's allegory of the cave, a return to the beginning. For Social Sciences 3 returns the student to the "cave" of his own society and culture, from which he started in Social Sciences 1. But, with the scientific and philosophic insight which he has acquired on the way, he should now be able to distinguish the shadows from the realities even while he remains and acts in the cave.

Reference to the necessities of action generally provokes two mutually contradictory objections to the type of program in the social sciences which we have just described. On the one hand, it provokes accusations of "indoctrination" on behalf of particular policies. On the other hand, there are those who will see in it an escape to the "ivory tower" and who regard rational deliberation as a paralysis of the springs of action, a process which makes cowards of us all. Neither of these objections can be sustained. The program of general education in the social sciences does have a positive relation to action, but it neither "indoctrinates" nor propagandizes for any particular course of action. It stays strictly within the proper functions of college and university education.

The positive relation to action is implicit in the aim to develop rational habits of deliberation about public policy. We as teachers would not organize a program aiming at this result if we did not expect that some day the student will himself exercise this habit in the making of real decisions in a free society. In reality, then, we have committed ourselves to the building and maintenance of a free society. Without this assumption, the ends of the program would make little sense. Further, we are committed to the use of those methods of free and impartial discussion which are essential not only for the continuance of a free society but for the very existence of the scientific spirit as well.

Although there is rarely any objection to these general commitments, there is frequently objection to some of their indirect effects, especially when these effects come into conflict with other special commitments that people have made. It is this conflict which gives rise to the mistaken impression of the social scientist as just another special pleader. This situation and its resolution have been clearly and forcibly described by a wise and humane social scientist:

"I think it is self-delusion for a social scientist to say that what he does has no concern with social values. I think that people are right when they express their feeling that social science does something to the values they hold with regard to such particular institutions as restrictive covenants or the tariff. For one thing social science tests these special values, by showing what they cost. It hears the people say, We want freedom. Social science listens, studies our society and replies, Very well, if you want freedom, this is what you will pay in one kind of freedom for enjoying so much of another. To every partisan the social scientist appears an enemy. The social scientist addresses himself to the question, How much security from idleness and want is compatible with developed capitalism? and equally to the question, How much political and civil freedom is compatible with socialism? To partisans on both sides he appears unsympathetic and dangerous.

"For social science, along with other science, philosophy and the general spirit of intellectual liberty, is asserting the more general and comprehensive values of our society against the more limited and special interests and values. It hears society say, We believe in the right of the human mind to examine freely, to criticize openly, to reach conclusions from tested evidence. Very well, replies social science, if this is your desire then you must endure the pain of the examination and the testing of the particular customs and institutions which you hold dear. Social science says to all of us: Except where your special interests are involved, you recognize that mankind has passed the period in which he took his ethical convictions from his grandfathers without doubt and reflection. Now we have to think, investigate and consider about both the means and the ends of life. Social science is that science, which in other fields you so readily admire, directed to human nature and the ways of living of man in society. By your own more general convictions you have authorized and validated its development."*

Apart from the far-reaching commitment to freedom, the program advocates no particular political position or course of social action. Even in the third year, when policy problems are analyzed, particular policy measures are discussed as hypothetical alternatives in terms of their respective costs and consequences. Such analysis never tells the student that such and such a measure is "the solution" to the problem, which he must accept and carry into action. Rather, what the analysis yields is insight into a wide spectrum of alternative measures, together with some sense of the direct and indirect consequences of each. The actual choice

* Robert Redfield, *The Social Uses of Social Science* (University of Colorado Bulletin [Boulder, Colo., 1947]), unpaged.

of a particular policy is left to the individual and to his delegated representatives.

Nor need it be feared that this process of analyzing alternatives dries up the springs of action. As soon as the student or instructor is out of the classroom, the pressures upon him to limit the range of alternatives and to choose a preferred one are virtually overwhelming. The College cannot hope to eliminate these pressures, but it can attempt to equip the individual with some rational principles for appraising and directing them for the common good. This is a proper function of general education, and, in performing it, the College is neither out of the world of action nor completely in it. It is an organic part of the community, a part whose purpose it is to develop truth and wisdom in its individual members, because these are intrinsic intellectual goods and because they will make such action as the individual takes more effective and wiser than it would otherwise have been.

Reading Lists

SOCIAL SCIENCES 1

AUTHORITY AND LIBERTY IN THE SEVENTEENTH CENTURY

Mayflower Compact, in WILLIAM BRADFORD, *History of Plymouth Plantation* ("Massachusetts Historical Collections" [Boston: Massachusetts Historical Society]), Fourth Series, III, 89–90.

WISE, JOHN, *A Vindication of the Government of New England Churches* (Boston, 1772), pp. 22–41, 62.

HOBBES, THOMAS, *Leviathan* (New York: E. P. Dutton, 1914), pp. 63–69, 87–97, 110, 114–16, 170–73, 176–78.

LOCKE, JOHN, *Second Treatise of Civil Government*, in *English Philosophers from Bacon to Mill*, ed. E. A. Burtt ("Modern Library" [New York: Random House, 1939]), pp. 403–23, 437–43, 449–69, 484–503.

THE AMERICAN REVOLUTION

Declaration of Rights of the Stamp Act Congress, October 19, 1765, in *Journal of the First Congress of the American Colonies, in Opposition to the Tyrannical Acts of the British Parliament* (New York: E. Winchester, 1845), pp. 27–29.

Declaratory Act—1766, 6 George III, c. 12, *The Statutes at Large*, ed. Danby Pickering (London, 1767), XXVII, 19–20.

Resolutions of the First Continental Congress, October 14, 1774, in *Journals of the Continental Congress, 1774–1789* (Washington: Government Printing Office, 1904), I, 63–73.

Virginia Declaration of Rights, in *The Federal and State Constitutions, Colonial Charters, and Other Organic Laws . . .* , ed. F. N. Thorpe (Washington: Government Printing Office, 1909), VII, 3812–14.

BOUCHER, JONATHAN, "On Civil Liberty, Passive Obedience, and Nonresistance," in *A View of the Causes and Consequences of the American Revolution* (London, 1797), pp. 495, 505–6, 507–21, 534, 543–44, 545–46, 549–50, 552, 553–58, 558–60.

The Declaration of Independence.

JEFFERSON, THOMAS, *Notes on the State of Virginia* (London, 1787), pp. 190–213, 243–49, 261–70, Correspondence of Jefferson and Adams on aristocracy, microfilm reproduction, Reels 77–78, of the *Papers of Thomas Jefferson* (Library of Congress), Vol. CXCVIII, fols. 35312–13; Vol. CXCIX, fols. 35381–82, 35425–26, 35488–91; Vol. CC, fols. 35526–27, 35378–79, 35638–40.

ADAMS, JOHN, *A Defence of the Constitutions of Government of the United States of America*, in *Works*, ed. Charles Francis Adams (Boston, 1851), IV, 402; VI, 145, 118; IV, 405; VI, 114–15; IV, 406–7; VI, 7–9, 10, 57–58; IV, 583–84.

CONFEDERATION AND CONSTITUTION

Articles of Confederation, in *Journals of the Continental Congress, 1774–1789* (Washington: Government Printing Office, 1912), XIX, 214–22.

The Constitution of the United States, in *Documents Illustrative of the Formation of the Union of the American States*, ed. C. C. Tansill (Washington: Government Printing Office, 1927), pp. 22–25, 989–1001, 1066–72.

Debates in the Federal Convention of 1787, in *Documents Illustrative of the Formation of the Union of the American States*, ed. C. C. Tansill (Washington: Government Printing Office, 1927), pp. 953–56, 124–27, 130–31, 159–67, 916–17, 967–70, 208–22, 233, 237–39, 487–91, 738–45.

HAMILTON, ALEXANDER; MADISON, JAMES; and JAY, JOHN, *The Federalist* ("Modern Library" [New York: Random House, 1941]), pp. 53–62, 79–82, 86–95, 327–31, 335–41.

JEFFERSON, THOMAS, Letters on the Constitution, in *The Writings of Thomas Jefferson*, ed. H. A. Washington (New York: H. W. Derby, 1861), II, 217–18, 260, 328–32, 404–5, 585–87.

PROBLEMS OF THE NEW REPUBLIC

SMITH, ADAM, *An Enquiry into the Nature and Causes of the Wealth of Nations*, ed. Edwin Cannan ("Modern Library" [New York: Random House, 1937]), pp. 531–33, 538–52, 579–91.

HAMILTON, ALEXANDER, *Report on Manufactures, December, 1791*, in Reports of the Secretary of the Treasury of the United States (Washington, 1837).

JEFFERSON, THOMAS, Remarks on the Hamiltonian System from The Anas, in *The Writings of Thomas Jefferson*, ed. H. A. Washington (New York: H. W. Derby, 1861), IX, 88–97.

———, "First Inaugural Address," in *A Compilation of the Messages and Papers of the Presidents, 1789–1897*, ed. James D. Richardson (Washington: Government Printing Office, 1896), I, 321–24.

Alien and Sedition Acts, 1 Stat. 570–71, 596–97 (1798), in SHALER, N. S., *Kentucky: A Pioneer Commonwealth* (Boston: Houghton Mifflin Co., 1884), pp. 410, 413–16.

ELLIOT, J. (ed.), *Debates in the Several State Conventions . . .* (Washington: J. Elliot, 1863), IV, 528–29, 533, 534, 538–39, 545, 547–50, 551–52.

Marbury v. *Madison*, 1 Cranch 137 (1803).

WASHINGTON, GEORGE, "The Farewell Address," in *Washington's Writings*, ed. John C. Fitzpatrick (Washington: Government Printing Office, 1940), XXXV, 198–201, 214–38.

EQUALITY IN JACKSONIAN DEMOCRACY

TOCQUEVILLE, ALEXIS DE, *Democracy in America*, trans. Henry Reeve, ed. Francis Bowen (4th ed.; Cambridge: Sever & Francis, 1864), I, 107–8, 109–10, 111, 115–16, 118–19, 120–21, 302–7, 310, 313–14, 319–23, 330–32, 335–38, 343–44, 558–59; II, 1–3, 5–6, 8–13, 37–39, 114–21, 124–27, 128–30, 132–36, 193–97, 325–29, 330, 331–34, 344–47, 356–58, 360–64, 380–81, 383–86, 391–93, 397–400, 400–401, 404–7, 410–12.

Commonwealth v. *Hunt*, 4 Metcalf 111 (Massachusetts, 1842).

MANN, HORACE, *Lectures and Annual Reports on Education*, ed. Mrs. Mary Mann ("The Life and Works of Horace Mann" [Boston: Walker, Fuller & Co., 1868]), III, 663–70, 686–89.

CLAY, HENRY, "The American System," in *Life and Speeches of the Hon. Henry Clay*, ed. Daniel Mallory (New York: A. S. Barnes, 1857), I, 647–52, 659–61, 662–63, 664–67.

JACKSON, ANDREW, Veto of the Bank Renewal Bill, in *A Compilation of the Messages and Papers of the Presidents*, ed. James D. Richardson (Washington: Government Printing Office, 1896), II, 576–91.

GOUGE, WILLIAM, *A Short History of Paper Money and Banking in the United States* (Philadelphia: T. W. Ustick, 1833), pp. 1–7, 41–44, 84–86, 123–28.

THOREAU, HENRY DAVID, "On Civil Disobedience," in *Aesthetic Papers*, ed. Elizabeth P. Peabody (Boston: G. P. Putnam, 1849), pp. 189–211.

THE CRISIS IN THE FEDERAL UNION

CALHOUN, JOHN C., *A Disquisition on Government*, in *Works* (New York, 1855), I, 1–107.

FITZHUGH, GEORGE, *Sociology for the South; or the Failure of Free Society* (Richmond: A. Morris, 1854), pp. iii, 7, 9–12, 20–40, 43–48, 82–87, 92, 94–95, 161–63, 169–71, 175–93.

EMERSON, RALPH WALDO, "Man the Reformer," in *Nature, Addresses, and Lectures* (Boston: Houghton Mifflin Co., 1884), pp. 217–44.

Dred Scott v. *Sandford*, 19 Howard 393, 399, 406–12, 426–27, 430, 432, 447–52 (1857).

LINCOLN, ABRAHAM, Springfield Speech, June 26, 1857, in *The Complete Works of Abraham Lincoln*, ed. John J. Nicolay and John Hay (New York: Tandy-Thomas Co., 1905), II, 319–39.

Mississippi Resolutions on Secession, November 30, 1860, in *Laws of the State of Mississippi* (Jackson, Miss.: E. Barksdale, 1860), pp. 43–45.

LINCOLN, ABRAHAM, First Inaugural Address, March 4, 1861, in *Messages and Papers of the Presidents*, ed. James D. Richardson (Washington: Government Printing Office, 1896), VI, 5–12.

———, "Letter to Horace Greeley," in *The Rebellion Record*, ed. Frank Moore (New York: D. Van Nostrand, 1871), XII, 482–83.

———, "The Emancipation Proclamation," 12 Stat. 1268–69 (1863).

———, Gettysburg Address, November 19, 1863, in *The Complete Works of Abraham Lincoln*, ed. John G. Nicolay and John Hay (New York: Tandy-Thomas Co., 1905), IX, 209–10.

———, Second Inaugural Address, March 4, 1865, in *Messages and Papers of the Presidents*, ed. James D. Richardson (Washington: Government Printing Office, 1896), VI, 276–77.

Mississippi Black Code, 1865, in *Laws of the State of Mississippi* (Jackson, Miss.: J. J. Shannon, 1866), pp. 82–93, 165–67.

Constitution and Ritual of the Knights of the White Camelia, in *Documentary History of Reconstruction* . . . , ed. Walter L. Fleming (Cleveland: Arthur H. Clark Co., 1907), II, 349–54.

Civil Rights Cases, 109 U.S. 3, 8–62 (1883); 163 U.S. 537, 540–64 (1896).

Plessy v. *Ferguson*, 163 U.S. 537, 540–44, 550–64 (1896).

SOCIAL CRITICISM IN THE INDUSTRIAL AGE

BELLAMY, EDWARD, *Looking Backward, 2000–1887* (New York: Houghton Mifflin, 1889), pp. 85–98, 123, 131–33, 225–37, 239, 241–44.

LLOYD, HENRY DEMAREST, *Wealth against Commonwealth* (New York: Harper & Bros., 1894), pp. 1–2, 6–8, 199–211, 494–97, 506–7, 510, 514–21, 523, 526–27, 532–33, 535–36.

SUMNER, WILLIAM GRAHAM, "The Challenge of Facts," in *The Challenge of Facts, and Other Essays*, ed. Albert G. Keller (New Haven: Yale University Press, 1914), pp. 17–18, 20–28, 30–35, 44–47, 49–52.

TURNER, FREDERICK JACKSON, "The Significance of the Frontier in American History," in *American Historical Association, Annual Report* (Washington: Government Printing Office, 1893), pp. 199–227.

THE POLITICS OF INDUSTRIALISM (1865–1914)

National People's Party Platform, in *The World Almanac, 1893* (New York: Press Pub. Co., 1893), pp. 83–85.

The Republican Platform of 1896, in *Republican Campaign Textbook, 1896*, ed. T. H. McKee (Washington: Harthan & Cadick, 1896), pp. 251–57.

The Democratic Platform of 1896, in *Official Proceedings of the Democratic National Convention Held in Chicago, Illinois, July, 1896* (Loganport, Ind.: Wilson, Humphrey & Co., 1896), pp. 250–56.

BRYAN, WILLIAM JENNINGS, The "Cross of Gold" speech, in *Speeches of William Jennings Bryan* (New York: Funk & Wagnalls, 1913), I, 238–49.

Slaughterhouse Cases, 16 Wallace 36, 57–62, 66–78, 83–89, 97–111 (1873).

Munn v. *Illinois*, 94 U.S. 113, 123–26, 131–34 (1877).

Wabash, St. Louis and Pacific Railway Co. v. *Illinois*, 118 U.S. 557, 560, 572–73, 575–77, 588–89, 595–96 (1886).

Allgeyer v. *Louisiana*, 165 U.S. 578–80, 583, 589–93 (1897).

Smyth v. *Ames*, 169 U.S. 466, 515, 526, 546–47 (1898).

Lochner v. *New York*, 198 U.S. 45, 52–66, 68–76 (1905).

STEFFENS, LINCOLN, *Autobiography* (New York: Harcourt, Brace & Co., 1931), pp. 187–96, 365–73, 416–29, 484–94, 703–11.

The Progressive Party Platform, 1912, in *The World Almanac, 1913* (New York: Press Pub. Co., 1913), pp. 693–97.

ROOSEVELT, THEODORE, *The New Nationalism* (New York: Outlook Co., 1910), pp. 3–5, 7–33.

WILSON, WOODROW, *The New Freedom* (New York: Doubleday, Page, 1913), pp. 3–32.

——, First Inaugural Address, 1913, in *Senate Document No. 3, SerialNo. 6507* (63d Cong.; Spec. sess. [Washington: Government Printing Office, 1913]), pp. 3–6.

The Sherman Antitrust Act, 26 Stat. 209–10 (1890).

The Federal Trade Commission Act, 1914, 38 Stat., 717–21 (1914).

The Clayton Antitrust Act, 1914, 38 Stat., 730–34, 738 (1914).

Standard Oil Co. of New Jersey v. *U.S.*, 221 U.S. 1, 30, 48, 50–52, 55–56, 58–60, 62, 75–77, 82–84, 98–99, 105 (1911).

United States v. *United States Steel Corporation*, 251 U.S. 417, 436–42, 444–45, 447–49, 451, 457–58, 463–66 (1920).

AMERICAN FOREIGN POLICY (1898–1920)

Mahan, Alfred Thayer, *The Influence of Sea Power upon History, 1660–1783* (8th ed.; Boston: Little, Brown & Co., 1894), pp. 1–2, 25–29, 50, 52–55, 57–59, 63–64, 66–67, 81–89, 225–27, 295, 324–26.

——, "The Peace Conference and the Moral Aspect of War," *North American Review*, CLXIX (October, 1899), 434–42, 444–47.

——, *The Problem of Asia and Its Effect upon International Policies* (Boston: Little, Brown & Co., 1900), pp. 4–18, 24–37, 55–62, 67–69, 72–75, 90–93, 96–100, 130–33, 145–46.

Beveridge, Albert J., Speech on the Annexation of the Philippines, *Congressional Record*, XXXIII, Part I (January 9, 1900), 704–5, 707.

Bryan, William Jennings, "On Annexation of the Philippines," in *Speeches of William Jennings Bryan* (New York: Funk & Wagnalls, 1913), II, 11–16, 19–22, 24–33, 39–49.

Hay, John R., Circular Letter on the "Open Door" Policy in China, in *Papers Relating to the Foreign Relations of the United States, 1899* (Washington: Government Printing Office, 1901), pp. 129–30.

The Platt Amendment (1901), in *Treaties, Conventions, International Acts . . .* , ed. W. M. Malloy (61st Cong., 2d sess., Senate Doc., Ser. No. 5646 [Washington: Government Printing Office, 1910]), I, 362–64.

Roosevelt, Theodore, "Corollary to the Monroe Doctrine," in *Messages and Papers of the Presidents (1798–1908)*, ed. J. D. Richardson (New York: Bureau of National Literature and Art, 1908), X, 831–34; XI, 1153–56.

Wilson, Woodrow, Address at Mobile, Alabama, in *Senate Document No. 226, Serial No. 6537* (63d Cong., 1st sess. [Washington: Government Printing Office, 1913]), pp. 3–6.

——, Appeal for Neutrality, in *Senate Document No. 566, Serial No. 6596* (63d Cong., 2d sess. [Washington: Government Printing Office, 1914]), pp. 3–4.

——, War Message, in *Senate Document No. 5, Serial No. 7264* (65th Cong., 1st sess. [Washington: Government Printing Office, 1917]), pp. 3–8.

——, "Peace without Victory," in *Senate Document No. 2685, Serial No. 7125* (64th Cong., 2d sess. [Washington: Government Printing Office, 1917]), pp. 3–8.

————, "The Fourteen Points," in *House Document No. 765, Serial No. 7443* (65th Cong., 2d sess. [Washington: Government Printing Office, 1918]), pp. 3–7.

Covenant of the League of Nations, in *The Aims, Methods, and Activity of the League of Nations* (Geneva: Secretariat of the League of Nations, 1935), pp. 169–209.

WILSON, WOODROW, Speech on the League at Pueblo, 1919, *Congressional Record*, LVIII, Part VII (October 6, 1919), 6424–27.

Excerpt from the Senate Debate on the League, November 19, 1919, *Congressional Record*, LVIII, Part IX (November 19, 1919), 8768–69, 8781–84.

FREEDOM IN AN INDUSTRIAL SOCIETY

SIMONS, HENRY C., "A Political Credo," in *Economic Policy for a Free Society* (Chicago: University of Chicago Press, 1948), pp. 1–39.

MEANS, GARDINER C., "The Separation of Ownership and Control in American Industry," *Quarterly Journal of Economics*, XLVI (November, 1931), 68–77, 80–84, 86–87, 94.

HOOVER, HERBERT, Speech on Relation of Government to Industry, October 22, 1928, *New York Times* (October 23, 1928), p. 2.

"No One Has Starved," *Fortune*, VI (September, 1932), 19–28, 80, 82, 84.

ROOSEVELT, FRANKLIN D., The Commonwealth Club Address, in *Public Papers and Addresses* (New York: Random House, 1938), I, 742–56.

JOHNSON, HUGH S., *The Blue Eagle from Egg to Earth* (New York: Garden City Pub. Co., 1935), pp. 158–64, 172–79, 188.

"Toward Stability," *Business Week* (May 10, 1933), 32.

LILIENTHAL, DAVID E., *TVA—Democracy on the March* (New York: Pocket Books, Inc., 1944), pp. 52–55, 65–67, 84–99, 119–20, 124–25, 138–41, 148–49, 152, 165–66, 171–72, 193–96, 199–200, 202–17, 233, 242.

THE TEMPORARY NATIONAL ECONOMIC COMMITTEE, in *Final Report and Recommendations* (77th Cong., 1st Sess., S. Doc. 35 [Washington: Government Printing Office, 1941]), pp. 11–17, 672–83, 686–87.

National Labor Relations Board v. *Jones and Laughlin Steel Corp.*, 301 U.S. 1, 22–37, 40–49, 76, 97–101 (1937).

The New Labor Law (Washington: Bureau of National Affairs, Inc., 1947).

Employment Act of 1946, 60 Stat. 23 (1946).

WALLACE, HENRY A., "An Economic Bill of Rights," *New York Times*, January 26, 1945.

TAFT, ROBERT A., "Shall the Government Guarantee Employment?" unpublished address to the National Industrial Conference Board, January 18, 1945.

COMMAGER, HENRY STEELE, "Who Is Loyal to America?" *Harper's*, CXCV (September, 1947), 193–99.

Gitlow v. *New York*, 268 U.S. 652, 654–59, 661, 664–70, 672–73 (1925).

West Virginia Board of Education v. *Barnette*, 319 U.S. 624, 625–35, 638–44, 646–52, 664–67 (1943).

Korematsu v. *United States*, 323 U.S. 214–26, 228–46, 248 (1944).

Hook, Sidney, "Academic Freedom and Communism"; originally appeared as "Should Communists Be Permitted To Teach?" *New York Times Magazine* (February 27, 1949), pp. 7, 22–24, 26, 28–29.

Meiklejohn, Alexander, "Professors on Probation"; originally appeared as "Should Communists Be Allowed To Teach?" *New York Times Magazine* (March 27, 1949), pp. 10, 64, 65, 66.

President's Committee on Civil Rights, *To Secure These Rights* (Washington: Government Printing Office, 1947), pp. 5–9, 20–30, 35–40, 53–57, 74–104, 151–73.

RECENT FOREIGN POLICY

Beard, Charles A., *A Foreign Policy for America* (New York: Alfred A. Knopf, 1940), pp. 134–40, 149–54.

Lippmann, Walter, *United States Foreign Policy: Shield of the Republic* (Boston: Little, Brown & Co., 1943), pp. 3–10, 27–49, 119–36.

Roosevelt, Franklin D., The "Four Freedoms" Speech, 1941, in *Development of United States Foreign Policy: Addresses and Messages of Franklin D. Roosevelt* (77th Cong., 2d sess.; Senate Doc. No. 188, Ser. No. 10676 [Washington: Government Printing Office, 1941]), pp. 81–87.

Atlantic Charter, in *Toward the Peace: Documents* (Pub. No. 2298 [Washington: Government Printing Office, 1945]), p. 1.

Willkie, Wendell L., *One World* (New York: Simon & Schuster, 1943), pp. 71–80.

Charter of the United Nations, 59 Stat. 1031 (1945).

Wallace, Henry A., Letter of July 23, 1946, to President Truman on American policy toward Russia, *New York Times* (September 18, 1946), p. 2.

X, "Sources of Soviet Conduct," *Foreign Affairs*, XXV (July, 1947), 566–69, 571–82.

Schuman, Frederick L., *Soviet Foreign Policy and Its Implications* (Chicago: Council on Foreign Relations, 1947), pp. 1–21.

Hutchins, Robert M., "The Constitutional Foundations of World Order," *Common Cause*, I (December, 1947), 201–8.

Truman, Harry S., Message to Congress Containing the "Truman Doctrine," *Congressional Record*, XCIII (March 12, 1947), 1999–2000.

The Foreign Assistance Act of 1948, 62 Stat. 137 (1948).

The North Atlantic Treaty, Supplement to *American Journal of International Law*, XLIII (1949), 159–62.

Charter of the Organization of American States, United States Department of State, *Ninth International Conference of American States* ("International Organization and Conference Series," Pub. 3263 [Washington: Government Printing Office, 1948]), II, 166–75.

These selections are contained in the two volumes of *The People Shall Judge* (Chicago: University of Chicago Press, 1949).

SOCIAL SCIENCES 2

PERSONALITY AND CULTURE: A CASE STUDY AND AN OVERVIEW

MYRDAL, GUNNAR, *An American Dilemma* (New York: Harper & Bros., 1944), pp. v–xx, xlv–lix, 23–112, 209–19, 573–604, 757–809, 927–55, 966–82, 1073–78.

FREUD, SIGMUND, "The Origin and Development of Psychoanalysis," in *An Outline of Psychoanalysis*, ed. J. S. Van Teslaar ("Modern Library" [New York: Random House, 1925]), pp. 21–71.

————, *Civilization and Its Discontents*, trans. Joan Rivière (London: Hogarth Press, 1930).

BENEDICT, RUTH, *Patterns of Culture* (Boston: Houghton Mifflin Co., 1934).

THE CHILD IN THE COMMUNITY

DAVIS, ALLISON, and DOLLARD, JOHN, *Children of Bondage* (Washington: American Council on Education, 1940).

PIAGET, JEAN, *The Moral Judgment of the Child* (Glencoe, Ill.: Free Press, 1948), pp. 1–103, 401–14.

THE INDIVIDUAL IN THE MODERN INDUSTRIAL SYSTEM

SMITH, ADAM, *An Inquiry into the Nature and Causes of the Wealth of Nations* ("Modern Library" [New York: Random House, Inc., 1937]), Book I, chaps. i, ii, iii, iv (in part), v, vi, vii; Book IV, chap. ii; Book V, chap. i.

MALTHUS, T. R., *An Essay on Population* ("Everyman's Library" [London: J. M. Dent & Sons, 1914]), I, 5–19, 304–15; II, 11–29, 151–73, 210–22, 256–62.

MARX, KARL, and ENGELS, FRIEDRICH, *The Communist Manifesto*, in *Capital, The Communist Manifesto, and Other Writings*, ed. Max Eastman ("Modern Library" [New York: Random House, 1932]), Parts I, II, and IV.

————, *Capital: A Critique of Political Economy* (Chicago: C. H. Kerr & Co., 1906), I, 91–93, 249–56, 385–94, 457–66, 530–35.

WEBER, MAX, *The Protestant Ethic and the Spirit of Capitalism*, trans. Talcott Parsons (New York: Charles Scribner's Sons, 1930), chaps. i, ii, iii, iv, v.

VEBLEN, THORSTEIN, *Theory of the Leisure Class* ("Modern Library" [New York: Random House, 1934]), pp. 1–114.

DURKHEIM, ÉMILE, *On the Division of Labor in Society* (Glencoe, Ill.: Free Press, 1947), pp. 39–46, 49–69, 129–32, 174–90, 226–29, 256–62, 283–303, 329–50, 353–73, 374–81, 396–409.

TAYLOR, F. W., *The Principles of Scientific Management* (New York: Harper & Bros., 1947), pp. 30–85, 114–32, 139–44.

HART, C. W. M., "Industrial Relations Research and Social Theory," *Canadian Journal of Economics and Political Science*, XV, No. 1 (February, 1949), 53–74.

IDEALS AND EXPERIMENTS IN THE FORMATION OF PERSONALITY

OWEN, ROBERT, *A New View of Society* (Glencoe, Ill.: Free Press [facsimile reproduction of the 3d ed.; London, 1817, 1948]), pp. iii–viii, 11–126.

SUMNER, WILLIAM GRAHAM, *Folkways* (Boston: Ginn & Co., 1906), pp. 2–39, 52–79, 84–88, 94–98, 107–8, 117–18, 201–2.

———, "The Absurd Effort To Make the World Over," in *Sumner Today*, ed. Maurice R. Davie (New Haven: Yale University Press, 1940), pp. 99–110.

DEWEY, JOHN, *Human Nature and Conduct* ("Modern Library" [New York: Random House, 1930]), Part I, Sec. VI; Part II; Part III, Sec. I.

EINSTEIN, ALBERT, and FREUD, SIGMUND, "Why War?" from an exchange of correspondence in *Civilization, War, and Death*, ed. John Rickman ("Psychoanalytical Epitomes," No. 4 [London: Hogarth Press, 1939]).

PARSONS, TALCOTT, "Certain Primary Sources and Patterns of Aggression in the Social Structure of the Western World," *Psychiatry*, X (1947), 167–81.

HUXLEY, ALDOUS L., *Brave New World* (New York: Harper & Bros., 1946).

SILONE, IGNAZIO, *The School for Dictators*, trans. Gwenda David and Eric Mosbacher (New York: Harper & Bros., 1938).

Some of these texts are included in *Social Sciences 2: Syllabus and Selected Readings* (3 vols.; Chicago: University of Chicago Press, 1949, 1950).

SOCIAL SCIENCES 3

THE NATURE AND VALUE OF FREEDOM

MILL, JOHN STUART, *On Liberty*, in *The English Philosophers from Bacon to Mill*, ed. E. A. Burtt ("Modern Library" [New York: Random House, 1939]), pp. 949–1041.

PLATO *Republic*, trans. B. Jowett, in *The Works of Plato*, ed. Irwin Edman ("Modern Library" [New York: Random House, 1937]), Books ii (in part), iii, iv, viii (in part).

DICEY, A. V., "The Period of Benthamism or Individualism," "The Growth of Collectivism," and "The Period of Collectivism," in *Lectures on the Relation between Law and Public Opinion in England during the Nineteenth Century* (London: Macmillan & Co., Ltd., 1930), pp. 126–210.

FREEDOM IN THE POLITICAL ORDER

HOBBES, THOMAS, *Leviathan*, in *The English Philosophers from Bacon to Mill*, ed. E. A. Burtt ("Modern Library" [New York: Random House, Inc., 1939]), pp. 129–30, 159–89, 192–212, 226–30.

LOCKE, JOHN, *An Essay Concerning the True Original, Extent, and End of Civil Government*, in *The English Philosophers from Bacon to Mill*, ed. E. A. Burtt ("Modern Library" [New York: Random House, Inc., 1939]), pp. 402–23, 453–75, 489–503.

MILL, JAMES, "Government," in *The English Philosophers from Bacon to Mill*, ed. E. A. Burtt ("Modern Library" [New York: Random House, Inc., 1939]), pp. 857–89.

RIESMAN, DAVID, "Civil Liberties in a Period of Transition," in *Public Policy*, III (Cambridge: Harvard University Press, 1942), 33–96.

Schenck v. *U.S.*, 249 U.S. 47 (1919).

Meyer v. *Nebraska*, 262 U.S. 390 (1923).

Gitlow v. *New York*, 268 U.S. 652 (1925).

Whitney v. *California*, 274 U.S. 357 (1927).

U.S. v. *Schwimmer*, 279 U.S. 644 (1929).

Near v. *Minnesota*, 283 U.S. 697 (1931).

Associated Press v. *National Labor Relations Board*, 301 U.S. 103 (1937).

LASSWELL, H. D., *Democracy through Public Opinion* (Menasha, Wis.: George Banta Pub. Co., 1941), pp. 14–34, 80–116.

COMMISSION ON FREEDOM OF THE PRESS, *A Free and Responsible Press* (Chicago: University of Chicago Press, 1947), pp. 30–68, 79–106.

MADISON, JAMES, *The Federalist*, No. 10 ("Modern Library" [New York: Random House, 1937]), pp. 53–62.

WEBER, MAX, "Politics as a Vocation," trans. Edward A. Shils from *Politik als Beruf* (2d ed.; Munich and Leipzig, 1926).

BURKE, EDMUND, "Excerpts Concerning the Theory of Party Government and of Representation: 'Speech at Bristol Previous to the Election in That City, 1780'; 'Speech to the Electors of Bristol, 1774,' " in *Writings and Speeches*, ed. F. W. Rafferty ("World Classics" [London: Oxford University Press, 1929]), II, 164–65; III, 13–14.

SCHATTSCHNEIDER, E. E., *Party Government* (New York: Farrar & Rinehart, 1942), pp. 35–64, 187–205.

DICKINSON, JOHN, "The Supremacy of Law and the Review of Administrative Determinations by the Courts," in *Administrative Justice and the Supremacy of Law in the United States* ("Harvard Studies in Administrative Law," Vol. II [Cambridge: Harvard University Press, 1927]), chap. ii.

GELLHORN, WALTER, *Federal Administrative Proceedings* (Baltimore: Johns Hopkins Press, 1941), pp. 1–40.

FREEDOM IN THE ECONOMIC ORDER

KNIGHT, FRANK H., "Social Economic Organization," and "The Price System, and the Economic Process"; from an unpublished manuscript printed in the *Syllabus and Selected Readings;* see note at the end of this list.

SIMONS, HENRY C., *A Positive Program for Laissez Faire* ("Public Policy Pamphlets," No. 15 [Chicago: University of Chicago Press, 1934]).

KEYNES, JOHN MAYNARD, "The End of Laissez-faire," in *Laissez-faire and Communism* (New York: New Republic, Inc., 1926), pp. 57–77.

MEADE, J. E., and HITCH, C. J., *An Introduction to Economic Analysis and Policy* (New York: Oxford University Press, 1938).

STIGLER, GEORGE J., "The Extent and Bases of Monopoly," *American Economic Review*, Supplement, XXXII, No. 2, Part II (June, 1942), 1–22.

WILCOX, CLAIR, *Competition and Monopoly in American Industry* (Temporary National Economic Committee Monographs," No. 21 [Washington: Government Printing Office, 1940]).

NUTTER, G. WARREN, "The Extent of Effective Monopoly in the U.S."; from an unpublished manuscript, printed in the *Syllabus and Selected Readings;* see note at the end of this list.

SIMONS, HENRY C., "Some Reflections on Syndicalism," *Journal of Political Economy*, LII, No. 1 (March, 1944), 1–25.

LESTER, RICHARD A., "Reflections on the 'Labor Monopoly' Issue," *Journal of Political Economy*, LV, No. 6 (December, 1947), 513–36.

West Coast Hotel Co. v. *Parrish*, 300 U.S. 379 (1937).

United States v. *F. W. Darby Lumber Co.*, 312 U.S. 100 (1941).

National Labor Relations Board v. *Jones & Laughlin Steel Corp.*, 301 U.S. 1 (1937).

National Labor Relations Board v. *Fruehauf Trailer Co.*, 301 U.S. 49 (1937).

National Labor Relations Board v. *Friedman-Harry Marks Clothing Co.*, 301 U.S. 58 (1937).

Apex Hosiery Co. v. *Leader*, 310 U.S. 469 (1940).

United States v. *Hutcheson*, 312 U.S. 219 (1941).

JOSEPH, MARGARET F. W., "Principles of Full Employment," *International Postwar Problems*, II, No. 4 (October, 1945), 463–69.

NATIONAL RESOURCES COMMITTEE, *Consumer Incomes in the United States, Their Distribution in 1935–36* (Washington: Government Printing Office, 1938), pp. 1–2, 5–7, 95.

———, *Consumer Expenditures in the United States, Estimates for 1935–36* (Washington: Government Printing Office, 1939), pp. 77, 83.

FREEDOM IN THE SOCIAL ORDER

MILL, JOHN STUART, "Some Requisites of Freedom," in *Dissertations and Discussions: Political, Philosophical, and Historical* (New York: Henry Holt & Co., 1874), II, 27–36.

MANNHEIM, KARL, *Diagnosis of Our Time* (New York: Oxford University Press, 1944), Preface and chap. i.

ZORBAUGH, HARVEY W., *The Gold Coast and the Slum* (Chicago: University of Chicago Press, 1929), pp. 1–16, 221–51.

SIMMEL, GEORG, "The Metropolis and Mental Life," trans. Edward A. Shils from "Die Grosstädte und das Geistesleben," in *Die Grosstadt*, ed. Theodor Petermann (Dresden: Zahn & Jaensch, 1903), pp. 185–206.

LYND, R. S. and H. M., *Middletown in Transition* (New York: Harcourt, Brace & Co., 1937), pp. 419–33, 443–65, 468–76, 482–86.

WARNER, W. L., and LOW, J. O., *The Social System of the Modern Factory* (New Haven: Yale University Press, 1947), pp. 181–216.

DURKHEIM, ÉMILE, "On Anomie," trans. William C. Bradbury, Jr., from *Le Suicide* (Paris: Felix Alcan, 1897), pp. 272–88.

MANNHEIM, KARL, *Man and Society in an Age of Reconstruction* (London: K. Paul, Trench, Trübner, Ltd., 1940), pp. 39–75.

MILL, JOHN STUART, "Inaugural Address at St. Andrews," in *Dissertations and Discussions* (New York: Henry Holt & Co., 1875), IV, 332–407.

DEWEY, JOHN, *The Public and Its Problems* (Chicago: Gateway Books, 1946), pp. 23–36 and chaps. iii and iv.

SCHUMPETER, J. A., *Capitalism, Socialism, and Democracy* (New York: Harper & Bros., 1942), pp. 121–34, 139–63.

FREEDOM IN ALTERNATIVE SOCIAL SYSTEMS

VON HAYEK, FRIEDRICH A., *Freedom and the Economic System*, ed. Harry D. Gideonse ("Public Policy Pamphlets," No. 29 [Chicago: University of Chicago Press, 1939]).

TAWNEY, R. H., "Social Democracy in Britain," in *The Christian Demand for Social Justice*, ed. William Scarlett (New York: Signet Books, 1949).

LINDSAY, A. D., "The Philosophy of the British Labour Government," in *Ideological Differences and World Order*, ed. F. S. C. Northrop (New Haven, Conn.: Yale University Press, 1949).

THORNTON, R. H., "Nationalization: Administrative Problems Inherent in a State-owned Enterprise," *Public Administration*, XXV, No. 1 (spring, 1947), 10–21.

LENIN, V. I., *State and Revolution* (New York: International Publishers Co., Inc., 1932), pp. 7–20, 69–85.

BIENSTOCK, G.; SCHWARZ, S.; and YUGOW, A., *Management in Russian Industry and Agriculture*, ed. A. Feiler and J. Marschak (New York: Oxford University Press, 1944), chaps. i, iii, iv, vi, x, and xvi.

MOORE, BARRINGTON, JR., "The Communist Party of the Soviet Union: 1928–1944," *American Sociological Review*, IX, No. 3 (June, 1944), 267–78.

PARES, B., *Russia* (New York: Penguin Books, 1943), chaps. viii–xi, xiv, xvii.

LEGISLATIVE REFERENCE SERVICE OF LIBRARY OF CONGRESS, *Fascism in Action* (80th Cong., 1st Sess., H. Doc. 401 [Washington, D.C.: Government Printing Office, 1947]), chaps. i, ii, vi, xii, xiv.

FREEDOM AND THE INTERNATIONAL ORDER

KANT, IMMANUEL, "Eternal Peace," in *Eternal Peace and Other International Essays*, trans. W. Hastie (New York: World Peace Foundation, 1914), pp. 66–127.

Minutes to Midnight: The International Control of Atomic Energy ("Atomic Science and Education Series," No. 1, published by the *Bulletin of the Atomic Scientists* [Chicago, 1950]).

General Conference Report of UNESCO (Document UNESCO/C/30), *First Session* (Paris, 1947).

Report of the UNESCO Committee on the Philosophic Principles of the Rights of Man to the Commission on Human Rights of the United States, Paris, 31 July 1947.

Charter of the United Nations, 59 Stat. 1031 (1945).

SOCIAL SCIENCE AND SOCIAL POLICY

KNIGHT, FRANK H., "Preface to the Re-issue," in *Risk, Uncertainty, and Profit* (London: London School of Economics, 1933), pp. xxv–xxxvi.

DEWEY, JOHN, *The Public and Its Problems* (Chicago: Gateway Books, 1946), chaps. v and vi.

Many of these texts are reprinted in *Social Sciences 3: Syllabus and Selected Readings* (3 vols.; Chicago: University of Chicago Press, 1948, 1949).

5

The Natural Sciences

I

THE THREE-YEAR PROGRAM

JOSEPH J. SCHWAB

THE three-year science program exists in organic connection with other parts of the College curriculum. Its structure and its function are therefore partly determined by the whole curriculum. In day-to-day practice, for instance, the discussion of materials in the science program takes cognizance of work which is going on serially or simultaneously upon related matters in the course in history, in the course in the interrelations of the fields of knowledge, and in the programs of the humanities and social sciences. Such day-to-day cognizance occurs in the sense that the work in science includes, on appropriate occasions, activities

NOTE.—For students entering at the first-year level (normally after two years of high school), the College offers a three-year program which parallels the other three-year programs of the curriculum. For students who enter the College at the third-year level (normally after graduation from high school), a modified program which usually requires two years for completion is offered. The three-year program consists of a physical sciences component and a biological sciences component of approximately equal lengths. In 1950–51 the two-year program will consist of a year of selected portions (as determined by placement test) of the physical sciences component of the three-year program, together with a one-year general course in the biological sciences. During this year the integration of the one-year general course in the biological sciences with the biological sciences component of the three-year program—an integration of the sort already achieved in the area of the physical sciences—will be under consideration by the College Faculty. Since 1948 a year course in laboratory physics, designed as an alternative means of preparation for the comprehensive examination in the physical sciences, has been offered for students who come to the College after graduation from high school and intend to enter the Division of the Biological Sciences.

149

which are associated with the main responsibilities of other fields and also in the sense that treatment of materials ancillary to the main business of science is confidently left to other courses and programs. The practical connection of science to the remainder of the curriculum is an expression of common principles. These are, in the first instance, formulations of the ends of liberal education as a whole, but they achieve substance and the possibility of practical realization only as they divide the whole of liberal education into parts and assign to them different duties and responsibilities.

The science program, then, is part of a whole in three ways. First, its activities are connected with the activities in other programs and can be fully understood only in the light of these connections. Second, its main business is the consequence of a division of labor between specialized parts of the curriculum; hence, the character of the science program is best understood in the light of the entire business being divided and in the light of the special aptitude of science (as against the special aptitude of the humanities, for instance) for certain parts of this business. Third, the science program expresses the principles of liberal education as a whole, but as mediated and modified by the qualities which distinguish science from the humanities and the social sciences; therefore, the science program is best understood in the light of what these principles become when expressed through the materials and procedures of science.

An adequate account of the science program will, in short, include a description of its matter and methods in relation to the matter and methods of other parts of the curriculum; it will state the specific aims and responsibilities of the science program in relation to the specific ends of other parts of the curriculum; and it will suggest the sense in which its specific materials, methods, and purposes realize the generic traits of the curriculum as a whole.

The subject matters treated in the science program reveal, at first glance, little effect of the operation of the principles of a liberal education. Taken separately, they show no notable departure from those which might be found in one or another conventional "survey" course or in one or another undergraduate pre-

professional program, but in their number, their interconnec-
tion, and their degree of depth and detail they exhibit some of
the significant features of the active plan of studies in the College.

As an introduction to the physical sciences the program begins
with the simple Archimedean laws of equilibrium and of the lever.
The first large unit, completed in about fifteen weeks, uses materials from the field of inorganic chemistry, with emphasis on
phenomena of chemical and physical change as these lead to the
development of molecular and atomic theories, which, in turn,
give rise to the periodic table of the elements.

The second major unit of the physical science part of the program, by beginning with descriptive astronomy, makes a new
start which appears, at first, to the student to be unrelated to the
earlier unit. From the treatment of astronomy, however, the
problems of motion develop, and, as solutions to them, the various conceptions and relations of classical mechanics and dynamics
are expounded. The concept of energy is thereby introduced and,
with it, the kinetic molecular theory. This is then seen as a solution to a number of unresolved problems deriving from the phenomena of chemical change examined in the first semester. In
this way a relation between a problem in physics and one in
chemistry is established as illustrative of the unifying function of
scientific inquiry. The unit ends with a treatment of the special
theory of relativity. The unity of this part of the program is
derived from the study of motions as phenomena to be accounted
for and as elements of theories which account for other phenomena.

The third unit deals with the rise of theories of atomic structure. The start is made not on the basis of materials already
treated (such as phenomena of chemistry), which could have
been employed to introduce theories of atomic structure, but by
the exposition of a new body of phenomena, those of radiation.
This provides a second illustration of the way in which scientific
theory functions in the unification of apparently diverse bodies
of phenomena. From the properties of visible light and the
theories developed to explain them, the course moves to other
forms of radiation and their connection with electric charge and
with magnetic and electric fields. These phenomena and the

problems which emerge from them are seen to be resolved in a progression of modern atomic theories, which includes Bohr's quantum theory of the hydrogen spectrum.

One and one-half academic years (i.e., four and one-half quarters, or three semesters) are assigned to the study of these phenomena, problems, and solutions.

The same amount of time is allotted to the biological part of the program. The first of its three units uses materials from physiology and anatomy, which treat two areas of problems and solutions: the transport and regulation of respiratory gases in the organism and the regulation and utilization of food material.

After a study of the gross anatomy and physiology of the heart and circulatory system, the unit turns to capillary anatomy and physiology as related to the transport of respiratory gases. It returns to a consideration of problems of the organism as a whole in relation to a changing environment involving the regulation of external and internal respiration and circulation.

To the previous exposition of the principles of structure and function, part and whole, and levels of organization, the second problem of the unit adds the factors of health and disease. These are treated both as problems for biological inquiry and as factors which contribute to the solution of its problems. The study of carbohydrate metabolism begins with an exposition of diabetic symptoms as a problem in the classification and description of disease. A characteristic contribution of pathology is exemplified by the identification of pancreatic lesions as a causal factor in diabetes, and clinical and pathological medicine are seen as contributing hypotheses to guide physiological investigations into structure and function. Exposition of the gross physiology of the pancreas, hypophysis, and liver as related to carbohydrate metabolism is followed by a view of the problem at the cellular and chemical levels. Finally, in order to illustrate the existence of still further levels of the problem of the organism and its parts, and also the tentative and incomplete character of scientific knowledge, the unit ends with a treatment of psychosomatic factors in sugar utilization.

The second biological unit considers the developmental history of the organism as an individual and as a member of a species. This unit is, therefore, concerned with phylogeny, ontogeny, and genetics. An exposition of Darwinian theory presents to the student a large body of phenomena, terms, and concepts and poses problems of genetics and embryonic development. These problems are pursued via experimental data and theories concerning nucleus-cytoplasm relations, embryonic regulation and induction, and the concept of organizers and gradients. Genetics is pursued through exposition of primitive Mendelian instances, the phenomena of linkage and crossing-over, and quantitative characters. The unit ends with the modern, quantitative treatment of mutation, migration, natural selection, and chance as factors of evolution.

The third unit of the biological part of the program draws its materials from psychology. The student examines problems and solutions which are characteristic of the Gestalt, the behaviorist, the Freudian, and the introspectionist conceptions of psychology.

In summary, the three years of the science program are divided approximately equally between biological sciences and physical sciences. Taken singly, the topics chosen for treatment are representative of these two major fields of scientific inquiry and exhibit no special features stemming from the defining principles of a liberal education. Taken together, on the other hand, the topics form a structure which departs from that of ordinary "survey" courses and also from that of pre-professional programs. From the point of view of pre-professional programs, the topical structure is characterized by an unusual variety of subject matters and of relation among the varieties. For instance, in the case of the physical sciences, topics range over the recognized areas of heat, light, mechanics and dynamics, inorganic chemistry, and astronomy; and each conclusion drawn from these fields is expounded not only in its own terms but also as relating to the problems, phenomena, and conclusions in other fields.

From one point of view, then, the science program is characterized by an unusual variety of subject matters and an unusual emphasis on the interrelations among this variety of specific and concrete matters of fact and theory. On the other hand, viewed from the vantage point of a conventional survey course in the biological or physical sciences, the topical structure of the science program is characterized by considerable incompleteness and lack of variety. For instance, the conventional topic of current electricity is missing. (To be sure, certain facts and theories concerning electrical phenomena are treated in connection with theories of atomic structure.) Similarly, in the case of the biological sciences, physiology is represented by only two topics rather than by a survey touching upon all the organ systems and most of the organs constituting the mammalian organism. The situation is similar in the case of embryology. This science is represented by a restricted series of experiments, with their data and conclusions, bearing upon a restricted but significant topic in the field rather than by a narrative of the development of the vertebrate or mammalian embryo.

In brief, by contrast with conventional survey courses, the science program treats a relatively small number of topics with an attention to detail and questions of evidence and interpretation reminiscent of a graduate seminar.

To combine what can be seen from these two points of view— that of the survey course and that of the pre-professional course— is to say that the unit elements of the program are not topics, strictly speaking, but problems. That is, the subdivisions of the physical and biological sciences drawn upon for materials are treated representatively, not exhaustively. The materials chosen to represent each field are, moreover, not only the conclusions of a representative part of that field but these conclusions together with the formulated problems, data, and the interpretations of data which yield the conclusions. Each field is taken, in short, not only as a body of knowledge but also as a field of inquiry, and one aim of this kind of material and treatment is to illuminate for the student the manner in which knowledge is obtained in each field, as well as the subject matters of the several fields (e.g., matter, motion, embryogeny). Further, the sequence and relation among the representative materials is made such that the problems, data, and conclusions of one field are often seen to have a bearing on similar factors in others. Problems in one field are viewed as stemming not only from previous solutions there but also from the knowledge and data of other, and sometimes remote, fields. Theories are presented as accounting for data in other fields, as well as for data in the field where they were developed; and theories arising more or less independently from diverse bodies of data are seen to pose problems of reconciliation and synthesis for the sake of unification of knowledge of nature.

A balance between depth and breadth is sought which is characteristic neither of the survey course nor of the pre-professional course but is somewhere in between. The excess of depth over breadth which appears by contrast with survey treatment of scientific material is constituted, in considerable part, of considerations bearing upon evidence and interpretation. For the rest, it consists of a concern for thorough treatment of conclusions as such and for avoidance of superficiality.

The excess of breadth over depth, on the other hand, which appears by contrast with pre-professional courses is constituted, in part, of a variety of problems and subject matters designed to exhibit the variety of ways in which the object of investigation of a science (e.g., the organism, in biology) can be examined in the light of varying principles, which pose different problems and suggest different kinds of evidence to be sought and conclusions to be formulated. For the remainder, the excess of breadth over depth which appears by contrast with pre-professional courses stems from the view that some aspects of the living and nonliving world are sufficiently important in themselves to be worth knowing about, even though the knowledge is gained only by some sacrifice of depth and of attention to questions of evidence and interpretation.

The present balance is the product of a long history of trials of differing proportions of these factors. The early efforts of the College science program were largely concerned with breadth, and with breadth of information about subject matter. Indeed, the earliest phase of development of the College science program was the prototype of the "survey" course. Its primary problem was choice of the subject matters appropriate to a "general education" and decision as to the amount of time and emphasis to be given to each. Its second problem was to choose a unifying theme which would bind together the diverse parts of its chosen subject matter so as to constitute a *narrative* whose structure would be an image or picture, which, though deficient in depth and detail, would be an informing and recognizable model of the world as then conceived by science. The name of the first University of Chicago science survey course, "The Nature of the World and of Man," is indicative of this goal.

This is not to say that science as a process of inquiry was ignored even in the earliest stages of development of the science program. Quite the contrary: a certain amount of time and considerable effort were devoted to an exposition of "scientific method." Nevertheless, the ratio of emphasis on conclusions to emphasis on scientific method was extremely high, and, moreover, method itself was primarily conceived as a subject matter. Its treatment was the same in kind as the treatment of other subject matters. It was the subject of a *narrative* account embodied in lectures and in chapters of a textbook. The student was expected to *know about* method in the same sense that he was expected to *know about* the structure of the atom or the age of the earth. Experience with a program characterized by relatively little emphasis on science as inquiry, by a tendency to understand inquiry in the narrow sense of "method," and by a reduction of "method" to the status of the subject matter of a narrative account led to dissatisfactions which promoted rethinking of all these matters. In 1943 a few members of the science staff were detached from duty in the parent-courses. They were expected to establish a new program in the sciences which, by practical operation, would provide a further and different body of experience wherewith to test our conceptions of the nature of scientific knowledge and the place of science in the liberal curriculum. The new program undertook neither to duplicate the method-content ratio of the parent-programs nor to invert it but, rather, to effect the union which is rather obviously suggested by the words "method" and "results." In other words, its responsibility was to avoid narrative discourse on either the conclusions of science or its method, by presenting "method" as the means by which conclusions are reached, verified, and related in science and "conclusions" as the consequences of the application of these means to an appropriate subject matter. By such a union, it was intended that the conclusions of science be given the cogency and meaning that is theirs when they are viewed in terms of the problems, the data, and the interpretations from which they stem. Furthermore, processes of inquiry which characterize science were to be exhibited only concretely and by example, that is, not as a doctrine about method but in the form of reports of problems formulated and data gathered and interpreted, which the student would need to grasp, point by point, as the necessary steps toward reaching a knowledge and understanding of conclusions.

The responsibility assigned to this new program was to effect a union of content and method in practice as well as in theory. A merely theoretical union would have admitted a continuation of narrative discourse as the principal means of instruction. The only change would have been that the units of the narrative would no longer have been aspects of the world or aspects of method, each taken separately, but units of analyzed and evaluated research. The mode of narrative discourse would have changed merely from the form, "The outer shell of the atom consists of . . . " or "There are N major divisions of the mammalian class," to the form, "On the heels of this discovery, Rutherford then investigated the magnitude of the charge . . . " or "The discovery of this particle forced a revision of the theory as follows. . . ." But a theoretical and practical union of "method" and "content" would assign to the student the task of understanding and following the stages of discovery and verification as the main route available to him for knowledge of the conclusions. By this means it was proposed to realize, in the area of the sciences, the notion, as stated by Mr. Faust in chapter 1 above: "It is not the purpose of the College to instruct members of the rising generation what to think, but rather to teach them how to think. Its purpose is not indoctrination but the development of power to form sound judgments. . . . This kind of competence, like skill in swimming, cannot be developed by learning rules but only by exercise, and, since the methods by which problems regarding the natural world are formulated and resolved differ from the formulation and resolution of problems [in other fields], education in the formation of sound judgments in these various areas requires practice in thinking about [these] different subject matters."

The practical union of "method" and "content" was effected

by putting into the student's hands, as his primary materials, neither a textbook of the philosophy of science nor textbooks of science but, rather, connected series of selected and edited papers and longer works drawn from the research literature of each of the scientific fields. Instruction consisted in careful reading and discussion of the papers, taken both individually and in relation to one another. The means used was laboratory work for two hours a week and discussion periods utilizing three hours per week. The aim of student and teacher was to take cognizance of the phenomena about which a paper is concerned, to understand the problem which is formulated in it, to see what aspects of the phenomena are embraced by the problem, and to follow the resolution of the problem. In similar fashion, student and instructor worked together to relate the researches and conclusions of the several papers of each series.

The experience of the staff members engaged in the development and teaching of this program produced both affirmative and critical judgments. The desirability and feasibility of using materials which enlisted the students' participation in the processes of evaluation and synthesis, which are ordinarily left to the instructor and lecturer, were confirmed. The desirability of laboratory work was confirmed. The propriety of a union of "method" and "content" was confirmed.

On the other hand, experience with the program in its earliest form disclosed certain unexpected weaknesses and omissions; and continued work with its later phases underlined the desirability of rectifying certain radical shifts in emphasis which at first were considered justified. The undesirable features with which the 1943 program could reasonably be charged were these:

In the first place, the laboratory program and methods of discussion which were developed in the course, though successful in guiding the student to an adequate habit of interpreting and understanding individual papers, were not effective in teaching students the skills necessary for relating the conclusions of a variety of papers to one another. As a result, the scientific model of aspects of the world which was present in the documents was not vividly grasped by a large proportion of students.

In the second place, the models, even as presented in the papers, had more numerous and larger gaps than were noticeable before actual trial in the teaching situation. Adding further papers was not feasible: the amount of reading would have required an investment in time and energy not justified by the relatively small increase in reading and interpretive skill which might have resulted.

In the third place, the method of treating the materials in discussion had the undesirable effects of maximizing their role to the student as examples of scientific inquiry and of minimizing their role as sources of knowledge about the world.

Finally, the practice of treating "method" only by example and eschewing such formulas and formula words as "induction," "deduction," "hypothesis," "empirical generalization," etc., had the effect of leaving the student capable of understanding and even evaluating the process of inquiry disclosed by a given paper, yet unable to formulate a statement concerning the nature of one or another pattern of inquiry.

The faults and overemphases of the 1943 program were, with the possible exception of the last-named, at the locus of the strengths of the older program. Conversely, the experience gained in developing and teaching the 1943 program was useful at those points where the older program could be said to have its principal vices. As more and more members of the science staff participated in both programs and brought their combined experience to bear upon them, the aims, content, and method of the two converged. The present curriculum is the result of this exchange and pooling of insights and experience.* In so far as the previous programs converged toward a common point, the present sequence is that point. On the other hand, there is one sense in which it is neither the older program, that of the 1943 experiment, nor an eclectic composite of the two but, rather, a third plan, developing from principles of its own, whose tentative validity is warranted by the amount and diversity of experience employed in choosing and interpreting them.

The present program, for instance, leans heavily upon the reading and discussion of original works, but the gaps between

* Under the administrative leadership of Benson Ginsburg, John W. Mayfield, Thornton L. Page, Aaron Sayvetz, and the author.

papers, which were a vice of the 1943 program, are filled by materials which supply necessary and useful information about phenomena and conclusions with the economy and in the manner of a good textbook. Moreover, the frequent appearance of these textbook materials and the manner in which they are treated in relation to the original papers appropriately bring to the student's attention questions both of the nature of scientific inquiry and of the nature of the world. The living organism, the nature of matter, and the nature of space and of motion are as much a concern of the student as are the patterns of inquiry which yield knowledge of matter, motion, and the organism.

Further emphasis upon the subject matter of science is achieved through the use of queries and problems which require, for solution, that knowledge of conclusions discovered in papers and textbook materials be brought to bear upon specific and concrete situations. Such queries and problems, together with textbook materials and a topical outline which contains the selected readings and textbook materials, also serve to achieve a connection between different conclusions. In the earlier years of the older program this connection was established by the instructor alone and communicated to the student by narrative; in the 1943 program it was not initially achieved to an adequate degree by any device.

These queries and problems are of different kinds. Some serve in a traditional way to illuminate the meaning and usefulness of scientific conclusions by applying them to practical or concrete situations. Some serve to interrelate different papers and textbook materials at the level of their conclusions. Others have the special function of bringing to students' attention the kinds of questions, which, by being asked of a given scientific paper, serve to connect its various logical parts (problem, evidence, interpretation, and conclusion). Queries of this last kind perform another function. They not only bring to the attention of the student the evidential relations of the parts of each individual paper to which they refer but, by an appropriate mode of repetition which introduces both specific variation and generic uniformity, teach students the kinds of questions and the various categories of answers which, together, constitute a knowledge of science as a process of inquiry. The chosen mode of repetition solves a problem which was not resolved satisfactorily either in the initial 1943 program or in the older one—the problem of a satisfactory and formulable notion of scientific method. If it could be charged that the older program, by expounding a narrative about method, reduced method to too simple a form, it could be charged with equal propriety that the initial 1943 program, by eschewing all reference to method as such, left its component parts so various and unconnected as hardly to permit an intelligent formulation by the student.

The materials, then, of the present program consist of series of research papers, monographs, and selections from textbooks representing the sciences by means of problems. Upon these papers and other materials a collection of queries and problems is directed in order to draw the papers together and to teach the student how to approach a statement in the field of science. Specimens of queries and problems are included in this chapter (pp. 181–86).

The use of primary or original source material in the program has elicited much comment and, apparently, much puzzlement also, for a variety of interpretations concerning the reason for their use has arisen, based on no more than the information that such materials were, somehow or other, employed in the course. It has been assumed, for instance, that the presence of original papers indicates that the science program has substituted the history of science for science proper. This would mean, supposedly, that the primary emphasis in the program is upon the shifts of research patterns or of principles or of scientific subject matter in succeeding epochs or in different places. This is not the case. It has been assumed that the presence of original papers indicates that the science program has substituted the sociology of science for science proper. This would mean, presumably, that the course conceives scientific investigation as largely or most significantly the creature of influences which lie outside science; for example, it might be thought that economic and technological factors are presented as determining problems chosen for research or that religious and philosophical factors are cited as determining the methods and canons employed for discovery and verification. This is not the case, either. Undoubtedly scientific inquiry is influenced by external factors, but such factors and their effects are not the concern of the science program, any more than the psychological determinants of a man's belief concern the scientist or detective who is trying to determine whether the belief is empirically warranted or not.

It has been assumed also that the presence of original papers means that the course has turned its back on science proper in order to treat scientific papers as humanistic objects, as creations of the human spirit. Nor is this the case. Undoubtedly, a few scientific works are works of art in the best sense. That is, they are complex wholes, woven of a multitude of parts whose relation to one another and to the whole are so complete and perfect as to constitute an aesthetic object. Darwin's *Origin of Species* is such a work. So also are Harvey's *Anatomical Disquisition* and Galileo's *Two New Sciences*. Parts or all of each of these works are used in the program. Nevertheless, the program is in no way concerned with these, or any other works, as works, i.e., humanistic objects.

An illuminating analogy for our use of primary source material is to be seen, rather, in a procedure found in the field of science itself—the practice of the graduate seminar. The "journal club," which meets to hear one or more of its members deliver an interpretation and analysis of a research paper or project, and the special-interest group, which meets to discuss current literature in its field of study, constitute practices familiar to most scientists, with aims and methods analogous to those of the three-year science program in its treatment of primary sources. The bibliographic graduate seminar, which systematizes the approach of journals clubs, is an even closer analogy. In such seminars the instructor presents a bibliography of papers and monographs from which each student selects his share of titles. Each student reads the articles chosen by him, writes abstracts of the papers for distribution among the members of the seminar, and delivers an extended interpretation and critical analysis of the work in question. Under the questioning of fellow-students and with the guidance of the professor, students participating in such a program learn what is relevant and what is not to the understanding and judgment of a scientific paper in the field and upon the kind of problem in question.

This practice is analogous to the use made of papers in the three-year program, but it is analogous only. It differs from that of a graduate seminar in ways which arise because the students are undergraduates and because the program is part of a liberal curriculum rather than a part of pre-professional training. The precise aim and practice in respect to the use of original papers are therefore best seen in terms of the educational principles which determine them.

The faculty of the College has chosen to divide its curriculum into three major parts, the humanities, the social sciences, and the natural sciences, because each of these areas of knowledge is large enough in itself and, further, because what is meant by knowledge in each of these areas differs sufficiently in origin and application. This division is made, however, without prejudice to the obvious (and sometimes subtle) relations which connect the fields of knowledge to one another. The problem of integration created by setting these boundaries is in part solved by integrative courses. Integration also takes place within the three principal programs as well as in the courses which are explicitly integrative, for this differentiation is a complex one whose basis is much broader than subject matter alone.

In fact, neither subject matter nor method nor purpose alone is an adequate criterion for discriminating and understanding the differences and similarities of the humanities, the social sciences, and the natural sciences. The end, method, and subject matter of each are found in some degree in each of the others. But it is also clear that any one of these criteria exhibits a predominant variant in each of the three fields. For example, in the area most relevant here, in respect to method and end, the process by which data are treated in ways which yield general truths, and primarily for the sake of these general truths, though to be found to a large degree in the social sciences and in the humanities, is nevertheless most prominent in the natural sciences. The same is true of subject matter. Nature, though treated by the humanities for its own purpose of finding models, means, and suggestions for its creations and though found in the social sciences in its specification to human nature, is pre-eminently the subject matter of the natural sciences.

The presence of all three components—humanistic, scientific, and social—in each of the three fields of activity is, therefore, one factor with which we must deal in understanding these fields. The predominance of each of these components in turn in the field which bears its name is another factor. These two factors, taken together in their bearing upon the differences and natures of the fields of the sciences, the social sciences, and the humanities, can be clarified by making explicit a distinction between a "field" and a "discipline." Let "field" stand for the combination of a plurality of subject matters, operations upon these subject matters, and the intentions of the operations, which are to be found in the clusters of organized studies that we call, respectively, the sciences, the humanities, and the social sciences. Let "discipline" stand for an organized activity brought to bear upon a subject matter, the activity achieving its organization in virtue of its purpose and in virtue of the way it takes (or views) its subject matter in order to make the activity, the purpose, and the subject matter appropriate to one another.

In these terms scientific discipline might be conceived as an activity of data-seeking and interpretation, brought to bear upon a subject matter viewed as a source of data capable of yielding general truths and pursued for the sake of such general truths. There would also be humanistic discipline, an activity of analysis and of recognition of relations, brought to bear upon a subject matter conceived as a human creation constructed of chosen parts and put together in chosen ways in order to constitute an envisaged whole, the end of the activity being a comprehension of the parts, their connections, and the whole; and that, in turn, is for the sake of appreciating the created object and for the sake of understanding the activity of choice and ordering of parts which produced it. There would be, finally, social-scientific discipline, an activity which orders knowledge of principles and grasp of particular situations and people to the determination of means-to-ends; this activity is brought to bear upon a dual subject matter, one conceived as giving rise to principles or general truths, the other conceived as setting a problem of choice of action; the activity is pursued for the sake of the choice of means-to-ends, or policy.

With these distinctions, we can then recognize the fields of the humanities, the social sciences, and the natural sciences as compounds of the same elements, but *chemical* compounds in which the characteristic differences of each field emerge as consequences of the differing proportions and connections *inter se* in which the three elements, the disciplines, appear in each field. For instance, the social sciences will have a humanistic and scientific component, but these will function primarily as they make it possible to know peoples, cultures, and societies for the sake of the ultimate determination of means-to-ends. In science, then, there will be a dole of humanistic and social-scientific disciplines, but only in so far as they serve the scientist in his elaboration of general truths from the particular facts of nature.

In terms of the three fields and their disciplines we may state the role to be played by each field in a liberal curriculum. First, each liberal program representative of a field will be concerned to convey to its students a knowledge of its subject matter. But it will be concerned to convey its knowledge to a degree and in a manner appropriate to its dominant disciplines: e.g., knowledge as an objective would loom largest in the field of science. Second, each program will accept responsibility for providing some practice in the liberal equivalent of those disciplines which are not primarily its own, though restricting this practice in kind and scope to the manner and extent that other disciplines function upon its own subject matter. Finally, each program will have a primary responsibility for providing the student with guidance and practice in the employment of the liberal equivalent of its own discipline.

The methods and materials of the natural science program of the College are determined by its share of these three aims. It is subordinately concerned with the disciplines of the other fields; but with these disciplines it is concerned only in so far as, and only on those occasions when, they are relevant to its major tasks. Its major concerns are to impart an understanding of the conclusions of science and to instil the abilities of thought and judgment by which the student may follow the application of scientific discipline in a particular instance to an understanding of the conclusions reached thereby: an understanding of conclusions both as warrantable interpretations of evidence and as instruments for the prediction and control of determinable aspects of nature.

The reason for the use of original research papers and the manner in which they are employed may now be clearer. The science program is not charged with responsibility for the humanistic disciplines, and its treatment of scientific papers does not take them as works of art, subject to the kind of analysis appropriate to a work of art. Therefore, the science program is not a reduction of science to the humanities. Similarly, because the responsibility for imparting knowledge of the social sciences is carried by the social science program and partly by the history course, the science program need not be, and is not, concerned with its material as evidence for conclusions about peoples, epochs, cultures, and trends. The science program is not a reduction of science to the history and sociology of knowledge, and its way of using scientific papers is not adapted to throw light upon such matters. The research papers are present as examples of inquiry, as containers of conclusions, and as centers for the kind of intellectual activity on the part of the student which will constitute practice of those abilities and powers of judgment which are appropriate to the discipline of science.

The student is concerned, in his reading of each reported investigation, with understanding its conclusions. He tries to determine and formulate the problem whose resolution is presented if that problem is not explicit. If the paper is a later one of a series, he tries to understand the problem in relation to the wider body of phenomena which the problems of other investigations have made clear to him. He then determines what kind of evidence is chosen for search by the scientist and why this kind of evidence is appropriate to the problem posed. The student then examines the data themselves and the degree to which they represent the phenomena for which they stand. He moves on to note the manner in which the data are interpreted so as to yield a conclusion, and he tries to determine the effects of the chosen method of interpretation upon the connection between the conclusions reached and the data. Now the student turns from conclusions as warrantable interpretations of data to conclusions as instruments of prediction and control. Through his knowledge of the sources and development of the conclusions, he attempts to understand to what phenomena they are applicable, under what limitations of circumstance and accuracy they may be applied, and with what power they may be expected to function.

The emphasis is also upon the paper as an exemplar of scientific inquiry. Although a single paper is but an instance of an isolated problem posed and solved, the variety of papers as a whole constitutes a cross-section of inquiry in their fields. As experience with one paper after another is established, there is a sifting of the numerous problems and solutions. Similarities and differences emerge. Questions to the students posed by query-sheets and discussions help him find, among the several varied papers, *patterns* of inquiry. He learns to recognize *types* of problems, *kinds* of data, and *modes* of formulation of knowledge.

He learns, for example, what causal inquiry aimed at biological subject matters is like: the kinds of data required, the difficulties of interpretation in such research. He will learn of the ways devised for resolving these difficulties or avoiding them. He will see differing conceptions of the constituent parts of an organism and of their relation to one another applied as tools for formulating problems and organizing research. He will note the advantages and disadvantages of differing principles by discovering what kind or degree of knowledge each yields and what each leaves unexamined. He will learn to distinguish such researches from those employing principles which lead to a different orientation of research, such as might be aimed at taxonomic schematisms or at comprehensive mathematical or mechanical theories. His study of the growth and development of the wave and the particle theories of radiation show him, for instance, what is involved in the development of such a model and what is done by science to combine breadth and flexibility of future application with precision of fit to existing data. He sees the differences in the sense of "verification" and what is experimentally and logically implied by "verification" when a taxonomic scheme is verified and how that differs from the verification of a mathematical model or the test of an assertion of causal relation.

The variety which is exhibited when each paper is treated as a singular solution to a singular problem is thus made intelligible by being seen as the expression of *types* of problem formulation and resolution. An inductive treatment of scientific inquiry replaces the more traditional narrative treatment, and inquiry itself is conceived as a process and an activity which is subject to indefinite variation and specification to particular problems, on the one hand, yet capable of intelligible formulations, on the other. This notion of inquiry is a far cry from its traditional treatment as a "method" to be formulated in a single set of general terms. The problems of inquiry, constituted of the special obstacles in the way of obtaining data and the special difficulties of interpretation which characterize different subject matters of science, as well as those which characterize particular problems, can emerge by an inductive treatment. An inductive treatment, moreover, provides a means by which the education of the student in respect to scientific inquiry can itself be an active scientific inquiry. The distinction of subject matter and student is made less rigid, and the student *does* what he is learning.

The textbook materials which accompany each set of original papers have their part to play as well. In respect to conclusions of science, the original papers cannot be expected to provide economically all that it is desirable to know about the phenomena treated in them. The textbook materials supply this lack: they occasionally provide the background of vocabulary or of unorganized knowledge of the situations with which the papers deal. More often they provide the background of previous theory and fact on which the papers depend or which they will reject, replace, or amend. The textbook materials are depended upon to enlarge and extend the conclusions reached in the papers read, and they supply links of knowledge between paper and paper and between the series of papers. In respect to inquiry, the textbook materials confirm and enlarge the students' understanding of various patterns of inquiry by tracing their effectiveness into areas not treated by the original papers.

The laboratory work of the program has special characteristics which parallel the use of original papers in the course; and, as a parallel to the presence of textbook materials among the readings, the laboratory work has its conventional side as well. The peculiar characteristic of the laboratory work is the marked paucity of explicit instructions for procedure and of predetermined "right" results, at which the student is supposed to aim.

Detailed procedural instruction and a mark to aim for are appropriate initiating devices for laboratory work, when the intention is to provide technique and to make vivid or meaningful the content of lecture and textbook. The laboratory of the science program accepts a measure of these responsibilities. It devotes much of its time to exhibiting the immediate phenomena with which papers or textbook materials will deal as problem situations. It must, for instance, exhibit the gross anatomy of the vertebrate animal; it must display such relatively commonplace phenomena as the solution and precipitation of solids, the behavior of gases during changes in temperature, and the behavior of solids in liquids relative to changes in density. At a more sophisticated level it must show the behavior of light, for example, in its passage through different media and the fact of the spectrum.

It is also through the laboratory that some features of the relation between fact and interpreted fact in science are conveyed. Here, for example, the student grasps by experience the difficulty, in experimentation, of realizing the conditions envisioned in a plan of experiment and the need and significance of the substitution of one procedure as the sign of another, as, for example, the chain of sign-signification relations which exist between the vertically falling body, the body on an inclined plane, and the pendulum. It is also through the laboratory that the difficulties in the way of attaining a required level of accuracy and precision of measurement can be appreciated and the importance of accuracy and precision be assayed.

A third familiar function of the laboratory work is that of making vivid and meaningful the conclusions of papers and text materials and the terms in which their problems are couched. The terms find their operational definition in the laboratory, and the conclusions find their extensional meaning and the limitations under which they have validity.

In a program aimed at comprehension of a discipline as well as at possession of information, however, the laboratory has a fourth function, and in this fourth function the initiating role ordinarily performed by detailed procedural instructions and a mark to aim at is more properly played only by a problem which is itself problematic, that is, a problem in the sense of a situation which invites investigation rather than a problem in the sense of a formulated query. The latter is, in fact, not a problem, strictly speaking, but a problem solved, the problem having been that of determining into what terms the problematic situation could be analyzed in a manner suitable for investigation. A formulated query, by indicating the terms in which the situation is to be analyzed, has also already solved the problem of determining what data are appropriate to solution and how such data are to be treated. A problematic situation, on the other hand, poses all these problems. And to be faced with all these problems is to be faced with the situation which confronts the scientist and which the discipline of science is intended to resolve.

It is for the sake of the light they can throw on the function and nature of the discipline of science that a very few (and these few only approximate) problematic situations confront the student in the three years of the program. Since the intentions of the program do not include the preparation of the student as a scientist, facility in the performance of the discipline of science is not an end, and therefore the number of such problematic situations is small. On the other hand, the responsibility of the program does include a comprehending and evaluating grasp of scientific discipline, and for this purpose a few confrontations with situations which are problematic to some degree have their use. This use has its analogy in the humanities, where some experience in the act of creating a poem or a painting has value not for the sake of making amateur painters or poets but for the sake of a more realistic and comprehending grasp of the artistic work.

Experience has taught us that multiplication of the number of confrontations with problematic situations beyond a few instances is unprofitable. They require much time and make demands upon qualities of originality and imagination which cannot be met by many otherwise highly competent students. It has been found more useful to inject a measured and appropriate degree of problematical quality into all laboratory functions rather than to employ dramatic instances of a wholly or largely problematical kind. This is achieved by reducing laboratory instructions to a minimum. Only a few instructions are written at all, and these in general terms. Rather, the laboratory work of a given week or period of weeks grows out of an initiating discussion of a selected facet of current work. This introduction serves to indicate the general problem area. Student teams then examine available equipment, formulate the problem to be solved, work out the details of experimentation, and proceed, on the basis of their own plans, to data-collecting and interpretation. Specimens of laboratory instructions are included in this chapter (pp. 179–81).

The same degree of independent work on the part of the student is achieved on the side of the discussions by a "reading period" which terminates the program. During this time the student pursues one topic through appropriate papers without the aid of class meetings and records the results of his independent investigation in an analytical and interpretive paper.

The distinction of discipline from field and the factors which this distinction emphasizes as aims of a liberal program in the sciences account for the presence and use of original papers and for some of the qualities of the laboratory work of the program. The specific mode of treatment of the papers, on the other hand —what is sought in them as relevant to their conclusions and to inquiry—is a consequence of the staff's conception of the nature of scientific discipline or inquiry.

Our conception of inquiry is an integration of two views which stem from a concern for subject matter, on the one hand, and a concern for skills and abilities, on the other, as the ends of education. Since the science program has both these aims and in relation to each other, its conception of inquiry must contain elements of both views, in proper relation to each other. If science in a curriculum is viewed solely or primarily as a body of conclusions to be narrated and learned, the appropriate view of scientific discipline is one which will assert the validity of scientific conclusions or state the component factors which constitute it. Validity is the only concern because, in respect to conclusions taken in relation to their objects, the principal question is only whether they are true or not. Moreover, where narration is the principal method of instruction, the validity of conclusions taken one by one is not a matter to be questioned or argued. That each separate conclusion is as valid as the method and subject matter permit is underwritten by the fact that they are chosen for narration by an able and informed authority, the teacher. What is required, therefore, is only that the *general* validity of the method employed in that given subject matter be conveyed. For this purpose, science may properly be conceived as a single, uniform procedure and the procedure be described within the limits of a single set of terms.

In point of fact, liberal programs in science concerned primarily or solely with conclusions hardly exist any longer. Yet the view of scientific inquiry appropriate to such a program persists as a vestige of the era in which the function of a general education was considered satisfied when a body of information was made available to the student. Views of this kind, which conceive science as a uniform procedure and describe it within the limits of a single set of terms, may be stated in a variety of ways. Science, for instance, is inductive, and what is not inductive is not science. Since induction implies a movement from particulars to more general statements, one can also say that science is a synthesis and interaction of facts and ideas. Or one can adopt procedural terms and describe science as a process with explicit steps (e.g., the observation of phenomena, the statement of a problem, the collection of relevant data, formulation of hypotheses, verification by prediction of consequences of hypotheses, and test for the presence or absence of predicted consequences).

Highly general formulations of this kind are true in their way, well adapted to a narrative method of instruction, and they serve well enough their purpose of conveying confidence to the student in the conclusions taught him. They have certain inherent limitations, however, and, practically, will not serve by themselves the purposes of a liberal program which is concerned with scientific discipline as well as information. Their limitation lies in the very generality and metonymy by which they are constructed.

Generality and its limiting effect can be seen in the stepwise formulation cited above. In order to reduce science to a conveniently narratable series of steps, the great variability which characterizes a given "step" when it is seen exemplified in different researches is lost. To refer to "formulation of hypotheses" as a step in scientific "method" is to give no hint of the great variety of *kinds* of hypotheses which are employed in different sciences and in different inquiries. Consequently, the fact that different kinds of hypotheses are so very different that each has its own definition of "relevance" in the notion of "relevant data" and confers upon verification its own operationally different meanings is hidden from view. The data and verification relevant to the hypothesis that *this* rather than *that* taxonomic schematism is best would involve an examination of the theories in which the schematism is grounded, a test to determine the value of the schematism in the solution of problems arising from these theories, as well as in a determination of the extent to which the schematism provides a place and only one place for each member of the universe to which the schematism is to be applied. A given taxonomic scheme is based upon a particular choice of qualities and properties of the objects to be classified, and the choice of qualities and properties is, in turn, determined by the use to which the scheme is to be put and the theories from which it arises. Therefore, a variety of taxonomic schemes applicable to a given universe and competent to provide each member of the universe with a place is possible. Verification of any one such scheme is therefore to be sought in a test of its usefulness upon problems and of its appropriateness to antecedent theories, as well as in a test by more immediate standards. A grasp of such ideas as these is not provided by the narration of a highly general, stepwise formulation of science, for, in their way, these ideas are themselves "steps" in scientific inquiry which are omitted from such a narrative.

The question of the data and tests relevant to the verification of a cause-and-effect hypothesis concerning a living organism and its parts presents its own complex features. Cause-and-effect researches in physiology involve notions of sufficient and necessary antecedent events and constituent parts. Hence one kind of relevant data and test of such a hypothesis will concern the consequence or lack of consequence of the presence or absence of designated parts or processes in the organism. "Part" and "particular process," however, are not objectively given pieces of the organism or of the life-process in time, and therefore the principles which determine the particular partitioning of the anatomy and activity of the organism are data relevant to a test of the hypothesis in question. Different researches employ different principles of partitioning which yield different parts (e.g., biochemical units as against organs, or organs as against organ aggregates), and therefore the test of a given hypothesis must include as relevant not only the data concerning ablation and replacement of parts characteristic of its own level of partitioning but also the facts concerning the consequences of the presence and absence of parts defined by other principles of anatomy.

Parts and particular processes in the living organism are also characterized by a peculiar fluidity. The structure and function of a given part, distinguished on whatever basis, varies with time and circumstance; its characteristics are a function of its environing neighbors and conditions, as well as of its own determination. Therefore, the changes in the organism as a whole under varied conditions and especially under the conditions of experimentation are valid data and part of the test of a causal hypothesis in the life-sciences.

Such matters as these escape a highly general presentation of the nature of science, in whatever terms it may be put. Large and important differences among various patterns of scientific inquiry are not raised for consideration. These differences need hardly be touched upon in a program concerned only with information, but a liberal program concerned also with scientific discipline requires a view of science which will permit a concrete and specific understanding of the individual examples of scientific inquiry examined by the student. A concrete understanding of particular researches requires a specification of general ideas to the matter in hand, and specification requires cognizance of sufficient diversity to make each paper intelligible in itself and capable of relation to other papers.

The need for simplicity and economy of narration which gives rise to highly general summaries of the nature of inquiry is also satisfied in many instances by metonymous procedures which achieve the same end by displaying a part of science as if it were the whole, that is, by describing a particular pattern of inquiry and omitting mention of others.

Metonymous formulations have the same limitation of usefulness to a liberal program as do highly general formulations: they do not suffice to make each inquiry intelligible in itself and capable of relation to other investigations. Metonymous constructions may, in fact, become more confusing than highly general constructions. The latter, though they fail to exhibit sufficient detail in a given example of research to permit its comprehension and evaluation, at least sketch a few broad lines which can be discerned in most papers. Metonymous constructions, on the other hand, may fail to fit (except by analogy) researches employing patterns of inquiry other than the one expounded.

At the other extreme from the general or metonymous narration of the nature of inquiry is the mode of presentation, with its attendant vices, which characterized the initial year of the 1943 science program. Then, as previously mentioned, formulation of the nature of inquiry in any terms whatever was eschewed. Inquiry was represented by individual researches examined in highly particular fashion; similarities and differences were sought, and thereby rough groupings of papers were noted; but the characteristics which bound one group of papers together as examples of inquiry and which separated that group from another were not distinguished and named, nor were the characteristics common to all the papers as examples of inquiry given adequate attention.

With such a procedure, the species of scientific inquiry become too numerous to function effectively as instruments of analysis; and the failure to establish them as species of a common genus by showing them as the varied application of common principles to a variety of problems leads to a failure to impart the notion of truth-seeking as such.

The failure to impart the notion of truth-seeking as such and a contrary failure in the case of general or metonymous narrations must be taken as representative of the inadequacies in practice of these ways of conceiving inquiry. General and metonymous narratives tend to lump all scientific conclusions together. Criteria of greater and lesser validity (as distinguished from true versus false) are not stated or applied. In consequence, all conclusions of science are understood as equally valid, and the level of validity is taken as absolute or very high. This view is likely to occur for psychological reasons, even if avoided in actual statement, for the lumping of all conclusions together at one level of validity requires that they all be accepted or rejected together. A total rejection is not likely. Total acceptance of conclusions requires acceptance of the allegedly common route by which they are reached. And the route itself has the same uniform validity conferred upon it that was attributed to the conclusions. Moreover, in the absence of a concrete study of varying scientific procedures and a consequent awareness of the complexity of the notion of validity, still a third mistaken factor colors the student's view of science: its conclusions are taken as all equally literal. The gram, the diameter of the earth, force in the Newtonian equation, the gene of Mendelian theory, the unseen x-tron of the latest mathematical exploration of atomic theory, and the automobile parked at the curb are assumed to have the same existential standing. That such a view leads to wild misunderstanding and confusion as to the meaning of conclusive statements in science goes without saying. The notion of science as a large body of equally true literal statements about nature, all arrived at by a common route, leads to a conception of problems and the difficulty of problem-solving equally wide of the mark. A problem appears to be something objectively given; the data seem to be waiting only to be recorded; and the solution seems to be something that supervenes automatically with the recording of the last datum gathered.

This simple and naïve empiricism finds its contrary error in the consequences of wholly individualistic treatment of inquiry. Many routes are seen to lead to as many conclusions, often mutually exclusive in their expression, yet, each in its own way, equally valid. The variety of procedures suggests the absence of canons of better and worse procedures. The variety of conclusions suggests the absence of canons of better and worse conclusions. Such a treatment often implants a conventionalistic view of scientific knowledge. Conclusions are conceived as mere plausible accounts stemming from the researcher's habitual choice of principles. Where the general narrative tends to implant naïve literalism, individualistic treatment tends to implant fictionalism —the notion that scientific conclusions are wholly metaphorical and to be judged only in terms of aesthetico-logical standards of unity, coherence, and economy. They come to be treated as useful myths among which choice is a matter only of custom and convenience. Problems appear to be merely invented, and data the product of an arbitrary choice.

Each of these approaches—the individualistic and the highly general—derives its prime weakness through ignoring the strength of the contrary view. The individualistic view tends to ignore the solid, factual basis of scientific knowledge. The general narrative ignores the constructive or inventive aspect of scientific theories and conclusions. A sounder view would incorporate and relate both. The science program attempts such an incorporation and relation of factual and ideational factors, both in its theory and in its practice. It does so by taking "problem" as a starting point rather than "data" or "conclusion." From "problem" it is possible to work in two directions. On the one hand, a problem can be seen in relation to nature as exhibited through other problems and thus be understood as an abstraction from the real and total situation with which nature confronts us. On the other hand, it can be seen as a statement which gives direction to inquiry and thus be understood as a meaningful question to which meaningful and valid answers can be given. From the first point of view, the incompleteness of scientific knowledge at any given moment and the significance of the variety of answers which it appears to give to a single question can be understood without recourse to conventionalism. They are seen as the consequence of the fact that problems are partial and abstract aspects of a larger complex of related matters. They are seen as consequences of a process by which more and more of the total situation called "nature" is encompassed and comprehended because the answers to partial problems lead to larger problems and their resolutions, which encompass more of the whole.

From the second point of view the validity of the knowledge of science at any given moment and the effectiveness of its answers as instruments for the control of nature can be understood without recourse to naïve literalism. They are seen as warranted answers to the questions-as-stated and also as milestones on the march of knowledge, since the amount of truth which they contain points to the knowledge which they do not contain and thereby they function as the germs of problems yet to come. By recognizing both the incompleteness of problems-as-formulated and the validity of solutions to such problems, a view of science is obtained in which its ongoing character, its continuing reconstruction of knowledge, and the practical truth of its views at a given moment in time are seen as faces of the same coin.

In practice, our treatment of instances of research follows this theoretical view. The student is concerned, first, with the problem stated, its relation to other problems, and, through these, its relations to nature. He then turns to the problem as relating to its resolution: he is concerned with matters of evidence, interpretation, and application. As experience with a variety of papers accumulates, he adds a concern for the modalities and the nature of inquiry itself: questions of types of problems and solutions and the canons of sound inquiry are raised and treated.

By thus distinguishing, but connecting, discipline and field, method and content, fact and idea, the science program attempts to determine its own duties, without neglecting the duties it shares with other programs of the curriculum, and to discharge these duties without doctrinaire adhesion to incomplete and warring dogmas. It can leave artistic analysis to the humanities and doctrines of knowledge and of being to philosophy, where these can be treated with wisdom and experience; it can concern itself with science; yet its treatment of science can be both sensitive and philosophical, without ceasing to be scientific. It is enabled to impart some knowledge of the world and yet construct a foundation for critical understanding of the limitations of human knowledge, without degrading the student to a parrot, on the one hand, or a snob, on the other. It can examine the contribution to science of both the eye and the human intellect without denigrating knowledge either to a catalogue or to a myth. Its attempt to do these things and its continuing effort to educate itself, to enlarge its competence for its task, and to subject its principles to continuing re-examination are the bases for calling it a *liberal* program in the sciences.

LABORATORY IN THE THREE-YEAR PROGRAM

While classwork in the natural sciences deals with reports of scientific investigation, the activities of the laboratory constitute attempts to gain knowledge of natural phenomena by actual observation and experimentation. The problems are selected and their investigation is planned to develop in students some understanding of the essential nature of experimental investigation and its relation to theoretical knowledge rather than to develop experimental skills. A concomitant objective is familiarity with the phenomena and experimental methods dealt with in the readings. Each instructor in the course either teaches or has taught laboratory sections, so that laboratory activities are frequent topics of class discussion and, conversely, the readings are frequently used in laboratory discussions and reports.

The methods used in the laboratory are revealed in part by descriptions of some specific problems in the account that follows. It should be noted, however, that any experiment is far too complex for exhaustive study. Thus only one or two aspects of experimental investigation are emphasized in each problem. By using different types of problems and emphasizing a different aspect each time, quite a number of aspects can be considered in the course of a year.

What follows is the first instruction sheet, "Laboratory Problem I," issued to the student.

THE INVESTIGATION OF FLOATING AND SINKING

The study of this Problem is to culminate in a paper which will be due at the third meeting of your laboratory section unless otherwise arranged by your instructor. The paper is to be based on your study of Archimedes treatise, "On Floating Bodies," and your experiences and results in the laboratory. Further directions are given below.

Approximately the first half of the first laboratory class meeting (about 50 minutes) will be allowed for planning. The remainder of the first meeting and all of the second meeting will be available for carrying out the laboratory tests. The paper is then to be written outside of class. You should begin active preparation for writing it immediately after the first laboratory meeting.

Laboratory Instructions. A. Examine with care the meaning of the two propositions below, from the treatise, "On Floating Bodies."

"Proposition 5. Any solid lighter than a fluid will, if placed in the fluid, be so far immersed that the weight of the solid will be equal to the weight of the fluid displaced."

"Proposition 7. A solid heavier than a fluid will, if placed in it, descend to the bottom of the fluid, and the solid will, when weighed in the fluid, be lighter than its true weight by the weight of the fluid displaced."

B. Devise a laboratory procedure for testing the truth of one of the two propositions. State *in writing and in considerable detail* how you will make the tests; i.e., state what articles and materials you will use, what you will do with these things, what data you will use, what you will do with the data. You may use any of the types of apparatus displayed in the laboratory or other simple equipment available in the supply room.

Submit your written plan to the instructor as early in the period as is practical. He will then arrange for you to work with some other student who chose the same proposition. With your partner, modify your plans as necessary.

C. Carry out the tests according to your modified plans. While you are manipulating your materials and making your observations, pay especial attention to all types of circumstances which cause difficulties and interfere with your getting what you might call "correct" results. Consider whether those circumstances can be eliminated. Repeat and improve your "tests" as far as possible.

If you need to weigh materials, be sure that you proceed correctly. The instructor will be glad to provide instruction in the use of balances and the metric system of weights. Experience has shown that instruction is necessary to avoid ridiculous errors in procedure with the type of balance that has two suspended pans.

A second laboratory problem is concerned with the pendulum. Study of this problem is initiated before students find, in *Two New Sciences*, how Galileo uses the pendulum to obtain knowledge about free fall, inclined planes, and even sound and music. After a very brief introductory discussion designed to stimulate questions, students experiment for a half-hour or more with a variety of pendulums, following which they are called together to report tentative answers to several of their questions.

The question, "How shall we achieve knowledge of the pendulum?" is then considered. The notion of variables and relations between variables has arisen in the preliminary studies and now becomes explicit. Students make up a list of observable variables inherent in the pendulum and select pairs for study of possible relations between them.

Other questions intrude at once. How shall period be measured? What is the length of a pendulum? Is it the distance from point of support to the top of the bob, bottom of the bob, or to some intermediate point? What experimental considerations might be of assistance in making a choice? If none, what about theoretical considerations? Is the choice arbitrary? Etc. After these matters are disposed of to the satisfaction of the class and the instructor, data are collected for a series of pendulums according to the operational definitions agreed on.

The data collected by the different teams are then given to two or three committees for collation before the next laboratory period. With the data presented by the different committees on the blackboard, the students and instructor consider how to use the data to find what relation, if any, exists between length and period. What period shall be selected for a pendulum of a given length? Do all pendulums of the same length have the same period? If so, what is the cause of the discrepancies that appear in the data? Invariably, an average of the values for a given length is proposed. But the instructor raises the question of which average should be used, the arithmetic average, the median, or the mode. The second and third of these measures are new to most students. After some discussion the choice as to which, if any, he will use is left to the individual. Next is the problem of how a mathematical relationship is evolved from data. Various algebraic and graphical devices are presented and discussed. The students leave with the assignment: "Find any relation that exists in the data and present evidence for it at the next meeting."

The qualitative and quantitative solutions proposed by the students are compared and criticized. Proposals for next steps in the experimental testing of their theories are elicited. Then each student is asked to write a paper which reports and justifies his solution of the problem and points out what other aspects of the pendulum need to be studied to obtain "complete" knowledge of the phenomenon. In each class a number of students will return to the laboratory to spend extra time checking their data and testing their theories.

QUERIES AND PROBLEMS IN THE THREE-YEAR PROGRAM

On the pages following are reproduced some sample "query-sheets" issued to students—sheets containing brief introductory guides to the readings, in addition to lists of questions and problems.

Of the numbered questions included in the specimens reproduced, the following are illustrative of questions concerning the meaning of a scientific paper. Such questions, which are numerous in the first weeks of the course, become progressively fewer (because less necessary) as time goes on:

Archimedes 1, 3, 7, 11
Galileo (First Day) 1, 2, 5, 12, 64
Galileo (Third Day) 78, 80

The following are illustrative of questions bearing on the applications of the conclusions of a paper. Such questions as these, which are the commonplaces of science instruction, continue throughout the program:

Archimedes 13
Galileo (Third Day) 83, 84, 102–4, 107, 109

The following are illustrative of questions bearing upon the choice of data and methods of their interpretation in relation to the meaning and validity of conclusions:

Archimedes 2, 5, 6
Galileo (First Day) 6, 57, 58
Galileo (Third Day) 77, 81, 82, 85, 87, 88, 90, 108

The following are illustrative of questions bearing upon the nature of scientific inquiry in general and upon different species of inquiry:

Archimedes 2, 8, 9, 15
Galileo (First Day) 2, 3, 5, 6, 57, 58
Galileo (Third Day) 77, 82, 85, 87, 88, 90, 108

ARCHIMEDES, *On Floating Bodies*

In this paper consider content and method as equally important. On the side of method, reading, discussion, and laboratory should culminate in your ability to apply the terms "theory," "empirical generalization," and "datum" to certain aspects of the paper or of the laboratory connected with it. At the conclusion of discussions and laboratory work, you should be able to define those words tentatively, discuss their interconnections, the usefulness of each, the difficulties which tend to produce characteristic imperfections in "theories" and empirical generalizations.

1. The postulate in this paper is divided into two parts. Distinguish them in terms of (1) the way parts-of-fluid are related, and (2) their treatment of the "thrusts" within a fluid.

2. (a) Are there really parts in a fluid as indicated in the postulate? (b) What advantage does Archimedes gain by thinking of parts of a fluid?

3. What, if anything, in the paper, *On the Equilibrium of Planes*, is analogous to the part of the postulate that reads, "that part which is thrust the less is driven along by that part which is thrust the more"?

5. In the proof of Proposition 2 what relation is assumed to exist between the amount of compression and the quantity of fluid that causes the compression? What must then be assumed about the nature of a fluid?

6. What relation does Proposition 1 bear to the postulate and to the later propositions?

7. Could the statement of Propositions 3–7 be improved by the use of modern terminology? If so, how would you state them? (What modern term indicates the relation between size and weight?)

8. How do you think Propositions 3, 4, 5, and 7 of this paper were originally arrived at? The postulate?

9. In view of your laboratory experiences would you prefer to say that the propositions named in Query 1 are "facts" or "generalizations"? Why?

11. In the figure for Proposition 3, is the portion *STUV* equal and similar to *BGHC* with respect to weight? to volume? to material?

13. If Propositions 3 and 4 are true, how is it possible that a ship made of steel, which is heavier volume for volume than water, carrying a cargo of materials also heavier than water, can float?

15. If Propositions 3–7 be known on an experimental basis, what are the possible advantages of proceeding as Archimedes did?

GALILEO, *Two New Sciences*, FIRST DAY

The First Day of *Two New Sciences* is one of the few readings in which the *apparent* subject matter (breakage) is less important than the problems of defining and creating a science which are illustrated step-by-step. Consider the First Day as unfolding the problems (and certain *tentative* solutions of them) which confronted a scientist in his attempt to construct a certain kind of theoretical science about a physical subject matter. Your principal problem of comprehension will be to discover the connections at the level of method which relate successive discussions in the dialogue on apparently diverse topics.

1. What significant distinctions are drawn in the first paragraph?

2. Does the first paragraph give any evidence of Galileo's opinion as to what constitutes science? If so, identify the evidence.

3. From the first few paragraphs what human faculty (or faculties) does Galileo seem to think necessary for the attainment of scientific knowledge? For the attainment of artisans' knowledge?

5. On pages 2 and 3 geometry is mentioned repeatedly. Does the term

have the same meaning in each case? Why is there sometimes agreement with geometry and sometimes not?

6. By what method does Galileo indicate that he will investigate the problem he sets himself? What are the conditions which must be imposed on the subject matter in order for this method to be applicable to the problem?

12. Galileo attempts to explain the coherence of the polished plates by "abhorrence of a vacuum." List the objections to this explanation raised in the dialogue.

57. What is Galileo's criterion for the truth or falsity of a scientific theory, as seen from the statement on page 73: "Employing this principle we shall, I believe, find a much closer agreement of experiment with our computation than with that of Aristotle"?

58. What are the variables which Galileo examines in attempting to formulate the laws of falling bodies? What does Galileo conclude to be the ideal situation with which to compare all others?

64. Draw curves illustrating the following relations:
    a) velocity vs. time for a body falling in a vacuum.
    b) velocity vs. time for a body falling in a medium of finite density, but considering only the effect of buoyance.
    c) velocity vs. time describing real fall of body in a medium. Divide this curve into (approximately) 3 parts and discuss the cause of the differences.
    d) acceleration vs. time for a body falling in a vacuum. (Acceleration is the modern term for increment of velocity per interval of time. See page 71.)
    e) acceleration vs. time for a body falling in a medium of finite density, but considering only the effect of buoyance.
    f) acceleration vs. time describing real fall of body in a medium.

GALILEO, *Two New Sciences*, THIRD DAY

The Third Day of Galileo's *Two New Sciences* and the material on falling bodies in the last pages of the First Day are important for their content concerning the physical world and as exemplars of scientific inquiry. Read closely from both these points of view.

77. Whenever a particle is moving uniformly, equal distances are traversed during any equal intervals of time. The equal distances may be measured by using the same yardstick. What must be assumed about the yardstick before one can declare that the distances are equal? How can one measure equal time intervals?

NOTE: In all algebraic equations requested below employ the following symbols for the quantities indicated:

s—distance
t—time
v—velocity
a—"acceleration," or increment of velocity per unit of time

78. Write an equation showing the relationship between uniform velocity, distance traversed, and time.

80. Write in algebraic form axioms I-IV on uniform motion.

81. *a*) Write the theorems on uniform motion in the form of proportions. Then solve each proportion for its second term.

    b) From what single algebraic equation may all of the theorems be derived?

    c) In Galileo's treatment of uniform motion what place does this single equation hold?

82. Is it possible to determine experimentally that a given motion in nature is uniform, as Galileo defines "uniform motion"? That a given motion is *not* uniform? Explain.

83. If it takes two hours for a boat to travel 42 nautical miles, how long will it take the boat to travel 63 nautical miles farther, proceeding at the same speed?

84. Two trackmen, Smith and Jones, are running at constant speeds, Smith at 18 feet per second and Jones at 15 feet per second. Two seconds after Smith passes Jones, how far will Smith be ahead of Jones? How long will it be after Smith passes Jones that Smith will be 15 yards ahead of Jones?

85. *a*) Select from the Third Day a series of quotations which indicate the aim of Galileo's second "New Science."

    b) Write a description of this method of obtaining knowledge about the natural world. Refer to the list of methods on page 1 of the introduction to these queries: which of them are represented in Galileo, the Third Day? which one is dominant in it?

    c) Compare the science of the Third Day with that of the First Day.

87. In what sense must Galileo "verify" his definition of uniformly accelerated motion? Compare this definition with Archimedes' postulate on floating bodies with respect to the possibility of direct experimental verification.

88. How does Galileo propose to "verify" his definition of uniformly accelerated motion, in the sense referred to in question 87?

90. For what experiment with inclined planes does Galileo substitute the pendulum experiment, pages 163–165? Why would the experiment with inclined planes be unsatisfactory?

102. A body, starting from rest, is uniformly accelerated. In three seconds after starting, it travels 27 feet; how far will it travel in eight seconds after starting? (Ans: 192 feet.)

103. An automobile starting from rest with uniform acceleration attains a speed of 10 feet per second after it has traveled 30 feet. How long was required to travel the 30 feet? What is the automobile's acceleration? (Ans: 6 sec; 5/3 ft/sec^2)

104. The speed of a uniformly accelerated body is increased from 8 to 18 feet per second in 8 seconds. What is the body's acceleration? How far does the body travel in the 8 seconds? (Ans: 1.25 ft/sec²; 104 ft)

107. An object slides 10 feet from its position of rest on an inclined plane in one second. What is the object's acceleration? How far will the object have traveled from its position of rest when it attains a speed of 60 feet per second?

108. List at least five points in Galileo's experiments of measuring the time of descent of a ball on an inclined plane at which errors of measurement could enter. Put a plus (+) mark after each error which would be likely to give too long a time for descent, a minus (−) mark before each error which would be likely to give too short a time for descent, and a zero (0) mark before each error of the sort that the average result of a large number of repetitions of the experiment would be more accurate than the result of a single performance of the experiment. Is it likely that the result would be greatly affected by these errors?

109. Two inclined planes, A and B, have the same height. A is 15 feet long; B is 9 feet long. If it takes an object 10 seconds to slide all the way down A, starting from rest, how long will it take the same object to slide down B? What is the velocity of the object when it reaches the lower end of either plane? (Neglect friction.)

II

BIOLOGICAL SCIENCES

MERLE C. COULTER*

THE INTRODUCTORY general course, Biological Sciences, is the only beginning biology course normally taken by students who enter the College after graduation from conventional high schools. It is therefore designed to serve the interests of both the prospective nonbiology majors and the prospective biology majors. Since the former group is in the majority (roughly 75 per cent), it is the primary obligation of the course to provide such biological training as is appropriate to general education. Under this limitation, the course also attempts to provide a substantial

* With the assistance of Dorothea Miller, Elizabeth Beeman, and Beatrice Mintz.

biological foundation for the smaller (25 per cent) group of students who plan to continue further in biology.

The guiding objectives of the course, Biological Sciences, have been:

1. To develop in the student an understanding of, a respect for, and some facility in the application of the clear and unbiased method of thinking that characterizes, or should characterize, workers in the field of natural sciences. For several years the course presented the "scientific method" in terms of a battery of admittedly formalized routines. With a growing feeling on the part of the staff that these routines do not conform closely enough with actual experimental practice, the procedures have been largely discarded. This year we have deformalized the presentation and have substituted a consideration of how representative problems in biology have been approached experimentally, how such experiments are conducted, and what evidence is required for the drawing of valid conclusions. In so far as possible, we have used experiments bearing upon the factual material covered in the course, particularly from the fields of plant and animal physiology and experimental embryology. We have hoped in this way to give the students an acquaintance with the methods used by the biologist and an appreciation of careful investigation and critical thinking. The staff hopes that students will apply their habits of thinking critically about classroom biological problems to the more general problems of everyday living.

2. To familiarize the student with biological facts and principles and to cultivate an intelligent understanding of biological problems with which he will be faced. The course makes no direct attempt to cover "practical" biology, but, wherever possible, practical illustrations are used to support the principles that are being presented.

3. To develop in the student an appreciation and some understanding of the grand machinery of the organic world.

As a fourth possible objective the staff believes that familiarity with biological objects and processes will almost certainly result in an aesthetic appreciation of the biological world.

The course serves these several objectives fairly continuously through the entire year, the actual organization being in terms of subject matter, as described below.

The Autumn Quarter opens with a consideration of some physiological processes (diffusion, osmosis, respiration) common to all organisms. The phylogeny of the major groups of plants is treated partially in the light of evolutionary trends which have contributed to the efficiency of these processes. In addition, selected problems in plant physiology, including photosynthesis, movement of materials, mineral nutrition, and growth and development, are considered. The major groups in the animal kingdom are studied in phylogenetic sequence, culminating in the evolution of man. This part of the course also considers how organisms adapt to and interact with one another and with the whole inanimate world to form groups and societies.

The Winter Quarter offers an introduction to regulatory mechanisms in the animal body. Major emphasis is placed on human physiology, with frequent comparisons to the physiology of other organisms and frequent references to the phylogenetic development of structure and processes considered in the previous quarter.

The Spring Quarter considers embryology, genetics, and evolution, and unlearned and learned behavior.

The course is scheduled on the basis of two lectures and two discussion section meetings a week. The lectures are given by about twenty-five different guest lecturers, most of whom are specialists from the various departments of the Division of the Biological Sciences.

Discussion sections of twenty-five to thirty students continue through the year under the guidance of the same instructors. It is this corps of instructors that constitutes the permanent staff of the course. Ordinarily operating under a chairman, this staff meets frequently to plan course policy and administrative details, revises the *Syllabus* and *Thought Question Booklet*, prepares numerous short and long practice tests, and assists the course examiner in the preparation of the comprehensive examination.

The text materials used in the course are: the *Syllabus*, the *Syllabus Supplement*, the *Thought Question Booklet*, and a rental set of textbooks.

The *Syllabus* outlines the subject matter, makes citations of "indispensable" readings, as well as optional readings, presents lists of questions by which the student can test his mastery of the readings, and supplements the readings by additional prose passages. The indispensable readings are selections from a rental set of nine books and reprints of several original papers that the student holds through the year. These books are of diverse origin, some having been produced locally to fit the needs of the course. The *Syllabus Supplement* is a collection of a number of original papers covering material which is not available in textbooks. Some of these papers are included in the indispensable readings, others are optional reading.

At the outset we recognized the necessity of reducing the amount of technical terminology and descriptive detail that is conventionally presented in introductory biology courses. Since the students are not burdened with the task of memorizing long lists of terms and anatomical details, more of their time and effort can be used for adequate mastery of the more important principles, theories, and methods of analysis of science. For example, in the presentation of the phylogeny of plant and animal groups, a few typical representatives of the major groups are considered, with the emphasis on how each has progressed in "solving the problems" of efficient living. Throughout the course the broad outlines appear more clearly than when cluttered with a bewildering array of details.

One of our educational experiments that has worked out well has involved the use of the *Thought Question Booklet*. This is a collection of provocative questions which go beyond the factual material presented in the course and require the application of facts, theories, and thought-processes already at the disposal of the students. Many of the questions were included because individual instructors had found them effective in stimulating discussion in sections. The questions are arranged to follow the subject matter of the course. We believe that their use reinforces the materials and facilitates transfer by pointing out the applicability of biological facts and principles to other fields and to everyday experience. Much of our discussion section time, as well as large fractions of our various tests and the comprehensive examination itself, is now devoted to the types of problems that are suggested in this booklet. The students react well to this procedure and have repeatedly testified that it makes the course more stimulating.

From the first, most of the members of the permanent staff have felt that the course should be reinforced by an appropriate program of individual laboratory. To date, physical and financial limitations have made this impossible, since in some years the course has been taken by more than nine hundred students.

After some years of experience with the course, the instructor usually inclines to the belief that the lack of individual laboratory work is less deplorable than he had felt at the outset. One reason for this qualification of his opinion is that the course does provide some measure of the laboratory type of experience. A substantial battery of exhibits and demonstrations is presented at frequent intervals in one of our biology laboratories. A trip through one of these exhibits occupies from thirty minutes to over an hour, depending on the nature of the exhibit and the intellectual curiosity of the student. One exhibit at the "Microworld" of the Museum of Science and Industry presents a variety of living invertebrates by microprojection. A guided tour through the exhibits of various classes of vertebrates at the Chicago Natural History Museum is also included in the course. In addition, our course has prepared an excellent set of eleven educational sound films which provide good demonstrations of laboratory procedures in a manner directly related to the other activities of the course.

During the year 1949–50, one pilot section of an individual laboratory program has been offered to twenty-four students. The laboratory has been "experimental," both in respect to the problem approach and in the opportunity to evaluate the effectiveness of such laboratory experience, in case it should eventually become feasible to include all the students. The students were chosen on the basis of interest, an effort being made to select a cross-section with respect to ability and aptitude (excluding the lowest group). The students received no credit and paid no tuition; the only promise of reward was in terms of satisfaction. The subject matter of the laboratory paralleled, to some degree, that of the course; but this was not a major policy, and the laboratory organization departed from the original sequence whenever it seemed advisable. Nor did we guarantee any degree of course coverage. The laboratory planning committee attempted only to present related problems for experimental solution.

The laboratory was organized around three major units, each occupying one quarter of the year: I, dynamics of protoplasm, II, dynamics of the organism, III, dynamics of the species. Within each large unit, representative problems were considered. Committees of from four to twelve students worked on related aspects of a problem, with a spokesman from each committee reporting to the entire group during a two-hour discussion period at the conclusion of each problem. A sample problem from the unit on the dynamics of protoplasm will illustrate the approach: "How does protoplasm react to changes in the environment?" Some of the topics considered by committees were: How do plants react to light and to gravity, and what is the mechanism underlying these responses? How do single-celled organisms respond to various stimuli? Is it possible to simulate any of the reactive, functional, or structural features of living protoplasm by preparing nonliving physical and chemical models?

The other large problems relating to the dynamics of protoplasm were "How does living protoplasm obtain and utilize food?" and "How does protoplasm reproduce, grow, and develop?"

Although it is too early to evaluate the contribution of the laboratory, we do have some impressions. Early in the year we realized that we had been too ambitious (1) in attempting too many concurrent problems, which resulted in some physical confusion during the laboratory and insufficient time for adequate discussion, and (2) in failing to appreciate the inexperience of the students and therefore gauging the procedures at too high a level, both in time requirements and in demand for technical skill. Consequently, the number and complexity of procedures were reduced. With this simplification, the students showed a better grasp of the problems and had more opportunity to relate their results to the major problem.

A second difficulty has arisen in regard to the extent to which the students can actually be left to their own devices for the solution of a problem. We found it expedient to compromise somewhat with our original aim of fairly complete freedom. Since the students are not familiar with the techniques available for the elucidation of a particular problem, we considered it advisable to supply some guidance on the technical level. Some of the students have requested more explicit guidance, others more complete freedom; many have expressed satisfaction with the middle course which we followed.

We believe that such a problem laboratory can make a real contribution to the course. Most of the students who are participating feel that it has increased their appreciation of how organisms function and of how experimental evidence is obtained and interpreted. This trial laboratory has proved educational to the staff as well as to the students; the experience should enable us to offer a more effective program in the future.

It is difficult to judge, in any very objective terms, the success that the course may have had during its nineteen years of existence in serving the educational needs of the two groups of students for whom it is intended: the prospective nonbiologists and the prospective biologists. A large number of students have testified—orally, on several printed questionnaires, and in unsolicited letters—that the course had made an attractive and effective contribution to general education. A number of teachers of advanced biology courses have asserted that students are better prepared for their work by Biological Sciences than by most other introductory courses. While conscious of such testimonials, the staff of Biological Sciences has continued to seek ways of making the course more effective.

Reading Lists

I. THE THREE-YEAR PROGRAM

PHYSICAL SCIENCES COMPONENT

MATTER: ITS NATURE, TRANSFORMATIONS, AND CLASSIFICATION

ARCHIMEDES "On the Equilibrium of Planes" and "On Floating Bodies," in *The Works of Archimedes*, ed. T. L. Heath (Cambridge: Cambridge University Press, 1897), Book i, pp. 189–96, 253–59.

GALILEI, GALILEO, *Dialogues concerning Two New Sciences* (Evanston and Chicago: Northwestern University, 1946), selections from First Day. Further selections from First Day and Third Day are used in connection with the topic "Motions and Interactions of Bodies."

LAVOISIER, ANTOINE, *Elements of Chemistry*, trans. Robert Kerr (Ann Arbor, Mich.: Edwards Bros., Inc., 1940), selections from Part I.

DALTON, JOHN, *A New System of Chemical Philosophy* (London and Manchester: R. Bickerstaff, 1808, 1810), selections from Part I, chap. ii; Part II, chaps. iv and v.

GAY-LUSSAC, JOSEPH-LOUIS, "Memoir on the Combination of Gaseous Substances with Each Other," in *Foundations of the Molecular Theory* ("Alembic Club Reprints," No. 4 [Edinburgh: Alembic Club; Chicago: University of Chicago Press, 1902]), pp. 8–24.

AVOGADRO, AMADEO, "Essay on a Manner of Determining the Relative Masses of the Elementary Molecules of Bodies, and the Proportions in Which They Enter into These Compounds," in *Foundations of the Molecular Theory* ("Alembic Club Reprints," No. 4 [Edinburgh: Alembic Club; Chicago: University of Chicago Press, 1902]), pp. 28–51.

CANNIZZARO, STANISLAO, *Sketch of a Course of Chemical Philosophy: Letter of Professor Stanislao Cannizzaro to Professor S. DeLuca* ("Alembic Club Reprints," No. 18 [Edinburgh: Alembic Club; Chicago: University of Chicago Press, 1911]), pp. 321–66.

MENDELEEV, DMITRI I., "The Relation between the Properties of Elements and Their Atomic Weights," trans. from *Die Beziehungen zwischen den Eigenschaften der Elemente und ihren Atomgewichten* ("Klassiker der exakten Wissenschaften," No. 68 [Leipzig: Wilhelm Engelmann, 1895]), pp. 20–40.

BERTHOLLET, CLAUDE, *An Essay on Chemical Statics*, Vol. I, trans. B. Lambert (London: J. Mawman, 1804), and *Researches into the Laws of Chemical Affinity*, trans. M. Farrell (Baltimore: P. H. Nicklin, 1809), selections.

MOTIONS AND INTERACTIONS OF BODIES

PTOLEMY, CLAUDIUS *The Almagest* i. 1–8, trans. Theodore Ashford and Thornton Page, from *Composition mathématique de Claude Ptolémée*, trans. Halma and Delambre (Paris: H. Grand, 1813).

COPERNICUS, NICHOLAS, "De revolutionibus," in *A Treasury of Science*, ed. Harlow Shapley, Samuel Rapport, and Helen Wright (New York: Harper & Bros., 1943), pp. 54–57.

KEPLER, JOHN, *Epitome of Copernican Astronomy*, Books iv and v, trans. Charles Glenn Wallis (Annapolis: St. John's Bookstore, 1939), selections.

HUYGENS, CHRISTIAN, "On the Movement of Bodies through Impact," trans. Bert Frank Hoselitz, from *Über die Bewegung der Körper durch den Stoss über die Centrifugalkraft*, ed. F. Hausdorff ("Klassiker der exakten Wissenschaften," No. 138 [Leipzig: Wilhelm Engelmann, 1903]), pp. 1–27.

NEWTON, ISAAC, *The Mathematical Principles of Natural Philosophy*, trans. Andrew Motte (New York: Daniel Adee, 1846), pp. 73–94, 383–402.

MAYER, JULIUS R., "The Forces of Inorganic Nature," in *Correlation and Conservation of Forces*, ed. E. L. Youmans (New York: D. Appleton & Co., 1865), pp. 251–58.

CLAUSIUS, RUDOLPH, "On the Nature of the Motion Which We Call Heat," *London, Edinburgh, and Dublin Philosophical Magazine*, Ser. 4, XIV (1857), 108–26.

EINSTEIN, ALBERT, *Relativity: The Special and General Theory*, trans. R. W. Lawson (New York: Hartsdale House, 1947), pp. 1–51.

NATURE OF LIGHT AND THE STRUCTURE OF ATOMS

NEWTON, ISAAC, "Opticks," in *Opticks, or a Treatise of the Reflections, Refractions, Inflections and Colours of Light* (New York: McGraw-Hill Book Co., Inc., 1931), pp. 1–20.

———, "The Motion of Very Small Bodies," adapted from *The Mathematical Principles of Natural Philosophy*, trans. Andrew Motte (New York: Daniel Adee, 1846), pp. 243–48.

———, "On Colour and Refrangibility," in *Physics: the Pioneer Science*, ed. L. W. Taylor (New York: Houghton Mifflin Co., 1941), pp. 474–77.

HUYGENS, CHRISTIAN, *Treatise on Light*, trans. Silvanus P. Thomson (Chicago: University of Chicago Press, 1945), pp. 1–45.

YOUNG, THOMAS, "Experiments and Calculations Relative to Physical Optics," *Philosophical Transactions of the Royal Society of London*, XCIV (1804), 1–6, 11–13, 15–16.

FRAUNHOFER, JOSEPH VON, *Prismatic and Diffraction Spectra: Memoirs by Joseph Von Fraunhofer*, trans. and ed. J. S. Ames ("Scientific Memoirs," ed. J. S. Ames [New York: Harper & Bros., 1898]).

KIRCHHOFF, GUSTAV ROBERT, and BUNSEN, ROBERT, "Chemical Analysis by Spectral Observations," in *The Laws of Radiation and Absorption*, ed. D. B. Brace ("Scientific Memoirs," ed. J. S. Ames [New York: American Book Co., 1901], No. 15), pp. 101–25.

BALMER, JOHANN JAKOB, "The Hydrogen Spectral Series," in *A Source Book in Physics*, ed. William Francis Magie ("Source Books in the History of the Sciences," ed. Gregory D. Walcott [New York: McGraw-Hill Book Co., Inc., 1935]), pp. 360–65.

THOMSON, J. J., "Cathode Rays," *London, Edinburgh, and Dublin Philosophical Magazine and Journal of Science*, Ser. 5, XLIV (1897), 293–316.

BOHR, NIELS, "The Quantum Theory of the Line Spectrum of Hydrogen," selections from "On the Hydrogen Spectrum," in *On the Quantum Theory of Line-Spectra* (Copenhagen: Andr. Fred. Host & Son, 1918), pp. 37–100, and from "On the Spectrum of Hydrogen," in *The Theory of Spectra and Atomic Constitution* (Cambridge: Cambridge University Press, 1922), pp. 1–19.

BIOLOGICAL SCIENCES COMPONENT

THE TOTAL ORGANISM: ANATOMY AND PHYSIOLOGY

FROHSE, FRANZ; BRÖDEL, MAX; and SCHLOSSBERG, LEON, *Atlas of Human Anatomy*, explanatory text by Jesse Feiring Williams (New York: Barnes & Noble, Inc., 1935).

HARVEY, WILLIAM, *Exercitatio anatomica de motu cordis et sanguinis in animalibus*, trans., with annotations, Chauncey D. Leake (Springfield, Ill., and Baltimore: Charles C. Thomas, 1928).

GERARD, RALPH W., *The Body Functions* (New York: John Wiley & Sons, Inc., 1941).

KROGH, AUGUST, *The Anatomy and Physiology of Capillaries* (New Haven: Yale University Press, 1929), pp. 1–4, 23–31, 90–93, 266–72, 293–314.

———, "The Supply of Oxygen to the Tissues and the Regulation of the Capillary Circulation," *Journal of Physiology*, LII (1918–19), 458–65, 469–70, 471–73.

HALDANE, JOHN SCOTT, *Organism and Environment as Illustrated by the Physiology of Breathing* (New Haven: Yale University Press, 1917), pp. 51–59, 89–119.

PROUT, WILLIAM, *On the Nature and Treatment of Stomach and Urinary Diseases* (London: John Churchill, 1840), pp. 26–41.

BERNARD, CLAUDE, "Lectures on Diabetes and Animal Glycogenesis," trans. and abridged from *Leçons sur le diabète et la glycogénèse animale* (Paris: Baillière, 1877), pp. 55–86, 262–92, 412–17.

OPIE, EUGENE L., *Disease of the Pancreas: Its Cause and Nature* (Philadelphia and London: J. B. Lippincott Co., 1903), pp. 215–29.

MERING, J. VON, and MINKOWSKI, O., "Diabetes Mellitus Following Extirpation of the Pancreas," trans. from "Diabetes mellitus nach Pankreasexstirpation," *Archiv für experimentelle Pathologie und Pharmakologie*, XXVI (1890), 371–87.

LAGUESSE, W. E., "On the Development of the Islets of Langerhans in the Pancreas," trans. from "Sur la formation des îlots de Langerhans dans le pancréas," *Comptes-rendus hebdomadaires des séances et mémoires de la Société de Biologie*, XLV (1893), 819–20.

BANTING, F. G., and BEST, C. H., "The Internal Secretion of the Pancreas," *Journal of Laboratory and Clinical Medicine*, VII (1921–22), 251–66.

HOUSSAY, B. A., and BIASOTTI, A., "Pancreatic Diabetes in Hypophysectomized Dogs," trans. from "Le Diabète pancréatique des chiens hypophysectomisés," *Comptes-rendus hebdomadaires des séances et mémoires de la Société de Biologie*, CV (1930), 121–23.

SOSKIN, SAMUEL, and LEVINE, RACHMIEL, *Carbohydrate Metabolism* (Chicago: University of Chicago Press, 1946), pp. 85–88, 247–61.

DANIELS, GEORGE E., "Present Trends in the Evaluation of Psychic Factors in Diabetes Mellitus," *Psychosomatic Medicine*, I (1939), 534–35, 540–41, 544–48.

THE HISTORY OF THE ORGANISM AND THE DYNAMICS OF THE SPECIES

DARWIN, CHARLES, *On the Origin of Species by Means of Natural Selection, or the Preservation of Favoured Races in the Struggle for Life* (London: J. Murray, 1859; New York: Modern Library, 1936).

———, "Provisional Hypothesis of Pangenesis," in *Variation of Animals and Plants under Domestication* (2d ed.; New York: D. Appleton & Co., 1876), II, 445–91.

WEISMANN, AUGUST, "The Continuity of the Germ-Plasm as the Foundation of a Theory of Heredity," in *Essays on Heredity and Kindred Biological Problems* (2d ed.; Oxford: Clarendon Press, 1891), I, 167–91.

SPEMANN, HANS, "The Normal Development of the Amphibian Egg Up to the Formation of the Principal Organs of the Embryo," in *Embryonic Development and Induction* ("Mrs. Hepsa Ely Silliman Memorial Lectures" [New Haven: Yale University Press, 1938]), pp. 6–13.

———, "On Delayed Nucleation of Half-embryos," trans. and abridged from "Über verzögerte Kernversorgung von Keimteilen," *Verhandlungen der deutschen zoologischen Gesellschaft*, XXIV (1914), 216–21. Figures reproduced from *Zeitschrift für wissenschaftliche Zoologie*, CXXXII (1928), 105–34.

WILSON, E. B., *The Cell in Development and Inheritance* (2d ed.; New York: Macmillan Co., 1900), pp. 1–14, 17–23, 30–31, 119–21, 234–40.

SPEMANN, HANS, and MANGOLD, HILDA, "On Induction of Secondary Embryos by the Implantation of Organizers from Different Species," trans. and abridged from "Über Induktion von Embryonalanlagen durch Implantation artfremder Organisatoren," *Archiv für mikroskopische Anatomie und Entwicklungsmechanik*, C (1924), 599–638, including Figs. 1–6 and 19–25.

CHILD, CHARLES M., *Patterns and Problems of Development* (Chicago: University of Chicago Press, 1941), pp. 175–83, 192–96, 272–82, 285–88, 321–23, 330–31, 470–80, 502–3.

WEISS, PAUL, "The So-called Organizer and the Problem of Organization in Amphibian Development," *Physiological Review*, XV (1935), 639–74.

MENDEL, GREGOR, "Experiments in Plant Hybridization," trans. from "Versuche über Pflanzen-Hybriden," *Verhandlungen des naturforschenden Vereines in Brünn*, IV (1865), 1–47.

SUTTON, WALTER S., "The Chromosomes in Heredity," *Biological Bulletin*, IV (1902–3), 231–51.

MORGAN, THOMAS HUNT, "The Mechanism of Sex Determination," in *Heredity and Sex* ("Jesup Lectures" [New York: Columbia University Press, 1913]), pp. 55–69.

———, "Linkage" and "Crossing Over," in *The Physical Basis of Heredity* ("Monographs on Experimental Biology" [Philadelphia and London: J. B. Lippincott Co., 1919]), pp. 80–95.

BRIDGES, CALVIN B., "Sex in Relation to Chromosomes and Genes," *American Naturalist*, LIX (1925), 127–37.

BEADLE, GEORGE W., "The Genes of Men and Molds," *Scientific American*, CLXXIX, No. 3 (1948), 30–39.

EAST, EDWARD M., "A Mendelian Interpretation of Variation That Is Apparently Continuous," *American Naturalist*, XLIV (1910), 65–82.

———, "Studies on Size Inheritance in Nicotiana," *Genetics*, I (1916), 164–76.

DOBZHANSKY, THEODOSIUS, *Genetics and the Origin of Species* (2d rev. ed.; New York: Columbia University Press, 1941).

MAJOR APPROACHES TO PSYCHOLOGICAL PROBLEMS

TITCHENER, EDWARD BRADFORD, *A Textbook of Psychology* (New York: Macmillan Co., 1916), pp. 45–57, 59–92, 201–23.

KOFFKA, KURT, "Perception: An Introduction to the Gestalt-Theorie," *Psychological Bulletin*, XIX (1922), 531–81.

HULL, CLARK L., "The Goal Gradient Hypothesis and Maze Learning," *Psychological Review*, XXXIX (1932), 25–43.

TOLMAN, EDWARD C., "Cognitive Maps in Rats and Men," *Psychological Review*, LV (1948), 189–208.

SPEARMAN, CHARLES E., *The Abilities of Men: Their Nature and Measurement* (New York: Macmillan Co., 1927), chaps. i and ii, pp. 26–38, 41–46, 55–66, 72–82, 87–89, 161–84, 329–39.

FREUD, SIGMUND, *A General Introduction to Psychoanalysis*, trans. G. Stanley Hall (New York: Boni & Liveright, 1920).

Many of the readings listed are reprinted in *Natural Sciences 1: Selected Readings* (4th ed.; Chicago: University of Chicago Press, 1948); *Natural Sciences 2: Selected Readings in Biology* (2 vols.; 4th ed.; Chicago: University of Chicago Press, 1949–50); and *Natural Sciences 3: Selected Readings* (2 vols.; 2d ed.; Chicago: University of Chicago Press, 1948–49).

II. GENERAL COURSE IN THE BIOLOGICAL SCIENCES

Introductory General Course in the Biological Sciences: Syllabus (13th ed.; Chicago: University of Chicago Press, 1949).

Thought Questions for the Introductory General Course in the Biological Sciences (6th ed.; Chicago: University of Chicago Press, 1949).

Introductory General Course in the Biological Sciences: Syllabus Supplement (Chicago: University of Chicago Press, 1949), the contents of which are:

RABINOWITCH, EUGENE I., "Photosynthesis," *Scientific American*, CLXXIX, No. 2 (1948), 25–34.

HOAGLAND, D. P., "Metabolism and Salt Absorption and Movement," from chap. ix, "Lectures on the Inorganic Nutrition of Plants," in *A New Series of Plant Science Books*, ed. Frans Verdoorn (Waltham, Mass.: Chronica Botanica Co., 1948), XIV, 73–81.

VAN OVERBEEK, J., "Plant Physiology and Recent Progress in Agriculture," *Scientific Monthly*, LXVII (1948), 236–37.

MEYER, B. S., "Photoperiodism in Plants," *Scientific Monthly*, LIX (1944), 73–75.

KROGMAN, WILTON M., "The Man-Apes of South Africa," *Scientific American*, CLXXVIII, No. 5 (1948), 16–18.

GRAY, GEORGE W., "The Great Ravelled Knot," *Scientific American*, CLXXIX, No. 4 (1948), 27–38.

BEADLE, GEORGE W., "The Genes of Men and Molds," *Scientific American*, CLXXIX, No. 3 (1948), 30–39.

"Guide to Present-Day Vertebrates in the Chicago Museum of Natural History."

BAYNE-JONES, STANHOPE, *Man and Microbes* (New York: Reynal & Hitchcock, 1933).

BUCHSBAUM, RALPH, *Animals without Backbones: An Introduction to the Invertebrates* (Chicago: University of Chicago Press, 1948).

————, *Readings in Ecology* (Chicago: University of Chicago Press, 1937).

CARLSON, ANTON J., and JOHNSON, VICTOR, *The Machinery of the Body* (Chicago: University of Chicago Press, 1948).

COULTER, MERLE C., *The Story of the Plant Kingdom* (Chicago: University of Chicago Press, 1935).

HOLMES, SAMUEL J., *Human Genetics and Its Social Import* (New York: McGraw-Hill Book Co., 1936).

MENDEL, GREGOR, *Experiments in Plant Hybridisation* (Cambridge: Harvard University Press, 1950).

MUNN, NORMAN L., *Psychology* (Boston: Houghton Mifflin Co., 1946).

NEWMAN, HORATIO HACKETT, *Evolution, Genetics, and Eugenics* (Chicago: University of Chicago Press, 1932).

ROMER, ALFRED SHERWOOD, *Man and the Vertebrates* (Chicago: University of Chicago Press, 1941).

III. PHYSICS

KOLIN, ALEXANDER, *Introduction to Physics* (2 vols.; Chicago: University of Chicago Press, 1948–49).

HOLLEY, CLIFFORD, and THORNTON, ROBERT A., *Problems in Physics* (Chicago: University of Chicago Press, 1949).

6

Mathematics

EUGENE P. NORTHROP

IN THE College's prescribed program of liberal education there is no problem of designing and presenting several courses in mathematics at the first-year level: one—presumably terminal—for students of the humanities, another for physical science majors, a third for engineering students, and so on. This fact appears to me to constitute a distinct advantage. A liberal education is presumably the kind of education everyone ought to have, regardless of the career he expects to enter. If this be true, then any mathematics course designed as an integral part of such an education should be one that every student ought to take, whether or not he plans to take further courses in mathematics. This is one of the assumptions on which the College program is based, and the greater part of this paper will be devoted to a discussion of the kind of course in mathematics which has emerged from this assumption and concomitant assumptions.

Actually, two one-year courses will be discussed. The first, Mathematics 1, is a required part of the College program. The second, Mathematics 2, is designed for those students who wish to pursue the subject further. Mathematics 2 is not an elective in the sense that it may be used to satisfy the requirements for the Bachelor's degree: these requirements may be met only by passing certain comprehensive examinations, one of which is Mathematics 1. Students who wish to make plans for specialized work in one area or another, however, are permitted to take advanced courses for which they are qualified concurrently with the specified courses in the College program.

A liberal education, properly speaking, is one which liberates the student's mind. It does so by providing him with intellectual disciplines of various kinds. He must be taught not only to read and write, but to analyze and interpret what he has read, to look for premises and conclusions of arguments, to recognize them when he has found them, and to discover the presuppositions which lead to the particular choice of the premises used. He must become acquainted not only with a part of humanity's store of knowledge, but with the various methods by which knowledge of different kinds is gained, with methods by which premises are formulated, with methods by which premises lead to conclusions, and with methods by which conclusions are validated. No single discipline can do all these things. Nor is it correct to assume that there exists a one-to-one correspondence between fields of knowledge and disciplines appropriate to them. There is a variety of disciplines, some of which are appropriate to one field and some to another field, with much overlapping among them.

Some of these disciplines involve the use of ordinary numerical reckoning. The value of mathematics in this very narrow sense is almost too obvious to mention. But consider mathematics as a discipline in itself—that is to say, as a body of concepts and methods which constitute a way of thinking. Mathematics deals almost exclusively with premises and conclusions and with deductive reasoning, which is one of the more important methods of drawing conclusions from premises. Moreover, clarity and precision of definitions and assumptions, and rigor in reasoning, can be more nearly attained and more simply studied in mathematics than in the other disciplines. Is not this the real place of mathematics in a liberal education—not simply as a subject matter or as a discipline applicable only to its own subject matter, but as a discipline which is pertinent to almost every intellectual activity of man?

If it be granted, for the reasons just stated, that the study of mathematics is an appropriate part of a liberal education, the aims of a mathematics course designed for such an education can be formulated somewhat as follows: The course should help the student acquire facility and precision in the statement, organization, and communication of scientific ideas (logical discourse and deductive systems). It should lead him to understand and to make use of the methods of mathematics (logic and intuition, analysis and construction, generalization and particularization). And it should supply him with certain facts, concepts, and techniques basic to exact science (relations and functions, number systems, analytic geometry, trigonometry).

The subject matter of Mathematics 1 has been selected and is presented with these aims in view.

The first part of the course presents conceptual apparatus adequate to the needs of elementary mathematics. The course begins with a study of sets, of subsets, and of ordered pairs. These notions, in turn, are used in formulating precisely the concepts of relation and function. Attention is then given to the logical meaning of propositions. Propositional functions are discussed, and the meaning of quantification is brought out. Finally, analysis is made of the processes of definition and proof, the structure of deductive and of mathematical systems, and the connections between a system and its models. These various concepts and methods are then utilized in a study of the commutative group.

In the middle part of the course certain features of numbers and number systems are discussed. In this connection the field is defined and its elementary properties explored. One model of the field—the system of rational numbers—is studied intensively, special emphasis being given to the transformation of rational expressions and the solution of rational equations. Next the "order" aspect of numbers is considered, and the ordered field is developed. The final phase of this discussion sees a postulational characterization of the system of real numbers and a treatment of real equations and inequalities.

The last part of the course centers on functions and relations in the set of real numbers. Since geometrical methods are particularly useful in this study, the elements of analytic geometry are first developed. Careful examination is then made of certain simple types of real functions and relations specified by algebraic equations. The course concludes with a treatment of the transcendental "circular" functions and their application to the solution of triangle problems.

The majority of the students in the College take no mathematics beyond the course which has just been described.* For such students it may be thought that the course is inadequate in its failure to include a number of topics for which various authors have argued with varying degrees of fervor. Although I cannot agree with such authors as those who would include number theory and permutations so that the student will be able to face later in life the problems he will find, respectively, in current popular magazines and in trying to arrange his dinner guests, I am quite ready to admit the desirability of giving the terminal student some idea of such topics as the calculus and statistical analysis. The difficulty, of course, is that of finding time for acceptable developments of these topics in a year course. The tendency in the College is to sacrifice breadth of coverage of many topics for depth of understanding of a few fundamental ones. The choice of those which are studied in Mathematics 1 is defended on the ground that any student who has successfully fulfilled the course requirements will be able to pursue, independently and with understanding, any further topics in mathematics in which he may have a genuine but nonprofessional interest.

It is apparent that students of the College who desire to continue their formal work in mathematics need some instruction designed to bridge the gap between the somewhat unconventional work of Mathematics 1 and the more advanced courses in calculus and post-calculus subjects offered by the Department of Mathematics in the Division of the Physical Sciences. The College provides such continuing instruction in Mathematics 2.†

The major objective of Mathematics 2 is to train the student in the fundamentals of differential and integral calculus. The

---

* For the sake of completeness it should be noted that Mathematics 1 presupposes only a grasp of elementary algebra and plane geometry such as is ordinarily acquired in the first two years of high school, that it meets four or five hours per week for three quarters (two semesters), and that the text for the course— *Fundamental Mathematics* (Chicago: University of Chicago Press)—first appeared in 1945–46 and is now in its third edition.

† Mathematics 2 meets five hours per week for three quarters. The texts are: *Mathematics 2 Notes* (Chicago: University of Chicago Press, 1947) and J. F. Randolph and M. Kac, *Analytic Geometry and Calculus* (New York: Macmillan Co., 1946).

course is based on—and uses extensively—the concepts, facts, and methods of Mathematics 1. In the first part of the course finite induction is developed and the theory of real numbers is reviewed and extended, with special emphasis on order and continuity. The remainder of the course is devoted to the calculus, the treatment including a review and extension of analytic geometry. This study is unified about the concept of limit, and an attempt is made to give the student a genuine and rigorous understanding of the concept and its significant role in the calculus.

It has been my conviction from the start* that such a course as Mathematics 1 is far more appropriate than most conventional courses for the college student who plans to study mathematics only one year. Several years of experience, together with favorable reactions from colleagues at Chicago and elsewhere, appear to support this conviction. I am equally convinced, however, that such a course, properly taught, is also more appropriate than most conventional courses at the same level for the student who plans to continue in mathematics or science. My belief that this is the case is based on the following ground: that an order of learning in which first emphasis is placed on the mastery of a conception of mathematical systems and of skill in following their development makes mastery of systems subsequently studied more rapid and more complete. Whereas to place first emphasis on the mastery of a large body of mathematical formulae and of skill in their manipulation makes mastery of subsequent formulae and manipulation almost as difficult as mastery of the first, and makes more and more difficult any later attempts to master and appreciate mathematical systems as such.

* Mathematics 1 was first offered in 1943–44; it became a required part of the College program in 1945–46.

7

Writing

HENRY W. SAMS

T<small>HE</small> conditions under which English composition is taught in the College are peculiar, in that all students are fully engaged in a prescribed program of courses. The English courses can be planned to exploit the context of the College, for the context is known. They can be made directly pertinent to the ideas and methods of work in other courses and therefore can avoid the insularity which has so often plagued composition instructors and driven them either into a forced identification with literary affairs or into a frantic simulation of topical and vocational interests.

However, since individual students in the College writing classes may be variously placed in the curriculum and may choose to schedule their courses in various combinations, English instructors cannot assume that all students in any particular class have identical programs. It would be quite impossible, even if it were desirable, to turn the English course into a device for directing and reading term papers for adjacent courses in literature and science. English composition is a separate and independent course. Nothing is admitted to it which does not serve the purpose of writing well.

There are two ways in which the context of the College assists instruction in composition: (1) it provides a body of information which may be used as a substantive basis for the development of writing exercises, and (2) it provides a consciousness of method which supports instruction in the ordering of paragraph and essay.

In the substantive courses of the College, in humanities, and in the social and natural sciences, selected units of material are studied with the intention of bringing the students to a thoroughness of knowledge that makes critical generalization possible. The units of work are limited in scope, but each unit is presented in such a way that it increases not only the student's local and specific knowledge but also his capacity for general application and reference of the knowledge he commands. In effect, each unit of work is developed to precisely the point at which writing about it becomes practicable and profitable. By exploiting the material so developed, the English staff avoids expenditure of time on the development of subjects for writing. It is also assured that essay assignments may be devised which will engage the students at a suitable level of complexity—a level high enough to entail exacting problems in composition, low enough to fall within the limits of the student's intellectual experience.

The consciousness of method which characterizes all instruction in the College gives point to that part of training in composition which is frequently called "logic." There is information about the syllogism and its fallacies which may be imparted in the composition class, but it is doubtful that any English course, alone and unsupported, has ever been able to make this information of genuine and permanent service to students in their writing. It is doubtful that, by defining the syllogism and its fallacies, one can bring them to function actively in student writing.

The concern with method characteristic of the College does not constitute a logical system. The English staffs do not attempt to make a system of it. In the substantive courses students find fragments of systems, local methods, and particular procedures which are in themselves reducible to rules of thought. They are capable of having names. Disjunction, alternation, equation, condition, for examples, are relations with which students are familiar, both as facts and as words. The English courses undertake not to systematize these relations but to apply them to the problems of writing. The relationship of systematic thought to written discourse, of logic to rhetoric, is important subject matter for the English teacher. Both the use and the limitations of logical principles may be taught. By a realization of the degree to which logical rigor must be qualified in rhetorical situations, the student learns what rhetoric is and where its virtues lie.

The prime objective of the English courses is to exercise students in the invention and ordering of persuasive English prose. This exercise is confined within the limits of what might be called "work-day" writing, for the literary niceties of phrase and cadence are never dealt with as ends in themselves. "Creative writing" is not taught in the College. Work-day writing includes, of course, grammar and spelling. Though the distinguishing emphasis of the program lies in its concern with the larger units of writing, every student must demonstrate his control of the mechanics of language, both in writing and in reading.

Perhaps the clearest definition of objectives may be derived from a description of the distribution of work within the English sequence of three courses. The first of these three, English Deficiency, is designed to remedy inadequacies in fundamental grammar and mechanics and to correct faults in reading traceable to habitual causes. The course is therefore divided into two parts: English Deficiency (Writing) and English Deficiency (Reading).

Students in English Deficiency (Writing) are drilled in sentence forms and grammatical relationships. There is some dependence upon the terminology of grammar, and students are able at the end of the course to talk about grammatical matters without being at a loss for words. Frequent brief writing assignments, repeated rewriting, and criticism, offered chiefly in conferences rather than in the classroom, are the devices which the course depends upon. All writing assignments are closely controlled. Each exercise presents a particular problem in sentence structure, punctuation, organization, transition, or diction. Students placed in the course remain in it until they demonstrate by their performance on a qualifying examination that they are ready for the work of the English course.

The objective of English Deficiency (Reading) is to improve reading speed to the level necessary for effective work in the College. The course in no sense duplicates the work of other courses in the College whose purpose is to enlarge the student's capacity for analysis and comprehension of different kinds of texts. By fre-

quent tests on the content of passages read, the instructor measures the student's comprehension; but the aim of the tests is to
furnish data by which the instructor may avoid advancing the
student's speed at the expense of comprehension. Speed is increased; comprehension is held to the level established by the
student at the beginning of the course. The methods of the course
are clinical: photographic analysis of eye movements, corrective
exercises, and drill at controlled speeds on reading boards. No
student is admitted to the course whom diagnosis does not show
to be in need of it and capable of benefiting by it. Fewer than 5
per cent of the students in the College ever register for English
Deficiency (Reading). These register for twelve or for six weeks
on the advice of the diagnostician and remain in the course until
they demonstrate by their performance on an examination their
ability to read at a rate suitable to the volume of work assigned
them in the College.

Most of the students in each entering class go directly into
English, the central course of the writing sequence. The course is
taught in sections of about twenty students which meet three
times each week throughout one year. The characteristic emphasis of the course is on the preparation, criticism, and correction
of student themes, of which approximately twenty-five are assigned in the year. In addition to the assignment of extensive
themes, there are detailed writing exercises on specific points of
style, and assignments and discussions in analysis of readings
chosen for their utility both as models and as sources.

It is by the consideration of readings as sources for ideas and
methods to be developed and imitated in student writing that the
course is brought into close association with the other courses of
the College. For example, the initial assignment in the course has
for several years been the late Carl Becker's "Everyman His Own
Historian," which was chosen (1) because it is on the general
subject of history as an intellectual construction, a topic thoroughly discussed, though in a different context, in Humanities 2
during the same period of the year and therefore capable of being
used in English classes at a fairly sophisticated level of complexity; (2) because it is developed by simple expository devices
of exemplification and analogy appropriate for discussion and

imitation in the English classes; (3) because it is written with admirable humor and style. Throughout the first quarter the subject matter of history and historical method is consistently exploited. By this means the product of discussions in the social science courses, and particularly in Humanities 2, is constantly reflected in student writing; the product of student writing may be to some extent reflected in the students' grasp of the social sciences and of Humanities 2.

English depends upon neighboring courses for material and for method, but the course must have, and does have, a structure of its own. This structure is determined by the considerations which become pertinent after the student has mastered an idea and is confronted with the problem of writing about it in a fashion appropriate to a particular purpose or situation. The course is divided into three parts which receive roughly equal emphasis: exposition, argumentation, and style.

During the first quarter students are introduced to the customary expository modes and are exercised in their application both to paragraph and to theme. It is not the intention of the staff to teach exposition as terminology or to expect pat identifications of narration, comparison, illustration, analysis, or enumeration of antecedents or consequences. It is rather their intention to encourage a habitual reference to these intellectual tags by bringing the students to recognize them in the readings which are discussed and to see how they are appropriate to ideas assigned for written development. A habit of reference to standard patterns, and of using them without being used by them, is the best reward that this portion of the course can offer.

During the second quarter the students advance from the bare presentation of ideas to argument for them. Practice in the use of expository patterns is continued, but the course is designed to suggest a fairly systematic evaluation of the various modes as they apply to particular ideas in particular situations and intentions. At this point, though the English course is not intended to include the study of formal logic, the logical formalities of method which are used elsewhere in the College may be related to written discourse. Students should know that, though a picturesque analogy may be excellent in a lecture intended for ladies' clubs, it may not get good results before a convocation of mathematicians; and they should be aware of the fundamental reasons for this difference.

During the third quarter the students are concerned primarily with the detailed execution of their themes. As the separation of the deficiency courses implies, it has not proved necessary in this or any other portion of the course to concentrate the attention of the class on rules for mechanical accuracy. The subject of the quarter is style. It would be somewhat visionary to suppose that in one quarter or in one year college students might be molded into "stylists" in any elevated or literary sense of the term. However, the attention of the student can be turned to criticism of his sentences as separate units of composition and as the basis of an aggregate effect. He can be made sensitive to figures of speech and encouraged to use them in a somewhat limited manner. He can discover the value of considering well before making a choice of word or phrase. If he can become familiar with the elements of style, he will have the equipment necessary to develop ultimately a mature style of his own. This portion of the course is designed to teach, by analysis and imitation, the simple elements of style.

Training in writing is continued in Humanities 3. The emphasis of this course with regard to writing, though it may not be contained within the word "style" in its usual signification, is yet centered upon the detailed resolution of specific problems in writing. Humanities 3 assumes the work of the first two quarters of English; it continues and expands the work of the third quarter of English. A complete description of the course may be found in the chapter of this book which deals with the humanities sequence.

In addition to the work of the humanities staff on the problems of writing, other courses in the College assign essays in the regular routine of instruction, in examinations, and in honors work. An experimental program to test the practicality of Bachelor's theses written as a part of the work of fourth-year, preceptorial classes is now under way. The faculty of the College as a whole has declared its resolution to extend responsibility for good writing into every phase of College work. However, the faculty has also recognized that the long divorce of rhetoric from the substantive courses cannot be made up by a simple declaration of good intentions. To bring all the College courses into focus upon a well-understood writing program, the faculty has included teachers of writing in the procedure for the supervision of honors work. It has welcomed qualified members of the English staff into other courses, so that the point of view of English may be represented there and, in turn, the interests of those courses fairly represented to the English staff. It has lent qualified members of other staffs to English from time to time and has co-operated in appointments of persons permanently valuable in English and in another discipline. This interchange has become so thoroughly established that at present there is no senior member of the English staff who is not, for at least one-third of his time, assigned to teaching outside the English courses.

The close knitting of English instruction into the curriculum of the College cannot overcome entirely the difficulties which, by its nature, accompany the teaching of writing. There is no easy way in which so complex an accomplishment as writing well can be imparted without labor and occasional failure. The English staff of the College has never supposed that it had found the pedagogical philosopher's stone.

However, the English staff feels confidence in the phases of its program which have been emphasized here. In weekly staff discussions and in frequent revisions and modifications of materials for teaching, it is apparent that ever larger parts of the course are gaining stability and that the staff as a whole is learning to conduct the course with constantly improving success. Its status as an independent staff in the faculty organization has contributed much to the sense of responsibility with which each teacher approaches his work and to the effective introduction of writing into other phases of College work. There is reason to hope that, by persistence in its present activities, by constant refinement of detailed classroom procedures, and by assimilation of ideas being developed in vigorous courses at other institutions, the College may in time bring rhetoric to the level of importance and utility in general education which it lost during the years in which undergraduate education was dominated by encyclopedic curriculums.

Texts Used

English: Selected Readings and Exercises (3 vols.; Chicago: University of Chicago Press, 1948–49).

TAFT, K. B.; McDERMOTT, J. F.; and JENSEN, D. O., *The Technique of Composition* (New York: Rinehart & Co., 1946).

NOTE.—*The Technique of Composition* is used very sparingly in the classroom but extensively for reference in correcting themes. The three volumes of readings and exercises are designed to support instruction in the principal topics of the course: exposition, argumentation, and style. For example, the section devoted to "Example and Illustration" (a part of the treatment of exposition) contains four readings:

PEIRCE, CHARLES, *Chance, Love, and Logic* (New York: Harcourt, Brace & Co., 1923), pp. 38–41.

THOREAU, HENRY DAVID, "Life without Principle," in *The Writings of Henry David Thoreau* (Boston: Houghton Mifflin Co., 1906), IV, 456–58.

EINSTEIN, ALBERT, and INFELD, LEOPOLD, *The Evolution of Physics* (New York: Simon & Schuster, 1938), pp. 47–51.

MENCKEN, H. L., "The American Language," *Yale Review*, XXV (1935–36), 538–52.

By the analysis and discussion of these readings the instructor seeks to develop in the student some sensitivity to this mode of exposition and an awareness of its advantages and limitations.

The third volume of *Selected Readings and Exercises* contains readings on the subject of the theory of style, as well as selections illustrating stylistic excellence.

8

Languages

IN RECENT years the place of language study in prescribed curriculums of general education has been the subject of much discussion and of various actions by college faculties. A few colleges have renounced the requirement of foreign language altogether, treating it as part of the preparatory work of some students but not as an appropriate part of the liberal education of all students. A few of these colleges, in turn, have substituted courses *about* language for courses *in* language, holding, apparently, that an inquiry into general problems of language may be carried on effectively by students who have never studied a foreign language and that such an undertaking is more easily defended as a requirement in general education than is the study of a single foreign language.

The College assumes that successful study of a foreign language is a proper part of general education, that students should be made aware of some of the general aspects and problems of language, and that the study of either of these things will not insure understanding of the other unless a deliberate effort to relate the two is made. Therefore, each student is required to pass a comprehensive examination in Greek, Latin, French, German, Spanish, Italian, or Russian and, concomitantly, an examination in general language problems, for which the course described in the second part of this chapter prepares students.

Seven accounts of seven different courses in foreign language would weary the reader of this book, and only the course in the general problems of language is separately described. However, since the major portion of the student's language study is devoted to a foreign language, something more should be said about the kind and quality of work done in the various foreign language courses. Perhaps the best way of doing this is to cite the texts which students read in these courses and to ask the reader to note, in the case of languages with which he is familiar, the level of competence expected of students who pass the comprehensive examination. These titles are supplied in the list of readings and textbooks at the end of this chapter. In noting differences among the foreign languages in these respects, it should be remembered that other languages vary in difficulty for English-speaking students and that the courses in the College differ somewhat in the emphasis which they place upon reading and vocabulary, as against grammatical analysis, on the one hand, and conversing and writing, on the other.

A course which places great emphasis upon reading is the course in French. A study of the results achieved by this course for more than twenty years is now being prepared for separate publication by its chairman, Otto F. Bond. His research shows that students at the end of the first third of French 1 are as competent in reading and vocabulary as are comparable students after two years of French in high school; that, after two-thirds of French 1, students are equivalent in reading competence and in vocabulary to comparable students who have taken three years of French in high school or nearly two years in college; and that, at the end of French 1, students have a control of reading and vocabulary which is equivalent to that normally achieved in four high-school years of instruction in French.*

If students who have attained this considerable competence in foreign language wish to continue language study and if the College is to be justified in prescribing foreign language for them, it

---

* The tests used in this study are those supplied by the Cooperative Test Service of the American Council on Education. The norms for high-school and college achievement in French are those based upon scores of students in "Type 1 colleges," this latter classification being based, in turn, upon the performance of entering students on the American Council on Education Psychological Examination.

seems both necessary and proper to see to it that students in the College are able to continue to use the language which they have been required to study. Elective, advanced courses are, it is true, available to students who are able to add them to their prescribed programs of study. However, the faculty of the College has been anxious to find means of extending the use of the foreign languages within the scope of the general courses which prepare students for the comprehensive examinations. Therefore, since the autumn of 1947, students who have done well in one of the required courses in foreign language are permitted to enrol in special sections of Humanities 3, in which texts in that foreign language are substituted for some of the texts read in English in the other sections of the course. A similar substitution is made in some of the examination questions for those sections of Humanities 3. In addition, the members of the foreign language staff of the faculty are now exploring the advantages and difficulties involved in requiring students to maintain their competence in language up to their graduation by reading in their original language some of the texts which are studied in English translation in the various general courses in the College. As in the case of English and mathematics, it would seem that the work in foreign language can and should be related closely to the context which a required curriculum in general education supplies.

I I

A GENERAL COURSE IN LANGUAGE

JAMES C. BABCOCK

In the last two decades general courses in language, often of the "exploratory" or "prognostic" variety, have become increasingly common in the junior and senior high schools of the United States. It is still unusual to find a general course in language of any sort included as a required part of a program of higher liberal education. This is true in spite of the fact that few, if any, planners of programs of liberal education would deny the importance of broadening one's views about language in general

and gaining insights into the nature and functions of an indispensable means of intellectual expression and communication.
It is felt, perhaps, that courses in logic, philosophy, and psychology (or the elements of these disciplines presented under different
curricular labels), plus required studies in English and foreign
languages, are adequate to produce the competence and understanding desired. Certainly, these studies may, if planned to do
so, contribute significantly to the attainment of the indicated
objective. In practice, however, important aspects of general
language study are either totally missing or barely touched upon
in college curriculums, and the student's competence in this area
is limited to what he may acquire more or less as a by-product of
courses which are primarily concerned with other matters.

In the College of the University of Chicago, a direct attack
upon general language problems was planned several years ago
by a group made up of instructors from the various foreign language staffs and Clarence H. Faust, then Dean of the College.
The present teaching staff includes, in addition to instructors in
the foreign languages, members of the English and social sciences
staffs. The role of the course, designated Language 1, in the College program remains essentially the same as that intended for it
by the original planning committee; it does not replace any part
of the regular work in foreign languages but is designed, rather,
to supplement the study of a particular foreign language (and to
some extent other courses in the College) by introducing or expanding topics of language study which contribute to the ends of
liberal education.

In general terms the aim of the course is to give the student
some understanding of the nature and functions of language.
Within the limits of a short supplementary course, meeting only
once a week during one quarter, the subject matter suggested by
this broad aim is restricted to the following topics or units of
study: phonetics, history and relationships of languages, grammar, and semantics. Corresponding to these four units of the
course, language is studied as (1) a system of vocal sounds, (2) a
changing historical phenomenon, (3) a system of symbols having
a structure that can be analyzed in various ways, and (4) a means
of symbolic expression and communication.

In each unit of study the materials that are read and discussed are original writings, ranging from Plato's *Cratylus* to chapters from Bloomfield's *Language*. No single textbook would serve so well the intention not only to increase the student's knowledge about language and languages but, especially, to acquaint him with the kinds of aims, methods, and subject matters which constitute attempts to arrive at solutions to language problems. Each assigned reading is discussed not only to examine its actual content but also with regard to the author's purpose in dealing with language, the assumptions concerning the nature and functions of language underlying the particular treatment offered, and the key terms used by the author in presenting his arguments or in defining, classifying, and distinguishing the elements of his subject matter.

Obviously, a short course for undergraduates can lay no claim to anything approaching completeness either with respect to "what is known" about language and languages or the numerous aims and methods of linguistic studies. The student does, however, acquire a significant amount of information about language, particularly in the historical portion of the course and in phonetics. Equally important for his future reading and thinking, he also acquires considerable competence in understanding books and discussions about language and in making informed, critical judgments of them.

The sort of reading and discussion which is typical of the course may be illustrated by reference to the unit which deals with grammar. In the preceding (historical) part the student has encountered brief statements concerning normative and universal grammar and a more extended treatment of descriptive, historical, and comparative grammar. He begins his study of grammar, therefore, with some awareness of the variety of purposes and points of view that have characterized grammatical studies. Previous class discussions have also taught him something about the kinds of questions that may properly be asked of each author. Of the writer on grammar he may ask such questions as the following:

1. What is the author's conception of grammar? Is he concerned with the structure of one language or more than one? Does

he deal with the standard literary language, colloquial standard speech, substandard speech, or other?

2. Is his study limited to a language or to languages of a specific time and place, or is he concerned with historical development and geographical variations?

3. Is the author's purpose practical or theoretical? If practical, what ends precisely are to be served by the results of the study?

4. What kind of distinctions are made, and what are the key terms employed? What, for example, are the criteria used in distinguishing the parts of speech (if these are distinguished): form, meaning, function in the sentence, or some combination of these?

5. Given the author's particular interests and purposes, is his formulation of the question or problem useful and clear, are his arguments well ordered, and are his conclusions based on adequate, appropriate examples or other data?

It is not intended, of course, that the same questions should be asked of every grammarian (or of every writer on any single topic), nor is any judgment of value attached a priori to the answers which identify the author's interests in a particular kind of speech, in synchronic or diachronic studies, or in practical or theoretical problems. But it is considered essential that the student be clearly aware of what a writer is trying to do and how, in his opinion, his purposes can best be accomplished.

As additional papers are read in the grammar unit, as in all other parts of the course, further questions call for comparison among the several authors, and relevant ideas found in preceding units are brought to bear upon a current topic. This procedure often throws additional light upon general questions that are pertinent to more than one part of the course. Thus, to take a simple example which can be set forth briefly, the student has encountered in the historical part Bloomfield's characterization of normative grammar as an unfortunate development (from universal grammar) which gave the authoritarian a chance to prescribe fanciful rules about how people ought to speak (chap. i of *Language*). This is recalled when, in the part on grammar, the class reaches the normative treatment of analogy and anomaly in Varro (Books viii and ix of *On the Latin Language*). The student has now progressed beyond the point at which he might ask whether Bloomfield is "right" and Varro "wrong." Instead, he recalls the context of Bloomfield's rapid survey of language study, with its emphasis upon the methods and values of descriptive, historical, and comparative grammar. It is clear that for Bloomfield's purposes normative grammar is worse than useless. It has been a waste of time and a stumbling block in the path of the development of the scientific study of languages. Moreover, the author's condemnation of a normative grammar which produces "logical" rules unrelated to actual usage is a needed corrective to the earlier grammatical training that some of the students have had in the schools. In short, Bloomfield's position is useful and necessary to the course. On the other hand, a careful reading of Varro shows that this author also has a legitimate purpose, that of investigating a particular kind of problem of usage with the practical aim of giving guidance to different speakers and writers (the people in general, orators, poets, and so forth) so that they may make more effective use of language in ordinary communication and in addressing audiences. Varro is clearly aware of the difference between descriptive and normative grammar. In this part of his work it is not his purpose to describe variations in usage but to indicate in a reasoned fashion the choice that should be made between existing equivalent variants when the user of language wishes to speak or write effectively. He writes a normative grammar, but he is not an authoritarian attempting to impose fanciful rules.

In the remaining papers on grammar, most of which present one or another basis for distinguishing grammatical categories, the ideas dealt with become necessarily somewhat more complex. The class procedure remains the same: the student is led to study and compare and to reflect upon the different methods, purposes, and interests represented. Not least important among the final outcomes of such a procedure is the student's realization that "truth" is not easily set forth in a single, tight system; that grammatical phenomena can profitably be examined from various (and often supplementary) points of view; and, finally, that grammar need not be a pedantic study but may reveal fundamentally different ways of looking at things.

The reading and discussion concerning grammar are, as was stated above, typical of the course. The phonetic and historical parts are more "factual" in nature, but in them as well as in the fourth and last part—semantics—the same principles of teaching and learning hold. It is felt that the kind of reading demanded in the course and the class discussions, when combined with the study of a particular foreign language and with other College courses, should stimulate the student to think intelligently about language. He may not have reached entirely satisfying solutions to the complex problems of linguistic study. He will have gained, however, a useful understanding of the nature of such problems, and he will be acquainted with a significant variety of methods which men have used in studying and reflecting upon their languages. He will also be aware of the correspondingly varied results which have been obtained and the ends which these may serve. This would seem to be a proper beginning.

Reading Lists

I. PARTICULAR LANGUAGES

FRENCH 1

BOND, O. F., *En Route* (Boston: D. C. Heath & Co., 1938).

———— (ed.), *Première étape, Deuxième étape,* and *Première étape* (alt.) ("Heath-Chicago French Series" [Boston: D. C. Heath & Co., 1936–47]).

LANDRY, JOSEPH A., *Graded French Word and Idiom Book* ("Heath-Chicago French Series" [Boston: D. C. Heath & Co., 1938]).

PARKER, C. S., and GRIGAUD, P. L., *Initiation à la culture française* (New York: Harper & Bros., 1944).

BERGSON, H., *Le Rire: Essai sur la signification du comique,* in *Œuvres complètes d'Henri Bergson* (Geneva: Skira, 1945), II, 15–26.

VOLTAIRE, "Le Monde comme il va," in *Contes et romans* ("Génie de la France" [Paris: Hilsum, 1931]), I, 97–114.

MICHELET, J., *Jeanne d'Arc,* ed. G. Rudler (Paris: Hachette, 1925), I, 77–120.

MÉRIMÉE, P., "Mateo Falcone," in *Œuvres complètes* (Paris: Champion, 1933), XIII, 3–22.

PALFREY, T. R., and WILL, S. F., *Petite anthologie* (New York: F. S. Crofts & Co., 1936).

MAUPASSANT, GUY DE, *Pierre et Jean,* ed. Aaron Schaffer ("Modern Students' Library, French Series" [New York: Charles Scribner's Sons, 1936]).

The texts from BERGSON, VOLTAIRE, MICHELET, and MÉRIMÉE are reprinted in *Lectures choisies: French 1* (Chicago: University of Chicago Press, 1950).

FRENCH 2

BARTON, FRANCIS B., and SIRICH, EDWARD H., *Simplified French Review* (New York: F. S. Crofts & Co., 1945).

MARCH, HAROLD, *Types of the French Short Story—Modern Period* (New York: Thos. Nelson & Sons, 1941).

KANY, CHARLES E., and DONDO, MATHURIN, *Intermediate French Conversation* (Boston: D. C. Heath & Co., 1941).

MUSSET, ALFRED DE, *On ne badine pas avec l'amour* ("Classiques Larousse" [New York: Appleton-Century-Crofts, n.d.]).

RACINE, JEAN, *Les Plaideurs* ("Classiques Larousse" [New York: Appleton-Century-Crofts, n.d.]).

MOLIÈRE, *Le Malade imaginaire* ("Classiques Larousse" [New York: Appleton-Century-Crofts, n.d.]).

NOTE.—French 2 is not required for the A.B. degree but is available to those wishing to study French beyond the level set for French 1.

GERMAN 1

CURTS, PAUL H., *Basic German* (New York: Prentice-Hall Book Co., Inc., 1946).

HAGBOLDT, PETER, *Graded German Readers* (Boston: D. C. Heath & Co., 1933 and 1942).

MEYER, ERIKA, *German Graded Readers* (Boston: Houghton Mifflin Co., 1949), Books I, II, III.

THOMA, LUDWIG, *Cora: Vier Lausbubengeschichten* (Boston: D. C. Heath & Co., 1933).

GERSTÄCKER, FRIEDRICH, *Germelshausen*, in RÖSELER, R. O., and BER, ADELAIDE (eds.), *Altes und Neues* (New York: Henry Holt & Co., 1934).

STORM, THEODOR, *Immensee*, in RÖSELER, R. O., and BER, ADELAIDE (eds.), *Altes und Neues* (New York: Henry Holt & Co., 1934).

SCHNITZLER, ARTHUR, *Der blinde Geronimo und sein Bruder* (Boston: D. C. Heath & Co., 1929).

KEYSERLING, EDUARD VON, *Abendliche Häuser* (New York: F. S. Crofts & Co., 1947).

GERMAN 2

CHILES, JAMES A., *German Composition and Conversation* (Cambridge: Ginn & Co., 1931).

ZWEIG, STEFAN, *Die unsichtbare Sammlung;* BINDING, RUDOLF, *Die Perle;* SCHOLZ, WILHELM VON, *Der Auswanderer;* WIECHERT, ERNST, *Der silberne Wagen;* all in COENEN, FREDERIC, *Auf höherer Warte* (New York: Henry Holt & Co., 1941).

MANN, THOMAS, *Tonio Kröger* (New York: F. S. Crofts & Co., 1932).

TIECK, *Der blonde Eckbert;* STIFTER, *Bergkristall;* MANN, *Das Wunderkind;* KELLER, *Das Tanzlegendchen;* WIECHERT, *Tobias;* RILKE, *Die Weise von Liebe und Tod des Cornets Christoph Rilke;* all in FLEISSNER, *Die Kunst der Prosa* (New York: F. S. Crofts & Co., 1941).

CHAMISSO, ADALBERT VON, *Peter Schlemihl* (any edition).

HEINE, HEINRICH, *Die Harzreise*, selections (any edition).

SCHILLER, FRIEDRICH VON, *Egmont* (any edition).

GOETHE, WOLFGANG VON, *Hermann und Dorothea* (New York: Oxford University Press, 1917).

Selected material (mimeographed) for translation with the aid of a dictionary.

NOTE.—German 2 is not required for the A.B. degree but is available to those wishing to study German beyond the level set in German 1.

GREEK 1

ABBOTT, E., and MANSFIELD, E. D., *Primer of Greek Grammar* (London: Rivingtons, 1937).

DYER, L., and SEYMOUR, T. D., *Plato: Apology and Crito* (Boston: Ginn & Co., 1908).

One Greek tragedy in an annotated College edition, e.g., EURIPIDES *Medea*, ed. D. L. Page (Oxford: Oxford University Press, 1938).

ITALIAN 1

YOUNG, RUTH E., and CANTARELLA, MICHELE, *Corso d'italiano* (New York: Macmillan Co., 1944).

GOGGIO, EMILIO, *A New Italian Reader for Beginners* (Boston: D. C. Heath & Co., 1941).

RUSSO, JOSEPH L., *Nel paese del sole* (Boston: D. C. Heath & Co., 1947).

BERGIN, THOMAS G., *Modern Italian Short Stories* (Boston: D. C. Heath & Co., 1938).

CIOFFARI, VINCENZO, and VAN HORNE, JOHN, *Graded Italian Readers* (Boston: D. C. Heath & Co., 1947), Books I–IV.

SWANSON, CARL A., *Modern Italian One-Act Plays* (Boston: D. C. Heath & Co., 1948).

DELEDDA, GRAZIA, *Marianna Sirca*, ed. Jones and Bissiri (Boston: D. C. Heath & Co., 1940).

PIRANDELLO, LUIGI, *Così è (se vi pare)*, ed. J. L. Russo (Boston: D. C. Heath & Co., 1930).

GOZZI, GASPARO, *La Gazzetta veneta* ("Cambridge Plain Texts" [London: Cambridge University Press, 1921]).

DANTE, *La Vita nuova*, ed. K. McKenzie (Boston: D. C. Heath & Co., 1922).

LATIN 1

HETTICH, E. L., and MAITLAND, A. G. C., *Latin Fundamentals* (New York: Prentice-Hall Book Co., Inc., 1947).

D'OOGE, B. L., *Cicero: Select Orations* (New York: B. H. Sanborn & Co., 1937).

GREENOUGH, J. B.; KITTREDGE, G. L.; and JENKINS, T., *Virgil and Other Latin Poets* (Boston: Ginn & Co., 1923).

Mimeographed selections from leading Roman authors, e.g., HORACE, CATULLUS, JUVENAL, LIVY, TACITUS.

RUSSIAN 1

BONDAR, *Simplified Russian Method*, rev. Mischa H. Fayer, A. Pressman, and Anastasia Pressman (7th ed.; New York: Pitman Pub. Corp., 1949).

LERMONTOV, *Taman'*, ed. F. Marshak-Sobotka ("Heath-Chicago Russian Series" [Boston: D. C. Heath & Co., 1945]).

PUSHKIN, *Two Short Stories*, ed. Fruma Gottschalk ("Heath-Chicago Russian Series" [Boston: D. C. Heath & Co., 1946]).

LERMONTOV, *Bela*, ed. F. Marshak-Sobotka ("Heath-Chicago Russian Series" [Boston: D. C. Heath & Co., 1947]).

SOLOVLYOVA, E. E., *et al.*, *Rodnaya Rech'* (3d ed.; Moscow: Uchpedgiz, 1946).

GORKI, MAXIM, *et al.*, *Rodnaya Literatura* (7th ed.; Moscow: Uchpedgiz, 1946).

SPANISH 1

BABCOCK, J. C., and TREVIÑO, S. N., *Introduction to Spanish* (Boston: Houghton Mifflin Co., 1944).

MÁRMOL, J., *Amalia*, ed. J. C. Babcock and M. Rodríguez (Boston: Houghton Mifflin Co., 1949).

CASTILLO, C., and SPARKMAN, C. F., *Sigamos leyendo* (Boston: D. C. Heath & Co., 1936).

KENISTON, H., *A Standard List of Spanish Words and Idioms* (Boston: D. C. Heath & Co., 1941).

GRISMER, R. L., and ARJONA, D. K., *Pageant of Spain* (New York: F. S. Crofts & Co., 1938).

ROBLES, J., *Tertulias españolas* (New York: F. S. Crofts & Co., 1938).

BENAVENTE, J., *Los Malhechores del bien*, ed. I. A. Leonard and R. K. Spaulding, (New York: Macmillan Co., 1933).

UNAMUNO, M. DE, *Abel Sánchez*, ed. Amelia and Ángel del Río (New York: Dryden Press, 1947).

SPANISH 2

CASTELLANO, JUAN, and BROWN, C. B., *Spanish Review Grammar* (New York: Charles Scribner's Sons, 1933).

CASONA, ALEJANDRO, *Nuestra Natacha*, ed. William H. Shoemaker (New York: F. S. Crofts & Co., 1937).

ADAMS, N. B., *España* (New York: Henry Holt & Co., 1947).

DEL RÍO, AMELIA and ÁNGEL, *Del Solar Hispánico* (New York: Dryden Press, 1945).

LÓPEZ Y FUENTES, GREGORIO, *Tierra*, ed. H. A. Holmes and W. A. Bara (New York: Ginn & Co., 1949).

CASO, ANTONIO, *México (apuntamientos de cultura patria)* (Mexico: Imprenta Universitaria, 1943).

NOTE.—Spanish 2 is not required for the A.B. degree but is available to those wishing to study Spanish beyond the level set for Spanish 1.

II. LANGUAGE 1

General Course in Language (Language 1), Selected Readings (3d ed.; Chicago: University of Chicago Press, 1949). This volume contains the following subjects and texts:

PHONETICS AND PHONEMICS

STURTEVANT, EDGAR H., *An Introduction to Linguistic Science* (New Haven: Yale University Press, 1947), pp. 9–18.

MARCKWARDT, ALBERT H., *Introduction to the English Language* (New York: Oxford University Press, 1942), pp. 19, 76–78.

THE HISTORY OF LANGUAGE

STURTEVANT, EDGAR H., "The Nature of Language," in *Linguistic Change* (Chicago: University of Chicago Press, 1917), chaps. vii and viii and pp. 23–31.

MOORE, SAMUEL, "Phonologic Change," adapted from *Historical Outlines of English Phonology and Morphology* (Ann Arbor: George Wahr, 1940), pp. 21–22, 42, 59.

BRYANT, MARGARET M., "Structure of Sentences and Connectives," in *Modern English and Its Heritage* (New York: Macmillan Co., 1948), pp. 223–25.

BUCK, CARL DARLING, "Introduction: The Indo-European Family of Languages," in *Comparative Grammar of Greek and Latin* (Chicago: University of Chicago Press, 1933).

GRAMMAR

BOAS, FRANZ, "The Characteristics of Language," in *Handbook of American Indian Languages*, ed. Franz Boas (U.S. Bureau of American Ethnology, Bull. No. 40 [Washington: Government Printing Office, 1911]), Part I, pp. 24–43.

HOIJER, HARRY, "An Indian Language of Texas," in *Handbook of American Indian Languages*, ed. Franz Boas (New York: J. J. Augustin, 1933), III, ix–x, 1–2, 23–27.

WAGNER, GUNTER, "Ideas Expressed by Morphological Devices," in *Handbook of American Indian Languages*, ed. Franz Boas (New York: J. J. Augustin, 1933), III, 310–15.

PAUL, HERMANN, *Prinzipien der Sprachgeschichte* (Halle, Germany: Niemeyer, 1880), selections partly translated from the 5th ed. (1920) and partly based on the adaptation of the 2d ed. (1886) by STRONG, LOGEMAN, and WHEELER, *Introduction to the Study of the History of Language* (London: Longmans, Green, 1891).

JESPERSEN, OTTO, *A Modern English Grammar* (Heidelberg: Carl Winters, 1927), I, 211–30.

HARRIS, JAMES, *Hermes, or a Philosophical Inquiry concerning Universal Grammar* (2d ed.; London: Nourse, 1765), pp. 1–32, 36, 87–99, 100–128.

FRIES, CHARLES, *American English Grammar* (New York: D. Appleton–Century Co., 1940), chap. i.

VARRO *On the Latin Language*, Books viii and ix, from an unpublished translation by P. H. De Lacy.

SEMANTICS

OGDEN, C. K., and RICHARDS, I. A., *The Meaning of Meaning* (8th ed.; New York: Harcourt, Brace & Co., 1946), pp. v, vii, ix, 1, 9–12, 15–16, 19, 21, 23, 48, 50–53, 56–57, 87, 88, 91–93, 101–7, 109, 113–15, 117, 118–20, 209, 223–26, 233, 239.

PLATO *Cratylus*, selections from an unpublished translation by Benedict Einarson.

HOBBES, THOMAS, *Leviathan* (London: J. M. Dent & Sons, Ltd., 1914), chaps. i–v.

NOTE.—In Chapter 8, Part II, reference is made to Bloomfield, *Language* (New York: Henry Holt & Co., 1933). Chapter I from this book appears in *General Course in Language* (*Language 1*), *Selected Readings* (2d ed.; Chicago: University of Chicago Bookstore, 1947).

9

Integration

I

HISTORY OF WESTERN CIVILIZATION

WILLIAM H. McNEILL

THE course entitled History of Western Civilization reflects the efforts of the College faculty to find a satisfactory place for the study of history in general education—a place in which it neither absorbs other intellectual disciplines nor is absorbed by them. The course normally falls in the student's last year, and it is expected that the student will have completed both Humanities 2 and Social Sciences 2. The history course has been put at the end of the curriculum because it is hoped that, in addition to introducing the students to a body of information about the past, a study of the development of Western civilization will bring into one sort of intelligible relationship many of the ideas and much of the information which students meet in other courses. The history course is conceived as a partner with the course entitled Observation, Interpretation, and Integration. Both strive to integrate the College curriculum: the one historically, by focusing attention on genesis and development, the other philosophically, by concentrating attention on intellectual analysis and methodology.

The ideal of a history course combining information with integration is relatively new in the College. In 1931, when general courses were first introduced, history had a prominent place in the curriculum; the humanities course was organized as a history of civilization, and this pattern was followed until 1942. In 1946 the faculty authorized the organization of an experimental course in the history of Western civilization; and in 1949 the resulting course was made a requirement for the Bachelor's degree. The committees which have co-operated to create the present course were instructed by the College faculty to design a course which would "acquaint the student with the history of Western civilization, and provide an historical integration of the College curriculum." Such an assignment raised two major problems: (1) how best to organize and select from the vast bulk of information which historians command and (2) what was, or could be, meant by the phrase "historical integration of the College curriculum."

The problem of organization and selection was approached with two principles in mind. Distrust and dislike of any course based primarily upon a textbook and lectures were widespread among the planners of the course; consequently, it was determined to construct a course based primarily upon readings and discussion of readings. Second, it was decided that a course so organized could not hope to deal equally with all the past but would have to concentrate mainly on selected periods while neglecting or minimizing others.

As a result, the course was divided into a series of "periods of concentration." In their present (1949–50) form the periods are as follows: the Greek polis to 404 B.C.; the Roman Empire and the rise of Christianity; Latin Christendom in the twelfth and thirteenth centuries; the Renaissance and Reformation; the French Revolution; Great Britain in the first half of the nineteenth century; and Russia in the twentieth century. (The history of the United States is omitted entirely, on the ground that it is treated in the Social Sciences 1 course.) Emphasis within the periods of concentration varies. For instance, the first topic is concerned with the Greek city-state—its rise, crisis, and failure —as exemplified in the history of Athens, with some side glances at other Greek states. In other words, it deals mainly with politics. On the other hand, the Renaissance and Reformation are treated primarily as intellectual movements; and Great Britain in the nineteenth century is studied as an example of the rise of an industrial society, with emphasis upon the social adjustments made to technological and economic changes. Other topics combine political, economic, and intellectual history in varying proportions.

Continuity between periods of concentration is not entirely neglected. A handbook has been prepared which amounts to a vest-pocket textbook. It was designed to serve two purposes: to fill in gaps between the periods of concentration in a very generalized fashion and to make easily available to the students information which will permit them to understand the readings better than they could otherwise do. In addition, "bridge" lectures attempt to sketch in necessary background for each period of concentration; and between successive topics open discussion periods are scheduled for which no specific readings are assigned. These class periods allow periodic backward and forward glances which may sum up old and introduce new periods of concentration.

The choice of periods of concentration was governed in part by the temporal distribution of materials studied in other College courses, for it was felt that, by so doing, a measure of historical "integration" would automatically result. This consideration dictated the starting point of the course, since Greek plays and philosophical and scientific writings are studied in various other College courses. In several instances deliberate overlapping of reading assignments has been provided for, with the thought that a demonstration of the diverse uses to which a given text may be put by social or natural scientists, by students of the arts, and by historians might be particularly illuminating to the students.

Another consideration was taken into account in the choice of periods for study: namely, the significance of an understanding of ideas, attitudes, or institutions developed at varying times in the past for an understanding of contemporary society. Thus, although the French Revolution is scarcely touched upon in other courses, it was judged proper to include some study of that period, on the ground that the French Revolution has been one of the principal formative influences of the modern European world.

In 1947–48 an experimental course, shaped according to these principles, was offered to a small number of students. Meanwhile, the second major issue—what was, or could be, meant by "historical integration of the College curriculum"—came under discussion in a Review Committee, appointed to represent the College Faculty as a whole and to pass judgment upon the success of the experimental course. Two distinct ways in which the study of history might serve as an integration of the College curriculum were formulated by the Review Committee. On the one hand, the course might try to make men, ideas, institutions, and events understandable by seeking to describe their relationship to the total society of a given period of the past and by tracing the gradual changes which came about in the general configuration of society, suggesting how changes in one segment of social activity led to other changes in related segments. This was the approach which had generally guided the planners of the course up to that time. But another possible method of historical study and integration was suggested: by restricting attention to the history of a particular concept or technique, it would be possible to construct a history which would show how men had successively formulated and solved (or failed to solve) a particular problem. A judicious selection of topics, it was urged, would permit the integration of much, perhaps of most, of the College curriculum in this more particularized form of historical study.

Perhaps an example will make the matter clearer. A course designed according to the first, more general, approach might study Leonardo da Vinci as a product of the Italian Renaissance and attempt to relate his artistic works to the social and political conditions of Italy, to the cultural stimulus of expanding contacts with the eastern Mediterranean and with northern Europe, to the personal peculiarities of Leonardo's life and character, etc. Information about these factors might permit students to see Leonardo's paintings in a new light and to understand them in a manner which cannot be achieved by simply looking at, or reflecting upon, the paintings themselves. Moreover, the student might be expected to connect Leonardo's paintings with Machiavelli's writings (met with originally in a different course) and detect a common denominator between the man who wrote about and the man who painted for Italian princes of the Renaissance.

The more particularized approach would not pay attention to such loose common denominators. Instead, Leonardo might be studied as a painter who dealt with the problems of pictorial technique, whose handling of such elements as perspective, media, shading, etc., would be compared with that of predecessors and successors in the history of painting.

It seemed clear in the course of the discussion that neither historical approach could claim exclusive or pre-eminent value. The generalized study of history was criticized for vagueness and superficiality; and it was suggested that the organization of the topics of concentration reflected certain principles and preconceptions which were in the minds of the men who had planned the course and which the students were not in a position to detect and criticize for themselves. The more particularized approach was criticized for its narrowness and technicality and for the disjointed character which a course constructed wholly on such lines would almost inevitably exhibit. To some it seemed that the weaknesses of the two approaches could in some measure cancel one another; and it was agreed that the history course should try both, by devoting a minimum of seven weeks to the study of particularized history and by retaining the generalized approach in the balance of the course. By this arrangement it was hoped that the potentialities and limitations of both forms of historical study might be suggested to the students.

Accordingly, in 1948–49 the course was reorganized, and, by compression and excision, room was made for three "special topics": conceptions of universal history, conceptions of space and time, and techniques for the representation of space in painting. The first two topics have, of course, an obvious relation to any study of history, which must presuppose some principles for selection and emphasis and which is concerned with events in space and time. Each was inserted in the general framework of the course at what seemed the most appropriate points. Thus, as the course now stands, a brief study of some of the leading conceptions of universal history serves as an introduction; conceptions of space and time are studied after the topic on the Roman Empire and the rise of Christianity—when classical preoccupation with the finite was replaced by Christian emphasis on the infinite; and the study of space in painting follows the topic on Renaissance and Reformation—pivoting on the introduction of mathematical rules for linear perspective which were introduced by Italian painters of the fifteenth century.

As may be seen from an examination of the current reading list which is appended to this chapter, each period of concentration and special topic is built around a series of readings assigned for class discussion. The readings have been chosen in large part from primary sources; but secondary works and interpretative essays by modern scholars have also been used fairly extensively. Classroom procedure naturally varies from instructor to instructor; but, in general, the effort is to elicit from the students themselves the information and ideas which make the reading relevant to the topic being studied.

An initial obstacle which must be faced in nearly every topic is the difficulty which many students have in understanding the text, especially when unfamiliar or technical terms are used and when the presuppositions of the writer are widely different from those familiar to the students. Consequently, paraphrase and exegesis of the text are frequently necessary. A second general difficulty arises from the students' frequent lack of interest in, or respect for, the importance of chronology. It has been found useful to prepare date lists for the students and to require memorization of about one hundred key dates. In addition, brief introductions to most of the readings have been prepared which make available a minimum of biographical and chronological information to the students before they read the assigned texts.

In the part of the course devoted to the special topics, these are the only important difficulties. The readings and the pictures are in a sense self-sufficient: material which, if well understood in a chronological context, may provide a sense of historical development. An additional difficulty besets the rest of the course, for there the readings must be understood in the light of the students' general knowledge about a period in the past—a knowledge which can be only gradually built up from the reading of a number of texts, from the handbook, from the lectures, and from the instructor's sharing of his habits of mind and his information with students in the classroom. At the beginning of the study of a period of concentration it is usually necessary for the instructor to spend a large proportion of the class time in exposition and in questions designed to test the students' comprehension of technicalities of the text; but, as study of the topic proceeds, one reading helps to illumine another, and a more genuine discussion, based upon a common fund of information and some measure of common understanding of the reading, becomes possible. Despite the limitations of the discussion method for the teaching of history, the staff of the history course is convinced that the informal atmosphere of a relatively small class and the free asking and answering of questions back and forth between students and instructor is a more successful way of teaching than any other.

Obviously, a great deal depends on the person of the instructor. Since one of the major aims of the course is to integrate the College curriculum, the principle has been adopted that the history staff should be drawn, as far as practicable, from persons who have taught or are currently teaching in other College courses. Only so can real familiarity with what is done elsewhere in the College be assured. The members of the staff meet weekly. Staff meetings sometimes are employed for a discussion of what is to be taught during the following week or weeks; in addition, more general historical problems—periodization, causation, theories of history, the organization and emphasis of the course, and its possible reorganization or redistribution, etc.—are debated; and an attempt is made to have each staff member present to the group some part of his own special knowledge or interests in informal seminars distributed through the year.

An effort is made to secure a circulation of staff members over a period of years. An instructor assigned to some other staff will teach history for a period of two or three years and then return to his parent-staff to make room for someone else. Approximately half the history staff is composed of professionally trained historians; the balance consists of other professional specialists: philosophers, students of literature, political scientists, etc. It is hoped that these practices will prevent the development of an excessively ingrown intellectual tradition, while the members of the staff will have the opportunity to deepen and broaden their own education constantly. These advantages are believed to outweigh the inevitably amateur status of some of the instructors when first they teach the course.

By means of the readings, discussions, lectures, and the handbook the history staff hopes that the course approaches the ambitious goals prescribed for it by the College faculty:

To locate major events and personalities in time and space; to give the students a sense of the continuity of Western civilization through an understanding of the manner in which one age influences another and particularly the extent to which their own civilization has drawn on the past;

To present certain personalities, periods, institutions and movements with such completeness that the student may understand the complexity and richness that lie behind the panorama presented in the historical textbooks used in the course;

To invite the students' critical judgement of particular formulations of history, and illustrate the way in which other disciplines make use of history; and

To place in their historical context the authors, materials, and ideas with which the students have become acquainted in other College courses.

That the course fully achieves these aims no one pretends; and it should be emphasized that the course is still very much in the making, so that details of organization and the particular choice of readings may be expected to change substantially from year to year in the foreseeable future.

I I

OBSERVATION, INTERPRETATION, AND INTEGRATION

WILLIAM O'MEARA

THE demand for integration in college education is a demand for some rationally defensible plan for choice and correlation among the large and apparently continually increasing number of subjects of study that compete for the attention of faculties and students. A reduction in the number of distinct courses in the College was achieved by the development of general courses in three major fields—the humanities, the social sciences, and the natural sciences—along with mathematics and auxiliary courses in English and foreign languages. While this constituted a practical solution in the organization of the curriculum of the College, the faculty realized that, over and above the program of general courses in the natural sciences, the humanities, and the social sciences, the students needed a treatment of intellectual problems, of both practical and theoretical importance, which could not be considered adequately in the courses restricted to particular ranges of learning.

We know that at various stages in the elaboration of a given discipline it is customary to offer views on the nature of knowledge in general and on the place and value of the given discipline in relation to other studies. Frequently the opinions held on these points suffer from a lack of learning and reflection, resulting from a too exclusive preoccupation with the established views of practitioners of the science in question. A common form of one-sidedness is to take one's own field as basic or primary and consequently to see other disciplines as derivative or even as unscientific. Two examples may serve to illustrate what I mean. In the Middle Ages the knowledge, service, and love of God, as elaborated in the study of sacred doctrine or theology was very generally held to be *the* science and its standpoint made to be the measure for the utility, the genuineness, and consequently the validity of all other fields of knowledge. St. Augustine had argued ably for the utility of all other learning on the grounds that it was necessary or useful in the fuller understanding of God's revelation to man. Other theologians, with less comprehensive views, did not hesitate to exclude profane learning, including the liberal arts, from the sphere of pursuits proper for the intellectual who would seek salvation. In modern times, physics is perhaps the science most frequently regarded as basic and primary, the science in terms of which all other knowledge is to be assayed. Thus, for many at the present time, the only sound way to carry on the study of biology, psychology, and every other discipline conceded to be genuinely scientific is to see them as elaborations or applications of the principles, methods, and criteria of physics. The present course has as its comprehensive purpose the examination of the problems posed by the divergence of opinion on matters of this kind.

The general purpose of the course may be stated in the words of the *Announcements:* it is designed "to equip the student with the knowledge and intellectual disciplines necessary for a theoretically and practically meaningful 'integration' of the different fields of knowledge which are the subject-matter of the other general courses." The student comes to the course with some ideas on the problem, but they are usually inexplicit. The previous courses he has pursued in the natural sciences and mathematics, the humanities and the social sciences, have directly and indirectly caused him to think about the nature of knowledge and the relations in which different fields of knowledge stand to one another. There remains to be done an explicit and extensive job.

The purpose of Observation, Interpretation, and Integration* is to give the student the opportunity to acquire the knowledge and ability necessary to work out for himself an intelligible theory on the interrelationships of the fields of knowledge. I should like to consider these aims with reference to the rest of the curriculum and to the capacities which the students who take the course may be expected to have. The three principal questions are: What relevant knowledge is it possible and necessary for the course to make available to the student at this stage in his education? What abilities is it desirable for the student to acquire and how is the program to see to the develop-

* A note on the name of the course. Before the changes in the curriculum of the College which took place in 1942, one of the general courses had the name, "Methods, Values, Concepts." This course was similar to courses in the introduction to philosophy and held a position in the old curriculum not unlike that intended to be occupied by the present course in the new curriculum. In the discussions of the faculty which led to the setting-up of the new curriculum, the present course was commonly spoken of as an "integration" course. When the time came to decide upon an official appellation, the proposal was made and adopted that the words "observation" and "interpretation" be added, resulting in the present name. The word "observation" was intended to indicate that the new course should have, as one of its primary aims, concern with scientific methods, and the word "interpretation" to express the course's concern with the humanities and the social sciences. Despite the awkwardness of the title, a less unsatisfactory one remains to be found. The course is commonly referred to as the "Integration Course" or by the abbreviation "O.I.I."

The course in its original form was developed by a committee appointed by Dean Clarence H. Faust and consisting of members of the staffs of the existing general courses. Richard McKeon, then Dean of the Division of the Humanities and a member of the College Humanities staff, was the principal author of the course, as regards both content and method.

ment of these abilities? And, finally, what is the nature and extent of the resultant "opportunity to work out for himself an intelligible theory on the nature and interrelationships of the fields of knowledge"?

In the first place, and in line with the practice of other courses in the curriculum, it was thought desirable to use, as the basic materials of the course, original readings concerned with an examination of the problems of integration which have been prominent and influential in Western culture. More will be said later about the details of this part of the course. For the present, let us consider the general approach.

Plans of integration may be regarded as falling into three different typical groups. One of the largest groups contains plans which may be termed "encyclopedic" in character. These are schemes of organization, the starting points of which are derived from the actually existing arts and sciences of a given time. The effort is largely to "cover the ground"; to take the existing situation and arrange the items, the bodies of knowledge, and the recognized arts in a comprehensive scheme. There is always a certain *practical* purpose involved, if only that of cataloguing in a convenient manner so that the knowledge at hand may be easily found; and there is frequently a theoretical basis for beginning at one point rather than at another or for at least the primary subdivisions of the scheme. But both practice and theory take a place secondary to comprehensiveness and generality, and such plans are usually capable of illustrating diverse theories or of being employed in the interest of diverse practical ends. In an encyclopedic organization, it is obvious, the integrative function is at a minimum. The point of view is pluralistic or eclectic, and little or nothing can be derived from such an organization which would permit judgment as to the relative importance of different fields of intellectual endeavors. In a word, the field is still open for plans of a more definite, or a more strongly integrative, kind. The encyclopedic integration involves few convictions or even assumptions, but it is for that very reason ineffective and unsatisfactory in meeting the demand for an organization of the arts and sciences which does answer questions of relative importance in a way which may have practical results for the individual or society.

Integrations of a more definite kind than the encyclopedic may be divided into those predominantly theoretical and those primarily practical. A theoretical integration is one derived from a developed doctrine on the nature of science, scientific subject matters, and scientific methods. It offers a solution of the problems of the unity or multiplicity of the sciences and of their relationships on the basis of the principles of its philosophy or world view. Integrations which are regarded as primarily practical are those which orient the sciences and education to particular applications in meeting the needs and solving the problems of individuals and groups. It must be emphasized that the designation "theoretical" or "practical" is given in view of the dominant characteristic of the scheme in question. In nearly every instance of each of the three kinds of integration some attention is given to theory, to practice, and to comprehensiveness, but usually one of these interests or aspects is primary.

In the case of a doctrine on integration of the theoretical kind, it is usual for the integrative scheme to be closely connected with a complete philosophy. The relation between the two may be more or less fully elaborated, but the doctrine on integration generally assumes theories elsewhere developed concerning fundamental principles of being and truth. Practical integrations, similarly, involve assumptions concerning the nature of value and use. In both cases the integrative doctrine tends to take for granted teachings which it does not itself include or expound. One difference between the two is that practical integrations do not appear to require examination of assumptions, since "success" or "failure" can be taken as the measure of correctness. Such a program of integration, however, is inevitably based upon unexamined and often unconsciously held assumptions, which determine not only the character of the integration but also the definition of success and its opposite. And this, obviously, renders verification by "success" a circular process. To choose intelligently among possible theoretic and practical integrations requires an ability to recognize, analyze, and judge the assumptions on which they are based. Of course, the exercise of these abilities, though indispensable, is not a guaranty of the achievement of certainty.

These considerations bring us to the most important matters for the understanding of the contents and methods of the present course. We have now outlined in general terms the kind of *knowledge* which the student is given the opportunity to acquire. In what follows we shall take up together the question of the inculcation of related *abilities* in the student, along with consideration of what is meant by saying that it is our aim to give the student the opportunity to attempt to work out for himself an intelligible integration of knowledge. In some programs which recognize the desirability of explicit study of the problem of integration, the instruction consists of what might better be called "indoctrination." The view of some school of philosophy is preferred by the instructor or staff in charge, and a course is given which attempts to convince the student that this view is *the* truth on the nature of knowledge and on the relation of one form of knowledge to another. Perhaps most frequently at the present time it is the philosophy of logical positivism which is set forth as a dogma. The student coming to college has already absorbed prevalent popular conceptions according to which mathematics and pre-eminently mathematical physics are the genuinely scientific disciplines, while the biological and the social sciences, in so far as they are scientific at all, are scientific because they are advancing toward the ideal embodied in the mathematical and physical sciences. The student is made acquainted with other comprehensive efforts to understand the nature of knowledge and the interrelationships of the sciences. Diverse plans of integration are studied, and their differing basic principles are analyzed and compared. Such questions as the following are raised: Is all science essentially of the same type, and, if so, what are the characteristics of the scientific? Are there several kinds of science, differing in their aims, methods, and subject matters? If there are several sciences, to what degree are they independent of one another, or are they arranged in an order of subordination to a primary science? Are sciences to be valued proportionally to their utility for the purposes of mankind or to their success in achieving objective truth? In this manner the assumptions underlying the various competing answers are brought to light and a better understanding is obtained of points in dispute. The student becomes aware that currently popular views are not the whole story and that, moreover, many of them are similar in type to such classical doctrines as those of Plato, Bacon, or Auguste Comte. In addition, he learns that there are other intelligibly defensible theories on the organization of the sciences which do not define science in a unitary way and which are consequently able to recognize nonmathematical disciplines, including theories on man and society, as no less scientific, though in different senses, than mathematics and physics.

The aim of our instruction is not to supply the student with final answers to the various problems which are taken up. In the study of the various types of integrations, we raise the questions whose answers are commonly taken for granted. Both the meaning and the value of certain important notions are often assumed without argument in schemes of integration. For example, differences of view, whose roots and, consequently, meaning are difficult to discover, may be found to arise from assumptions unconsciously held concerning the nature and mutual relations of fact and idea and the related faculties of sensation and understanding. The meaning and role of factors such as these must be carefully examined. Through the analysis, by the discussion method, of the assumptions, principles, methods of argumentation, and conclusions of the texts assigned for study, the student *may* acquire the ability to compare, contrast, and relate different answers to questions, together with the ideas, principles, and methods used to arrive at the answers, so that he will know not merely that they are the same or different but what the differences and similarities are and how, in terms of the principles and methods used by the answerer, the differences arose.

The question may well be raised whether our plan is not too ambitious, whether the college student is able to profit by this kind of course, using this method of instruction. The short answer, of course, is that we do not believe that we have aimed too high. This conviction is supported by seven years' experience in teaching the course. A further consideration is our opinion that nothing short of this kind of course would be worth doing in the College's program of general education. In the light of the accomplishments, and not merely the ideals, of the other courses that the student has taken previously or is taking along with O.I.I., it is clear that a course in integration which aimed to present *the* answer to the problem or even a conspectus of answers, presented in the mode of conclusions, would be definitely beneath the student's level. The continual emphasis in every other course is upon reasons and methods and never merely upon achieved results. The whole character of the curriculum calls for an integration course of the kind which has been described. A merely informational or eclectic survey of theories on the nature and interrelationships of the fields of knowledge would do little for students already to some degree skilled in examining serious treatments of fundamental problems in the fields of the other general courses. A dogmatic type of integration course, whether of secularist or of religious inspiration, would be unfitting for obvious reasons. The present course may properly be said to offer an *instrumental* integration—instrumental in the sense that its aim is to give the student the means to achieve his own answers to the problems proper to the course. To the extent to which this can be done, it can be best achieved by the method of systematic discussion, exercised upon important original works.

We have the conviction that the opportunity which training in this knowledge and ability gives to the student to achieve an answer of his own to the problems raised in the course is considerable. In common with the other parts of the College curriculum, O.I.I. is both terminal and preparatory. There is little or no difficulty in seeing the suitability of the present course as part of a general education which is preliminary to more advanced studies. Whatever specialized work he may enter upon, the student has been equipped with the fundamental knowledge and ability needed to see his chosen field in relation to other specialties. His views will, no doubt, go on growing and changing, but, in view of the discipline of O.I.I., such development should take place critically and with fuller awareness of the commitments involved in adopting a particular point of view. He has been trained to be critically self-conscious, and thus he has a foundation for making up his own mind as he works out for himself an integration of the fields of knowledge. Much the same may be said of those for whom O.I.I. is part of their concluding formal education. They should possess the means for critical reflection and action on the problems that they will face in their lives as individuals and as citizens. To this general aim of the College program, O.I.I. has made its distinctive contribution.

The readings for the course have been chosen from the history of thought from the time of Plato to the present. These readings have been grouped under the following titles: "Organization of the Sciences," "Methods of the Sciences," and "Principles in the Sciences," used successively in the three quarters of study given to the course. At the outset it will be well to explain the relation between the three words used in the title of the course—"observation," "interpretation," and "integration"—and the three words used in the names of the three parts of the course—"organizations," "methods," and "principles." The circumstances which led to the choice of a title for the course have been explained above.

As the work of selecting and arranging the readings went on, it was decided that the most suitable topic to treat at the beginning would be that of *organizations* of the sciences. This part was to be followed by readings on the topics of methods and principles.

It is obvious that there is a certain correspondence between observation and methods, between organizations and integration, and between principles and interpretation. Observation is often a prominent factor in theories of method; an organization of knowledge is usually a part or a consequence of a theory of integration; and interpretation in any comprehensive sense is difficult to think of without some elaboration of the principles of construction and meaning belonging to the scientific propositions being interpreted. The order—organizations, methods, principles—then, was adopted as the problems of interpretation were divided into three parts for pedagogical reasons and for convenience of arrangement in a curriculum extending over the three quarters of the academic year. Thus, when the student is first introduced to the problems of integration, he studies plans which

consist of comprehensive essays of organization or classification
of the arts and sciences. This provides a general background, but
one in which many questions are raised which are not fully
answered. The student sees that assumptions concerning the
definition of science and assumptions concerning the methods of
acquiring and testing knowledge are often prominent factors in
the organizational schemes proposed. Moreover, the operation
of principles, both tacit and avowed, is constantly noted. Hence
the need for a more explicit consideration of methods and principles, which is met in the second and third parts of the course.
Thus we may say that throughout the course the emphasis is on
integration, seen in the three parts or sections from the vantage
points of organization, methods, and principles. In each part's
work the problems common to the course as a whole are taken
up primarily from the point of view of one of the three main
heads, while those of the other two are in a secondary position.
Organization, methods, and principles are understood in senses
sufficiently inclusive for the three taken together to make a place
for the consideration of the leading problems raised by treatments
of the nature of knowledge and its kinds.

Questions concerning organizations of the sciences have to do
with the relation of propositions or items of information or sciences to one another. They are questions such as: What does a
given author mean by science or learning in general? Are there
many sciences or only one? If there are many, how are they
related? What is the bearing of the asserted unity, plurality, or
interdependence of the sciences on their methods and on the interpretation of their conclusions? What is the result of using biological principles in the interpretation of social phenomena,
physical principles on biological phenomena, logical principles
on the social sciences, or sociological principles on the humanities? Questions of this sort are intended to bring forward for examination the usually half-formed views which students have
already developed in their earlier courses. For example, the implicit conviction that works of art must be understood in terms
of social conditions would affect the significance and cogency of
propositions in literary and artistic criticism. Similarly, views on
the interrelations of various fields will influence the questions

that can be asked meaningfully in those fields and the significance
of the answers given to them. Thus, if it is conceived that physics
is basic in respect of other forms of knowledge to such a degree
that the statements of other "sciences" must be similar to physics
in method of discovery and in form, it is obvious that disciplines
concerned with judgments of value, such as political science and
the humanities, will be interpreted in a manner very different
from that in a scheme in which physics does not occupy such a
position. Such implicit convictions are in the background whenever statements about the nature of anything are questioned, as,
for example, when the definition of man as a rational animal is
disputed either by the argument that man does not "think" or by
evidence that animals do "think"; when "justice" is asserted to
have only rhetorical bearings on decisions of law; or when art is
held to be, not an "imitation," but a creation or an expression.

The bases upon which each author defines and classifies the
sciences are examined. Differences are noted, and reasons why
sciences appear in, or disappear from, the different schemes proposed are analyzed. If the same name is found in otherwise differing plans, does the science named continue to have its original
subject matter, method, and purpose? Again, what happens to
such disciplines as metaphysics, politics, psychology, or physics,
which sometimes dominate a hierarchy of sciences, when they
are made subordinate or removed from the category of science,
and to the subordinate sciences under their respective domina-
tions? Finally, in what, if any, sense are literature, history, philosophy, and theology sciences? And what is the relation of the
sciences to technology, the fine arts, and morals? These and many
more are the kinds of questions to which attention is given in the
first part of the course.

In that part of the work, theories concerning methods are noted
as sources of differences of doctrine concerning the nature and the
interrelationships of the fields of knowledge. However, at that
point in the course, time cannot be taken to examine in detail
everything relevant and interesting which comes up. The general standpoint of the first part's work is that of considering the
sciences as already constituted. It is noted frequently, but only
in passing, that views on method, i.e., on how knowledge is to be

achieved, seem to have importance for this or that author in his theory on the integration of knowledge. It is in the more general or comprehensive treatment of the problems of the course in the first part that the topics especially studied in the second and third parts are found. The second part of the course, then, has the aim of analyzing diverse theories of method, in so far as these may be seen to have relevance for the study of the integration of knowledge.

Excerpts from the following authors are read in the section on methods in the sciences: Plato, Aristotle, Francis Bacon, Descartes, Newton, De Morgan, Whewell, J. S. Mill, Böckh, Durkheim, Poincaré, John Dewey, Einstein. Principal topics are: the roles of sense and intellect in scientific discovery; the place and techniques of induction; the nature and use of hypotheses; method in mathematics, the natural sciences, the social sciences; the relation of world view to method; methods in the humanities. The students' attention is directed to many fundamental questions. The sources and outcomes of different theories of method, whether of a unitary or of a pluralistic kind, are subjected to careful study. Various doctrines on the relation of knowledge to reality and criteria for the identification of "truth" are examined. The section on methods in the sciences throws light on some of the sources, frequently difficult to discover, of the major differences between alternative plans for the integration of knowledge.

The work of the third part consists of a study of principles in the sciences, to the extent that differences of view on principles are relevant to problems of integration. The two first parts have amply shown that diversity in doctrine always involves some differences concerning the nature and function of principles. In this part we consider how various thinkers state their principles, what sorts of entities these principles are, how their relation to other parts of the science is conceived, and how the different thinkers vary in regard to these matters. Our primary concern is with the internal structure of a given science or system of the sciences. This study is complementary to the study of methods, conceived as ways of acquiring scientific knowledge, in that it inquires into the nature and role of principles in sciences when they are regarded as relatively fully elaborated. Two groups of readings are used to accomplish this result of bringing into sharp focus a system of knowledge as determined by principles.

The first group of readings presents four treatments, in terms of four different sets of principles, of what appears to be a single subject matter, while the other presents, from the point of view of one principle, discussions of different subject matters. The first group is constituted by four readings concerning "pleasure" by Plato, Aristotle, Hume, and Mill; the second by selections from two works of Kant. The two groups are in a sense the inverse of each other. That is, in the case of the first, we have chosen what seems to be the same problem—the function of pleasure in moral philosophy—and try to see what difference four sets of principles make in its statement and solution. In the second case there is a single principle, the categorical imperative, and our effort is to see how it is possible to distinguish different problems and subject matters and state and resolve problems in terms of different formulations of this principle, as it is employed, for example, in distinguishing ethical duties from duties of right.

The continuing aim is to make the student aware of the complexities which are encountered in attempts to solve fundamental problems of both theoretical and practical import when there is disagreement on the nature and functioning of principles in the variously distinguished disciplines, and thus to provide a basis for an intelligent approach to such problems.

It may be possible, at the end of this paper, to add a word to the earlier statement to the effect that a course in addition to the general courses in the three major fields and to the auxiliary courses was felt to be needed when the present curriculum was introduced. Observation, Interpretation, and Integration is intended to meet this need by offering to the student the knowledge and abilities required to place in their context—to locate, so to speak—many of the most important issues with regard to which discussion or deliberation takes place. While many problems may be placed clearly enough in one or another field and thus may be tackled by the means provided by education and experience in that field, there are others which involve knowledge and skills drawn from more than one branch of learning. Where such problems are in issue, critical awareness is essential concerning what one is doing when one makes a commitment—more simply, when one reaches a decision or makes up one's mind. In these cases the resources of the ordinarily recognized fields of study may well be insufficient. There are needed further knowledge and abilities which can come only from acquaintance with and reflection upon the various fields of knowledge, the arts and sciences, and the multiple relations in which they stand to one another. Hence the aim of the present course—to give to the student an opportunity to work out for himself an integration of knowledge.

Reading Lists

I. HISTORY

McNEILL, WILLIAM H., *History Handbook* (Chicago: University of Chicago Press, 1949–50).

CONCEPTIONS OF HISTORY

BOSSUET, J. B., *Discourse on Universal History*, trans. W. H. McNeill (unpublished), from *Discours sur l'histoire universelle* (New York: Roe Lockwood, 1856), pp. 1–5, 337–42, 422–29.

CONDORCET, MARQUIS DE, *Outlines of an Historical View of the Progress of the Human Mind* (Baltimore: J. Frank, 1802), pp. 7–19, 154–78, 197–200, 203–11.

HERDER, J. G., *One More Philosophy of History for the Cultivation of the Human Mind*, trans. C. M. Mackauer (unpublished), from HERDER, J. G., *Auch ein Philosophie der Geschichte zur Bildung der Menschheit* (Riga: J. F. Hartknoch, 1774).

RANKE, LEOPOLD VON, Preface to *Geschichten der Römischen und Germanischen Völker*, trans. W. H. McNeill (unpublished), in *Sämmtliche Werke* (Leipzig: Duncan & Humbolt, 1874), XXXIII, v–viii.

Three letters on the materialistic interpretation of history, in MARX, KARL, and ENGELS, FRIEDRICH, *Correspondence 1846–1895*, trans. Dona Torr (New York: International Publishers, Inc., 1936), pp. 472–73, 475–77, 516–19.

TOYNBEE, A. J., "The Tragedy of Greece," in *The Tragedy of Greece* (Oxford: Clarendon Press, 1921), pp. 2–42.

THE GREEK "POLIS"

THUCYDIDES *History of the Peloponnesian War*, trans. Richard Crawley ("Modern Library" [New York: Random House, 1934]), i. 1–24, 67–88, 139–46; ii. 35–46, 59–66; iii. 70–85; v. 86–116; Books vi and vii.

HERODOTUS *The Persian Wars*, trans. George Rawlinson ("Modern Library" [New York: Random House, 1947]), i. 28–33; Books vii and viii.

PLATO *Apology* and *Crito*, trans. B. Jowett in *The Works of Plato*, ed. Irwin Edman ("Modern Library" [New York: Random House, n.d.]).

ARISTOTLE *Constitution of the Athenians*, trans. Livio Stecchini (unpublished), chaps. 1–41.

AESCHYLUS *The Persians*, in *The Tragedies of Aeschylus*, trans. R. Potter (London: J. & J. Allman, 1819).

ARISTOPHANES *The Knights*, in *The Comedies of Aristophanes*, trans. William James Hickie (London: G. Bell, 1869), i. 53–114.

THE OLD OLIGARCH *On the Athenian Republic*, trans. Livio Stecchini (unpublished).

THE ROMAN EMPIRE AND CHRISTIANITY

Gospel of St. Matthew, Epistle to the Galatians, Acts of the Apostles.

ADCOCK, F. E., "The Achievement of Augustus," in *Cambridge Ancient History*, ed. J. B. Bury, S. A. Cook, and F. E. Adcock (Cambridge: At the University Press, 1938–39), X, 583–606.

TACITUS *Annals*, the Oxford translation (New York: Harper & Bros., 1858), i. 1–7.

AUGUSTUS *Res gestae*, in SHUCKBURGH, E. S., *Augustus* (London: T. Fisher Unwin, 1903), pp. 293–301.

ORIGEN *Against Celsus*, in *The Ante-Nicene Fathers*, ed. Alexander Roberts and James Donaldson (Buffalo: Christian Literature Pub. Co., 1885), IV, 395–401, 665–69.

"The Edict of Milan," in *The Ante-Nicene Fathers*, ed. Alexander Roberts and James Donaldson (Buffalo: Christian Literature Pub. Co., 1885), VII, 320.

Three letters by CONSTANTINE, in *The Works of St. Optatus*, trans. O. R. Vassall-Phillips (New York: Longmans, Green & Co., 1917), pp. 384–87, 395–98, 412–15.

ST. AMBROSE, two letters (Nos. XVII and LI), in *The Letters of Ambrose* (Oxford: James Parker & Co., 1881), pp. 88–94, 324–29.

The Nicene Creed, in *A Select Library of Nicene and Post-Nicene Fathers of the Christian Church*, ed. Henry Percival (2d ser.; New York: Charles Scribner's Sons, 1900), XIV, 3.

ROSTOVTZEFF, M. I., "The Oriental Despotism and the Problem of the Decay of Ancient Civilization," in *Social and Economic History of the Roman Empire* (Oxford: Clarendon Press, 1926), pp. 449–87.

BAYNES, N. H., "The Decline of the Roman Power in Western Europe: Some Modern Explanations," *Journal of Roman Studies*, XXXIII (1943), 29–35.

ST. AUGUSTINE *Confessions*, trans. F. J. Sheed (New York: Sheed & Ward, 1943), pp. 3–13, 105–14, 157–61, 164–79, 183–87, 192–203.

DAWSON, CHRISTOPHER, "St. Augustine and His Age," in *A Monument to Saint Augustine* (London: Sheed & Ward, 1930), pp. 43–77.

HORACE Epode XVI, in MARIN, SIR THOMAS, *The Works of Horace Translated into English Verse* (Edinburgh: Blackwood, 1888), II, 25–27.

VIRGIL Fourth Eclogue, in BOWEN, SIR CHARLES, *Virgil in English Verse* (London: Murray, 1889), pp. 25–28.

DAWSON, CHRISTOPHER, *The Making of Europe* (London: Sheed & Ward, 1932), pp. 1–66.

CONCEPTIONS OF SPACE AND TIME

ARISTOTLE *Physics*, trans. R. P. Hardie and R. V. Gaye, in *The Basic Works of Aristotle*, ed. Richard P. McKeon (New York: Random House, 1941), Book iv.

PLOTINUS "Of Time and Eternity," *Third Ennead* vii. 8–13, in *Complete Works*, trans. K. S. Guthrie (London: Geo. Bell & Sons, 1918).

AUGUSTINE *Confessions*, xi. 10–31, trans. F. J. Sheed (New York: Sheed & Ward, 1943), pp. 268–86.

CASSIRER, ERNST, discussion of time and space in Nicolaus Cusanus, trans. from *Individuum und Kosmos in der Philosophie der Renaissance* (Leipzig: B. G. Teubner, 1927), pp. 185–94, 43–45.

NEWTON, ISAAC, Definition VIII and Scholium, in *Mathematical Principles of Natural Philosophy*, trans. Florian Cajori (Berkeley: University of California Press, 1934), pp. 4–12.

BERKELEY, GEORGE, *A Treatise concerning the Principles of Human Knowledge* (La Salle, Ill.: Open Court Pub. Co., 1920), pp. 86–87, 94–98, 100–101.

LEIBNIZ, G. W., "Correspondence with Clarke," in *Philosophical Writings* "Everyman's Library" [New York: E. P. Dutton & Co,, Inc., n.d.]), excerpts from pp. 198–224.

KANT, IMMANUEL, "Transcendental Aesthetic," in *Critique of Pure Reason*, trans. J. M. D. Meikeljohn (London: Geo. Bell & Sons, 1893), pp. 21–44.

MEDIEVAL SOCIETY IN THE TWELFTH AND THIRTEENTH CENTURIES

POWER, E. E., "Peasant Life and Rural Conditions (*ca.* 1100–1500)," in *Cambridge Medieval History*, ed. H. M. Gwatkin and J. P. Whitney (New York: Macmillan Co., 1911–36), VII, 716–50.

WALTER OF HENLEY *Husbandry*, trans. Elizabeth Lamond (New York: Longmans, Green & Co., 1890), pp. 3–15, 27–31.

PIRENNE, HENRI, "Northern Towns and Their Commerce," in *Cambridge Medieval History*, ed. H. M. Gwatkin and J. P. Whitney (New York: Macmillan Co., 1911–36), VI, 505–27.

PRÉVITÉ-ORTON, C. W., "The Italian Cities till *ca.* 1200," in *Cambridge Medieval History*, ed. H. M. Gwatkin and J. P. Whitney (New York: Macmillan Co., 1911–36), V, 208–41.

Documents on English towns and guilds, in *Translations and Reprints from the Original Sources of European History*, ed. E. P. Cheyney (Philadelphia: University of Pennsylvania Department of History, 1895), Vol. II, No. 1.

"Regulations Respecting Manufacture and Sale of Cloth at Douai," in CAVE, R. C., and COULSON, H. H., *A Source Book for Medieval Economic History* (Milwaukee: Bruce Pub. Co., 1936), pp. 253–57.

JOHN OF SALISBURY *Policraticus*, in *The Statesman's Book of John of Salisbury*, trans, John Dickinson (New York: Knopf, 1927), pp. 3–8, 32–36, 335–49.

BRYCE, JAMES, *The Holy Roman Empire* (8th ed.; New York: Macmillan Co., 1887), pp. 89–132.

Documents illustrating the conflict of Empire and Papacy, 1076–1122, in HENDERSON, E. F., *Select Historical Documents of the Middle Ages* (London: George Bell & Sons, 1892), pp. 366–77, 380–84, 385–87, 394–405, 408–90, 432–37.

DANTE, "De monarchia," in CHURCH, R. W., *Dante* (London: Macmillan & Co., Ltd., 1879), pp. 184–210, 257, 268–70, 275–304.

STRAYER, J. R., "The Laicization of French and English Society in the Thirteenth Century," *Speculum, a Journal of Mediaeval Studies*, XV (April, 1940), 213–23.

Maddox, Margaret, unpublished notes relative to the development of the English government, 1066–1307.

Constitution of Clarendon, trans. Sylvia Thrupp (unpublished).

Assize of Northampton, trans. Sylvia Thrupp (unpublished).

Magna Carta, trans. Sylvia Thrupp (unpublished).

St. Francis of Assisi, *The Mirror of Perfection*, chaps. 67–75, trans. Sebastian Evans (2d ed.; London: D. Nutt, 1900), pp. 114–134.

"The Testament of Our Seraphic Father St. Francis," in *The Writings of St. Francis of Assisi*, trans. Constance, Countess de la Warr (London: Burns & Oates, 1908), pp. 37–41.

St. Francis of Assisi, "Hymn to the Sun," in Arnold, Matthew, *Essays in Criticism* (London: Macmillan & Co., Ltd., 1865), pp. 204–5.

"The Rule of the Friars Minor from the Text of 1223," in *The Writings of St. Francis of Assisi*, trans. Constance, Countess de la Warr (London: Burns & Oates, 1908), pp. 28–36.

St. Bonaventura *Breviloquium*, trans. Erwin Esser Nemmers (St. Louis: B. Herder Book Co., 1946), pp. 81–93, 109–11, 114–19, 128–37, 175–77, 237–44.

RENAISSANCE AND REFORMATION

Petrarch, *Secret, or the Soul's Conflict with Passion*, Dialogue II, trans. William H. Draper (London: Chatto & Windus, 1911), pp. 47–106.

Troeltsch, Ernst, "Renaissance and Reformation," trans. Henry A. Finch, from *Historische Zeitschrift*, CX, 519–56.

Machiavelli, *The Prince*, ed. Thomas G. Bryan (New York: F. S. Crofts & Co., 1947), pp. 12–33, 41–45, 65–68, 72–78.

———, "Discourses on Livy," in *The Historical, Political, and Diplomatic Writings of Niccolò Machiavelli*, trans. Christian E. Detmold (Boston: James R. Orgood & Co., 1882), pp. 104–7, 120–31, 137–40, 169–71, 208–12, 214–21, 229–35, 419–20.

More, Sir Thomas, *Utopia*, ed. H. S. V. Ogden (New York: Appleton-Century-Crofts, 1949).

Luther, Martin, *A Treatise on Christian Liberty* (Philadelphia: Muehlenberg Press, 1947).

The Twelve Articles of the Revolting Peasants (1525), in *Works of Martin Luther*, trans. C. M. Jacobs (Philadelphia: A. J. Holman Co., 1931), IV, 210–16.

Luther, Martin, *Against the Robbing and Murdering Hordes of Peasants*, in *Works of Martin Luther*, trans. C. M. Jacobs (Philadelphia: A. J. Holman Co., 1931), IV, 248–54.

TECHNIQUES OF REPRESENTING SPACE IN ART

Alberti, Leone Battista, *On Painting*, Book I, trans. Richard Scofield (unpublished), from *Il Trattato della pittura e i cinque ordini architettorini* (Lannano: R. Carabla, 1913), pp. 1–18.

BUNIM, MIRIAM SCHILD, *Space in Medieval Painting and the Forerunners of Perspective* (New York: Columbia University Press, 1940), pp. 3–11, 12–13, 14–17, 20–26, 27–30.

PANOFSKY, ERWIN, "Perspective as Symbolic Form," trans. Richard Scofield (unpublished), from *Vorträge der Bibliothek Warburg, 1924-25* (Leipzig: Teubner, 1927), pp. 258–330.

Selected University prints.

THE FRENCH REVOLUTION

ROUSSEAU, J. J., *Social Contract*, ed. Charles Frankel (New York: Hafner, 1947), pp. 5–9, 14–30, 32–43, 46–60, 80–89, 92–94, 110–13, 115–25.

SIEYÈS, EMMANUEL JOSEPH, *What Is the Third Estate?* trans. W. H. McNeill (unpublished).

Declaration of the Rights of Man and of the Citizen (1791), trans. Margaret Maddox (unpublished).

Declaration of the Rights of Man and of the Citizen (1793), trans. Margaret Maddox (unpublished).

BRISSOT, J. P., *To His Constituents* (London, 1794), pp. 1–9, 15–22, 55–79, 93–121.

ROBESPIERRE, MAXIMILIEN, "Letter to His Constituents, No. 2, 1793," trans. Edward Bastian (unpublished), from *Lettres de Maximilien Robespierre* (Paris: Chez P. J. Duplain, 1792–93), II, 49–60.

———, "Dedication to Jean-Jacques Rousseau," trans. H. S. Mims (unpublished), from *Œuvres complètes de Maximilien Robespierre* (Paris: Leroux, 1910–26), I, 211–12.

———, "Catechism," trans. Edward Bastian (unpublished), from COURTOIS, E. B., *Rapport fait au nom de la commission chargée de l'examen des papiers trouvés chez Robespierre* (Paris: Maret, 1795), pp. 180–81.

———, *Report upon the Principles of Political Morality* (Philadelphia, 1794).

BABEUF, F. N., "Manifest of Equals," from BUONARROTI, FILIPPO, *History of Babeuf's Conspiracy for Equality*, trans. Bronterre (London: Hetherington, 1836), pp. 314–17.

Three letters from Jullien fils to Robespierre, trans. H. S. Mims (unpublished), from *Collection des mémoires relatifs à la Revolution Française* (Paris: Baudonin Frères, 1828), LVIII, 4–8, 13–17, 19–25.

ROBESPIERRE the YOUNGER, "Account of His Activities in the Department de Haute-Saône, trans. H. S. Mims (unpublished), from *Œuvres complètes de Maximilien Robespierre* (Paris: Leroux, 1926), III, 257–61.

GREAT BRITAIN AND NINETEENTH-CENTURY INDUSTRIALISM

BURKE, EDMUND, *Reflections on the Revolution in France* (London: Dodsley, 1790), selections.

MILL, J. S., *Autobiography* (New York: Henry Holt & Co., 1883), pp. 63–67, 105–9, 190–97, 230–36.

DICEY, A. V., "Law and Public Opinion in England," in *Lectures on the Relation between Law and Public Opinion in England* (London: Macmillan & Co., Ltd., 1905), pp. 62–65.

WESLEY, JOHN, *The Character of a Methodist* (7th ed.; London: Cock, 1751).

BENSON, JOSEPH, *An Apology for the People Called Methodists* (London: Story, 1801), pp. 129–33, 140–51, 179–83.

WILBERFORCE, WILLIAM, *A Practical View of the Prevailing Religious System of Professed Christians in the Higher and Middle Classes in This Country Contrasted with Real Christianity* (Philadelphia: Key & Biddle, 1835), pp. xiv, xxii–xxv, xxxiii–xxxiv, xliii, 75–76, 292–93, 296, 313–15.

KNOWLES, L. C. A., *The Industrial and Commercial Revolutions in Great Britain during the Nineteenth Century* (London: George Routledge & Sons, 1933), pp. 1–25, 79–84, 102–8, 162–70, 177–78, 363–75.

MARSHALL, L. S., "The Emergence of the First Industrial City: Manchester, 1780–1850," in *The Cultural Approach to History*, ed. Caroline F. Ware (New York: Columbia University Press, 1940), pp. 140–61.

SMILES, SAMUEL, "William Fairbairn," in *Industrial Biography; Iron Workers and Tool Makers* (London: Murray, 1863), pp. 314–16, 323–33.

CARLYLE, THOMAS, *Past and Present* (London: Chapman & Hall, 1843), pp. 1–2, 4–8, 197–99, 201–2, 253–55, 258–59, 260–62, 353–60.

HAMMOND, J. L., "The Industrial Revolution and Discontent," *Economic History Review*, II (1929–30), 222–28.

RUSSELL, LORD JOHN, "Speech Introducing the Reform Bill," in HANSARD, *Parliamentary Debates* (3d ser.; 1831), II, 1061–65.

WELLINGTON, DUKE OF, Letter on Parliamentary Reform, in GLEIG, G. R., *The Life of Arthur, First Duke of Wellington* (London: Longmans, Green, Longmans & Roberts, 1862), pp. 630–31.

COBBETT, WILLIAM, "On the Reform Bill," *Cobbett's Political Register*, LXIII (1831), 306–10, 312–19; LXXVI (1832), 539–42.

OASTLER, RICHARD, "Letter on Yorkshire Slavery," *Leeds Mercury*, October 16, 1830.

Extracts from SADLER COMMISSION, *Evidence, Great Britain, Parliamentary Papers, 1831–32*, XV, 44, 95–97, 115, 195, 339, 341–42.

Debate on factory legislation, in HANSARD, *Parliamentary Debates* (3d ser.), LXXXVI (1846), 1029–38, 1040, 1043; LXXXIX (1847), 487–91, 1074–81; XC, 768–72, 772–74, 812–18.

"Factories—Owners and Inspectors," *Economist, Weekly Commercial Times, Bankers' Gazette, and Railway Monitor; A Political, Literary, and General Newspaper* (March 10, 1855), pp. 251–52.

HOLYOAKE, G. J., *Self-help by the People: The History of the Rochdale Equitable Pioneers* (London: S. Sonnenschein, 1893), pp. 1, 2–3, 7–8, 9–10, 11–12, 16, 19–20, 26–27, 41.

"A Strike in 1838," *Annual Register, or a View of the History and Politics of the Year 1838* (London: Rivington, 1839), pp. 203–5, 206–7.

CHEYNEY, E. P., "The Rise of the Working Classes, 1796–1929," in *Modern English Reform* (Philadelphia: University of Pennsylvania Press, 1931), pp. 120–50.

THE RUSSIAN REVOLUTION

MAYNARD, SIR JOHN, *Russia in Flux* (New York: Macmillan Co., 1948), pp. 1–13, 178–96.

HERZEN, A. I., "The Russian People and Socialism," in *My Past and Thoughts*, trans. Constance Garnet (New York: Knopf, 1928), VI, 210–48.

WALLACE, SIR DONALD MACKENZIE, *Russia* (London: Cassell & Co., Ltd., 1912), pp. 122–41.

TURGENEV, I., "Hor and Kalinich," in *A Sportsman's Sketches* (New York: E. P. Dutton & Co., 1932), pp. 1–18.

KROPOTKIN, P. A., *Memoirs of a Revolutionist* (Boston: Houghton Mifflin Co., 1899), pp. 296–302, 304–9.

LENIN, V. I., "What Is To Be Done?" in *Collected Works of V. I. Lenin* (New York: International Publishers, Inc., 1929), IV, 94–97, 121–23, 124–25, 157–62, 164–67, 187–88, 198–200, 205–12, 213.

LENIN, V. I, "Speech Delivered at a Caucus of the Bolshevik Members of the All-Russian Conference of the Soviets of Workers' and Soldiers' Deputies, April 17, 1917," *ibid.*, XX, 95–103.

———, "Speech on Peace and Speech on Land," in BUNYAN, JAMES, and FISHER, H. H., *The Bolshevik Revolution, 1917–1918: Documents and Materials* (Stanford, Calif.: Stanford University Press, 1934), pp. 124–32.

"Documents on Nationalization of Industry" and "Constitution of RSFSR," in BUNYAN, JAMES, *Intervention, Civil War, and Communism in Russia, April–December 1918: Documents and Materials* (Baltimore: Johns Hopkins Press, 1936), pp. 397–402, 507–12.

GORKI, M., *Days with Lenin* (New York: International Publishers, Inc., 1938), pp. 44, 49–50, 52.

LENIN, V. I., "State and Revolution," in *Collected Works of V. I. Lenin* (New York: International Publishers, Inc., 1929), XXI, 149–50, 153–66, 215–31.

MARTOV, J., *The State and the Socialist Revolution*, trans. Inkger (New York: International Review, 1938), pp. 16–26, 33–34, 55–56, 63–64.

MAYNARD, SIR JOHN, "Collective Farming in the USSR," *Slavonic and East European Review*, XV (1936–37), 47–69.

BIENSTOCK, GREGORY; SCHWARTZ, S. M.; and YUGOW, AARON, *Management in Russian Industry and Agriculture* (Ithaca, N.Y.: Cornell University Press, 1944), pp. 3–8, 47–57, 66–86.

HARRIS, S. E., "Appraisals of Russian Economic Statistics," *Review of Economic Statistics*, XXIX (1947), 213–14.

TROTSKY, LEON, *The Real Situation in Russia*, trans. Max Eastman (New York: Harcourt, Brace & Co., 1928), pp. 37–45, 48–59, 83–87, 111–21, 155–60, 193–95.

CILIGA, ANTON, *The Russian Enigma*, trans. F. G. Renier and Anne Cliff (London: George Routledge & Sons, Ltd., 1940), pp. 135–38, 243–60.

People's Commissariat of Justice, U.S.S.R., *Report of Court Proceedings: The Case of the Trotskyite-Zinovievite Terrorist Centre* (Moscow: State Pub. House, 1936), pp. 9–11, 98–101.

———, *Report of Court Proceedings: The Case of the Anti-Soviet Trotskyite Centre* (Moscow: State Pub. House, 1937), pp. 17–19, 55–69, 539–41.

Trotsky, Leon, *I Stake My Life* (New York: Pioneer Publishers, 1937), pp. 3–24.

"Communist International Manifesto, 1919," in Trotsky, Leon, *The First Five Years of the Communist International*, trans. and ed. J. G. Wright (New York: Pioneer Publishers, 1945), I, 19–30.

"Condition for Admission of the Parties into the Communist International," trans. Edward Bastian (unpublished), from *Thèses, manifestes et résolutions adoptées par les I., II, III., et IV. Congrès de l'Internationale Communiste (1919–23)* (Paris: Librairie du travail, 1934), pp. 39–41.

The Stalin-Howard Interview (New York: International Publishers, Inc., 1936), pp. 3–15.

Litvinoff, Maxim, "Speech, 21 September 1938," in League of Nations, *Official Journal*, Special Suppl. No. 183, pp. 74–78.

Molotov, V. M., "Speech to the Supreme Soviet, 31 October 1939," *New York Times*, November 1, 1939, p. 8.

Most of these readings are included in the three volumes of *Selected Readings: History* (Chicago: University of Chicago Press, 1948 and 1949).

II. OBSERVATION, INTERPRETATION, AND INTEGRATION

ORGANIZATIONS OF THE SCIENCES

Plato *Republic*, trans. J. L. Davies and D. J. Vaughan (London: Macmillan & Co., Ltd., 1925), vi. 506–vii. 541.

Aristotle *Physics*, trans. R. P. Hardie and R. K. Gaye, in *The Basic Works of Aristotle*, ed. Richard McKeon (New York: Random House, 1941), ii. 1–2.

——— *Metaphysics*, trans. W. D. Ross, *ibid.*, ii. 1–3; vi. 1; xi. 7; xii. 1; xiii. 1–3.

——— *Nichomachean Ethics*, trans. W. D. Ross, *ibid.*, iii. 1–3; vi. 3–8.

——— *Politics*, trans. B. Jowett, *ibid.*, iii. 12; iv. 1; Book viii.

Boethius *Dialogue on Porphyry's "Introduction,"* i. 2, trans. Richard McKeon.

——— *On the Trinity*, chap. 2, trans. Richard McKeon.

St. Thomas Aquinas, *Summa theologica*, Part I, Question 1, Art. 1, trans. W. O'Meara; Arts. 4–5, trans. Richard McKeon.

——— *Commentary on Boethius' "Treatise on the Trinity,"* Question 5, Arts. 1–4; Question 6, Art. 1, trans. Richard McKeon.

——— *Commentary on the Nichomachean Ethics*, Preface, trans. Richard McKeon.

St. Augustine *City of God*, viii. 3–8, trans. Richard McKeon.

——— *On Order*, ii. 11–16, trans. Richard McKeon.

Bacon, Francis, "Of the Proficience and Advancement of Learning," in *Ad-*

vancement of Learning and the New Atlantis (London: Oxford University Press, 1919), pp. 67–68, 74–164, 190–91, 219–30, 234.

COMTE, AUGUSTE, *Course of Positive Philosophy* (Paris: J. B. Baillière and Sons, 1877), chap. ii, trans. A. C. Benjamin.

———, *System of Positive Polity*, trans. J. H. Bridges, R. Congreve, and H. D. Hutton (London: Longmans, Green & Co., 1875), I, 354–68; IV, 161–68; 549, 597–98.

KANT, IMMANUEL, *Introduction to Logic*, trans. T. K. Abbott (London: Longmans, Green & Co., 1885), chap. i, pp. 1–6.

———, *Fundamental Principles of the Metaphysics of Ethics*, trans. T. K. Abbott (London: Longmans, Green & Co., 1916), Preface, pp. 1–9.

———, *Critique of Pure Reason*, trans. F. Max Müller (New York: Macmillan Co., 1922), Preface to the 2d ed., and Part II, chap. iii, pp. 688–97, 667–82.

CARNAP, RUDOLPH, "Logical Foundations of the Unity of Science," in *International Encyclopedia of Unified Science* (Chicago: University of Chicago Press, 1938), I, No. 1, 42–62.

METHODS OF THE SCIENCES

ARISTOTLE *Organon: Posterior Analytics* i. 1–4; ii. 19; *Topics* i. 1, 12, 15 (in part); trans. William Kent.

NEWTON, ISAAC, *Mathematical Principles of Natural Philosophy and the System of the World*, trans. Florian Cajori (Berkeley, Calif.: University of California Press, 1934), pp. 2–6.

———, *Opticks: Or a Treatise of the Reflections, Refractions, Inflections, and Colours of Light* (4th ed.; New York; G. Bell & Sons, Ltd., 1931), pp. 397–406.

DESCARTES, RENÉ, *Discourse on Method*, trans. John Veitch (New York: E. P. Dutton & Co., 1912), pp. 33–37, 48–52.

———, *Meditations on the First Philosophy*, in *A Discourse on Method and Other Works*, trans. John Veitch (New York: E. P. Dutton & Co., 1912), pp. 79–94, 111, 120–26.

BACON, FRANCIS, *Novum Organon*, in *English Philosophy from Bacon to Mill*, ed. E. A. Burtt ("Modern Library" [New York: Random House, 1939]), excerpts from pp. 5–114.

WHEWELL, WILLIAM, *Novum organon renovatum* (3d ed.; London: Parker & Sons, 1858), Book II, chaps. i–viii, pp. 27–136 (in part).

———, *On the Philosophy of Discovery* (London: J. W. Parker & Sons, 1860), pp. 285–89.

DE MORGAN, AUGUSTUS, "On Bacon's *Novum organum*," in *A Budget of Paradoxes* (London: Longmans, Green & Co., 1872), pp. 48–57.

EINSTEIN, ALBERT, "Geometry and Experience," in *Sidelights on Relativity*, trans. B. J. Jeffery and W. Perrett (New York: E. P. Dutton & Co., 1922), pp. 27–56.

POINCARÉ, HENRI, "Science and Hypothesis," in *The Foundations of Science*, trans. G. B. Halstead (New York: Science Press, 1914), pp. 55–80.

MILL, JOHN STUART, *A System of Logic* (8th ed.; New York: Longmans, Green & Co., 1884), pp. 125–26, 153–54, 207–10, 214–32, 272–74, 276–77, 278–83, 284–91, 307–11, 349–59, 397–405, 579–81, 586–89, 607–25, 630–31.

DURKHEIM, ÉMILE, *The Rules of Sociological Method* (Chicago: University of Chicago Press, 1938), pp. 1–17.

DEWEY, JOHN, *The Public and Its Problems* (New York: Gateway Books, 1927), pp. 185–219.

———, *Logic: The Theory of Inquiry* (New York: Henry Holt & Co., 1938), pp. 81–98.

BERGSON, HENRI, *An Introduction to Metaphysics*, trans. T. E. Hulme (New York: Liberal Arts Press, 1949).

BÖCKH, AUGUST, *The Encyclopedia and Methodology of the Philological Sciences*, trans. Richard Hocking, from *Encyklopädie und Methodologie der philologischen Wissenschaften*, ed. Ernst Bratuscheck (Leipzig: Teubner, 1877), pp. 1–20, 52–61, 80–88, 170–71.

PLATO *Protagoras*, trans. B. Jowett, in *The Works of Plato* (New York: Random House, 1937).

PRINCIPLES IN THE SCIENCES

PLATO *Republic*, trans. A. D. Lindsay (New York: E. P. Dutton & Co., 1946), Book ix.

ARISTOTLE *Nichomachean Ethics*, trans. W. D. Ross, in *The Basic Works of Aristotle*, ed. Richard McKeon (New York: Random House, 1941), i. 5, 8; vii. 11–14; x. 1–5.

HUME, DAVID, *An Inquiry Concerning the Principles of Morals* (La Salle, Ill.: Open Court Pub. Co., 1938), pp. 46–67.

MILL, JOHN STUART, *Utilitarianism*, in *English Philosophers from Bacon to Mill*, ed. E. A. Burtt ("Modern Library" [New York: Random House, 1939]), pp. 895–916, 923–28.

KANT, IMMANUEL, *Fundamental Principles of the Metaphysics of Morals*, trans. T. K. Abbott (London: Longmans, Green & Co., 1916), Sec. I, pp. 9–22.

———, *The Metaphysics of Morals*, in *Selections from Kant's Moral Philosophy*, trans. Charles Wegener (Chicago: University of Chicago Press, 1949), Introd., Sec. III; "Metaphysical Elements of the Doctrine of Right," Introd., Secs. A–E; "Metaphysical Elements of the Doctrine of Virtue," Introd., Secs. I–X.

Many of the readings listed are reprinted in *Organizations of the Sciences* (2d ed.; Chicago: University of Chicago Press, 1946) and *Methods of the Sciences* (3d ed.; Chicago: University of Chicago Press, 1948).

PART III

On Method

10

Teaching

ALBERT M. HAYES

THE truest thing one can say about teaching in the College, and
perhaps the most important, is that practically everyone who
does it enjoys it. Most of the other generalizations of this chapter should be qualified with such phrases as "Many teachers believe . . . " or "The best practice in the College is . . . . " But, however varied may be the methods employed by the hundred and
fifty men and women who constitute the College faculty and however mixed may be the attitudes toward other aspects of the work,
there is general agreement on this: that our classroom experiences
afford a unique kind of satisfaction.

This universal feeling arises in part from the native excellence
of the students who come to be taught, but more (I think) from
qualities evoked in these students by certain characteristics inherent in the structure of the College. No man is unaffected by
the patterns of the society he lives in, least of all students in an
educational institution. That is why to this account of teaching at
Chicago I must preface some observations concerning the structural patterns which condition the kind of teaching we do.

The most important single influence is the system of comprehensive examinations. Every student knows that his educational
success, his attainment of a degree, is determined solely by these
examinations, and that no individual teacher can choose what
grade shall be received by any individual student since, at the
time when grades are decided on, the authorship of particular
papers is unknown. It is a system involving certain dangers, as

we are well aware, and I would not claim that we have completely averted all of them. There is one tremendous advantage, however, which most of us feel outweighs all the evils, and that is the effect of this system on classroom attitudes. There is no apple-polishing. Winning the good will of a teacher may bolster a student's self-confidence, but it cannot alter his grade. With respect to the external criteria of educational success, performance in the classroom is a useful, for most students even a necessary, preliminary; but it can be by-passed. It meets no formal requirements. In such a system it behooves the teacher to make his classroom a place where real learning can occur, for the students soon recognize that this is the sole function of classes. If our objectives were less fundamental or our examinations more narrowly factual, classes could easily degenerate into cram sessions. They do not, however, and the students usually show a gratifying concern with the real business of education.

The fact that examinations occur only at the end of a whole year's work contributes to this effect. June is a long way off, and the social sciences teacher feels he can easily afford to postpone that important discussion of Gresham's Law if the response of some student chances to raise a related problem that seems worth discussing. We all complain at times, of course—it is an occupational trait—about the difficulty of covering the ground we have proposed to ourselves; but in a very real sense we do have leisure to teach *ad hominem*, to seize the opportunities presented by an accidental turn of the discussion, to encourage intellectual curiosity, to stimulate real thinking, in general to incite active learning at whatever point shows most promise. There is a sense of spaciousness in the College classroom which is good for the faculty and good for the students.

There is a sense, too, that a real object of knowledge exists somewhere outside our individual consciousnesses, waiting for us to master it. Too often, I am afraid, students dimly suspect that their teacher has invented a special body of knowledge; that he and they are playing a game in which their part is to discover the contents of his mind without worrying about where the contents came from. In the College, however, where the staff of a single course may number as many as thirty teachers and where the examination is somewhat detached from the operation of the classes which prepare for it, a tradition of joint investigation has developed: students and teachers feel they are reaching out together to explore a field of possible knowledge. As they succeed in finding what is really there, they will succeed in the examination, for the examination is accepted as a reasonably accurate measure of what a person really knows.

A second factor which exercises major influence on the patterns of teaching in the College is the freedom of the student to come or to stay away. It is true that the younger students, those who are in the eleventh or twelfth year of their schooling, are required to attend classes; but there are only four courses in the College which are primarily occupied by students of this level. In the others, the levels are so mixed that the mores of voluntary attendance are dominant. To some teachers this may seem a frightening phenomenon—classes in which neither the teacher nor the Dean of Students has any power to compel attendance. Oddly enough, the system works. Repeated surveys have consistently shown that, on the average, three students out of four will be in the classroom on any given day. They float about a bit, sampling the wares of various instructors. A small minority grossly abuse their freedom. But the great majority accept the responsibility they have been given and act as mature individuals. For the teacher, of course, this is a great advantage. He knows that the students who appear are there for a serious purpose. He knows, too, that the students expect him to lead them in a serious discussion. If he fails to meet their demands, they may not return tomorrow. I know it is possible to exaggerate the power of students over a teacher in this respect; he retains, of course, his natural intellectual advantage. But the system is one which focuses the attention of the faculty upon their real job, the education of the young,* and the faculty have responded well to the challenge of this pattern. Teachers initiate lines of investigation which students freely choose to follow. The classroom becomes a

* Among the other factors which help to create an atmosphere favorable to good teaching, one might mention that each year the University makes three awards of $1,000 each for excellence in undergraduate teaching.

place where teacher and students together explore whatever there is to be known.

In these preliminary remarks I have been speaking of certain external conditions which affect the character of teaching in the College. All human activity is subject to some such predisposing factors. But external conditions can do no more than limit the choices from which the individual instructor may make his selection. The actual decision must be made in terms of his general and particular purposes, the educational beliefs of the faculty—singly and collectively.

At Chicago we have chosen discussion as our primary instrument of instruction. Let us explore a bit the grounds of our choice. The kind of knowledge we are concerned with is a matter of reasons and relationships, not of isolated pieces of information. It comes to be in the mind through an active taking hold of the object and making it, as it were, its own, and not through the passive retention of the memory. Usually there is involved a groping about in the dark, followed, if the activity is successful, by a sudden illumination. Different men have used different figures to express this fact of experience. Socrates, for example, was so impressed with the uniqueness of this act (one may surmise) that he felt compelled to think of it as a recollection of what the soul had known before it was born into the body. Whitehead speaks of an awakening, of imagination, joy, and cyclical rhythms. But, whatever the metaphor, all agree that what is significant is an individual act of the individual mind. It will occur more readily in a mind which has been subjected to appropriate discipline; it may be guided by another mind which has walked the same road already. But each individual must finally grasp the object of knowledge for himself; and, once he has grasped it, it is as though it were there forever.

It is in terms like these, or their equivalents, that any good teacher might begin his account of discussion. The aim is to generate an activity in the minds of individual students, each of whom is different from everyone else in some portions, at least, of his experience, of his developed knowledge. That is why at Chicago we meet students in groups small enough to permit dealing with these unique particulars; we want to test through question and answer whether the act of knowing is really happening. As Plato puts it in the *Phaedrus*, the teacher is concerned with the "intelligent word graven in the soul of the learner, which can defend itself, and knows when to speak and when to be silent." Discussion differs, that is to say, from recitation in that it requires the student to produce, by way of answer, something that has not been given him previously from outside (i.e., in text, lecture, or the like)—to produce from himself restatements of an argument, analyses of its course of movement, illustrations of an idea or principle, connections with other facts or ideas. For the intelligent word is one that has been so assimilated to the mind that the mind can produce such things as these, and, in fact, it is by producing them that the mind comes to know what it knows.

Perhaps an illustration would clinch the point. In the Natural Sciences sequence students read original scientific papers both for their content and for the understanding they can give of scientific problems and methods. My illustration is drawn from a discussion of diabetes based on a reading from a treatise on stomach and urinary diseases by William Prout in the light of certain other papers on the same subject. The problem is that of the classification of diseases, and the chapter (published in 1840) is significant for its clarification of the problem at that date. The instructor began by posing this question: Since Prout was working at a time when little was known about the physiological cause of diabetes, how did he recognize that there was a single disease entity to be studied? The class explored various solutions. First, they fixed on the complex of associated symptoms which Prout reported. At one level this answered the question, but only by raising another. For only two of the symptoms were invariably present, thirst and a saccharine condition of the urine, and each of these was known to exist separately—how then could Prout know that these symptoms belonged together as signs of a single disease? Perhaps, the discussion continued, classification of diabetes as one disease depended on some single cause of these varied symptoms. Exploration of this possibility, however, revealed several senses for "cause"; and several different experiments with bodily organs were cited as capable of producing or affecting the symptom complex. One student even tried the modern treatment by a single drug, insulin (unknown to Prout, of course), as a sign of a single disease, but he was quickly beaten down by a reminder of the diverse diseases to which penicillin had been successfully applied. How was it possible to say that there existed one thing to be called "diabetes"? And then the light began to appear. The most prominent symptom was sugar in the urine. This sugar should normally have been (in Prout's term) assimilated, i.e., converted into bodily tissue. "Assimilation" of sugar was a normal function of the body. Whenever something went wrong with this function, from one or another cause, some components of the symptom complex appeared. For Prout, then, diabetes could be classified as a single disease through defining it as the derangement of a specific bodily function.

Such examples could be drawn from other subject matters—discussion, for instance, of Malthus' principles of population, Aristotle's concept of plot in a tragedy, or Madison's argument from the nature of factions in No. 10 of *The Federalist*. Since the teacher's aim is to plant understanding in the mind of the student, or to discover that it has already started to grow there, the teacher commonly finds it useful to begin the period by creating a problem for the students to solve, by making the question of the day seem real and the discovery of its answer an urgent necessity. It may be through calling attention to the paradox of some apparent contradiction in the materials to be discussed; it may be through relating the "academic" subject matter to the immediate experience of the students; it may be through provoking two students to take strikingly opposed positions, or through leading the whole group out on the precarious limb of an untenable position and then starting to saw it off. For the ingenious teacher the material in hand will suggest some appropriate device for generating a starting point, for impelling motion in the direction of knowledge. The whole art of teaching may almost be defined in terms of the power to make minds really active and to make them act on reality.

Knowledge in this sense, as I said above, is not the product of habituation; but its development depends upon and itself creates intellectual habits. Each time the mind really knows, it becomes a little surer in its recognition that this experience is a knowing and not merely verbalizing or opining. Each time the mind reaches out to grasp knowledge, it becomes a little surer in its technique of grasping; it develops, as it were, rules for its own operations. These, of course, are among the skills or disciplines which each course in the College sets up as objectives for its instruction, and their sum is that wisdom whose cultivation the opening chapter of this book has defined as the ultimate purpose of the College—wisdom, "the competence to establish an adequate relation of the mind to the things which it undertakes to grasp."

Our aim, then, is to foster the growth of certain habits of activity (the "competence to establish") rather than the passive retention of information, through providing opportunity in discussion for repeated experiences of the act of knowing and through suggesting ways of systematizing the process of coming to know. In the second year of the Humanities sequence, for example, the students develop arts of interpretation through practicing them on various literary works. Repetition is of the essence here. The student who has come to know dramatic irony in Oedipus' curse upon the as yet unknown murderer of Laius is the readier by that knowledge to know the effect of Gloucester's speech on the heath to the disguised Kent in the presence of the disguised Edgar:

> His daughters seek his death. Ah, that good Kent!
> He said it would be thus, poor banish'd man!
> Thou say'st the King grows mad; I'll tell thee, friend,
> I am almost mad myself. I had a son,
> Now outlaw'd from my blood; 'a sought my life,
> But lately, very late. I lov'd him, friend,
> No father his son dearer; true to tell thee,
> The grief hath craz'd my wits.

In dealing with this passage, of course, the teacher would not be content with eliciting from the students recognition of the similarity of the *Lear* passage to the one in *Oedipus Rex* (that in each the audience, having greater knowledge than the speaker, understands his words in a sense he does not intend) but would invite the class to investigate also the differences (in the kind of fact that the speaker is ignorant of, in the extent to which others on the stage share the audience's recognition of the irony, in the character of the emotion with which the scene is regarded); for by such an investigation the students will gain not only a more complete "knowledge" of this part of the play but also, by example, understanding of the kinds of questions by which they may thereafter acquire similar knowledge of other plays they may read.

The first course in the Social Sciences sequence examines the history of the United States as one extended example of the way in which the society best known to the students has arrived at the decisions which have shaped its present. One of the principal intentions of this study is to develop in each student the capacity to deliberate rationally on matters of social policy, to participate wisely in the decisions which will determine our society's future. Critical periods in American history serve as focal points, and documents containing significant arguments on public questions provide the material for this training. Appropriate devices are employed by the teacher to make these issues real ones for the student, who may then participate, in some sense, in rendering judgment. Thus each successive stage in the development of our society, though it presents a new problem and involves some new principles, may be regarded as a repetition, for the student, of a single process—weighing facts and arguments, considering ends and means, making choices—and through this repetition he develops the skills he will need as a citizen.

Some of my readers may at this point be perplexed by the disparity of my examples of knowledge. Knowing Shakespeare appears to be very different from knowing diabetes, and both, in turn, from knowing social science. I agree. The point lies at the heart of the College curriculum. If we are to cultivate true wisdom in the minds of our students, we must develop various competences which are relevant to the various "things which the mind undertakes to grasp." This is not the place to enumerate the several skills which the College attempts to develop in its students. Those have been presented in the chapters dealing with the separate courses and sequences which constitute our curriculum. It is appropriate, however, that I point out here the implications of this conception for teaching.

For if, by repeated acts of knowing, a teacher is to develop

habits which will make students competent to go on knowing in
the future, and if these habits must have a specific appropriateness to the things which the students will seek to know, then the
teacher is obligated to adhere conscientiously to the real facts of
his subject matter. He must constantly seek to know more clearly,
more deeply, more comprehensively the essential nature of the
"things which the mind undertakes to grasp" in his field of
knowledge, to know them especially in those particularities which
differentiate them from the things to be known in other fields.
He must know in this fashion not only for his activity as a member of a staff planning a course but also for his activity as a
teacher; for he must teach his students to direct their attention
to that which is relevant to the knowledge they are seeking.

Our system of education through a limited number of required
general courses is one that provokes reflection on the nature of
"a course." When one man offers a course on "British Socialism"
or "The Physiology of the Nervous System" or "The Literary
Epic," it is easy enough to say what that course is: it is a structure within the mind of that teacher—a structure, no doubt, intended to represent some external reality; but, as a human construction, one having its primary existence in his mind. Not so
with a general course planned democratically by a group of
teachers—a course planned, further, as one unit in an integrated
program of general education. If such a course exists as a single
thing in the minds of the several individual teachers—and this
is certainly to be desired—it must derive its singleness from a
common reference of each mind to the external "things which
the mind undertakes to grasp." These "things" cannot be simply a reading list, for the books on that list are there for the sake
of the course and not as ends in themselves. *The Federalist* will be
treated as a historical event in Social Sciences 1; the *Areopagitica*
as a discussion of the problem of liberty in Social Sciences 3; but
in Humanities 2 both will become occasions for rhetorical analysis. The materials and procedures of a course must equally be
dictated by its ends. Hence in teaching any class it is necessary
constantly to bring before the minds of the students the purpose
of a particular discussion, that they may direct their intellectual
activity toward the appropriate object of knowledge. Each course

in the College has its own objects and, with a certain amount of overlapping which is both natural and desirable, its own set of relevant intellectual habits. To these ends our teaching is oriented, course by course.

There remains one word in our definition on which I have not explicitly commented: "the competence to establish an *adequate* relation of the mind to the things which it undertakes to grasp." Adequacy may be defined, in outline at least, as occurring when the mind brings the right facts and the right ideas together in the right way. But such a definition may mean anything to anybody. In the College I think we would take it to mean that adequacy is relative to three variables: the stock of facts, the stock of ideas, and the skill developed by practice in putting these together. Accordingly, we are concerned day after day with seeing that our students have knowledge of some facts; that, more important, they know what makes a fact a fact, and under what circumstances; that they learn, further, how to find the facts they need when they cannot supply them from memory. We are concerned equally—but no more—that they be acquainted with a variety of ideas, with their interrelations, and with their relevance to one kind of fact rather than to another. And always we are trying to give them practice in putting these elements together so that they may acquire skills—the skills which are appropriate to the things the mind may grasp.

It is this concern for adequacy which has formulated the courses of the College in terms that seem to the outside observer very "fancy," unrealistically ambitious. No one denies that wisdom is an ambitious goal, in any age; but it is the only goal worth aiming at. How near a particular college comes to it can be determined only by the future of its graduates. In this place it is fitting to report merely that the height of our general aim is reflected in the height of our general teaching practice. We do not aim our teaching, most of us, at the level which can be attained easily by all but the lazy and among them by those of quick wit. We hold, rather, with Browning that "a man's reach should exceed his grasp." In planning our courses, in planning our classroom discussions, we aim to stretch the reach of our ablest students. I would not go so far as to say that we direct all our teaching to the

A students, but the tendency is in that direction. This may sound like the educational equivalent of feeding the poor with the crumbs that fall from the rich man's table, and I grant there are students who get very little nourishment from the fare offered. The great majority, however, including many of very ordinary ability, are stimulated by this technique to intellectual achievements they would not otherwise attain. Students are much more sensitive than their elders to what is expected of them and much more ready to try to meet that expectation. In the light of the existing pattern of actual student behavior at Chicago, the sequences of courses are simply what they have to be if they are to continue to "stretch the reach" of those who take them sequentially. The philosophical breadth and complexity of the final courses, moreover, is absolutely essential if our students are ever going to be able to judge whether the relations their minds are establishing are really adequate to the things they are undertaking to grasp. The materials these courses deal with are hard nuts for the students to crack, but, recognizing the importance of the kind of knowledge involved, the students respond to the intellectual challenge with enthusiasm; they make the necessary effort. And so, though the program is ambitious, yet, with respect to the kind of general education which is its proper end, it is realistically designed. To a larger extent than one might think possible, students do attain wisdom.

This account I have given of the use of discussion in the College has dealt more with the theory than with the practice. It has sought to explain intentions rather than to describe procedures. This emphasis has been deliberate. The most striking characteristic of our teaching as it appears to observers is precisely its purposiveness. It is in aims that we are a united faculty. In classroom techniques the common ends permit a high degree of individuality. Instructors are constantly experimenting—singly and in groups—to find new and better ways of actualizing knowledge in their students. Some of the experiments are extremely interesting—student-planned discussions, classless weeks, preceptorial sections—but there would be little point in describing them here. Experiment is their essence, which standardization would destroy. Individually they have no part in the general

picture of teaching in the College, though collectively their existence is one of the cardinal facts. Discussion may properly be
called the "method" of teaching in the College, but only if it is
clearly understood that there is no single method of discussion.

Of course, we also have lectures—but not many. Only two
courses ask the students to spend as many hours in lecture halls
as in discussion classes. Eight of the fourteen courses in the curriculum make no use whatever of lectures. In recent years every
change has been away from the lecture system and toward discussion. Still, for the sake of completeness, I should say something
about this method of instruction.

Some courses regard their lectures as means of unification. By
this they sometimes intend to suggest the psychological effect
upon the students of coming together en masse and thus realizing
how many of them are united in the single intellectual enterprise
of the one course. Others, aware of the important role in education played by informal discussions, regard the lectures as providing a common basis of intellectual experience for dormitory
"bull-sessions." Most of the faculty, however, would maintain
that the common materials and objectives of a course are sufficient of themselves to rise above the narrow boundaries of separate discussion sections and provide the students with an appropriate psychological unity. In this sense lectures are unnecessary.
Certain courses, nevertheless, feel a need for lectures to tie together scattered reading materials and give them the unity of
connected discourse which, they feel, is often lacking in classroom discussions. Others use lectures to introduce the concepts
in terms of which the class sessions may subsequently deal with
the reading materials.

It is assumed in such views of the lecture that certain ideas are
better communicated by the spoken than by the written word and
that mimeographed copies of the lecture would not serve the
same function. The difference lies in the personality of the lecturer; and all of us can testify from the history of our own development that particular individuals can exercise a decisive influence on young men and women through the challenge which
a concrete example presents to the imagination. A sequence of
assorted lecturers greatly extends (in fifty-minute samples) the

range of a student's experience of informed and disciplined minds coping with a problem and solving it. For one of the most common patterns of lecturing is that in which the teacher illustrates a method—one which he hopes the student will acquire in the course—by demonstrating its actual use on a particular problem or a particular body of facts. In certain areas, moreover—the social sciences are the most obvious example—both methods and conclusions are major points of controversy; and lectures, given by men of diverse views, are one means of protecting the student against what must be recognized, despite all efforts to avoid it, as the unconscious bias of the discussion leader. In other areas, of course, the lectures make available to all students the specialized knowledge of individual members of the faculty, including men from outside the College faculty, in a way that carries with it the special mark of the speaker's distinctive authority.

In the last analysis, it is about the role of authority in teaching that debates concerning lectures center. For though the lecture, at its best, is a genuine act of knowing—the establishment of an adequate relation of the mind to a fairly complex object of knowledge—it is such an act chiefly for the lecturer. The listener can do little but follow. If he is a good listener and the lecturer intends to teach (not merely to inform), the student may be able to follow through all the stages which lead on to the understanding reached—though this occurs less frequently, I would guess, than most lecturers suppose: yet even under these most favorable circumstances the listener's knowledge is only derivative; he does not possess it as the lecturer did. And for the great majority— since there is never time for everyone to get answers to all his questions, and usually there is no opportunity for anyone even to ask—the conclusions must be accepted on faith, if they are understood at all. It is good for students to see at first hand— not simply in the written discourse of a great book—a mind operating at a level which can be only their goal for the present; there is a place in any college for a limited program of lectures. But the major job of teaching, granted the objectives defined earlier in this chapter, must be "accomplished in face-to-face relationships by means of give and take. Logic in its fulfillment recurs to the primitive sense of the word: dialogue. Ideas which are not communicated, shared, and reborn in expression are but soliloquy, and soliloquy is but broken and imperfect thought."*

These words of Dewey are taken from a work in which he argues that the solution of social problems presupposes the establishment of true communities. As the first chapter of this book indicates, the College is concerned with similar social ends: the curriculum is designed to supply students with the knowledge and intellectual habits which they will need as citizens; the common training provides a common language for the give-and-take of real discussion; and in the College itself the students find a prototype of the genuine community, at least in that aspect with which Dewey is most concerned. In so far as this chapter has been successful, it will have given the reader some sense of what sort of community of faculty and students has come into being at Chicago. For the kind of teaching I have described, though it exists also in many classrooms elsewhere, has here become the animating principle of a small society. It is not a perfect society, even intellectually, but it offers satisfactions which both faculty and students carry with them into the other societies of which they are, or will become, members. And it is to the character of this community that I would finally point when anyone asks me to tell him what we are trying to do by our teaching in the College.

* John Dewey, *The Public and Its Problems* (New York: Gateway Books, 1927), p. 218.

NOTE

As this chapter goes to press, the University of Chicago has taken a most heartening step toward the further encouragement and recognition of good teaching. With the aid of the Carnegie Corporation, it has established three special professorships in the College, comparable in dignity and in stipend to those which it awards to members of its graduate faculties for distinction in research, to be awarded for "excellence in teaching and in reflection upon the problems of undergraduate education." Two other professorships are to be added during the next two years. Thus, for perhaps the first time in the history of American universities, the delight in good teaching which Mr. Hayes describes above will be dislodged from its traditional association with "an honorable poverty."

—F. C. W.

11

Examining

I

THE GENERAL PLAN

BENJAMIN BLOOM

The plan of the College which was instituted in 1931 proposed to place a great deal of the responsibility for securing an education directly on the shoulders of the students. Under this plan the requirements for graduation were set in terms of demonstrated competence rather than in terms of the length of time a student must attend class. It was assumed that students could secure the required competence in a variety of ways. Although the majority of them would probably find it profitable to attend the lectures and discussions in each of the courses and to do the readings and other assignments, it was recognized that some students might secure this competence through independent study.

The College Plan envisioned a somewhat different relationship between instructors and students than had hitherto prevailed. It was assumed that, if instructors were not the assigners of academic rewards and penalties, the more serious students could discuss problems with instructors without feeling that other students might regard this association as an endeavor to secure high grades. The instructor, in turn, could feel that his task was to aid students in achieving the desired competence without fear that this relationship would be sullied by efforts of the student to extract special rewards or favors from him.

Since great emphasis had from the beginning been placed upon demonstrated competence, the faculty worked out a system of comprehensive examinations in the major fields of knowledge. Students have been given an opportunity to demonstrate the competence they have developed out of whatever educational experiences they found useful and valuable. Comprehensive examinations, offered several times each year to any student who believed that he was adequately prepared, have been administered in each of the fields of knowledge in which the general courses of the College are offered. Thus, in the social sciences at the present time, a student held for the full requirement in the field would take three six-hour comprehensive examinations.

This emphasis on demonstrated achievement rather than on the amount of time devoted by the student to class attendance, study, or cultivation of the instructors made it essential that the comprehensive examinations be so designed as to give the student the fullest opportunity to demonstrate the competence acquired from his total educational experience. The University reorganization of 1931 provided for the establishment of a University Examiner, assisted by a technical staff. At the time of its inception it was natural that this staff should consist of individuals who were especially well qualified in statistics and in tests and measurements. In addition to taking major responsibility for the construction of the various examinations, they did much to train various College instructors in the methods of test construction. Over a period of eighteen years the examiners have changed from an initial group with major training in tests and measurements, but with little training in the specific College subject fields, to a group of individuals with major training in the specific subject fields supplemented by additional training and experience in the theory and techniques of test construction.

Although the examination system was originally set up primarily for the purpose of certifying that students had the required competence in each of the subject fields before being granted a certificate or degree, work on the examinations and with the various instructional groups revealed many uses and effects of examinations which were not originally contemplated. It was soon recognized that the preparation of the comprehensive examinations required very clear statements as to the types of competence that instructors were seeking to develop in the students. It also required that the examiner be perfectly clear as to the kinds of tasks the students must do in order to demonstrate possession of these types of competence. The preparation of these specifications for the comprehensive examinations became a major task, involving a series of conferences between the instructional staff in a course and the appropriate examiner. This work of defining the ends of instruction and the actual construction and discussion of the test material served to focus the attention of all the instructors in a particular course on the purposes of the course and on the kinds of instruction which might develop the appropriate types of competence in students. As a result of these conferences, the instructors were able to achieve some unanimity of opinion concerning the ends of the course, although rarely did they reach such unanimity concerning the methods of instruction which would best develop the types of competence desired.

It was soon discovered that the nature of the examination had a profound influence on the extent and type of preparation which the students made. Students quickly discovered the kinds of questions which they would be expected to answer on the various examinations. If the students expected to be questioned on only a limited number of topics, they would devote their major attention to these topics. If, however, they thought that the examination would sample a very broad range of material included in a course, they prepared for such a range of questions. If the students discovered that for a particular examination they would be held only for such things as they could memorize, their preparation stressed the memorizing of a great many particular items of information, and they made efforts to "learn" as much as possible at the last minute. Again, if students discovered that the examination would require applications of the ideas discussed in lectures and classes, they would devote a great deal of attention in their preparation to thinking about possible applications of such ideas.

In order to improve the quality of the examinations, the examiners made use of various kinds of statistical analyses of the results. For example, they used these analyses to find the kinds of questions which did not discriminate between students who performed well or poorly on the examination as a whole. In addition to this technical use, the statistical analyses of the students' responses to test questions proved to be useful in enabling instructors to find the portions of the course and the ideas presented in the course which students were able to grasp, as well as to find those portions and ideas which were not so readily grasped. Thus, over a period of years, the examinations became a kind of mirror in which the instructors, by analysis of the responses to test questions, could determine the extent to which students were able to demonstrate types of competence that courses sought to develop.

From time to time students requested more information about their performance on the examinations than was provided by a letter grade. The analysis of the examinations for this purpose revealed that the examinations could be used to diagnose the strengths and weaknesses of individual students. It was found that in some cases the student had the greatest difficulty with certain types of subject matter, while in other cases the difficulties were primarily with certain kinds of understanding, ability, and skill. Thus it might be found that the student possessed all the necessary information in the various subject fields but could make little use of this information when given problems different from those discussed in the classrooms. Again, some students could make an excellent analysis of a document that had been discussed in class but could not do so well with documents that had not been analyzed in class.

As these various uses and effects of measuring achievement became clearer, the methods of constructing appropriate examinations also became clearer. It was recognized that the development of specifications for the tests was a major and all-important task. Although the original specifications were in the form of an outline of the course, it became evident that such an outline of the major topics to be treated in the course did not fully reveal what the student was expected to do with them. Thus, if the examiner started with the topical outline of the course as a specification for the examination, the questions in the examination would merely reveal the extent to which the student had the kinds of information which might be gained by the study of each of the topics. The instructors made it clear to the examiners that in addition to demonstrating the possession of information about important topics the student should be expected to give evidence that he was able to use that information in a variety of situations. They also believed that the students should be required to devise new kinds of support for some of the theories discussed in the course and to apply major generalizations and principles to predict, explain, and analyze unfamiliar problems. In addition, they expected students to possess a variety of analytical skills as well as reading and writing skills.

In clarifying and establishing specifications for examinations, a two-dimensional table has been used in most cases. One dimension of this "table" lists the topics or subjects which are treated in the course. The other dimension lists the kinds of behavior that students are expected to demonstrate in connection with each of the topics. The topical outline was easily determined from the outline of the course and from the syllabus which was prepared for each of the courses. The behavior to be developed and displayed in connection with each of the topics was not so easily discerned, and there were marked differences from course to course. However, despite these differences, certain purposes of instruction emerged as common to the various courses.

A major purpose of instruction in the College is that the student possess a useful and workable body of information at the completion of the program. The student should possess this information in each of the fields of knowledge, and he should be able to demonstrate it in a number of different ways. He is expected to show an understanding of the meaning and appropriate use of the more important technical terms in each field. He should know certain facts, generalizations, laws, theories, and concepts. He should be acquainted with the chronological development of certain ideas or the point in time at which certain specific events occurred. The student is expected to know the evidence, such as axioms, observations, and experiments, on which some of the more important theories and laws depend. He should also know the characteristic methods of inquiry and the role of evidence in each of the fields of knowledge. He is also expected to be acquainted with the sources he might consult to secure additional information on specific problems in each field.

In addition to demonstrating possession of information, the student completing the College program is expected to be able to use this knowledge in a variety of unfamiliar situations. Thus the student should demonstrate an ability to apply principles and generalizations to explain given phenomena, to predict the outcome of a particular situation, to determine a course of action, or to interpret a work of art. In so doing, he should make use of certain skills: logical reasoning, careful interpretation of data and texts, clear presentation of ideas in writing, accurate manipulation of mathematical and other nonverbal symbols, and sound judgment of experimental procedures used in testing given hypotheses.

There are several other important objectives of instruction in the College which are not represented in the comprehensive examinations. The instructors seek to have students develop certain habits of thinking. It is difficult to determine whether the student's performance on a comprehensive examination is a reflection of a habit or whether it is an ability or skill which is brought out only for academic exercises of a particular type. Clear-cut evidence of the presence of habits would require the collection of data based on observations of the student over a relatively long period of time and under a great variety of conditions. Although this is theoretically possible, it is impractical under the present comprehensive-examination system. In addition to habits, instructors may encourage the development of certain interests and attitudes in students. These have not been represented in the comprehensive examinations because of the difficulty of finding methods of securing valid evidence of their presence. Students who are faced with the rewards and penalties of examination grading may be tempted to express interests and attitudes which they do not really possess.

The preparation of specifications, then, represents the first step in securing examinations that have a high degree of validity. A second step in securing a valid examination is to find test problems and situations which are really appropriate to the specifications. The instructors and the examiners propose test material which they believe is suitable. This material is discussed until all are satisfied that it really will measure the knowledge and competence sought in the course. The discussion also insures that the examination will be at the appropriate level of difficulty, complexity, or depth and that the examination questions will be clear, unambiguous, and free of special "catches" and tricks.

In addition to emphasis on high validity, every effort is made to insure that the tests have a high degree of reliability. Since the student's entire grade depends upon a single examination, the error of measurement must be as small as possible. High reliability of the examination is insured by the use of a large number of examination problems and by seeing to it that the various kinds of competence sought in the course are represented in proper proportion. Most of the examinations are six hours in length, and the reliability coefficients are in the neighborhood of .95, which is usually judged sufficiently high for individual measurement.

A third characteristic which is sought in constructing each examination is high objectivity. Obviously, if two readers or graders judged the student's paper quite differently, it would be unfair to the student to assign a grade on the basis of either judgment. The problem of objectivity is one of securing as high a consistency among judges of the student's work as is possible. This objectivity is secured in part by clarifying to a maximum the directions to the student and the statements of examination problems, so that the student has little room for doubt as to what he is asked to do. In addition, readers of essay questions are asked to agree in advance on the points to be considered in grading the papers and the standards to be used in appraising them. Finally, identifying data are removed from the examination at the time it is graded, so that the reader's attention is confined to the examination itself rather than to the personality of the student, the amount of effort he has expended previously, or other individual characteristics.

Although the major examinations called for in the New Plan were the comprehensive examinations, other examinations have been included in the College program as the need for them arose. These now include: (1) entrance tests, which are taken by students who are applicants for admission to the College; (2) placement tests, which are designed to determine the proper starting point and pace of work for each entering student; (3) advisory tests, which are taken in the course of study during each academic year; and (4) evaluation tests, which are designed to reveal the changes taking place in students as a result of the College program.

The placement tests and comprehensive examinations are the special subjects of discussion in later parts of this chapter. A word about the advisory and evaluation tests will suffice to complete this introduction.

The advisory tests are designed to give the student numerous opportunities during the academic year to determine whether or not he is proceeding in a satisfactory manner. Quizzes, mid-quarterly, and quarterly examinations are offered. The scores and kinds of errors made on these tests and any other pertinent disclosures help the instructor, the student's adviser, and the student to assess the progress made. The taking of these tests is voluntary, and the results, since the tests are advisory in nature, do not appear on the student's official record.

The evaluation tests are given to sample groups of students when they enter the College and again at later points in their College careers. Since some of the tests are also given to students in secondary schools and in other colleges, it is possible to compare the progress of students in the College with that of other students who had equal initial competence. From time to time the evaluation tests have included tests of objectives not included in the comprehensive examinations, such as interests, attitudes, emotional adjustment, and the like. Techniques of testing other than the usual paper-and-pencil method have been used, e.g., projective testing techniques, such as the Rorschach test, and an oral test making use of special interviewing techniques. In addition to the tests, social-history studies using case-work methods have been made on small samples of students, in order to investigate the relation between many aspects of the individual's personal and home background and his work in the College. Various aspects of the College program and its courses have been studied intensively by questionnaire techniques. In connection with selected courses, students have been asked questions designed to determine whether they understand the aims of a course and the extent to which they believe them to have been achieved; their reactions to various parts of the course, such as the readings, the discussions, and lectures; the extent and type of study that they did in connection with the course; and their reactions to the comprehensive examinations and advisory tests related to the course.

Some of the findings of such investigations have been quite interesting and suggestive for educational methodology. In the humanities courses the primary emphasis in the teaching is on the methods of analyzing literary and artistic works, and this is clearly reflected in the changes in the appropriate test scores. Yet while little emphasis is given in the courses to information about artists, writers, and the names of works and their major characteristics, very great changes in the extent of such information about artistic and literary works and their makers have been disclosed by the tests. Thus gains in knowledge appear to be a concomitant of emphasis on skills of analysis. Another interesting finding centers around retention of various types of competence. In general, it has been found that retention on the tests intended to measure knowledge is quite good, with little or no loss evident a year after the course has been completed. On the other hand, in the case of several skills, not only is there no loss, but frequently there are sizable gains in scores over a period during which no relevant formal course work was given. It would seem from these results that, if a minimal competence has been developed as a result of a course, the skills will continue to develop if the student has opportunities to use them in connection with his daily experience.

II

DEVELOPING A PLACEMENT-TEST PROGRAM

BENJAMIN BLOOM AND JANE ALLISON

SINCE the reorganization of the College in 1931, placement tests of some kind have been given new students during the orientation week to assist advisers in planning appropriate programs of study. The first tests were essentially predictive instruments and were of value in helping a student to decide whether he should take a particular course in his first or second year of the College, how heavy an academic load he could successfully carry, which of the fields of specialization he might plan to enter, and which elective courses he should take. But with reliance on comprehensive examinations—rather than course credits—as the measure of achievement and the provision of a single, sequential required curriculum which students were permitted to enter after two or more years of high school instead of after four, the value of predictive tests was greatly reduced. On the other hand, placement tests which could be used to determine the appropriate level at which each student should start his work became necessary.

From 1940 to 1943, various faculty groups discussed several problems connected with the placement of entering students. Where, it was asked, should a student start his work in the social sciences—in the first, second, or third course of the sequence? The record of the student's previous academic work was not very useful in answering this question, since grades from different institutions mean different things and since it was impossible to determine the equivalence of the College courses with courses having the same names in other schools. The faculty pointed out that students are not required to attend classes in the College and that some students are able to demonstrate adequate performance on the comprehensive examination without such formal class attendance. Would it not be possible for entering students to have a competence exceeding that revealed by the academic records which they present? The faculty was also concerned with the great range of ability of students within a particular College course. Although each of the general courses involves a year of work, the faculty recognized that some students could probably complete the examination requirement satisfactorily with less than a full year of study in that course.

With these problems in mind, the faculty, in the spring of 1943, recommended that students be placed in the College program on the basis of competence demonstrated on tests in each of the subject fields. A placement-test committee, consisting of representatives of the various instructional staffs and members of the University Examiner's Office, was appointed. As the committee worked on the problems in this field, it became increasingly aware that the nature of the placement-testing program, the kinds of tests to be used, and the ways in which the results were utilized would be determined by the educational philosophy and academic program of the College. A placement-testing program was fundamentally necessary because the entering students were heterogeneous with respect to educational and experiential background and because the College emphasized the level of achievement attained rather than the means by which it was attained.

If all the students have very similar educational backgrounds, there is little reason for a placement program. If, however, students have come from a great variety of schools, reveal little uniformity in the pattern of courses they have had, and differ with respect to the kind and extent of independent reading and studying they have done, it is difficult, if not impossible, to determine precisely from records of previous academic work the level of the student's competence or the point at which he should begin his advanced work.

Many of the difficulties encountered in the appraisal of the student's previous background and training have been recognized by colleges throughout the country. Recently, consideration of these problems was stimulated by the necessity of insuring that veterans were properly placed. Veterans had, in many instances, taken correspondence courses or studied many different subjects in special training programs. Seldom had these courses been the equivalent of the usual college courses, and academic institutions had difficulty in assessing the educational value of such varied study and experience. Some schools met this problem by developing special placement tests, while others made use of standardized achievement tests, such as those prepared by the Cooperative Test Service and by the examination staff of the United States Armed Forces Institute.

The placing of students on the basis of records of courses taken elsewhere assumes a similarity of courses between one school and another. It assumes that if a student has had a course with a particular name at a previous school, it is the equivalent of a course with a similar name at the school to which he is applying. The principal defect in any appraisal of scholastic records as the basis for placement of students is that courses may and do vary considerably. In addition, it disregards the fact that a record of completion of a course at some time in the past is no guaranty that the student still possesses the competence which the course was presumed to have developed. Moreover, it does not take into consideration the possibility that a person lacking some formal educational experiences may have acquired an equivalent competence by other means.

Students enter the College of the University of Chicago after having attended any of several hundred schools and after having completed from ten to fifteen years of schooling. Although most students enter directly from other schools, many have been out of school for a number of years—some after several years of military experience. Some are as young as thirteen, while others are thirty. The problem of assessing previous educational experience is further complicated because the general courses in the College are quite different from the usual courses that the student may have had in secondary school or college. It has been impossible to relate the student's experience in various combinations of courses taken in other educational institutions to specific requirements in the College.

In addition to evidence of achievement, such as final examinations, term papers, and level of classwork, most schools place emphasis on class attendance as a requirement for certification. Few schools will permit students to submit evidence of achievement if they do not meet the minimal requirement of class attendance. This requirement usually involves the assumption that the competence required for graduation can be achieved only if the student has a prescribed set of educational experiences. It also involves the assumption that there are important outcomes of education which are not readily defined and included in the more explicit evidences of achievement represented by examinations, term papers, and the like.

Since the requirements for graduation in the College are stated in terms of comprehensive examinations, the principle of placing emphasis on the level of achievement rather than on the means of developing such achievement was established. The comprehensive examinations do, however, tend to contain many questions and problems which are specifically related to the particular courses in the College. A student who had previously acquired equivalent competence but who was unacquainted with the specific formulations of the problems, the particular readings, and the exact details of the subject matter dealt with in a College course might not be able to pass the comprehensive examination. If he were held for the comprehensive examination, he would usually have to go through a specific set of educational experiences—whether he needed them or not to complete this general education. On the other hand, it seemed possible that tests could be constructed which would give all students an opportunity to demonstrate the major understandings, intellectual abilities, and skills emphasized in a course, even though they have not acquired these as a result of instruction on the specific materials used in the College.

In the early years of the placement-test program the placement committee was not willing to abandon completely consideration of the amount of previous schooling that the student had had. In large part, this was because it did not have complete confidence in the results of the placement tests. It was also a reflection of its belief that the number of years of school attendance make a difference, whether reflected in demonstrated achievement or not. Several members of the placement committee argued that even though an eleventh-grade student could demonstrate satisfactory achievement over the first course in a subject field, he was too young to take the second course and, therefore, should enter the first course in order to secure whatever the course might offer for his further growth. Some also held that to require older students to take the full four-year program of the College would be to require too much of them and that some compromise should be effected in order to reduce the amount of time such students would need to meet the requirements. As the placement program has developed, there has been more and more emphasis on achievement; and, at present, in only three of the fourteen requirements is any attention given to students' previous scholastic records.

A major problem for any educational institution is the level of achievement to be required of a particular student. Should a student be excused from a program of work if he has already demonstrated the minimal competence to be required of students? If he already has this minimal competence, is it making the best use of his time and the school's resources to require him to spend additional time in such a program? What should decide whether the student should continue to attend a course for which he has already demonstrated acceptable competence?

The comprehensive-examination system at the University of Chicago permits a student to complete a requirement with a grade of D or higher. This means that a capable student must determine for himself whether he shall strive for a high or only for a passing grade. While this same decision is offered to students in other colleges, the consequences are different. If a student in the College is of the opinion that he already has the minimal competence necessary, he may elect to take the course and do all the work involved; he may decide to work independently and do only part of the course work; or he may do no course work at all in preparation for the comprehensive examination. In contrast to this, the usual college program demands that the student attend class regularly and do all the work required.

The placement committee conceded that a student who could satisfy the College examination requirements at time of entrance might profit to some extent from further work in the course or courses from which he was excused. On the other hand, since the minimal requirements were quite high, the committee doubted whether such attendance would constitute the best use of a student's time. The committee also recognized the possibility that such students might be poorly motivated and more likely to develop poor habits of work and study unless they were constantly challenged by more and more complex ideas. The specification of a minimal standard of achievement does seem to be defensible in connection with general education, where the attempt is to insure that each citizen will have at least a minimal competence in certain general fields. In a specialty it might be more justifiable to insist on maximum achievement and to have students take work even though they have already satisfied the minimal requirements. The point of view that students should continue to attend classes even though they can demonstrate attainment of the minimal requirements can be best defended if additional experiences are provided for such students to broaden their understanding of the field or to intensify their understanding by going deeper and deeper into some of the more complex aspects of the subject.

The assignment of course grades has always been a rule-of-thumb affair in institutions of higher education. The criteria used in grading have varied considerably from course to course and from instructor to instructor. Even the same instructor varies his standards from time to time. Very rarely has an instructor attempted to define the level of achievement that he will regard as passing. Even when lengthy and objective tests have been given, little has been done to give meaning to the various scores other than to describe their distributions.

For placement purposes it is not sufficient to describe score distributions. If a placement program is to be meaningful, it is necessary to have some definition of levels of competence as well as some stable techniques for determining when that competence has been achieved. It is imperative that there be some method of determining what score or pattern of scores is indicative of the minimal level of competence to be required.

Since comprehensive examinations have been used for nearly twenty years in the College of the University of Chicago, the problem of relating examination scores to standards of achievement has been given much attention. For some time the procedure was to set grades by reference to a normal distribution such that a definite proportion of the students received A, B, C, D, and F. More recently, attempts have been made to use such other criteria for setting grade standards as the pooling of instructors' judgments on the test performance to be required for each grade, anchoring test material from one examination to another, and setting absolute standards which continued from one examination to another.

The standards of achievement for the comprehensive examinations became the basis for setting the placement-test standards. Since the test material for placement purposes is selected from or is parallel to the comprehensive examinations, it is possible to determine whether a student's placement performance is the equivalent of a particular grade on the comprehensive examination. The faculty has decided that a student may be excused from a comprehensive-examination requirement if his performance on a placement test is the equivalent of a C and, in some cases, a high D on the appropriate comprehensive examination.

The committee recognized that the exact nature of the placement program would be determined by the extent to which the academic program was well integrated and sequential and that this would be best determined when the objectives of the College as a whole and the specific courses were well defined. The development of the placement tests, in turn, helped to reveal a number of points at which the academic program was not sequential and where objectives were not clearly defined.

Unless the specific outcomes of a course or subject have been defined, it is impossible to determine whether entering students have or have not already acquired what the course can give them. Since the objectives of a course indicate the ways in which an instructional staff believes that it can change the behavior of a group of students, the task of a placement program is to determine whether the students have already reached the levels and the varieties of competence which the course can develop. The definition of the objectives of a course or subject field enables one to specify the kinds of evidence necessary to determine whether students have reached the desired types of competence.

Each of the courses in the College has defined its objectives as a basis for the preparation of comprehensive examinations. These statements of objectives were of great value in planning the placement tests. Perhaps the problem of defining objectives can be clarified by an illustration. One of the course outlines indicated a series of literary works that the student was expected to read. The instructors made it clear that mere knowledge of these particular readings did not represent the ends of the course and was not sufficient to warrant excusing the students from the course. They further made it clear that other comparable books might be substituted for the particular ones on this list. The faculty were using the reading materials as means rather than as ends, since they were seeking to develop certain skills of interpretation in students through the use of these materials. The placement test, then, had to be designed to secure evidence of the extent to which the students could interpret certain literary works through the application of the intellectual abilities and skills taught in the course. The definitions had to be sufficiently clear to enable one to determine what some of the permanent outcomes of a course were expected to be and what equivalent types of experience might be sufficient to enable a student to satisfy the require ments. One value of the placement tests was, therefore, in stimulating the instructional staff to produce clearer and clearer definitions of the outcomes of a course. These definitions also served to focus the attention of the instructional staff on some objectives which they regarded as important and desirable but which they did not, at present, believe were being satisfactorily achieved.

Very early in its explorations the placement committee had to face the problem of what should be done with students whose scores were just below that chosen as the minimum grade for exemption from a comprehensive-examination requirement. In the early years of the use of placement tests it was recommended that all such cases be given special attention. Where it seemed clear that the students did have courses or training approximating that required in the College, they were excused from the particular examination requirement, although others with similar scores who had not taken "equivalent" courses elsewhere were held for the requirement. This, however, was regarded as a compromise measure. It is clear that when any standard is applied there must be a substantial number of students having borderline scores. These are students who have some, but not all, of the competence required. It would not seem fair to have such students spend a full year of work in a course because they missed a few points on a placement test. Experience with these borderline individuals has indicated that many of them have patterns of knowledge, skill, and ability such that they can complete the requirements in much less than the usual length of time.

It has been found possible for many such students to round out their competence in a field sufficiently to pass the comprehensive examination with relatively high grades by attending only certain sessions of the regular classes or by taking specially designed abbreviated courses. In individual cases it has been possible to give a student special guidance as to the books he should read, the specific classes he should attend, and the educational experiences he should acquire before taking the comprehensive examination. These have proved to be very satisfactory techniques and have enabled many students to move ahead at a rate commensurate with their competence.

The placement tests have also led the faculty to face the problem of what to do with students who are unusually deficient on a placement test. It was found that some students' knowledge, ability, and skill in a field were so meager that they were quite likely to fail the comprehensive examination if given only the regular instruction in a course. The placement tests made it possible to detect many of these students; this, in turn, led the faculty to provide deficiency and remedial classes for them. In some cases it was possible to have extra meetings of a class to give these students additional instruction and to help make clear many of the points they were not able to grasp at the regular pace of the course. Procedures such as these have tended to reduce the proportion of failures in the College.

If a student is to profit most effectively from the time that he spends in an educational program, it is necessary to insure that he begins his work at the proper point. This is especially necessary where the student leaves one type of school for another with a very different educational philosophy, curriculum, and pedagogical technique. If one is willing to grant the possibility that (a) students may acquire some of the competence stressed in educational programs through experiences outside the school; (b) a particular competence, though once attained, is not necessarily permanent; and (c) academic standards and course classifications may be different from one school to another, then one must have some misgivings about assessing the students' competence on the basis of the usual academic record or transcript. It therefore becomes evident that techniques must be devised for appraising the competence of a student at the time of entrance to a new school. Placement tests, if made carefully with due consideration for the relevant kinds of competence which a student may attain, can serve as the basis for assembling such evidence. We have here stated a number of principles and criteria by which a place-

ment program can be organized and on the basis of which placement tests can be constructed. It is recognized that the educational and testing programs are closely interwoven and have
many possible forms of interaction. As the educational program
is clearly defined, it is possible to determine the tests and testing
techniques which are most appropriate. When such tests have
been devised and used, they help to determine whether the program is achieving the ends desired and at what points the program can be improved.

The problem of establishing the validity of placement tests is
a complex one and requires the use of a number of distinct kinds
of evidence. One way is to have experts judge whether the test
situations used are appropriate to the specifications set by the
instructional staff, as well as whether they meet the requirements for placement testing. The experts, who are members of
the instructional staff, examine each item as it relates to the
specifications. Since many of the placement-test items are drawn
from comprehensive examinations, another method of validation
is to correlate the performance of students taking the comprehensive on the items to be used on the placement test with their
performance on the remainder of the comprehensive. Where the
sample of placement-test items represents about one-fourth or
one-third the total comprehensive examination, the correlation
between this sample and the remainder of the examination is
usually above $+.85$ and in most cases is $+.90$ or higher. However, it should be recognized that these correlations are based
on comprehensive examinations which are generally taken after
the student has completed the appropriate courses. The entire
case for validity cannot rest on such correlations, since the
placement tests are to be given to students before they take the
college courses. However, this validation technique does yield
some supporting evidence. Both the expert opinion and the
correlational method of validating the placement tests are
methods used in the selection and construction of test material
and thus provide checks on validity before the placement tests
are given.

A method of validating the tests which yields an a posteriori type of evidence is to determine the relationship between students' previous academic training and their placement-test results. It would be expected that, with increased amount of relevant previous training, there should be some increment in the placement-test scores. Since the placement tests measure a specific type of competence at a particular point in time and since the data on amount of training do not make allowances for variations in quality and relevance of training from one school to another, variations in quality of previous work from one student to another, or variations in retention, one would not expect a perfect relationship between amount of training and placement-test results.

We have chosen the four subject fields in which the secondary-school courses are likely to be most relevant to and most nearly approximate some portions of the College work. These are in the fields of mathematics, social science, English, and foreign languages. Table 1 shows the proportion of students held for the full requirement in selected subjects in the College as related to the amount of previous training which they have had. It will be noted that in each case there is a decrease in the proportion held for the full requirement as the amount of previous training increases. The change is particularly great in mathematics and foreign language.

The most important type of evidence in support of the placement program is the subsequent performance of students on comprehensive examinations. One group of students whose performance provides significant evidence is made up of those whose placement-test scores indicate that they have satisfied part, but not all, of a particular requirement; such students are given special instruction and counsel on the specific work which they should do in preparation for the comprehensive examination. This usually means that the students can prepare for the comprehensives by attending only certain meetings of the course and by doing specified readings and individual study. Data are available on 217 students who were given advice on comprehensive examinations in 1945. Seventy per cent of these students made grades of A or B on the relevant comprehensives, as contrasted with 28 per cent of the total group of college students taking these examinations. Only 3 per cent of the students given advice on the comprehensive received grades of D or F, as contrasted with 21 per cent of the total student population. These results would seem to indicate that the placement procedures for this group were more than justified by the large proportion of the students who made high grades. It is evident that some students when given the proper advice and counsel can complete requirements at a very high level with much less than the usual amount of study and preparation.

TABLE 1

PERCENTAGE OF STUDENTS WITH DIFFERENT AMOUNTS OF PREVIOUS TRAINING IN A SUBJECT WHO ARE HELD FOR THE FULL REQUIREMENTS IN EACH SUBJECT

Years	Mathematics 1*	Social Sciences 1*	English†	Foreign Language†
1 or less......	57.1	34.1	....	80.5
1–2..........	54.8	24.7	96.0	64.2
2½..........	23.0	....	....	....
3..........	9.0	24.3	89.6	38.0

* Based on a sample of 195 students who entered the College after twelve years of previous schooling.

† Based on a sample of 336 students with ten, eleven, or twelve years of previous schooling.

Significant evidence is also obtained from the performance of those students who have been excused from the first-year requirement in a subject field on examinations over the second year's work in the same field. In 1945, 115 students who had entered at the end of ten years of school were excused from the Humanities 1 or Social Sciences 1 comprehensive examinations. On the second-year comprehensive-examination requirement, Humanities 2 and Social Sciences 2, 35 per cent of these students made grades of A or B, while 22 per cent made grades of D or F. The corresponding figures for all students taking those comprehensives are 29 per cent A or B and 21 per cent D or F. These accelerated students, thus, do as well as the regular College group taking the comprehensives. That 22 per cent received grades of D or F may be regarded as some indication that these accelerated students did not profit as much from the placement procedures as might have been expected. One would expect more of these students to continue doing superior work on subsequent examinations in the same field.

The relation of student performance on the comprehensives to their previous academic training and their placement-test record is worth noting in the light of the conclusions to be drawn from Table 1. It might be expected that, if placement on the basis of academic credit is valid, a student's performance on the comprehensives would, like his placement-test record, vary with the amount of his previous training. Thus it might be expected that a higher proportion of students with three or more years of previous mathematics would receive grades of A or B in the Mathematics 1 comprehensive than would be true for students with less than this amount of training. However, analysis of the four subject fields in which secondary-school training is most relevant to the work of the College does not give this result. It can be seen in Table 2 that, with the exception of English, students with less training tend to do somewhat better on the comprehensive examination than do students with more training in that field. It is evident from these data that those students who, in spite of relatively more training, are held for the requirement on the basis of their placement-test record are the ones who have difficulty in that field. The placement tests are thus especially useful in pointing out deficiencies or weaknesses not discernible when students are placed on the basis of their academic record.

The effect of the placement program may be seen most clearly when the length of the students' programs as determined by placement tests is contrasted with that to be expected by the customary appraisal of transcripts of academic work. If students were placed in the College program on the basis of their transcripts, those who enter the College after ten years of previous work would require three and one-half years to complete the degree requirements.* The placement results show that 54 per cent of these students require this amount of time, 42 per cent three years, and 4 per cent can complete the College in two years or less. Thus, for a large number of students entering the College after ten years of previous school work, the placement tests serve to decrease the amount of time spent in fulfilling requirements

* Assuming that a student is held for fourteen examinations and takes four comprehensive examinations in each academic year of three quarters.

for the Bachelor of Arts degree. For the students who enter the College after the completion of twelve years of previous schooling (customarily high-school graduation), the College program, if it were based on transcript credit and if it gave full credit to their previous years of school, could be completed in about two and one-third years.* On the basis of the placement-test results, 60 per cent require three years or more, 36 per cent require two years, while 4 per cent can complete the College in one and one-third years or less. For these students the placement program generally results in a longer program of work.

TABLE 2

GRADES ON COMPREHENSIVE EXAMINATIONS MADE BY STUDENTS HELD FOR PARTICULAR REQUIREMENT AS RELATED TO EXTENT OF PREVIOUS TRAINING IN SUBJECT (IN PERCENTAGES)

GRADES	MATHEMATICS 1		SOCIAL SCIENCES 1		ENGLISH		FOREIGN LANGUAGE	
	2 Yrs. or Less	2½ or More Yrs.	1 Yr. or Less	2 or More Yrs.	2 Yrs. or Less	3 or More Yrs.	2 Yrs. or Less	3 or More Yrs.
A–B........	41	35	48	30	26	29	37	22
C.........	37	39	36	55	42	44	33	44
D–F........	22	26	16	15	32	27	30	34
	100	100	100	100	100	100	100	100
No. of students..	137	23	73	93	123	155	113	32

A study of the placement of 750 students entering the College with ten, eleven, or twelve years of previous schooling shows that only 45 per cent of the students are placed at a level which might have been expected from an analysis of their previous transcripts, 25 per cent are excused from examinations which would have been required on the basis of the usual evaluation of the transcripts, while 30 per cent are required to do more work in the College than might have been required if the transcript had been the sole basis for deciding placement in the College program.

The effect of the placement program may also be seen in connection with specific subject fields. Sixteen per cent of students with two or less years of previous work in mathematics are ex-

* Assuming that a student is held for nine examinations and takes four comprehensive examinations in each academic year of three quarters.

cused from the Mathematics 1 requirement and thus have a competence exceeding that represented on the transcript of academic credit. On the other hand, of those students with two and a half or more years of previous training in mathematics, 16 per cent are required to take the Mathematics 1 examination. These students do not have the competence which might have been inferred from the academic credit. In the case of Social Sciences 1, 34 per cent of the students with one year or less of secondary-school social sciences are excused from the full requirement, while 44 per cent with two years or more of previous work in the field do not demonstrate sufficient competence on the placement test to be excused from the full requirement. In the foreign languages, 12 per cent of students with two years or less of training in the foreign language evidence sufficient competence to be excused from the requirement, while 68 per cent of the students with three years or more do not give sufficient evidence of competence to be excused from the requirement. Thus there appears to be a significant disparity between the specific work required of the student on the basis of placement tests and that which might have been required on the basis of transcripts of credit.

The evidence cited in connection with placement-test procedures indicates that a college which places its students on the basis of demonstrated competence at the time of entrance will find the program required of students to be substantially different from that which might have been required on the basis of evidence of similar or parallel work elsewhere.

III

THE EFFECTS OF INDEPENDENT COMPREHENSIVE EXAMINATIONS

PAUL B. DIEDERICH

THE College has completed eighteen years of operation under a system of comprehensive examinations which are prepared and marked by the Office of the University Examiner and which are the sole basis for granting degrees. While a similar system is very common abroad, it is relatively uncommon here, and any institution which has tried it for so long a period has an obligation to report how it works. What are the advantages and disadvantages that one of the examiners sees in the system?

One of the early objections was that students would probably neglect their work through the first two quarters of each year and "cram" desperately in the third. It also implied that students would devote their whole attention to the recall of facts, with no regard to the use of those facts in their thinking or to the development of interests, attitudes, and appreciations. It was feared that the system would not only compel all teachers to teach exactly the same things in the same ways but would reduce instruction to the level of that found in the coaching schools, which endeavor to guess what will appear in the forthcoming examinations of the neighboring university and to "cram" their clientele with the requisite information in the shortest possible time. It was feared that any instructor who tried to lead his students in the adventures of the soul among masterpieces would be met by a cold stare and the question, "Will that be in the examination?"

While these dangers always have to be guarded against, they have not proved serious in practice. The examinations do not place undue emphasis on the recall of facts. Even in the sciences, the time and weight given to the recall of facts are never more than 30 per cent of the examination. Chief emphasis is given to the use of facts in solving problems that have not been discussed in the course. In literature, half or more of the examination is based on works studied independently by students, without class discussion, to demonstrate their mastery of the methods of analysis taught in the course. They cannot merely remember the instructor's interpretation; they must work out their own. If students focus their attention on such examinations, they will be learning exactly what their instructors want them to learn anyway. These general principles and intellectual skills are retained unusually well. There have been many opportunities for retesting, as students come back for further study, and no serious loss has been discovered in the kinds of outcomes which are given greatest weight in the comprehensives. While no college knows the extent to which its students use for their own purposes what they have learned, there is at least no evidence that these students forget what they have learned as soon as possible after the examination.

The College offers fourteen general courses to prepare students for the comprehensive examinations required for the Bachelor's degree. Each of the general courses enrols hundreds of students and is taught by a staff of from ten to thirty teachers. All teachers of a given course use the same syllabus, which is prepared and revised annually by the staff, and they meet once a week to discuss ways of dealing with the materials which they are about to teach. It becomes apparent in these meetings that the materials are used in the greatest diversity of ways. The examiner attends all these meetings, notes the divergent views which are expressed, and obtains from them a clearer view of the more basic matters which are to be tested and which underlie the diverse procedures used by various staff members. As a result, he prepares questions that deal with the general objectives of the course rather than with any particular means of reaching these objectives.

Since the University Examiner is an independent officer, it was once feared that the staff of examiners would dictate the curriculum. This danger has been avoided through the convention that the examiner in a particular subject area must secure the agreement of the teaching staff to every objective covered by the examination. He has no authority to tell the staff what to do; he has to find out what they are trying to do and then prepare questions related to these purposes and no others. He need not secure staff agreement to every question, but, if a question could be shown to bear no relation to any of the announced purposes of the staff, the examiner would be subjected to severe censure.

The chief criticism of the teaching staff is that the examination system gives them no control over students. They admit that, if they were perfect teachers, they would not need a goad; students would follow willingly wherever they led. But in this imperfect world, they contend, a goad is sometimes necessary. If they make an assignment and students disregard it, the worst they can say is, "If this neglect continues, you will probably get an F on the comprehensive." They cannot say, "I will give you an F." They know, and the students know, that instructors have no control over marks.

On the other hand, this lack of control over marks has its compensations. It is a blessed relief to most teachers to be freed from the pressure of the importunate student—sometimes that of his parents as well. In most colleges some students contest every mark, from the first paper in the course to the final examination. Some try to influence marks by the procedures known as "apple-polishing," while others argue or cry. Under an independent examination system it is easy to explain to students that all preliminary marks, such as those on assigned papers, quizzes, and quarterly examinations, represent only an estimate of progress toward passing the comprehensive. They will not stand in the record, and there is no point in arguing about them. If a student fails the comprehensive examination, the instructor can explain, in all sincerity, that he had nothing whatever to do with setting the mark and has no power to alter it. In most cases he does not even know the mark until the student tells him. He never has to look a well-meaning but incompetent student in the eye and tell him, "I gave you an F." The terrible responsibility of judging people at the end of every course is taken off his shoulders. Shelving this responsibility has a most beneficial effect on the relations of students and teachers. They are both on the same side of the fence. It is up to the students to pass the examination; the teacher is there only to help them as much as he can. He is not their taskmaster and judge. He assigns no rewards or penalties. He is their friend and guide.

There is no evidence of widespread or serious neglect of assigned work. On the contrary, students work uncommonly hard. If an occasional assignment is disregarded, it may, or may not, be a real loss. If students did everything that all their instructors wanted them to do, they would soon be working sixteen hours a day. Furthermore, it must be granted that not all assignments are so carefully considered that students will really suffer if they omit them. Some of them deserve to be disregarded. A system which allows some latitude in this respect is probably healthier than one which requires conformity to every whim of the instructor.

The question may still be raised, however, whether the final judgment of the student's competence in a given field should not be filtered through the mind of someone who knows the student. Perhaps the examination should be used as a doctor uses a clinical thermometer. The doctor wants the thermometer to register the correct temperature, uninfluenced by any sentiment toward the patient; but his final diagnosis of the case is a human judgment, taking into account everything he knows about the patient. In the same fashion, perhaps, the result of the examination should be reported to the instructor and be used by him, along with any other evidence at his disposal, to determine the student's mark. Isn't it true that some students who have worked very hard and who desperately need encouragement still fail the examination? And that some shiftless ones who have never been near the course manage to slip by?

It is true that these things happen, but it is still questionable whether the responsibility for determining marks should be thrown back on the instructors. Students respect the mark more and work harder to earn it when they know that it stands for sheer competence, uninfluenced by docility, regularity of attendance, completion of assignments, participation in class discussion, promptness, neatness, appearance, affability, and other irrelevant matters. Also it is arguable that the "doctor" in this case is not properly the instructor but the adviser, who is selected and trained especially for this work, who knows more of the student's background and circumstances, and who has more sources of information about him than any one instructor. The adviser should have at his disposal marks which mean exactly what they are supposed to mean and then have the power to save a deserving student from any harsh consequences. The shiftless students can be caught by the mechanism of reports to the adviser, in which the instructor can speak his mind fully, without restricting himself to five letters of the alphabet, and the adviser can take any action which seems warranted. When one further considers the extreme variability of instructors in assigning marks, the great difficulty of approximating a common standard, and the substantial benefits which instructors gain from not having this responsibility, one is glad to leave the determination of marks to an impersonal examining agency.

Another criticism of comprehensive examinations is that they are probably conducive to the development of neuroses. This charge would be so serious, if true, that it would outweigh all the benefits of the system; but thus far there is no evidence, or even any substantial probability, that it is true. The incidence of actual breakdown, for example, is negligible—if even one such case could be called negligible—and is certainly no higher than in other colleges of comparable size. Examiners and instructors frequently observe students during examinations with a watchful eye for signs of anxiety or undue strain, but they rarely find cause for alarm. What takes the curse off the system is that students need not register for an examination until they feel prepared for it, and some put off the examination for three months or more after completing the course. If they fail or make a low mark at their first attempt, they have only to find out what they did wrong, remedy their weaknesses, and try again three months later. Many students repeat examinations when their initial grade was C or even B, because they will be satisfied with nothing less than an A. They run no risk, for whichever mark is higher stands in the record. With all these safeguards, it is hard to imagine why comprehensive examinations in themselves should induce neuroses. It is probably true that students who are already neurotic will manifest anxiety toward examinations, as toward any other threat to their security, but it seems highly improbable at present that such anxiety could cause a neurosis. If it combines with the underlying causes to bring out an incipient neurosis, it may be just as well to bring the condition to light while the student is young enough to achieve a cure with relative ease and while he can spend the money set aside for college on the course of treatment that he needs.

On the positive side, the system seems to give students a lively sense of responsibility for their own education. It has repeatedly been found that there is little difference in average scores between different sections of the same course. Students know what they are expected to learn, from the syllabus, from quarterly examinations, and from copies of past examinations, and, if their instructors do not teach them these things, they manage to learn them by themselves.

The effect on standards of accomplishment is salutary. If each teacher sets his own examination, he tends to ask only those questions which most of his students will be able to answer. On the other hand, if the examination is produced by an agency which has no interest in fortifying the ego of the instructors and if it is to be published and subjected to every sort of criticism, it tends to demand whatever the liberally educated man ought to know about the subject. Students know that they cannot rely on any favorable impression which they may have made on the instructor. Their only safety lies in knowing how to answer these hundreds of merciless questions. New instructors are often appalled by the difficulty of the questions, but students somehow rise to them.

The examinations produced by a full-time professional staff in constant association with a teaching staff are not only more difficult but also better examinations—more valid, more objective, and more reliable—than the examinations ordinarily produced by teachers. Many a professor thinks of his examination questions while walking to the examination and then writes them on the blackboard. In some cases, they turn out to be brilliant questions and are marked with great insight and fairness, but in many other cases it is largely a matter of chance whether the students happen to be well prepared on these particular questions. In hardly any case could these questions compare with the hundreds of penetrating questions devised by an experienced examiner after months of work which covers every aspect of the course and every type of competence which it is expected to produce.

The manner in which the examinations are prepared tends to make the teaching staff unusually conscious of the objectives of the course. A careful analysis of the results of the examination can also give them a clear picture of their successes and failures. It is a chastening experience to select typical questions representing each objective and to count how many students got them right.

Finally, the examination serves as a focal point around which to organize the work of the course. It is a psychological advantage to have a very concrete goal to aim at, with progress toward it indicated by marks on assignments, quizzes, and mid-quarterly and quarterly examinations. The final comprehensive examination reviews the work of the whole course, brings all parts of it into fruitful interplay with one another, and shows clearly what the student is now able to do with all the facts and skills which he has learned.

ITEMS FROM COMPREHENSIVE EXAMINATIONS

NOTE.—These items have been chosen to illustrate some of the examining techniques used in the College. It has not been possible to include samples from every course or field.

ENGLISH

Three weeks before the examination selections from the following works were distributed:

PLATO *Republic*, iii and iv.
ARISTOTLE *Politics*, ii. 5.
LOCKE, *Second Treatise on Civil Government*, chap. v.
MARX and ENGELS, *The Communist Manifesto*.
WILLIAM GRAHAM SUMNER, *The Challenge of the Facts*.
R. H. TAWNEY, *The Acquisitive Society*, chap. iii.
POPE PIUS XI, *Quadragesimo anno*.

All these passages bore on the theme of "private property," but no hint was given as to the exact nature of the essay to be assigned. When the students came to the examination, they received the following instructions:

Write a unified paper on some restricted aspect of the question of the future of private property in America. The paper may be either an argument in support of some form of ownership which you favor, or an attack upon some form which you oppose, or both. It must, however, observe the following stipulations:

1. It must include a discussion of the *moral bases* and *social effects* of the kind of ownership which you favor or wish to attack. For example, what ultimate right has anyone to claim anything as his own? What should he be allowed to do with what he owns? How should such rights be achieved, or protected, or limited? What will be the effects on society of the policies which you discuss?

2. It must relate to your thesis the relevant arguments pro and con of the *passages* distributed before the examination. It must not merely report what these passages said in the order in which they were printed. In the course of developing your own position you must make use of the arguments which support it and refute the arguments which oppose it.

3. It must show some *application* of your theoretical position to one or more examples of property rights drawn from your own experience, observation, or reading. The following examples may suggest possibilities: Private property in the family, or in the dormitory; rented, owned, and co-

operative housing; public and private schools; independent, chain, and cooperative stores; making the University Bookstore a cooperative; municipal ownership of utilities and transportation; nationalization of banks, coal mines, railroads, and communications; national developments such as TVA; the rights of capital, management, labor, and consumers in the control of large corporations, etc.

4. In form, the paper must be an *argument*. It must not be a mere assertion of your opinions supported by a description of the practices which you favor. It must give reasons for the position which you favor and against the positions which you oppose. The reasoning must be logical, but it need not make explicit reference to logical forms.

5. The argument should be clear, interesting, and acceptable to the *audience* to which it is addressed. In a preliminary paragraph, separate from the rest of the paper, describe briefly the traits of your audience which you intend to keep in mind while writing your paper.

6. The paper must be effectively organized and well written. It must not follow the points given above as a writing outline. It must not ignore them, however. Students are expected to deal with the assignment.

7. The nature of the opinions expressed in this paper will have no effect on grades, and will never be revealed.

8. You will have three hours in which to plan and write this paper. It will be wise to spend about half an hour thinking about the assignment and planning the paper, and to reserve half an hour at the end to read over and revise what you have written. Do not attempt more than you can treat adequately in two hours of writing. A careful limitation of the scope of the paper is one mark of a good essay. The first pages may be used for notes, an outline, or a rough draft; but draw lines through this material to indicate that it is not a part of the finished essay. Please write in ink, and as legibly as you can. Since there will not be time to make a fair copy of the essay in its final form, portions may be crossed out and corrections inserted between the lines and in the margins, but please make the corrections as clearly and neatly as possible. Dictionaries may be used, and any notes which you have written on your copy of the Passages for Study.

NATURAL SCIENCES 1

The following questions refer to a paper by Hooke distributed for study prior to the examination.

DIRECTIONS: *Blacken* the answer space corresponding to the letter of the *one best* answer or completion, unless otherwise directed.

1. In developing his law relating the tension and power of springs, Hooke's crucial observation was that

A—$F_1/F_2 = B_1/B_2$, where F_1 and F_2 are the forces exerted *by* the spring, and B_1 and B_2 are the degrees of bending of the spring.

B—$F_1/F_2 = B_1/B_2$, where F_1 and F_2 are the forces exerted *upon* the spring, and B_1 and B_2 are the same as above.

C—$W_1/W_2 = B_1/B_2$, where W_1 and W_2 are the weights of bodies fastened to the spring, and B_1 and B_2 are the same as above.

2. The law itself states that

A—$F_1/F_2 = B_1/B_2$, where F_1 and F_2 are the forces exerted *by* the spring, and B_1 and B_2 are the degrees of bending, of the spring.

B—$F_1/F_2 = B_1/B_2$, where F_1 and F_2 are the forces exerted *upon* the spring, and B_1 and B_2 are the same as above.

C—$W_1/W_2 = B_1/B_2$, where W_1 and W_2 are the weights of bodies fastened to the spring, and B_1 and B_2 are the same as above.

3. In measuring the power of a spring in terms of force as defined by Newton, it was necessary for Hooke to make

A—the assumption that, if a system is in equilibrium, all its parts are at rest.

B—the assumption that, if a system is in equilibrium, there is no net force acting upon it.

C—the assumption that, if a system is in equilibrium, there must be some unbalanced force acting upon it.

D—none of the above assumptions concerning the properties of a system in equilibrium.

4. According to Hooke's law relating the tension and power of springs,

A—any finite force, no matter how small, must cause a finite bending of any spring.

B—certain finite forces may be too small to cause finite bending of certain springs (i.e., a certain minimum force may be required to cause any finite bending of a certain spring).

5. The statement completed in Question 4 probably is

A—a summary of experimental data obtained in the laboratory.

B—an extrapolation from laboratory data to a limit which cannot be experimentally tested.

C—a theoretical deduction which has no relation to experimental data.

6. According to Hooke, ". . . if one . . . weight lengthens it [a spring] one . . . length, then two . . . weights will extend it two . . . lengths. . . ." On the basis of your laboratory experience, it is probable that this sentence

A—is a report of data actually obtained by Hooke in experiments with springs

B—reports an arithmetic mean of data obtained in experiments with springs.

C—states a relation from which laboratory data are assumed to be accidental deviations.

7. A certain spring is stretched 10 centimeters by a 1-kilogram weight. According to Hooke's law, what is the weight of a body which stretches the same spring 25 centimeters?

A—0.25 kilogram
B—1 kilogram
C—2 kilogram
D—2.5 kilogram
E—25 kilogram

Hooke's law relating the tension and power of springs might be variously interpreted as: a definition of the term 'spring"; a definition of the term "equal weights"; or as a proposition derived by experiment.

8. This law, stated as a definition of the term "spring," would read: "A spring is a body

A—which has a tendency to return to some normal or natural state."
B—which requires a finite, constant force for its distortion."
C—which is equally distorted by equal weights."
D—the distortions of which are proportional to the weights causing them."

9. In his discussion of uniformly accelerated motion, Galileo proceeded by first constructing a definition and then deducing consequences from it. According to Galileo, such a definition and its consequences constitute a contribution to natural science

A—only if a phenomenon fitting the definition can be shown to exist in nature by direct observation
B—if the consequences deduced from the definition can be shown to exist in nature by direct observation, even if the phenomenon fitting the definition cannot be similarly shown to exist.
C—whether or not any phenomenon fitting the definition or the consequences deduced from the definition can be shown to exist in nature by direct observation.

10. Hooke's law, stated as a definition of the term "equal weights," would read: "Equal weights distort a given spring by the same amount." Which of the following could *not* be used as a definition of the term "spring," as it appears in this definition?

A—"A spring is a body which returns to some normal or natural state when external forces are removed."
B—"A spring is a body which is equally distorted by equal weights."
C—"A spring is a body which behaves like a 'standard' spring chosen by agreement among scientists."

11. According to Newton, as the altitude of a given body is increased,

A—both the accelerative and motive forces exerted upon it by the earth remain constant.

B—both the accelerative and motive forces exerted upon it by the earth increase.

C—both the accelerative and motive forces exerted upon it by the earth decrease.

D—the accelerative force exerted upon it by the earth increases, but the motive force decreases.

E—the accelerative force exerted upon it by the earth decreases, but the motive force remains constant.

12. Therefore, assuming Newton's position concerning the variation of accelerative and motive forces (as in Question 11), it would be concluded that the degree of bending produced in a given spring by a given body

A—remains constant, as the altitude of the spring and attached body is increased.

B—increases, as the altitude of the spring and attached body is increased.

C—decreases, as the altitude of the spring and attached body is increased.

13. In his experiments, Hooke observed that the degree of bending produced in a given spring by a given body

A—did not change noticeably as the altitude was increased.

B—increased as the altitude was increased.

C—decreased as the altitude was increased.

14. On the basis of these observations, Hooke

A—accepted the position that the tendency of bodies toward the earth's center remains constant as their altitude is increased, since it had been demonstrated by experiment.

B—rejected the position that the tendency of bodies toward the earth's center remains constant as their altitude is increased, since it had been refuted by experiment.

C—accepted the position that the tendency of bodies toward the earth's surface increases as their altitude is increased, since it had been demonstrated by experiment.

D—rejected the position that the tendency of bodies toward the earth's center decreases as their altitude is increased, since it had been refuted by experiment.

E—neither accepted nor rejected the position that the tendency of bodies toward the earth's surface decreases as their altitude is increased.

The behavior of Hooke's particles before and after impact is like the behavior of elastic bodies in that the relative velocities are the same both before and after impact. However, it would constitute nonsense rather than theory to consider these particles as elastic (i.e., as capable of deformation and return to their original shape). Instead, it is necessary to consider them as perfectly hard (i.e., undeformable). Why?

15. Which of the following observations could be most easily (i.e., with little or no revision) accounted for by Hooke's explanation of springiness?

  A—Certain finite forces do not produce any infinite distortion in a given spring.

  B—A spring has a certain maximum compression; no finite force, no matter how great, can compress it further.

  C—The tendency of a spring to return to its undistorted form is not proportional to the degree of distortion, if it is extended sufficiently.

  D—A certain spring, when extended sufficiently, does not return to its undistorted form.

16. The character of the forces which exist between the particles of springs, according to Hooke, most closely resembles the character of those forces postulated by Clausius to exist between the molecules of

  A—solids.
  B—liquids.
  C—real gases.
  D—perfect gases.

17. According to Hooke, the average velocity exhibited by any spring in returning the whole distance from any deformed position to its undeformed position is equal to

  A— ks^2, where k is a constant, and s is the distance returned.
  B— ks.
  C— $k\sqrt{s}$.
  D— s.
  E— k/s.

18. This proposition relating average velocity and distance makes it possible to deduce the proposition concerning time, since

  A— $t = s/v$, where t is the time of a motion, s is the distance, and v is average velocity.

  B— $t = s/v^2$.
  C— $t = sv$.
  D— $t = sv^2$.

19. Certain similarities of mathematical interrelationship exist between the terms used by Hooke to describe the phenomena of springs, on the one hand, and the terms used by Galileo to describe the phenomena of uniformly accelerated motion, on the other. Thus, for Hooke, f (distorting force) is related to s (distance to which a given spring is distorted) as, for Galileo, v (instantaneous velocity of a body which starts from rest and has a given uniform acceleration) is related to

  A—acceleration.
  B—distance traversed.
  C—time.

20. Furthermore, for Hooke, P (aggregate of powers released from a distorted to the non-distorted position) is related to s (distance distorted) as, for Galileo, s (distance traversed) is related to

    A—acceleration.

    B—time.

    C—instantaneous velocity.

21. Thus Galileo's definition of uniformly accelerated motion is mathematically analogous to Hooke's statement that

    A—the power of a spring is proportional to its degree of bending.

    B—the aggregates of powers received are proportional to the squares of the space bended.

    C—the velocities of a body moved are proportional to the square roots of the aggregates of powers by which it is moved.

22. And Galileo's Theorem II of uniformly accelerated motion ("for a given uniformly accelerated motion, the distances traversed are as the square of the times") is mathematically analogous to Hooke's statement that

    A—the power of a spring is proportional to its degree of bending.

    B—the aggregates of powers received are proportional to the squares of the space bended.

    C—the velocities of a body moved are proportional to the square roots of the aggregates of powers by which it is moved.

23. There is a very close analogy between a pendulum and a spring having the properties described by Hooke. Thus, each one, after being initially distorted from its equilibrium position and released, moves toward and then beyond that equilibrium position. The reason that the velocities of both spring and pendulum are finite, rather than zero, when they attain the equilibrium position after having been distorted and released, is:

    A—since the potential energy gained by the original distortion from equilibrium cannot be lost (by the law of conservation of energy), the spring or pendulum must always retain its tendency to motion.

    B—although the potential energy becomes zero at the equilibrium point, the sum of the kinetic and potential energies remains constant (neglecting friction and air resistance), and therefore the kinetic energy at the equilibrium point must have a finite value.

    C—although the kinetic energy becomes zero at the equilibrium point, the potential energy gained during acceleration is finite at that point, and consequently the spring or pendulum must have a tendency to motion.

HUMANITIES 2

Note to student: In the following set, you are asked to consider two statements about Shakespeare's *Hamlet;* the questions following each statement deal with evidence for or against the statement, with the implications of the position taken in the statement, and, finally, with the most significant difference between the statements.

DIRECTIONS: For each item blacken the answer space corresponding to the letter of the *one* best completion or answer.

STATEMENT I

"(1) One of Hamlet's characteristics is the tendency to idealize the world about him. (2) This tendency explains why he is, before the action begins, and at significant points in the action, unsuspicious of base motives on the part of those who have not given him reason, by any overt action, to suspect them. (3) This attitude of Hamlet's explains, then, why he is so affected emotionally by base actions (or what appear to him to be base actions) when he becomes aware of them."

1. Which piece of evidence, among the following, best supports the contention concerning Hamlet's behavior made in the second sentence in Statement I, and could therefore indirectly be used to support the characterization made in the first sentence?

   A—Hamlet's plan to feign madness.
   B—Hamlet's attitude toward Claudius *before* the interview with the ghost in Act I.
   C—Claudius' prediction that Hamlet would not examine the foils.
   D—Ophelia's description of Hamlet as she knew him before the beginning of the action of the play.

2. Which piece of evidence, among the following, could best be used to support the contention concerning Hamlet's behavior made in the third sentence in Statement I, and could therefore indirectly be used to support the characterization made in the first sentence?

   A—The "prophecy" of Hamlet's "prophetic soul" in Act I.
   B—Polonius' theory that Hamlet has gone mad because of Ophelia's rejection of his suit.
   C—Hamlet's attitude toward Laertes in the fifth act before the duel takes place.
   D—Hamlet's attitude during, roughly, the first half of the play, toward his mother.

3. *Assume, temporarily, complete agreement* with the analysis of Hamlet's character which is given in Statement I. Which of the following comments would you accept?

   A—There are no explicit examples of Hamlet "idealizing" during the course of Act I. A reader or spectator must wait until Act II when Hamlet's madness (feigned or not) shows his emotional instability; the inference must be that the cause of that instability is the rude shock occasioned by the ghost's revelation.

B—There are no explicit examples of Hamlet "idealizing" in the entire play. But such an inference must be made, for no other hypothesis can explain why he continually postpones direct action.

C—There are a number of explicit examples in the play of Hamlet "idealizing," and the first of them appears early in the first act; the description he then presents of his father and of the relationship between his father and mother is an idealized one.

D—There are a number of explicit examples in the play of Hamlet "idealizing," but these do not appear until Act II, when his attitude toward Ophelia is made clear.

4. If the analysis of Hamlet's character given in Statement I is a significant one, it may aid in explaining the cause for Hamlet's delay in murdering Claudius. Which of the following hypotheses as to the nature of this cause follows most logically from Statement I?

A—Hamlet does not act because he is not certain of Claudius' guilt.

B—Hamlet is prevented by external circumstances from killing Claudius until Act V.

C—Hamlet is unable to act because his disillusionment brings on a mental state of severe depression.

D—Hamlet is unable to act because he is following a set of principles according to which a man, no matter how just his cause, may not take the law into his own hands.

STATEMENT II

"Throughout the whole course of the play, Hamlet repeatedly makes plans without carrying them out; for he is essentially a speculative person—the kind of man who is always substituting thinking for acting, except when he is forced by external circumstances to act on the instant."

5. Statement II asserts that Hamlet is continually making plans without carrying them out. Let us assume (in this and in succeeding items involving this point) that by "plans" is meant "definite plans for action." We would suppose that evidence supporting this assertion might be found in some of the soliloquies. Is it true of any of the soliloquies that in it Hamlet does make a *definite plan* for action which later he does not carry out?

A—The soliloquy in Act I which begins, "O, that this too, too solid flesh. . . ." (This occurs just before he is informed of the ghost's visit.)

B—The soliloquy in Act II which begins, "O, what a rogue and peasant slave am I!" (This occurs shortly after the arrival of the players.)

C—The soliloquy in Act III which begins, "To be or not to be. . . ." (This occurs just before the "Get thee to a nunnery" scene.)

D—The soliloquy in Act IV which begins, "How all occasions do inform against me." (This occurs just after he sees Fortinbras's army.)

E—It is not true of any of the above soliloquies.

6. Statement II makes the point that Hamlet is always substituting thinking for acting *except* when he is forced by external circumstances to act on the instant. In this way certain events are explained which would seem to contradict the generalization that Hamlet is "always substituting thinking for acting." An event that would be covered by this "except-clause" is

  A—the affair with the pirates.
  B—the presentation of the play within the play.
  C—Hamlet's behavior when he finds Claudius praying.
  D—Hamlet's greeting of Rosencrantz and Guildenstern when he first meets them.

7. Statement II maintains that Hamlet repeatedly makes plans without carrying them out *throughout the whole course of the play;* the implication is that this is *habitual* in action. Opponents of this view claim that there is evidence from one of Hamlet's speeches which would lead to the conclusion that during a period of time within the action of the play, Hamlet could not be so characterized. Which of the following quotations would best constitute such evidence?

  A—"I do not know / Why I yet live to say 'This thing's to do,' / Sith I have cause, and will, and strength, and means / To do 't." (From the soliloquy he speaks after he sees Fortinbras's army.)
  B—"Here, thou incestuous, murderous, damned Dane! / Drink off this potion!" (From the last act.)
  C—"And praised be rashness for it; let us know, / Our indiscretion sometimes serves us well / When our deep plots do pall." (To Horatio, after the scene of the grave-diggers.)
  D—"I'll lug the guts into the neighbor room. / ... Indeed this counsellor / Is now most still, most secret, and most grave, / Who was in life a foolish prating knave." (After the murder of Polonius.)

8. Assume that you are convinced, *on the basis of the specific evidence presented in the preceding item,* that the phrase in Statement II "throughout the whole course of the play" is inaccurate. In the light of the evidence presented in the preceding item, which of the following statements best explains *why* the phrase is inaccurate?

  A—The phrase implies that Hamlet *never* carried out any of his plans; whereas the evidence presented shows that one plan at least—feigning madness—was actually carried out.
  B—The phrase implies that Hamlet is already making plans at the beginning of the play; whereas the evidence presented shows clearly that he did not begin to make plans until *after* he had spoken with the ghost.
  C—The phrase implies that Hamlet was making plans not only at the beginning of the play and at the end but also during the middle of the action; whereas the evidence presented shows that in the very middle of the play, he reprimands himself for *not* having any plans in mind.

D—The phrase implies that no change takes place in Hamlet's habit of making plans; whereas the evidence presented would lead to the conclusion that such a change has taken place between the time of his departure from Denmark and the time of his return.

9. A consideration of the evidence given in *the four items which precede* might very likely lead to

A—the view that Hamlet is not "essentially a speculative person" but, on the contrary, essentially a man of *action*.

B—the view that Hamlet delays in carrying out the ghost's command because he has *moral scruples* against the act of murder.

C—a serious doubt of the validity of characterizing Hamlet as "the kind of man who is always substituting thinking for acting."

D—a serious doubt of the validity of the final "except-clause" of the statement; "except when he is forced by external circumstances to act on the instant."

HUMANITIES 3

Write an essay of about five pages on *one* of the following two topics, both dealing with the same novel. Take time to organize your essay into a well-shaped whole. Do *not* take any space for a re-telling of the story; but, of course, it is appropriate to refer to any part or the whole of the story whenever you think it a useful way of presenting the ground of your judgment. It is recommended generally that you apportion your time about as follows: organizing, 20 minutes; writing, 80 minutes; revising, 20 minutes.

A. Write a critique of *The Age of Innocence*. Your central task is to say in what respects and to what degree you find this book good or bad. The development and defense of your judgment will involve reference both to particulars in the novel and to specific criteria. In your references to the novel be sure that you make clear how each citation is relevant to some aspect of your judgment. In your use of criteria make clear what your basic assumptions are without introducing these premises too explicitly. Remember that your essay is to be an evaluation of the novel rather than a discussion of critical principles or a synopsis of the action. In the course of your essay indicate briefly what differences, if any, there would be in your final judgment of the book if you had chosen to use other basic assumptions.

or

B. "At least," she continued, "it was you who made me understand that under the dullness there are things so fine and sensitive and delicate that even those I most cared for in my other life look cheap in comparison" (p. 243).

It would be possible to take this statement of Countess Olenska to Newland Archer as expressing the "idea" of *The Age of Innocence*, and to explain the action and significance of the novel in terms of this "idea."

It would also be possible to view the novel as a tragedy, the action of which is the failure of these two persons to complete the relationship toward which they seem to be moving through the first half of the story.

Write a critique of the novel, following one of these two interpretations, or fusing both of them. In the course of the essay indicate, with reasons, whether you consider the two views compatible or contradictory; account for the title of the novel, for its satirical treatment of New York society (e.g., in chap. i), and for its epilogue (chap. xxxiv); in addition to making an interpretation of the novel, state and justify your evaluation of it.

SOCIAL SCIENCES 2

In the past year, you have analyzed various theories and case histories dealing with problems of personality and culture. The concepts developed in this study should be useful in understanding and evaluating the significance of other data, such as those presented below. These data were collected about 1925. They are concerned with the attitudes expressed by certain social groups about the type of personality development regarded as desirable.

Study the following table. Summarize the important generalizations which you think can be made about the results. Formulate your own hypotheses as to the meaning and explanation of these results. The table summarizes the answers to a questionnaire which were given by mothers in a middle-sized American town. The answers were obtained in interviews, and every effort was made to check their accuracy by outside means. The respondents were presented with a list of fifteen traits which might or might not be considered important to develop in children. Each mother marked the *three* traits she considered *most important* as X, the *five next most important*, Y, *all other important or desirable*, Z, and all *unimportant* or *undesirable*, 0. Then, if possible, each woman also marked traits as she thought *her* mother would have checked them. The same rating scheme was used for this. Thirty-seven mothers interviewed were married to business and professional men, while another 104 were wives of laborers. In the table, the first group is denoted "business class," and the second "working class." The business- and working-class mothers had come from families in those respective groups.

The results are given in the table as percentages. For example, 14 per cent of the business-class mothers thought appreciation of art, music, and poetry one of the three most important traits; none of the business-class mothers thought it unimportant or undesirable.

In comparing percentages, a difference of 3 per cent or less may well be due to the fact that the groups interviewed were so small, and not to any real difference in attitudes.

The headings "34 mothers in 1890" and "67 mothers in 1890," refer to the answers which the *present-day* mothers thought their mothers would give, for business- and working-class groups respectively. There are fewer answers about mothers in 1890 than in 1925 since some women said they were uncertain, and some answers which later proved inaccurate when checked against other sources, were eliminated.

For purposes of interpreting the study, assume that the answers which are reported are typical of the answers which would have been given if all the mothers in the community had been interviewed.

	PER CENT OF RESPONDENTS PLACING EACH TRAIT IN A GIVEN CATEGORY*															
	BUSINESS CLASS								WORKING CLASS							
RATED BY:	37 Present-Day Mothers				34 Mothers in 1890, as Seen by the Present-Day Mothers				104 Present-Day Mothers				67 Mothers in 1890, as Seen by the Present-Day Mothers			
No.　　RATES GIVEN:........	X	Y	Z	0	X	Y	Z	0	X	Y	Z	0	X	Y	Z	0
1—Appreciation of art, music, and poetry..............	14	32	54	0	9	29	61	0	8	33	58	2	3	20	61	17
2—Concentration..........	19	59	22	0	6	26	64	3	6	11	84	0	3	17	81	0
3—Curiosity..............	0	8	78	14	3	3	73	20	1	7	64	28	0	3	69	29
4—Desire to make a name in the world..............	0	8	70	22	3	35	46	15	7	38	48	7	6	36	51	8
5—Economy in money matters..................	8	40	51	0	6	58	32	3	31	49	19	1	30	60	10	0
6—Frankness in dealing with others................	43	19	38	0	38	32	29	0	21	46	32	1	18	48	35	0
7—Getting very high grades in school..............	3	24	68	5	12	46	41	0	25	44	31	0	17	49	33	2
8—Good manners..........	19	54	27	0	38	55	6	0	35	49	16	0	42	44	15	0
9—Independence..........	46	32	22	0	18	27	49	6	17	36	47	0	15	27	57	2
10—Knowledge of sex hygiene.	16	51	32	0	0	15	20	64	14	32	48	6	3	18	32	48
11—Loyalty to the church....	35	32	27	5	67	17	9	6	56	31	12	2	71	25	4	0
12—Patriotism..............	22	35	43	0	12	44	38	6	20	45	33	2	20	50	28	2
13—Social-mindedness........	22	30	46	3	9	58	23	9	10	26	64	1	6	36	59	0
14—Strict obedience.........	43	27	24	5	70	23	6	0	46	38	14	1	61	33	6	0
15—Tolerance..............	11	46	43	0	6	29	55	9	4	16	77	3	4	18	74	4

* This table is adapted with permission from Robert S. and Helen Merrell Lynd, *Middletown* (Harcourt, Brace & Co., 1929).

NOTE: The following is a brief selection from a lengthy exercise interpreting these data and relating them to various theories of culture analyzed in the course.

DIRECTIONS: The following items consist of various interpretations of the table contained in Selection I of your reading materials. You may refer to this table and any other notes during this part of the examination. For each item, *blacken* the answer space corresponding to the letter of the *one best* answer or completion.

1. The two traits considered of greatest importance by business-class mothers in 1890

    A—are also regarded as most important by present-day mothers in the business class, although there is less agreement about them.

    B—have been partially replaced by "more liberal" attitudes.

    C—are generally regarded as positively undesirable.

    D—have been partially replaced by "more conservative" attitudes.

2. The three traits considered of greatest importance by working-class mothers in 1890

    A—are also regarded as most important by present-day mothers in the working class, although there is less agreement about them.

    B—have been partially replaced by "more liberal" attitudes.

    C—are generally regarded as positively undesirable.

    D—have been partially replaced by "more conservative" attitudes.

3. Changes in attitudes between 1890 and 1925

    A—have occurred to an approximately equal extent among both business and working-class mothers.

    B—were greater among business-class mothers than among working-class mothers.

    C—were less among business-class mothers than among working-class mothers.

    D—have not been significant in either class.

4. Which of the following constitutes the best explanation of the trends pointed out in items 1–3?

    A—There is a relatively greater class consciousness and solidarity in the working class, which is increasing as social barriers to opportunity increase.

    B—There is a relatively greater disposition among members of the business class generally, to maintain the status quo, which disposition is becoming strengthened as pressures from the increasingly frustrated lower class become greater.

    C—There has been a decline in the importance of informal social controls.

    D—There has been an increased disposition to obtain conformity by legislation rather than by agreement, and childhood training.

    E—Contacts have become more impersonal and have increased, and provincialism has been reduced in all classes, but these changes are more quickly apparent in the business classes.

5. The relative importance of "economy in money matters" has apparently

    A—declined since 1890 in the business class, but remained the same in the working class.

B—declined since 1890 in the working class, but has risen in the business class.

C—declined since 1890 in both the business and working classes.

D—not changed significantly in either class.

6. In the business class, this change in attitudes towards "economy" in money matters

A—may be due to a higher evaluation of the ideals of Puritanism, as described by Weber.

B—could be the result of greater indifference to the "things of this world."

C—may indicate the beginning of a leisure-class ethos, as described by Veblen.

D—is so small that it seems business-class mothers are following strictly the ideals held by their own mothers.

7. This theory (item 6) is supported by

A—the change in business-class attitudes towards "appreciation of art, music and poetry,"

B—increased desires in the business class for their children to "make a name in the world,"

C—the relatively high value in the business class placed on "loyalty to the church,"

D—the relatively high value in the business class placed on "strict obedience,"

8. because

A—obedience to parents' ideals was so strongly inculcated by business-class upbringing.

B—aesthetic abilities, according to Veblen, provide one basis for invidious comparison.

C—success is the mark of certainty of salvation.

D—religious codes require honesty in economic dealings with one's fellows.

SOCIAL SCIENCES 3

DIRECTIONS: This year is Presidential election year in the United States. It is appropriate, therefore, that you, as an actual or potential voter, should formulate the *grounds* (i.e., *the general values and the concrete policy proposals*) which you would use as a basis of evaluation with respect to *five topics*. The topics do not constitute a complete list of the areas of policy relevant to choice. However, you should limit discussion to them unless you are explicitly directed to bring in topics of your own. *In respect to each topic, discuss (i) the general objectives toward which public policy should be directed in that area and (ii) concrete policy proposals for achieving those objectives in view of the relevant contemporary trends which you indicate are of crucial importance.*

NOTE: Certain sources are suggested following each topic. You are not to regard these as a complete list. Refer to other topics and authors as relevant.

You will not be judged on the position which you choose but rather on the *consistency, completeness,* and *cogency* of your argument. The various parts of this essay are weighted in proportion to the suggested time for each.

TOPIC I (20 minutes): On what grounds would you favor or oppose any party *as a party, apart from its program?* That is, in terms of what values or standards do you propose to measure its general characteristics—its leaders, its composition, its sources of support, its history, or other features you believe relevant? You should make clear (i) both the relation of these values to the structure of the party *and* (ii) the bearing of that structure on the likelihood that the party will employ and develop effective techniques of administration. (Some suggested sources: Burke, Dickinson, Gelhorn, John Stuart Mill, Weber.)

TOPIC II (20 minutes): On what *grounds* would you judge a party's proposals in respect to the government's monetary and fiscal (taxation and expenditure) policies? Your answer should include an account of (i) the general objectives which such monetary and fiscal policies should be designed to serve and (ii) concrete policies for achieving these objectives. In discussing the latter, you should show how in the light of current conditions they will contribute to your objectives. (Some suggested sources: Hansen, Meade and Hitch, President's Report to Congress, Simons.)

TOPIC III (20 minutes): On what *grounds* would you judge a party's proposals in respect to the role of the government in achieving directly or indirectly the kind of consensus you think desirable? Your answer should include a discussion of the nature of this consensus, the trends which now are favorable or unfavorable to its achievement, and concrete policies which the government should undertake in view of these trends. (Some suggested sources: Durkheim, Mannheim, J. S. Mill, Plato, Simmel.)

TOPIC IV (20 minutes): On what *grounds* would you judge a party's proposals in respect to U.S. participation in the United Nations and other international organizations? Your answer should include a brief discussion of the objectives which you think U.S. foreign policy should serve and concretely the type and extent of participation (or non-participation) which would help to realize these objectives under contemporary conditions. (Suggested sources: Bulletin of Atomic Scientists, Carr, Hansen, Kant, UN documents, Veblen.)

TOPIC V (30 minutes): (i) Explain in summary which of the above topics, or what other one or more, seem to you of decisive importance in deciding how to cast your vote. In explaining why certain topics are of strategic importance, make explicit your assumptions regarding *the relative importance of various general social values* and your assumptions regarding *the relation of social knowledge to social policy* (including *man's capacity* to acquire and employ such knowledge in 20th century society). (ii) Show how the views of one or more of the following authors coincide, wholly or in part, with your assumptions and how one or more of them is in disagreement with your assumptions.

AUTHORS: Dewey, Hobbes, Locke, Kant, Knight, J. S. Mill, Plato. If none of these authors agrees at many points with you, elaborate the point of view of some other author whose approach you find more congenial.

HISTORY

This essay consists of *two parts*, which will be graded *separately* according to a scale of points proportional to the time allotted for each part. In effect, therefore, you are being asked to write two brief and separate, though closely related essays, and you are advised to follow the recommended time-limits rather closely. The total time suggested for *both parts* is *90 minutes*. It would be wise to spend about 20 minutes organizing your thoughts about the essay problems *before* you begin to write. Quality is much more important than quantity, and you will not be expected to write more, for example, than is usually required in a 60-minute essay. As the correctness and clarity of your expression will affect your grade, you should reserve a few minutes to look over your paper at the end. Unless there is some good reason to the contrary, *please write in ink*.

PART I (about 25 minutes): Discuss critically Becker's concept of "climate of opinion," and indicate whether you would accept, modify, or reject it as an approach to the understanding of a historical period.

PART II (about 45 minutes): Answer *either* A *or* B.

A. If you *accept* the concept (with or without modification or qualification), apply it by describing or characterizing the climate of opinion in *one* of the following periods:

1) Athens in the fifth century
2) The later Roman Empire
3) The Renaissance-Reformation
4) The French Revolution
5) England in the age of the Industrial Revolution
6) Russia in the twentieth century

Support your conclusions (to the extent that time will allow) by concrete reference to the materials of this course or of other courses with which you are acquainted, or to any other pertinent materials at your command.

B. If you *reject* the concept, discuss *one* of the above periods in your terms, and indicate why you refuse to apply Becker's concept as an organizing principle for your discussion. Support your conclusions as in A, above.

OBSERVATION, INTERPRETATION, AND INTEGRATION

DIRECTIONS: In questions 1–10 you are to consider pairs of quotations taken from the selected readings for the course. For each pair, blacken the answer space corresponding to the completion which best accounts for the *real or apparent difference* between the positions represented. Each quotation is to be understood as it was meant in its original context.

1. (*a*) "Neither is pleasure the good nor is all pleasure desirable" (Aristotle *Ethics* x. 3).
   (*b*) "To think of an object as desirable (unless for the sake of its consequences), and to think of it as pleasant, are one and the same thing" (Mill, *Utilitarianism*, chap. iv).

The *difference* between these statements may be accounted for by considering that

  A—Aristotle holds that there is a hierarchy of pleasures, whereas Mill believes any pleasure to be fundamentally as desirable as any other.
  B—Aristotle holds that some pleasures are more appropriate to man than are others, whereas Mill believes all pleasures to be equally appropriate to man.
  C—Mill holds that all pleasures are in themselves desirable (though some more so than others), whereas Aristotle, who distinguishes between activities which are pleasant without qualification and activities which are pleasant only with a qualification, holds that some pleasures are not naturally desirable.
  D—Mill holds that all pleasures are in themselves desirable (though some more so than others), whereas Aristotle holds that no pleasure is good without qualification, and can only be called good incidentally.

2. (a) "There are many things we should be keen about even if they brought no pleasure, e.g., . . . possessing the virtues" (Aristotle *Ethics* x. 3).
  (b) "Virtue, . . . if it were not a means to anything else, would be and remain indifferent" (Mill, *Utilitarianism*, chap. iv).

The *difference* between these statements may be accounted for by considering that

  A—Mill makes happiness or pleasure the ultimate end of all actions, whereas Aristotle holds that pleasure only supervenes, and is not what is primarily desired.
  B—Mill identifies happiness with pleasure (and the absence of pain), whereas Aristotle holds that happiness is not pleasant.
  C—Aristotle identifies virtue with happiness, whereas Mill distinguishes them.
  D—Aristotle is speaking of what people ought to do, as determined by their obligation to be virtuous, whereas Mill is referring to the empirical fact that people actually never desire virtue as an end in itself.

3. (a) "The mind is not in a right state . . . unless it does love virtue . . . as a thing desirable in itself" (Mill, *Utilitarianism*, chap. iv).
  (b) "Virtue, . . . if it were not a means to anything else, would be and remain indifferent" (Mill, *Utilitarianism*, chap. iv).

The *difference* between these statements may be accounted for by considering that, according to Mill,

  A—virtuous actions increase the total amount of happiness in the world only when they are desired as ends in themselves.
  B—men have no original desire for what men call virtue, but they can come to take pleasure in virtuous actions. When this happens, their

actions will more readily tend to promote the greatest general happiness.

C—virtue can be desired either as a means to the ultimate end of happiness, or as identical with happiness. The natural tendency of mankind is to desire it as a means; the proper attitude is for them to desire it and only it.

D—virtue can be desired either as a means to happiness or as a part of happiness. The natural tendency of mankind is to desire it as a means; the proper attitude is for them to desire it as a part of that happiness towards which there are no attainable means, happiness and its parts being ends in themselves.

4. (a) "Virtue is its own end" (Kant, *Metaphysics of Morals*, p. 19).

(b) "Virtue, . . . if it were not a means to anything else, would be and remain indifferent" (Mill, *Utilitarianism*, chap. iv).

The *difference* between these statements may be accounted for by considering that

A—Kant is speaking of what all men do take as an end, whereas Mill is referring to the fact that men ought to seek that pleasure to which virtue is a means.

B—Kant is speaking of what men ought to take as an end, whereas Mill is referring to what men do take as an end.

C—Kant is speaking of free actions, whereas Mill is speaking of actions which are indifferently free or compelled.

D—Kant is speaking of a virtue that involves only one's own perfection, whereas for Mill virtue is an attitude towards the happiness of all men.

5. (a) "Pleasure, and freedom from pain, are the only things desirable as ends" (Mill, *Utilitarianism*, chap. ii).

(b) "Happiness is desirable, and the only thing desirable, as an end" (Mill, *Utilitarianism*, chap. iv).

The *difference* between these statements may be accounted for by considering that, according to Mill,

A—the two ends of (a) are not ultimate ends, but only means to the single end referred to in (b).

B—pleasure and freedom from pain are desirable as ends if no distinctions are made between the higher and lower faculties of man; but if these distinctions are made, then happiness rather than pleasure is desirable.

C—pleasure and pain are "desirable" in the sense of "what actually is desired," whereas happiness, which sometimes is not actually desired, is nevertheless "desirable" in the sense of "what ought to be desired."

D—"happiness" means "pleasure, and the absence of pain."

6. (a) "Self-love is a principle in human nature" (Hume, Section V, Part II).

   (b) "There is a principle, supposed to prevail among many, which is utterly incompatible with all virtue. . . . This principle is, that . . . all of us, at bottom, pursue only our private interest" (Hume, Appendix II).

The *difference* between these statements may be accounted for by considering that, according to Hume,

     A—self-love is a principle of the actions of immoral men only, and moral men act from benevolence instead.

     B—immoral men desire only their pleasure, whereas moral men also seek the objects of their secondary desires or inclinations.

     C—all men pursue their own interests, but they also have a direct urge to seek the interests of others.

     D—self-love is an internal principle of all human nature, but private interest is an external principle, in the sense of an end which is desired only by vicious men.

7. (a) "We have pointed out in what sense pleasures are good without qualification" (Aristotle *Ethics* vii. 12).

   (b) "Nothing can possibly be conceived in the world, or even out of it, which can be called good, without qualification, except a Good Will" (Kant, *Fundamental Principles*, p. 9).

The *difference* between these statements may be accounted for by considering that

     A—what Aristotle means by "good" is pleasure, while what Kant means by "good" is the conformity of actions to law.

     B—what Aristotle means by "without qualification" is "having no quality but pleasure," whereas Kant means "having no quality but conformity to law."

     C—what Aristotle means by "pleasure" is "activity," and what Kant means by "Good Will" is activity.

     D—Aristotle does not mean that pleasures can be good in and of themselves, but only through their association with good activities. Kant, however, is looking for something which is good in itself.

8. (a) "The Investigation of difficult Things by the Method of Analysis, ought ever to precede the Method of Composition. This Analysis consists in making Experiments and Observations, and in drawing general conclusions from them by Induction" (Newton, *Methods*, p. 25).

   (b) "I have pointed out what are the laws of nature; and, with no other principle upon which to found my reasonings except the infinite perfection of God, I endeavoured to demonstrate all those about which there could be any room for doubt" (Descartes, *Methods*, pp. 53–54).

The *difference* between these statements may be accounted for by considering that

    A—Newton believes the senses to be usually trustworthy, whereas Descartes believes them to be almost always misleading.

    B—Newton believes the mind must operate on material provided to it by sense, whereas Descartes believes that the mind can arrive at truths without consulting sense experience.

    C—Newton's interest is in accounting for the motions of bodies, whereas Descartes also wants to explain the phenomena of his own mental existence.

    D—Descartes believes that God is the first principle of natural motion whereas Newton's principles are mathematical.

9. (a) "I have pointed out what are the laws of nature; and, with no other principle upon which to found my reasonings except the infinite perfection of God, I endeavoured to demonstrate all those about which there could be any room for doubt" (Descartes, *Methods*, pp. 53–54).

   (b) "I have ever remained firm in my original resolution to suppose no other principle than . . . to accept as true nothing that did not appear to me more clear and certain than the demonstrations of the geometers had formerly appeared" (Descartes, *Methods*, p. 52).

The *difference* between these statements may be accounted for by considering that, according to Descartes,

    A—the principle referred to in (b) states the criterion by which truth is judged, whereas the principle referred to in (a) is a principle from which true laws of nature are deduced.

    B—the principle referred to in (a) is a principle of mathematics (including geometry), whereas the principle referred to in (b) is a principle of physics.

    C—the mind is the starting point of mathematical reasonings, whereas God is the starting point of reasonings which require a reference to experience.

    D—absolute clarity and certainty are obtainable only in metaphysics and mathematics, not in physics.

10. (a) "Hypotheses are not to be regarded in experimental philosophy" (Newton).

   (b) "The function of hypotheses is one which must be reckoned absolutely indispensable in science" (Mill).

The *difference* between these statements may be accounted for by considering that

    A—Newton holds that science ("experimental philosophy") must consist of necessary and universal propositions, whereas Mill admits degrees of probability, and therefore hypothetical reasoning.

B—Newton bases natural philosophy upon God as first cause of the laws of nature, whereas Mill's doctrine, dealing only with laws of nature, has no such absolute principle.

C—Newton opposes occult causes, whereas Mill holds that some causes can be inferred only from their effects.

D—Newton means by "hypotheses," "suppositions not based upon or verifiable by experience," whereas Mill views hypotheses as suppositions which suggest experiments by which the hypotheses can be verified.

12

Advising

JOHN R. DAVEY

STUDENTS in the College are assisted by faculty advisers in planning their academic work. These advisers constitute the staff of the Dean of Students in the College, whose immediate responsibility it is to co-ordinate the relations of each student in the College with the University.

The advising of students is one of the noncurricular services administered by the Dean of Students in the University. The other functions which are brought together under this one head include entrance counseling and the admission of students; the administration of entrance tests, placement tests, and comprehensive examinations prepared by the University Examiner; the recording and reporting of grades; the awarding and handling of fellowships, scholarships, and other financial aids for students; the supervision of residence halls; the care of students' health; physical education; the supervision of student organizations and social activities; the co-ordination of veterans' affairs; vocational guidance and placement; and specialized counseling. This unified direction of student personnel services promotes a clear understanding of the business of each service and of its relation to the other noncurricular services. As a result of the inclusion of the College advisory service in this administrative organization, a closer connection than would otherwise be possible between students' academic work and their extra-curricular interests is achieved.

The advisers in the College are members of the faculty who are relieved of approximately one-third the instructional duties which would normally be assigned to them. This plan has several advantages over the practice observed in many colleges, where advising is conceived as an activity to be carried on by all or some members of the faculty in addition to their full-time work as teachers. Since no adviser takes on more than two-thirds the normal quota of instruction, research, or examining in the College, he can give from six to eight hours a week to conferences with students and can have these conferences at times which are convenient for them. Under this arrangement, advising becomes a significant part of the total service rendered by some members of the College faculty. The relatively small number of persons involved in advisory work is another advantage, for their activities can be closely co-ordinated and therefore made more effective than they might be otherwise. And, finally, since advisers remain as teachers in close contact with the curriculum of the College, they are able to help the faculty define and conduct the academic program with a better understanding of what students need.

Members of the faculty are asked to serve as advisers only if they are interested in this type of service and have demonstrated their ability to work with students individually. Professional training in counseling is not, of course, expected; but those personal qualities are sought which will enable the adviser to gain the confidence and co-operation of students. Although advising students introduces one quickly and extensively to the aims, practices, and policies of the College, it would not be proper to regard this service as a device for the orientation of new members of the faculty. They are not considered for appointment as advisers until they have had sufficient experience in College courses and have become familiar with the structure of the University. A further condition taken into account in making appointments concerns distribution: an effort is made to obtain advisers from each of the instructional staffs in the College. One consequence of this is that the inclusion of a certain number of advisers is figured in the personnel plans of each staff. An advising assignment usually specifies at least three years of service. This term is long enough for the adviser to become proficient in all aspects of the work and to become well acquainted with the students in his group. Often he serves the same ones throughout all or most of their residence in the College.

There is no formally organized training for new advisers, although the various aspects of their work are discussed with them frequently and regular meetings are held for considering particular phases of their business. No fixed manual on advising is used. Instead, they follow as guides general bulletins and special instructions prepared by the Dean of Students in the College. New appointees to the staff become familiar with their work by doing it; and the most effective training they can receive is provided by the more experienced advisers, with whom they share offices. In order that the relationship between the counseling of students and other noncurricular affairs may be made clear, the directors of the special services meet with advisers at frequent intervals.

Both men and women serve as advisers, each one counseling both men and women students. At present there is an advisory staff of 20 for a student body of approximately 2,400 students, so that no one has more than 120 charges. Some advisers counsel only those students who enter the College after graduation from high school, while others advise only those students who enter after having completed the tenth or eleventh grade. This arrangement, which takes cognizance, on the one hand, of differences in the maturity and needs of these two groups and, on the other hand, of differences in the personalities and interests of advisers, has been found more effective than the assignment of students to counselors strictly in terms of their expressed plans for later and more specialized study.

Nevertheless, whenever possible, a student is given an adviser whose instructional work is in the field of his principal interest. Thus a student who intends to study English literature after he has completed his general education in the College plans his program with a member of the English or Humanities staff. The advice of specialists is particularly necessary, however, for those who expect to do advanced work in one of the physical or biological sciences, since they must complete certain prescribed predivisional or pre-departmental courses, in addition to satisfying the requirements for the College degree. Such students are under the guidance of an adviser in the field of their special interest either from the time they enter the College or after they are ready to undertake pre-divisional courses. The most systematic arrangement of this kind has been made for premedical students, who are counseled by the same special adviser during their last two years of work in the College and in their final premedical year (when they are registered in the Division of the Biological Sciences).

Proper liaison between advising in the College and the academic counseling of all divisions is made easy by the fact that the offices of the advisers, the Dean of Students in the College, and the divisional Deans of Students are all located in one area. Students with questions about particular (i.e., post-A.B.) lines of study may be readily referred to the proper dean. Many are also referred to the departmental counselors during the final year of residence in the College, since over 80 per cent of the College students expect to enter a Division or a Professional School.

The advisers are frequently consulted for information or advice on matters not directly related to a program in general education. For example, students often express concern about the choice of a vocation and ask for help in making their plans. Since members of the advisory staff are not experts in vocational guidance, they can deal with such problems only in general terms. For further suggestions students are encouraged to consult the Office of Vocational Guidance and Placement. The results of special tests administered by the Office may be furnished to the adviser if the student so requests; and they are often useful not only in clarifying a student's ultimate plans but also in fixing his immediate course of study.

The first contact between a new student and his adviser occurs in a specially arranged group discussion of the regulations of the University, registration procedures, and other matters of immediate, practical interest. Then the two get together for a registration conference. By this time the results of the placement tests are known, and also the requirements remaining to be satisfied for the Bachelor's degree. With this information in hand and with regard for the student's interests, educational expectations, and vocational preferences, the adviser draws up the first registration plan.

From this general account of an initial registration conference it should not be inferred that the planning of a student's academic program is a simple and mechanical matter. The requirements for the degree are not stated as courses to be taken or credits to be earned, but in terms of the knowledge and competences which the student must possess and be able to demonstrate on placement tests or comprehensive examinations. The results from placement tests do indicate the conditions to be fulfilled, but the academic means of fulfilment must fit each particular case. Differences in the extent to which students have already achieved the objectives of the College are obvious; differences in the ability to learn are much less so. But the adviser must take both factors into account in helping the individual he has before him to chart his preparation for meeting the remaining requirements. A few are counseled to study independently for all or part of an examination. For most of them the recommendation is to take the entire course which is designed to prepare one for the examination. Some may be encouraged to get themselves ready for more than the normal number of examinations during their first year in the College, while others are advised to prepare for only two or three. Those who are deficient in reading or writing or the fundamental mathematical skills are required to plan programs which make it possible to remove these deficiencies without delay. Students in this category are usually discouraged from registering for a full load of courses during their first year.

It should be clear, then, that, in order to counsel students effectively, the adviser must be familiar with the aims of the whole curriculum, must know how to interpret the data drawn from aptitude and placement tests, and must be able to explain clearly to each student how he may best prepare to meet the requirements left on his program. To insure that the best use is made of placement-test scores, the examiners provide their recommendations, and special placement advisers are present at registration to review any recommendation which may be questioned or to counsel students who are thought to be capable of preparing for a comprehensive examination without attending all of the course.

About six weeks after classes have begun, the new student has his next planned conference with his adviser. Together they review his progress in his studies and his adjustment to the life of the University community. An attempt is made to come to a realistic evaluation of the extent to which a balance has been achieved between academic work and other activities. At least one such conference is required every quarter; students are urged, however, to come in whenever they encounter a difficulty of any kind. One adviser stated recently that in the course of an academic year he had an average of six interviews with each member of his group, and as many as twelve with some. In any case, whenever there is a report of unsatisfactory progress, the student is summoned for a special conference.

Most of the difficulties which disturb new students in the first weeks of the year stem from their lack of familiarity with the University and with the methods of instruction used in College classes. Later more serious problems are likely to be presented to the advisers. Instructors are expected to inform the Dean of Students in the College of unsatisfactory work done by any student. Although these reports may be submitted at any time, they are generally sent in after mid-term or quarterly examinations. Both instructors' reports and advisory grades are referred to the adviser, and, where the work is generally substandard, an immediate conference is arranged. The most common causes of trouble appear to be inadequate study skills, irregular preparation, and the distracting influence of personal problems or non-academic activities. It may be that the adviser can give all the assistance and encouragement necessary; or he may find that the difficulties are too deep-seated to be analyzed and relieved except by an expert.

If the student has not followed a regular schedule of study, he is helped to plan one. If he complains that he does not know how to do his work and does not understand what is expected of him, he may be told of study techniques that others have found effective, or he may be asked to consult his instructor for concrete suggestions. Occasionally, the adviser asks the instructors concerned to meet with him and the student to consider how the level of achievement may be raised. If it seems that the stumbling block is lack of skill in reading (and such evidence will be available in the scores on reading tests already taken by the student), the adviser may send him to the instructor in charge of the English Deficiency (Reading) course for further diagnosis and assistance. If the trouble appears to be poor physical condition, the Student Health Service is asked to examine the student and to make a recommendation as to the amount of work he should undertake.

Parents of students often consult advisers, and advisers often ask that parents confer with them. Many of these conferences reveal a lack of communication or understanding within the family and indicate that an important function of an adviser is that of interpreting, as well as he can, the views of one generation to another, without identifying himself with either. A similar position is commonly held by the resident head of a College house or residence hall, for he serves as a general counselor for the students who are living there. Truly effective guidance of resident students requires, as a matter of fact, close co-operation of the heads of the College houses and the academic advisers. Reports of academic progress go regularly to the heads of houses, and they, in turn, submit to the Dean of Students in the College their observations with regard to the study habits and the interests of students. At general meetings of heads and advisers, the tasks of each group are defined; informal consultations between particular members of the two staffs occur whenever the academic work of a student or his conduct in the house calls for joint action.

Some of the problems met by the adviser and some of the means he uses in solving them have now been indicated. It should be clear that he tries to help each student as much as he can but does not undertake to deal with difficulties which are beyond his competence. Obviously, one of the marks of a successful adviser is this ability to recognize a situation requiring the attention of an expert in personal counseling. In the case of emotional or social maladjustment, it may be suggested that the student go to the University's Counseling Center. Here specialists, using the "nondirective" technique, are available to help the student help himself by developing his capacity to cope with problems independently. If he is severely disturbed, however, the adviser may refer the student to the Health Service for psychiatric treatment. In other words, he is not responsible for counseling those students assigned to him on all kinds of problems, but he is expected to locate the general nature of a student's trouble and to know to what other service an appeal must be made. It often happens that he serves as one who co-ordinates the advice given by several of these agencies, or even brings together the other persons whose collaboration is essential to the student's welfare. However, the adviser soon realizes that he is not the only one to whom a student turns for advice and that he may do more harm than good if his interest comes to be viewed as interference in personal matters. In no instance does he act as a disciplinary officer, although he is naturally expected to bring any matter requiring disciplinary action to the attention of the appropriate official of the University. Nor is an adviser responsible for determining the academic status of any student. His opinion may be sought, however, in determining the appropriateness of probation or suspension when someone has consistently failed to meet the standards for continuation in the College.

At present most of the counseling is done in conferences with individual students. The few group conferences which have been arranged are largely for the purpose of informing students about general policies and practices; they cannot be considered as the employment of group counseling techniques. Plans have been prepared, however, for conducting a series of group advisory conferences for students during their first year in the College and for so arranging the schedule of these students that twenty-five or thirty who have the same adviser will be registered in the same sections of each course. It is hoped that this will make it possible for each group to meet with its adviser and instructors to discuss common interests and will promote close social and personal relations in a way which may break down some of the barriers between the academic and the noncurricular aspects of a student's experience in the College.

The question of what counseling technique should be used is discussed frequently, but few advisers consciously attempt to follow either the "directive" or the "nondirective" method. Each one conducts the advisory conference in the manner that seems most suitable to the topic at hand and to the personality of the student. He tries to answer the questions put by the student, or he directs him to the person or service which can best provide the needed assistance or information. As the adviser becomes experienced in his work, he usually sees that in most instances he can only inform students of the possible consequences of the choices they make. This is probably the best kind of advising that can be done as part of a program of general education designed to help students develop the ability to think for themselves.

[PRINTED IN U·S·A]